D0049075

Surviving Wounded Knee

Surviving Wounded Knee

The Lakotas and the
Politics of Memory

DAVID W. GRUA

OXFORD
UNIVERSITY PRESS

OXFORD
UNIVERSITY PRESS

Oxford University Press is a department of the University of
Oxford. It furthers the University's objective of excellence in research,
scholarship, and education by publishing worldwide.

Oxford   New York

Auckland   Cape Town   Dar es Salaam   Hong Kong   Karachi
Kuala Lumpur   Madrid   Melbourne   Mexico City   Nairobi
New Delhi   Shanghai   Taipei   Toronto

With offices in

Argentina   Austria   Brazil   Chile   Czech Republic   France   Greece
Guatemala   Hungary   Italy   Japan   Poland   Portugal   Singapore
South Korea   Switzerland   Thailand   Turkey   Ukraine   Vietnam

Oxford is a registered trademark of Oxford University Press
in the UK and certain other countries.

Published in the United States of America by
Oxford University Press
198 Madison Avenue, New York, NY 10016

A version of Chapter 4 has appeared in an earlier form as David W. Grua, "'In Memory
of the Chief Big Foot Massacre': The Wounded Knee Survivors and the Politics
of Memory," *Western Historical Quarterly* 46 (Spring 2015): 31-51. Copyright by
the Western History Association. Reprinted by permission.

Book proceeds benefit the Oglala Lakota College Archives, Kyle, South Dakota.

Library of Congress Cataloging-in-Publication Data
Grua, David W., author.
Surviving Wounded Knee : the Lakotas and the politics of memory / David W. Grua.
pages cm
Includes bibliographical references and index.
ISBN 978-0-19-024903-8 (hardcover : alk. paper)   1. Wounded Knee Massacre, S.D., 1890.
2. Dakota Indians—Government relations.   3. Dakota Indians—Wars, 1890–1891.
4. Wounded Knee Massacre, S.D., 1890—Claims.   5. Memorialization—Political aspects—United
States.   6. Collective memory—South Dakota.   7. Dakota Indians—Claims.
8. South Dakota—Race relations.   9. Memorialization—South Dakota.
10. Memory—Political aspects—United States.   I. Title.   II. Title: Lakotas and the politics of
memory.
E83.89.G78 2016
973.8'6—dc23
2015035931

1 3 5 7 9 8 6 4 2
Printed in the United States of America
on acid-free paper

Contents

Acknowledgments

ANY AUTHOR CAN tell you that while research is often a solitary activity, writing a book results from many hours of conversation and assistance from interested friends and colleagues. My debts to these individuals are many. At Brigham Young University, Susan Rugh introduced me to both the history of the American West and collective memory, two interests that Brian Cannon and Ignacio Garcia subsequently cultivated and expanded. At Texas Christian University, Todd M. Kerstetter taught me to see the West from the perspective of Native America, as he shepherded this manuscript when it was still an evolving dissertation. Greg Cantrell, Rebecca Sharpless, and Peter Szok provided valuable encouragement and feedback on the manuscript. Fellow TCU graduate students Lisa Barnett, Jensen Branscombe, Rebekah Crowe, Brett Dowdle, Beth Hessel, Dustin Naegle, Jacob Olmstead, and Jeff Wells gave much appreciated friendship and support.

Two historian-mentors deserve special comment. Ari Kelman is not only among the leading practitioners of the historian's craft—he is also one of the most genuine human beings I have ever known. Long before we met in person, Ari was generously answering emails, reading rough chapter drafts, and providing invaluable feedback. Ari also put me in contact with Oxford University Press editor Susan Ferber. Jeffrey Ostler's groundbreaking scholarship on Lakota history and American colonialism was deeply influential as this project developed. He subsequently answered email queries, read chapter drafts, and served as an outside reviewer for Oxford. Both of these individuals left an indelible mark on the dissertation and then the revised book.

This book has also benefitted from the generosity and insights of many friends and scholars. Philip Burnham, Kent Blansett, Matthew Bokovoy, Boyd Cothran, Raymond DeMallie, W. Paul Reeve, and Sherry L. Smith read and commented on chapters or conference papers. Rani-Henrik Andersson, Andrew R. Graybill, Jerome A. Greene, Margaret Jacobs, Jeffrey Means, Jean O'Brien, Akim Reinhardt, Larry Skogen, Robert Wooster, and John R. Wunder freely shared ideas and sources that enriched this book. Bryon Andreasen, Mark Ashurst-McGee, Matthew Bowman, Jeffrey Cannon, Matthew Godfrey, Kurt Graham, Matthew Grow, Amanda Hendrix-Komoto, Robin Jensen, Christopher Jones, Spencer McBride, Reid Neilson, Benjamin Park, Andrea Radke-Moss, Jenny Reeder, Brenden Rensink, and Brent Rogers offered advice and encouragement during the revision and publication process.

I owe some of my greatest debts to the Lakotas who agreed to discuss the Wounded Knee survivors' fascinating lives and histories with me, a non-Indian scholar. Mario Gonzalez, former attorney for the Wounded Knee Survivors Association and a key figure in the Lakotas' historic legal battles surrounding the Black Hills, allowed me to interview him in his law office in Rapid City, South Dakota. Mike Her Many Horses shared his files accumulated from many years of archival research and his memories of his own contributions to the Survivors Association's memorial activities. The late Marie Fox Belly-Not Help Him, former president of the Survivors Association, hosted me in her home on the Pine Ridge Reservation, and described her powerful memories of her great-grandfather Dewey Beard. Leonard Little Finger, a descendant of Big Foot, Joseph Horn Cloud, and other survivors answered my questions in phone interviews.

The assistance of various institutions made this book possible. I am indebted to the dedicated staffs the following archives: Assumption Abbey Archives, Richardton, North Dakota; Brigham Young University, Provo, Utah; Dakota Wesleyan University, Mitchell, South Dakota; Indiana University, Bloomington, Indiana; Kansas State Historical Society, Topeka, Kansas; The Little Bighorn Battlefield National Monument, Crow Agency, Montana; National Archives and Records Administration, Kansas City, Missouri; National Archives and Records Administration, Washington, DC; Nebraska State Historical Society, Lincoln, Nebraska; South Dakota State Historical Society, Pierre, South Dakota; University of South Dakota, Vermillion, South Dakota; and the US Cavalry Museum, Fort Riley, Kansas. I also benefitted from the financial assistance of Texas Christian University's Department of History and Geography, Graduate Student Senate, and Graduate School, each of which provided grants that made research at distant archives possible. In addition, I thank Susan Ferber and the dedicated staff at Oxford University Press. Finally, I thank the Church History Department of The Church of Jesus Christ of Latter-day Saints for providing institutional resources as I completed the dissertation and revised the manuscript into a book.

My last and most deeply felt thanks go to my family. My parents, Marilyn and Corey W. Grua, instilled in me a love of books and learning that sustained me through the grueling—yet rewarding—rigors of writing a book. They also kindly read and commented on the manuscript twice. My twin sons, Caleb and Daniel, have provided much-needed balance and unconditional love as they've grown alongside this manuscript. My wife, the former Hope Hendricksen, accompanied me emotionally and intellectually through the entire process of researching, writing, and revising. She even scrolled through microfilms of old newspapers and searched dusty archival boxes for references to Wounded Knee. For her, I reserve my most profound gratitude.

Surviving Wounded Knee

Introduction

THE POLITICS OF WOUNDED KNEE MEMORY

IN THE EARLY 1970s, Wounded Knee—a small valley in southwestern South Dakota—became a household name in the United States. The site was known for what had occurred there eight decades before, when the US Seventh Cavalry killed more than two hundred Lakota followers of the Lakota Chief Big Foot on December 29, 1890, ostensibly for their adherence to the Ghost Dance indigenous religion. For Americans growing increasingly aware of past racial injustices and weary of the military's entanglements in the Vietnam War, Wounded Knee was the culmination of a previous era's expansionist impulses and their devastating effects. Simultaneously, American Indian activists came to see the 1890 Lakota deaths as exhibit A of the United States' past treachery toward Native peoples and the nation's reckless disregard of solemn treaty obligations. The Wounded Knee Massacre therefore assumed great symbolic significance in American collective memory at a time when many in the United States were willing to question and critique a heroic account of the country's past in the service of seeking a more inclusive and just national future.

Ironically, Wounded Knee had also been central to the traditional interpretation of the history of American expansion into the West following the Civil War. In the 1890s, the Department of War celebrated the "Battle of Wounded Knee" as the culminating event of the four-hundred-year conflict between civilization and savagery for North America by awarding twenty Medals of Honor to the Seventh Cavalry for gallantry, and by erecting a monument to the thirty-five soldiers who were either killed or fatally injured on December 29, 1890. William "Buffalo Bill" Cody brought this view of Wounded Knee as a heroic battle to the silver screen in his 1913 silent film *The*

Indian Wars. The late nineteenth-century conflicts with Native peoples were therefore seen as necessary for the progress of the nation and foundation for the prosperity that followed in the twentieth century.

When it appeared in 1970, Dee Brown's *Bury My Heart at Wounded Knee: An Indian History of the American West* reversed this heroic interpretation, by seeking "to fashion a narrative of the conquest of the American West as the victims experienced it, using their own words whenever possible. Americans who have always looked westward when reading about this period should read this book facing eastward."[1] In Brown's account, Wounded Knee culminated "an incredible era of violence, greed, audacity, sentimentality, undirected exuberance, and an almost reverential attitude toward the ideal of personal freedom for those who already had it."[2] *Bury My Heart at Wounded Knee* remained on the bestseller list for over a year, making the name Wounded Knee instantly recognizable for many Americans.[3]

For seventy-one days in early 1973, Wounded Knee was the site of a major occupation by the American Indian Movement (AIM) and local Lakota activists on the Pine Ridge Indian Reservation in South Dakota. The protesters' immediate concern was corruption in the reservation's tribal government, which was supported by the Bureau of Indian Affairs. However, the protest also included a broader critique of the federal government's failure to uphold treaties and recognize past wrongs. For more than two months federal agents, backed by armored vehicles, laid siege to the protesters occupying Wounded Knee, which was widely described in the media as the site of the last major nineteenth-century massacre of Native peoples. Celebrities such as Marlon Brando publicly expressed their support for the activists. Americans told pollsters that they had followed the occupation closely as time passed, with a slight majority of respondents stating that they supported the Indians. By the time the occupation ended in early April 1973, the name Wounded Knee had become closely associated not only with the violent legacies of American expansion, but also indigenous demands that the United States respect treaties and recognize Native American sovereignty.[4]

Bury My Heart and the 1973 occupation helped elevate Wounded Knee—both the place and the 1890 event—into a place of prominence on the American memorial landscape during the 1970s. However, it was rarely recognized at the time that both Brown and the AIM occupiers had relied heavily on the endeavors of an earlier group of activists—the Lakota survivors of Big Foot's band—who had worn out their lives pursuing justice for their relatives killed at Wounded Knee on December 29, 1890. Brown's chapter on Wounded Knee relied almost exclusively on first-hand accounts given by the survivors during the 1930s. The symbolic center of AIM's occupation was the Wounded Knee mass grave where Big Foot and his slain followers were interred, marked by a monument erected by the Lakotas in 1903 to commemorate the "Chief Big Foot Massacre." Both the written accounts and the granite monument had emerged in the context of the survivors' sustained demands for compensation within the government's claims system, a pursuit of justice that ultimately brought them before the United States Congress in 1938 to testify of the wrongs committed against their people nearly five decades before. *Surviving Wounded Knee* recounts the largely unknown story of the remnant of Big Foot's band—those who survived—and their prolonged engagement with the politics of memory surrounding the event that not only shattered their world, but also framed how many Americans in the twentieth century and beyond understood their nation's history.

The Politics of Memory

Surviving Wounded Knee is not a traditional history of the killings that occurred on December 29, 1890. The event has attracted the attention of several scholars, beginning with Robert M. Utley's 1963 *Last Days of the Sioux Nation* and most recently with Jerome Greene's *American Carnage: Wounded Knee, 1890*. Readers interested in the history of Wounded Knee itself within the context of the late-nineteenth century Indian Wars are encouraged to consult these and other works.[5] *Surviving Wounded Knee* is instead a history of ways that Wounded Knee has been remembered, contested, and reimagined during the five decades after 1890. Whereas the aforementioned works explore what led to the confrontation between the Seventh Cavalry and Big Foot's people in late December 1890, *Surviving Wounded Knee* examines what came after.

Following the ideas of French sociologist Maurice Halbwachs, this book defines collective memory as a social construction. Rather than preserving a complete record of past experiences waiting only to recalled, the human mind only captures fragments of experience, which are later reconstructed to address present concerns. Memories are constructed within social frameworks, meaning that people filter and organize their memories according to the values and concerns espoused by whatever group or groups to which they belong. Collective memory refers to socially framed memories of individual experiences, as well as information about a group's past that is derived from written or oral sources, but not through direct observation.[6]

Collective memory is central to understanding how identities are formed in society. Socializing into a group means adopting not only communal norms, but also learning a group's historical memory.[7] Whereas small-scale groups often transmit historical memory orally, large-scale groups such as nations rely on written texts to create, in Benedict Anderson's term, "imagined communities."[8] In speeches, monuments, commemorations, pageants, and holidays, national elites invoke a heroic version of the nation's past that inspires and unifies a diverse and divided citizenry, encouraging patriotism, loyalty, and sacrifice for the national cause.[9] Collective memory is therefore inherently political, or what is termed here the politics of memory, as dominant groups in society struggle over how collective memory is produced and represented in official records and in public spaces.[10]

Although advocates of dominant or official memories often seek to silence, obscure, and contain competing memories of the past, marginalized groups in societies employ countermemories, or alternative understandings of history, to sustain distinct identities and pursue justice for past wrongs.[11] For Native peoples in modern America enduring the onslaught of the government's educational system that was intent on assimilating Indians into mainstream society,[12] countermemories have proven essential to the survival and persistence of indigenous cultures. The first generation of Indian students who entered the boarding schools, however, left with the tools of education that allowed them to "talk back to civilization" and critique the United States' past treatment of the Native nations within its borders, including treaty violations.[13] These critiques relied heavily on understandings of history that differed from those advocated by the federal government. This memory activism played out in negotiations with government officials and in the government's claims system, including the US Court of Claims.[14] Within this context, the Lakota survivors pursued compensation for the wrongs committed at Wounded Knee.

Chapter Overview

Chapter 1 of *Surviving Wounded Knee*, "Race War and Wounded Knee," explores the history of US–Lakota relations on the northern Great Plains and the events leading to Wounded Knee. In the early nineteenth century, the United States recognized the Lakota nation as a great power and initiated formal relations. The chapter explores the discourse of "race war," meaning the idea that Euro-American "civilization" was locked in a struggle with "savagery" for the continent. This logic shaped US–Lakota relations as the century progressed. When the Lakotas embraced the Ghost Dance, an indigenous religious movement that swept across the West in the late 1880s, army officials labeled Big Foot's band as "hostile," "fanatical," and "savage," words that created the tense atmosphere on December 29, 1890. Race war logic also shaped the earliest accounts that described Wounded Knee, written by reporters and army officers at the scene, which celebrated the event as a heroic victory over "treacherous" Ghost Dancers.

Chapter 2, "Exonerating the Seventh Cavalry," examines the emergence of competing explanations of what happened at Wounded Knee. Although the earliest accounts of the killings omitted reference to noncombatant deaths, the bodies found on the field confirmed reports that the troops had pursued and killed fleeing men, women, and children. Major General Nelson A. Miles, who oversaw the army's operations against the Ghost Dancers, launched an investigation in January 1891 into the conduct of Colonel James W. Forsyth, the commanding officer at Wounded Knee. Although Miles intended to compile evidence against his subordinate, the witnesses who testified at the court of inquiry were primarily Forsyth's own officers, who closed ranks in support of their commander. The inquiry also led to the recording of the first accounts of Lakota survivors, who argued that the cavalrymen had massacred a peaceful Lakota chief and his people. Ultimately, Secretary of War Redfield Proctor used the authority of his office to exonerate Forsyth and his men, and the court of inquiry's papers became the official "objective" government record of the event.

The third chapter, "Honoring Gallant Soldiers," analyzes the efforts by the Seventh Cavalry and the Department of War to memorialize Wounded Knee as a heroic victory. Following Forsyth's vindication he returned to Fort Riley, Kansas, determined to defend his reputation and his men from charges of perpetrating a massacre. Through Forsyth's instigation, the War Department awarded twenty Medals of Honor to the Seventh Cavalry, placing Wounded Knee among the most decorated engagements of the post-Civil War frontier army. In 1893, the Seventh Cavalry erected a monument to honor the men killed in 1890 in South Dakota. The dedication ceremony of the monument reinforced the emerging narrative that Wounded Knee culminated the four-hundred-year struggle between Euro-Americans and indigenous peoples for North America. The chapter concludes with a discussion of Buffalo Bill's 1913 *The Indian Wars*, which brought the "Battle of Wounded Knee" to American theaters.

Chapter 4, "In Memory of the Chief Big Foot Massacre," discusses the Lakota survivors' early efforts to obtain compensation for Wounded Knee and erect a monument to honor their dead. In 1891 Congress appropriated $100,000 to compensate "friendly" Lakotas—those who had not embraced the Ghost Dance—for losses incurred during the army's 1890 operations in South Dakota. Since the government had labeled Big Foot's band as hostiles, the survivors were excluded from compensation despite the fact that they had inarguably lost the most during the conflict. The chapter introduces Joseph Horn Cloud—who as a teenager in 1890 lost his parents, two brothers, and other relatives at Wounded Knee—and describes how he used his limited education to initiate claims for the survivors in the mid-1890s. Although these early claims were unsuccessful, Horn Cloud and other survivors raised funds to erect a monument in 1903 at the mass grave that commemorated "the Chief Big Foot Massacre." In the claims and the monument, the survivors engaged in the politics of memory by using the English word "massacre" to define Wounded Knee.

Chapter 5, "We Never Thought of Fighting," analyzes the survivors' efforts to work with sympathetic whites to record and disseminate the Lakotas' memories of Wounded Knee. During the first two decades of the twentieth century, several ethnographers and amateur historians interviewed the survivors. In the resulting accounts, the survivors argued a central point: the Seventh Cavalry had massacred a friendly band of Lakotas in 1890, who, in spite of embracing the Ghost Dance, had not adopted a hostile stance toward the US government. This reflected the survivors' awareness of the army's 1890 categorization that continued to impede the Lakotas from obtaining justice. In the process the survivors and their interlocutors created an alternative set of written records, now preserved in archives, which challenged the Seventh Cavalry's official record.

The sixth chapter, "Irreconcilable Memories," examines a series of official government investigations of Wounded Knee conducted during the 1910s. Securing the high-profile support of retired Lieutenant General Nelson A. Miles—the same man who had launched the investigation of the Seventh Cavalry's conduct in 1891—required the Office of Indian Affairs to at least appear like it was interested in fairly evaluating the survivors' claims. However, the officials assigned to evaluate the petitions repeatedly did so within the framework of the friendly/hostile binary, arguing that because army officials had labeled Big Foot's band as hostiles in 1890, the survivors were ineligible for compensation. The chapter compares the Lakota survivors' experience with that of the Blackfeet survivors of the 1870 Marias Massacre, who also submitted compensation claims during the 1910s. In both cases the government rejected the Natives' claims, concluding that the petitioners' memories could not be reconciled with the army's contemporary reports.

The seventh chapter, "Liquidating the Liability of the United States," examines the survivors' campaign for congressional compensation in the 1930s. The Great Depression and the restructuring of the New Deal's federal Indian policy created a somewhat favorable environment for the survivors' claims in the nation's capital. The Lakotas, drawing on a new awareness of treaty rights, reframed their memories of Wounded Knee as a violation of the 1868 Treaty of Fort Laramie. In 1933, Pine Ridge Superintendent James H. McGregor recorded the Lakotas' statements and lobbied the state's congressional leaders, which eventually produced Representative Francis Case's bill to "liquidate the liability of the United States" for Wounded Knee. Two survivors testified in support of this bill in 1938, culminating nearly five decades of memory politics. The army opposed Case's bill, basing their opposition entirely on official documents produced during the Miles-Forsyth controversy of 1891. Although concerned about the potential of setting a precedent for other compensation claims for nineteenth-century massacres, the House Committee on Indian Affairs nonetheless approved the bill. But with the onset of World War II and opposition among fiscal conservatives toward any bill that included payments for Indians, the survivors' window of opportunity closed prematurely.

The conclusion, "Surviving Wounded Knee," reviews the life of Dewey Beard. Beard was a key participant in the survivors' half-century engagement with the politics of memory. Although Beard's pursuit of justice essentially ended in 1940 when Case's bill failed, he and other survivors laid a foundation upon which Dee Brown and the American Indian Movement activists later built.

PART I

Official Memory

I

Race War and Wounded Knee

WHEN THOMAS JEFFERSON commissioned Meriwether Lewis and William Clark to lead the Corps of Discovery into the western interior of North America in 1803, the president was well aware of the "immense power" on the northern Great Plains, the Lakota nation. The Lakotas had built their power and prestige over the previous century, as they incorporated horses, guns, and buffalo hunting into their economy. They expanded their influence by cultivating relations with French traders and other Natives who had connections with the Spanish in New Mexico. The Lakotas were also known as fearsome warriors, as willing to extend their dominion through warfare as through trade. Jefferson instructed Lewis and Clark to engage Native peoples in a "most friendly & conciliatory manner," to inform them of "the object of [the Corps'] journey," and to convey the United States' desire to open "commercial intercourse" with them.[1]

In late September 1804, Lewis and Clark entered Lakota territory along the Missouri River in present-day South Dakota. For reasons that remain obscure, the American captains completely ignored the president's instructions and nearly blundered into several armed confrontations with their Native hosts. The Corps had apparently hoped to slip past the Lakotas on the Missouri River and avoid them altogether. Instead, the Americans were discovered and detained for more than a week. Rather than arriving prepared with generous gifts—an expected diplomatic gesture—Lewis and Clark only reluctantly parted with tobacco, pork, alcohol, and other small gifts. Exacerbating the problem, the captains accepted some gifts from the Lakotas while declining others.[2] Tense situations, however, were usually diffused by Black Buffalo, the Lakotas' "grand chief" whom Clark described as "a good man." Black Buffalo smoked a peace pipe with Lewis and Clark, invited the newcomers into his lodge—representing "a Great Mark of friendship"—and held a great feast in their honor. Although Black Buffalo was willing to defend and represent his people's interests, he was also fair and diplomatic with the Americans.[3]

Expedition member Patrick Gass summed up the paradoxical nature of this first official encounter between representatives of the United States and the Lakota nation. Although Gass considered the Lakotas "the most friendly people [he] ever saw," he also feared that they would steal from him if given the opportunity. His comment reflected American racial assumptions about indigenous peoples in general and the Lakotas in particular, that they were "savages," "hostile," and "treacherous."[4] These assumptions reflected broader ideas among Europeans that they were engaged in a "race war" between "savagery and civilization" for the Americas.[5] Beginning with the French and continuing with the Americans into the nineteenth century, interactions between Europeans and Lakotas were framed by the notion of race war. Ultimately, this framework would pave the road to Wounded Knee in 1890, when Black Buffalo's descendant, Big Foot—renowned as a diplomat and peacemaker in his own right—was unable to diffuse a difficult situation with the US Army, one that would only end with the deaths of hundreds of men, women, and children.

Colonialism on the Great Plains

The events that led to Wounded Knee had their roots in the 1600s, when French explorers, trappers, and missionaries established an empire, New France, in the Great Lakes region. In search of furs that could be transformed into commodities sold in European markets, the newcomers offered Native peoples European goods. To facilitate trade the French learned Native languages, intermarried with Indian women, sent Catholic missionaries, exchanged gifts, and formed alliances with indigenous nations. The French also trafficked in Indian slaves, tapping into and transforming Native trade networks that transported captives throughout New France. Native peoples, eager for trade themselves, obtained guns, horses, and new technologies that dramatically transformed their societies. Unanticipated germs accompanied the Europeans and devastated Indian populations within New France's sphere of influence.

As the French expanded their empire westward, they sought out and made trade pacts in the late 1600s with a people that they called the "Nadouesioux" (later shortened to Sioux), a loose confederation of three allied groups, the Santee Dakotas, the Yankton-Yanktonai, and the Lakotas (also known as

Tetons) that were closely related through kinship, intermarriage, and language. The French estimated at the close of the eighteenth century that there were at least 24,000 Sioux, numbers that far exceeded those of French settlers in North America.[6] Although the French saw the Sioux as valuable trading partners, the newcomers also saw these new allies in much the same light as other Natives—as savages. Like all savages, the French believed that the Sioux were inherently warlike, perhaps even exceptionally so compared to other indigenous peoples. Without a strong military presence in North America, the French had to rely heavily on more subtle strategies to enforce their sovereignty over claimed territories in the continent. The solution was to "Frenchify" or civilize Native peoples (including the Sioux) through trade, intermarriage, education, and religious conversion, and in the process transform savages into civilized subjects and bring about peace and prosperity for the New France empire.[7]

The Sioux, like other Native peoples, were happy to receive French gifts and trade goods, but they did so on their own terms and for their own purposes. In the eighteenth century Lakota and Yankton-Yanktonai bands migrated from present-day Minnesota onto the northern Great Plains, separating themselves geographically from their Dakota cousins, who remained in their traditional homelands. Although membership in Lakota bands was fluid, seven groups would become dominant on the Plains: the Oglalas (Those Who Scatter Their Own Grain), Sicangus (Brulés or Burned Thighs People), Minneconjous (Planters by the Water), Itazipcos (Sans Arcs or Those Without Bows), Oohenumpas (Two Kettles or Two Boilings People), Sihasapas (Blackfeet or Wearers of Black Moccasins), and Hunkpapas (Campers at the Entrance of the Camp Circle). These bands, empowered by guns, horses, and other European-derived goods, were attracted to the Plains by prospects of buffalo hunting and the expanses of grass that would support the Lakotas' burgeoning horse culture. Gradually, the Lakotas made incursions into the territories of other equestrian groups such as the Crows, Cheyennes, and Arapahoes that had earlier adopted horses into their economies.[8]

Lakota ascendancy as a Native power on the Plains also benefitted from the invisible threat of European germs that spread quickly with devastating effects, especially among sedentary nations such as the Mandans, Hidatsas, and Arikaras that had built large villages based on agriculture along the Missouri River. The palisades that surrounded these villages, once an effective means of keeping out nomadic raiders, could not protect those inside from the silent invasion of smallpox and other European diseases in the late eighteenth and early nineteenth centuries. By contrast, horses gave the

Lakotas sufficient mobility to minimize the impact of dangerous microbes. The decline of the sedentary nations allowed the Lakotas to gain control of a large territory between the Mississippi and Missouri Rivers that was rich with beaver and buffalo on the northern plains.[9] In spite of French efforts to civilize and control the Lakotas, interaction with New France's representatives had ultimately contributed to the Lakota nation's rise as a power and the decline of other Native peoples in the northern Great Plains region.

By the time the United States acquired France's Louisiana territory in 1803, the Lakotas had already had a long history with European peoples and goods that had transformed their nation into a dominant power intent on expanding its influence in the region. Although the US claimed sovereignty over Lakota-dominated lands, that control was on paper only. When Meriwether Lewis and William Clark reached the northern Great Plains in 1804, they recognized the Lakotas as the principal obstacle to American expansion. Like the French, the Americans viewed their relations with the Lakotas and other Native peoples through the lens of race war, as savages opposing the rightful advance of civilization. Lewis characterized the Lakotas as "the vilest miscreants of the savage race" and the "pirates of the Missouri," a Native nation that the United States would need to reduce to a state of "dependence" upon American goods.[10] A half century later, the United States again acknowledged the Lakota nation's dominance in the 1851 Treaty of Horse Creek, which recognized the tribe's conquests over other Native nations and its extensive territory covering more than half of present-day South Dakota as well as parts of Nebraska, Wyoming, Montana, and North Dakota.[11]

The 1851 treaty was designed to protect overland emigrants and secure the government's right to maintain roads and forts in territories controlled by Indians. As white incursions into Lakota lands increased during the 1850s conflict between the United States and the Lakotas came to a head, resulting in all-out war by the mid-1860s. The primary point of contention was the Bozeman Trail, which miners had been using to cross Lakota territory into Montana. In spite of obvious treaty infractions in such crossings, Americans simplified the struggle into a contest between civilization and savagery, with "friendly" Lakotas supporting the expansion of American sovereignty and "hostiles" opposing the miners' incursions. This rhetorical strategy had roots stretching back to the beginnings of European colonization of North America and the emergence of race war ideology. In December 1866 the army suffered a devastating defeat—later known as the Fetterman Massacre—when the Lakotas ambushed and killed eighty soldiers. Such events reinforced white stereotypes of the inherently warlike nature of savages.

The United States, fearing an extended military campaign after the Civil War when many wanted to reduce the size of the army, decided to seek peace. Additionally, the government hoped to protect workers building the Union Pacific railroad, which, once completed, would render the Bozeman Trail unnecessary. In 1868 militants under the leadership of Oglala chief Red Cloud signed the Treaty of Fort Laramie, which called for permanent peace between the United States and the Lakotas, established mechanisms to settle disputes and provide compensation for damaged property, defined the boundaries of the Great Sioux Reservation (comprising the western half of present-day South Dakota), and promised provisions and farming equipment. Although the treaty reflected some Lakota perspectives, it nonetheless limited Lakota sovereignty and authorized the United States to build railroads within Lakota lands.[12]

Under the leadership of Hunkpapa medicine leader Sitting Bull and Oglala warrior Crazy Horse, other Lakotas rejected the treaty and continued to oppose American incursions into Lakota lands. Conflict with nontreaty bands came to a head in the early 1870s, when President Ulysses S. Grant moved to seize the Black Hills, a site where gold had recently been discovered, but also a religious, economic, and cultural center of Lakota life. The ensuing war included the Lakotas' resounding victory over Lieutenant Colonel George Armstrong Custer at the Little Bighorn on June 25, 1876. This defeat would have a profound impact on the American psyche and memory, with reverberations that would manifest themselves fourteen years later at Wounded Knee. In spite of the Lakota victory, after a long winter, starving tribal militants began surrendering due to lack of provisions and after negotiating some concessions. Sitting Bull and his followers regrouped north of the border in Canada. George W. Manypenny subsequently led a government delegation charged with acquiring the Black Hills from the Lakotas. Although the 1868 Treaty of Fort Laramie specified that three-fourths of all adult Lakota males needed to approve any land sales, the commission could only muster a small number of signatures.[13]

During the 1880s, the Lakotas experienced in microcosm the broad assimilationist assault on tribal societies that the government waged against indigenous nations confined to reservations, an assault intended to eliminate savagery and inculcate civilized habits among Native peoples. With the reorganization of federal Indian policy in the decade, the American settler colonial project was fully implemented in Indian Country. As scholar Patrick Wolfe has argued, "invasion is a structure not an event," meaning settlers are immigrants who come to stay, eliminate indigenous competitors for territory, and establish a new colonial society on the expropriated land.[14] This elimination did not always involve outright murder. According to Wolfe, "the settler colonial logic of elimination in its crudest frontier form [was] a violent rejection of all things Indian." Once Indians were confined to reservations, however, the logic of elimination "was transformed into a paternalistic mode of governmentality which, though still sanctioned by state violence, came to focus on assimilation rather than rejection. Invasion became bureaucratised, a paper-trail of tears that penetrated Indian life in the form of Bureau of Indian Affairs officials rather than the US Cavalry."[15] In the 1880s, the government implemented new policies to accelerate Native assimilation.[16]

Within the Great Sioux Reservation, federal authorities established agencies to distribute treaty annuities, which white officials hoped would induce Lakotas to adopt farming, cattle-raising, and permanent homes in place of seasonal hunting migrations—a transition that the rapid disappearance of buffalo herds would facilitate.[17] These officials coerced families to send their children to schools, both on and off reservations, where their hair was cut, their traditional clothing was exchanged for "citizen clothes," they were given English names, and they were punished for speaking Lakota. This effort to "kill the Indian, save the man," however, resulted in many young Lakota—including future survivors of Wounded Knee—becoming literate in English, a skill they later used to protect against further land loss, seek to regain land that had previously been taken, and inscribe their memories of a violent past in written form.[18] Agency officials also attempted to suppress Lakota religious customs deemed savage—such as the Sun Dance, death and mourning rituals, and traditional healing practices—all while encouraging conversion to western religions.[19] Officials intended the assimilation program to replace tribal political, cultural, and economic structures with individualism.[20]

Transforming indigenous relationships with the land was central to assimilation policy. Reformers argued that because Indians misunderstood the notion of private property, they lacked the traits necessary for civilized life. Additionally, settlers, capitalists, and state and territorial officials pressured the federal government to open up "unused" tribal lands to whites for development. In 1889, a government commission pressured the Lakotas into an agreement that divided the Great Sioux Reservation into six smaller units: the Standing Rock, Cheyenne River, Pine Ridge, Rosebud, Crow Creek, and Lower Brulé reservations. The deal transferred nine million acres—nearly half of the Lakotas' remaining territory—into non-Indian hands. Paralleling the logic behind the 1887 General Allotment Act, the agreement also provided that each smaller reservation would eventually be divided into one-hundred and sixty or three hundred and twenty acre allotments, one assigned to each head of house, thereby teaching Natives the virtues of private property.[21]

The assimilation program divided the Lakotas between those who endorsed accommodation—progressives—and those who advocated continued resistance against the United States—traditionalists. Whites viewed these divisions as evidence that some Natives were more inclined to accept civilization, while others remained irreconcilably opposed to it. Traditionalists were often labeled "hostiles," the same name given previously to militants who

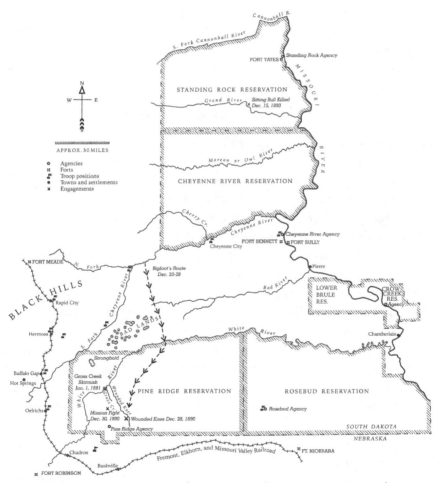

FIGURE 1.1 Lakota Reservations and Vicinity, 1890–1891. *American Carnage*, by Jerome A. Greene. Copyright 2014 University of Oklahoma Press. Reproduced with permission. All rights reserved.

armed themselves and physically opposed the consolidation of American sovereignty. The logic of race war therefore continued to shape white perceptions of Indians even after the latter's confinement to reservations. However, as historian Jeffrey Ostler notes, it is crucial

> to realize that Sioux leaders adopted a *range* of strategies based on reasoned assessments of changing conditions and possibilities. Sioux leaders were not always locked into polar antagonisms. Rather, they adjusted their tactics in light of new circumstances and were responsive to changing opinion among their people. Leaders cooperated among themselves on some initiatives and engaged in the tough political work of mending fences and building unity.[22]

Despite the labels applied to them, Lakotas continued to seek solutions to the problems that beset them and their people.

The Ghost Dance and Fanaticism

In the late 1880s, a Paiute prophet named Wovoka preached a powerful message from Nevada: Indians' deceased relatives would soon return, disease would be no more, and everyone would be young. Buffalo and other game would reappear, and, through supernatural means, Euro-Americans would be removed from North America. This message spread rapidly from tribe to tribe throughout the West, and various nations, including the Lakotas, sent delegations to Wovoka for first-hand instruction.[23] To usher in this millennium, Wovoka advised his disciples to avoiding harming others, to do good to whites, and to perform the Ghost Dance (*wanáǧi waćhípi*), which involved fasting and dancing until exhaustion induced a visionary experience.[24]

The press interpreted the Ghost Dance within the framework of fanaticism, or irrational behavior that fell outside of mainstream acceptability. Fanaticism described an entire system, requiring an imposter who claimed visions and dupes who uncritically accepted the false prophet's delusions. The concept emerged in the context of the Protestant Reformation, when it was used to describe individuals who claimed direct revelation, either from a divine or demonic source. Mainstream Protestants such as Martin Luther who worked within the confines of established society governments condemned adherents of the Radical Reformation (Anabaptists and others) as fanatics, claiming that their zeal to build the City of God would destroy civil society itself. Fanaticism served as a foil to reason, placing fanatics and lunatics in a broad category opposite of sane people. Only violence, in Luther's view, could stop fanatical madness from dismantling not just the Reformation, but European society as a whole.[25] Prophets proliferated in the transatlantic world from the seventeenth through nineteenth centuries, with millennial "doomsayers" proclaiming the fulfillment of biblical prophecy and the end times.[26]

Anglo-Americans employed the framework of fanaticism to describe indigenous prophets who led resistance movements against European expansion in the late eighteenth and early nineteenth centuries. When applied against indigenous peoples, the polarity between rational civilization and savage fanaticism became explicit. British soldier and American frontiersman Robert Rogers, for example, wrote that "religious impostures are not less frequent among the Indians of America, than among the Christians of Europe," with indigenous prophets "persuading the multitude that they are filled with a divine enthusiasm." Additionally, "they often persuade the people that they have revelations of future events" and that they understand "the mysteries of religion and a future state," offering promises to their credulous followers of the "inexhaustible plenty of every thing desirable" in the world to come.[27] The framework was used to dismiss Neolin, the Delaware Prophet during the Seven Years' War and the Shawnee Prophet Tenswatawa during the War of 1812, as well as their followers.[28] This language extended and reinforced notions of race war between civilization and savagery for the continent.

The Ghost Dance was therefore seen as simply the latest manifestation of indigenous fanaticism. Rumors circulated in the press that the Ghost Dance had inspired tribes throughout the West to form a military conspiracy of historic proportions against American sovereignty and white settlement in the region. Washington, DC's *The Daily Critic* quoted "Captain Trimbleton ... commandant at Fort Sill [Oklahoma]" as saying that "the greatest Indian uprising of modern times is certainly to come soon." Trimbleton claimed that five thousand Natives of unidentified tribes were performing "a series of incantations and religious orgies" as they waited for the "Great Medicine Man" to come and "wipe out the whites and restore to them the ownership of the country."[29] The Chicago *Inter Ocean* placed the "Messiah Craze" within a long history of "bogus Messiahs" who offered vain promises of immortality and a coming millennium to their "deluded enthusiasts." While these "false prophets and pseudo Christs" could be found in all cultures, the Ghost Dance was the latest in a line of Indian "crazes" stretching back to colonial times.[30]

However, there were some observers who believed that there was something far more sinister at work. Major General Nelson A. Miles, for example,
informed the *New York Times* that it was his belief after a careful investigation that "the impersonator of the Messiah . . . is a full-blooded white." In
fact, Miles contended that "the Mormons are the prime movers in all this."[31]
The general played on a long-standing distrust of the Church of Jesus Christ
of Latter-day Saints, informally known as the Mormon Church. Protestants
had deployed the fanaticism framework to describe Mormonism, casting
the sect's founder, Joseph Smith, as an imposter, his claim to new revelation
as a delusion, and his followers as dupes. Aside from polygamy, communal-
ism, and incipient theocracy, opponents denounced the church's attempts
to evangelize Native peoples—efforts that stemmed from a belief that indigenes were a remnant of scattered Israel—as "tampering" with Indians and a
threat to American sovereignty.[32] Historians have been skeptical of a direct
tie between the Mormons and the Ghost Dance, since Wovoka himself had a
Presbyterian background and indigenous converts to Mormonism were evidently not attracted to the Ghost Dance. Observers like Miles, however, saw
Mormonism and the Ghost Dance as two manifestations of the same fanatical threat to the American nation.[33]

Toward Wounded Knee (Čhaŋkpé Ópi)

By the end of the 1880s, the economic and social situation on the South
Dakota reservations had reached a nadir. A decade of relentless governmen-
tal assault on Lakota customs and land base, the steady decline of the buffalo
population, drought-inflicted poor harvests that limited food supplies, and
disease combined to depress the population severely. Furthermore, Congress
reduced the Lakotas' beef rations by twenty-five percent. The promises of government officials and Lakota leaders who argued for accommodation with
whites seemed hollow.[34]

In late summer 1890, after a severe drought brought crop failures and
famine, the Lakotas on various reservations embraced Wovoka's message. As
anthropologist Raymond DeMallie has shown, the Ghost Dance resonated
with Lakota beliefs regarding the relationship between humans and the natural world. They understood the disappearance of buffalo herds, the crop
failures, and their declining land base as the result of a failure to access and
channel spiritual power through traditional practices such as the Sun Dance,
which had been banned during the previous decade. Adopting the Ghost
Dance was therefore an attempt to reestablish a connection with spiritual

forces that could reverse the misfortunes that had undermined their society and culture since the US government and army began pressuring the Lakota people onto reservations.[35]

Ghost Dance camps formed on the Pine Ridge and Rosebud Reservations in the south, with Chief Red Cloud offering tacit support. In the north, Ghost Dancers gathered under the protection of Chiefs Hump and Big Foot on Cheyenne River, and on Standing Rock with Sitting Bull as the primary leader. It is unclear how much these chiefs participated in the dance—Sitting Bull, for example, admitted publicly his failure to experience a vision—but each leader encouraged his followers to dance.[36] At the movement's height in fall 1890 there were perhaps four to five thousand Ghost Dancers, comprising nearly thirty percent of the Lakota population.[37] Although the Ghost Dance primarily appealed to those Lakota bands with a history of resisting the federal government's assimilation project, disillusioned advocates of accommodation to white demands also joined the Ghost Dancers.[38]

Observers speculated that the Lakotas had twisted Wovoka's peaceful religion into a militaristic cult intent on destroying whites, citing as evidence the adoption of ceremonial Ghost Shirts, which were believed to make their wearers invulnerable to bullets.[39] Although it is true, as historian Rani-Henrik Andersson notes, that the "Lakotas were extremely unhappy and longed for the traditional way of life and for the time before the white man interfered with their lives," no surviving evidence suggests that the dance had militaristic elements or that the Lakota adherents were plotting attacks on white settlements. The dance would bring about a spiritual transformation of the world, with the Messiah bringing about supernatural changes, rather than Lakota warriors physically ushering in the anticipated great reversal.[40] In DeMallie's words, "from the 1850s through the 1870s the Lakotas tried to get rid of the whites by war; in 1890 they tried ritual dancing and prayer."[41]

Indian Office agents, many of whom were political appointees with little experience with Indians, responded with alarm to the new movement at the various reservations. President Benjamin Harrison's Interior Department, eager to keep the newly created states of North and South Dakota in the Republican electoral column, departed from the policies of previous administrations by allowing local party leaders to appoint Indian agents, rather than tapping them in Washington, DC. "Home Rule," as political historian Heather Cox Richardson has described this change in policy,

was terrible for the Indians. State officials would simply hand out the lucrative agency appointments to local political supporters. The quality of Indian agents plummeted: the new agents were men who were out of work and money . . . and were unlikely to be skilled administrators. And because they were local appointees, bred of a culture that was determined to get Indians out of the way of American development, the new agents had no sympathy for their charges.[42]

For example, Daniel F. Royer was a failed South Dakota medical doctor who nonetheless could deliver votes. After his appointment as Pine Ridge Agent in October 1890, Ghost Dancers defied his orders that they cease dancing,

FIGURE 1.2 Chief Big Foot, second from right, and Horned Cloud, first on left, ca. 1889–1890, photographer unknown. Photo courtesy of Her Many Horses Family Collection.

causing him to panic and ask for troops to restore order. On neighboring Rosebud, temporary agent E. B. Reynolds also suggested the need for troops.[43]

Standing Rock Agent James McLaughlin and Cheyenne River Agent Perain P. Palmer advised that rather than bring in troops, the reservation police should instead arrest Sitting Bull, Big Foot, and other leaders. McLaughlin, a longtime Indian Office employee and strict administrator of the government's assimilation programs, described Sitting Bull as the "high priest and leading apostle of this latest Indian absurdity."[44] Palmer, a recent appointee, met with Hump and Big Foot to assess the situation. Although Big Foot advocated traditional ways, he was nonetheless a peacemaker who preferred negotiation to violent resistance. Palmer noted that "Big Foot talked freely in regard to the ghost dance, claiming that he was only leading or advising with a view to thoroughly investigate the matters." The agent opined that "Big Foot appeared friendly," but nonetheless labeled the chief a "hostile" leader who should be removed from the reservation.[45] Palmer's inexperience with Indians led him to vacillate between seeing the Ghost Dance as a threat and considering it harmless, but his recommendation that Big Foot be arrested and removed from the reservation shaped perceptions of the chief that ultimately set the stage for both Wounded Knee and subsequent remembrance of the event.[46]

Although military authorities initially hesitated to send soldiers, on November 13 President Benjamin Harrison ordered troops to maintain control of the Lakota reservations, avert an uprising, and protect settlers. Over the next few weeks, as many as seven thousand soldiers—including members of the Seventh Cavalry—arrived on the Lakota reservations.[47] Since 1876, the Little Bighorn had entered American memory as the hallowed resting place for two hundred and sixty-eight soldiers who had shed their blood for American civilization. The War Department designated the grounds as a national cemetery, erected an imposing monument at the site, and awarded twenty-four Medals of Honor to the surviving cavalrymen.[48] William "Buffalo Bill" Cody reenacted Custer's Last Stand in his Wild West shows, poets and novelists heralded the "boy general," and artists rendered his last moments on canvas.[49] Many observers in late 1890 anticipated a concluding, more favorable, chapter in the Custer saga. "The sending of the Seventh cavalry to the Sioux agency may afford it an opportunity to take long delayed vengeance on Sitting Bull and his warriors," noted one paper. "Pride in its name and fame as the organization and the memory of the misfortune which befell it on the Little Big Horn in 1876 will give it an increased desire to once again meet Sitting Bull and his braves in deadly combat, and to the cry of 'Remember Custer.' "[50]

As Jeffrey Ostler has noted, "because there was no real evidence that the ghost dancers threatened settlers' lives, the decision to send troops arguably violated Article I of the 1868 Treaty," which pledged the United States to maintain peace with the Lakota nation.[51] While many Lakotas sought security in the agencies, frightened Ghost Dancers congregated in remote villages and in an area of the Badlands known as the Stronghold, northwest of the Pine Ridge Agency.[52] Although they hoped to survive through the winter using cattle and other supplies confiscated from "friendly" Lakotas who had abandoned their homes for the agencies, army officials successfully exploited divisions among the Ghost Dancers, convincing the majority to surrender by mid-December.[53] At Cheyenne River, Major General Nelson A. Miles contacted prominent Ghost Dancer Hump, with whom he had a prior relationship, and convinced the Minneconjou leader to abandon the dance and enlist as a government scout.[54] At Standing Rock, Agent McLaughlin sent the agency Indian police to arrest Sitting Bull on December 15, which resulted in the police shooting and killing the Hunkpapa holy man.[55]

Between one hundred and fifty and two hundred of Sitting Bull's followers, fearing that they would be pursued and killed, fled to the Cheyenne River Reservation, setting off a chain reaction that led to Wounded Knee. While most of Sitting Bull's people stopped at the agency to accept provisions, nearly four dozen continued on to Big Foot's camp. Miles dispatched Lieutenant Colonel Edwin V. Sumner to arrest Big Foot, whom the general identified as dangerous and casting the band as "hostile." However, upon witnessing the impoverished state of Big Foot's followers and Sitting Bull's refugees, Sumner believed he could convince the Ghost Dancers to surrender voluntarily and accompany him to nearby Fort Bennett. He allowed them to camp in their own village on December 22, expecting them to continue with him to the fort the next day. During the night on December 23, however, Big Foot and four hundred followers—nearly two-thirds of whom were women and children—slipped away to the south.[56] Members of Big Foot's band later explained that a local rancher had warned them that soldiers were coming to attack them. Some frightened warriors argued they should flee south to Pine Ridge. Big Foot initially hesitated, stating that he did not want to leave his home, but eventually acquiesced, explaining that Red Cloud had previously promised the Minneconjou chief one hundred horses if he would help resolve the Pine Ridge troubles.[57]

Although the band covered fifty miles during the first night and day of travel, on Christmas Day they were forced to stop and rest, since Big Foot had developed pneumonia. After messengers informed Red Cloud at Pine Ridge of the situation, the Oglala chief warned the Minneconjous that soldiers were looking for them. Meanwhile, the remaining Ghost Dancers in the Stronghold, hearing promises of good treatment if they surrendered, continued their steady stream into Pine Ridge.[58] Despite the waning likelihood of Big Foot joining other "hostiles" in the Stronghold, Miles believed that Big Foot's move south revealed his hostile intentions. The general ordered that the Minneconjou chief should be located, arrested, and disarmed, authorizing troops to "destroy him" if he resisted. This order would have profound ramifications. Despite Red Cloud's warning of soldiers, Big Foot's illness required the band to move straight for the agency. On December 28, Major Samuel M. Whitside of the Seventh Cavalry intercepted the Minneconjous, who voluntarily surrendered under a white flag. Whitside met with the ailing chief and demanded that Big Foot's warriors give up their weapons. The chief agreed, but indicated that his men were nervous and would prefer to deliver their guns at Pine Ridge. Unable to force the Indians to disarm, the major moved the Lakotas to a camp on Wounded Knee Creek (*Čhaŋkpé Ópi*), where they spent a restless night.[59]

The next morning, the Seventh Cavalry, comprising more than five hundred men, surrounded the Minneconjous at Wounded Knee. Colonel James W. Forsyth, a distinguished Civil War and Indian Wars veteran, had assumed command of the regiment. He ordered Big Foot's warriors, numbering just over one hundred men, to surrender their weapons. The soldiers separated the Lakota men from the women and children, as the warriors began depositing their weapons nearby. Forsyth, believing that the Lakotas were hiding weapons in the camp, ordered a few of his men to search the wagons and tents. As they did so, the troops agitated the women and children, as well as the men who stood helpless while the soldiers harassed their families. During the disarmament a shot rang out, precipitating the bloodshed that followed. When the smoke cleared hundreds of Lakota men, women, and children lay dead, some miles away from the initial campground. Twenty-five cavalrymen also lost their lives, and several more sustained injuries.[60]

Wiping Out Inhuman and Bloodthirsty Brutes

The first written accounts of Wounded Knee were consistent with the race war assumptions that had defined Lakota interactions with Europeans since

FIGURE 1.3 James W. Forsyth, ca. 1890, photographer unknown, James W. Forsyth Family Collection, UW32357. Photo courtesy of University of Washington Libraries, Special Collections.

the seventeenth century. The earliest recorded descriptions of the event, recorded within hours of Wounded Knee, came from journalists who witnessed the fight and from Colonel James W. Forsyth of the Seventh Cavalry. These individuals had a great deal of power to shape how Wounded Knee would be remembered. Gilded Age journalists wielded the cultural authority of the printed word to shape the views of tens of thousands of readers.[61] As a respected field commander, Forsyth enjoyed substantial clout in the army. Sharing a common vocabulary, these early accounts were framed by the logic of race war. The journalists assumed that the Seventh Cavalrymen had

performed their duty at Wounded Knee and had gallantly conducted themselves according to the laws of civilized warfare: they honored the white flag
of truce, they restrained themselves in the face of attack, and they protected
noncombatants.[62] The Lakotas of Big Foot's band, conversely, demonstrated
all the characteristics of savages: they violated the white flag and treacherously
attacked unsuspecting soldiers.[63] Rendered irrational by the Ghost Dance,
the warriors were deemed fanatical and dangerous, launching their attack
against a superior force and in the process endangering their own women and
children. Wounded Knee was therefore a heroic battle, for which the soldiers
who gave their lives should be honored.[64]

It has been said that reporters write the first draft of history, and such
was the case at Wounded Knee. *Omaha Daily Bee* correspondent Charles
H. Cressey claimed to have been "within touching distance of the treacherous devils" during the disarmament. In an article entitled "A Bloody Battle,"
Cressey explained that "while [the disarmament] was going on the warriors
held an incantation pow-wow," referring to the Ghost Dance. "All thought
of any trouble was evidently wholly out of mind with the soldiers," Cressey
noted. "About a dozen of the warriors had been searched [for weapons], when,
like a flash, all the rest of them jerked guns from under their blankets and
began pouring bullets into the ranks of the soldiers."[65] In Cressey's view, by
catching the soldiers unawares, the Lakotas epitomized stereotypical treacherous savages, or Indians who feigned friendship before attacking opponents.
By claiming that the warriors had acted treacherously, Cressey was tapping
into a tradition of seeing whites as innocent victims of Indian aggression.
Euro-Americans had long portrayed Indians as inherently warlike, launching
unprovoked attacks on settlers and soldiers.[66]

The troops, in Cressey's treatment, showed great forbearance in the face of
this onslaught. The journalist related that the Lakotas' "first volley was almost
as one man, so that they must have fired a hundred shots before the soldiers
fired one. But how they were slaughtered after that first volley!"[67] Since the
troops were simply defending themselves, they were not responsible for the
subsequent carnage. The *Bee* reporter, however, nowhere indicated in his
article whether women and children were among the Indians "slaughtered"
at Wounded Knee. His language was sufficiently vague that a casual reader
might have assumed that the fight was between soldiers and warriors and that
all the women and children were among those who escaped "to the small hills
to the southwest."[68] The *New York Herald*'s Charles W. Allen was likewise
vague in his published account, describing the battle in detail but neglecting
to mention the fate of women and children.[69] These reporters composed their

"instant histories" within hours of Wounded Knee, transmitted them via telegram that evening, and saw them published the following morning, with newspapers copying their articles nationwide.[70]

In his first account of the engagement, Colonel James W. Forsyth reported to his superiors that some warriors had been killed, but he was silent on noncombatant deaths.[71] On December 30, Major General Nelson A. Miles received word that Forsyth's men had counted eighty male bodies around the site of the disarmament and had seen other dead warriors in the ravine, but the need to return to the agency precluded a full body count. Miles learned that "the women and children broke for the hills when the fight commenced, and comparatively few of them were hurt." The cavalrymen had transported thirty-nine women and children to the agency, twenty-one of whom were injured. Forsyth, therefore, strongly implied that no women or children had been killed. Assuming that Wounded Knee was a fight against warriors, Miles concluded that the Lakotas' "severe loss at the hands of the 7th Cavalry may be a wholesome lesson to the other Sioux."[72] Writing from Washington, DC, John M. Schofield, Commanding General of the Army, asked Miles to "give [Schofield's] thanks to the brave 7th Cavalry for their splendid conduct."[73]

On New Year's Eve, Forsyth wrote his official Wounded Knee report. In it the colonel explained that the trouble began when a medicine man "in Ghost Dance costume, began an address to which I paid no attention, as the Interpreter [Philip H. Wells] told me he was talking of wiping out the whites. I then made him cease his address."[74] After ordering his men to search the one hundred and six warriors, "the bucks made a break, which at once resulted in a terrific fire and a hot fight lasting about twenty minutes, followed by skirmish firing of about one hour," thereby paralleling the reporters' descriptions of fanatical treachery.[75] When the fighting ceased, Forsyth's men counted ninety dead warriors, and the colonel reiterated that "from the first instant the squaws started for the hills and it is my belief that comparatively few of them were injured." Forsyth did, however, acknowledge that his men had pursued and killed three Lakotas whose gender "could not be determined."[76] The Seventh Cavalry's losses included Captain George D. Wallace and twenty-four other soldiers. The colonel closed his report by praising his men's "gallant conduct" against "Indians in desperate condition and crazed by religious fanaticism."[77]

The race war logic that framed Forsyth's official report reflected the long-standing Euro-American views of Native peoples generally and Lakotas specifically. The French were the first to cast the Lakotas as savages who, although valuable trade partners, were nevertheless dangerous and treacherous and needed to be "Frenchified" and civilized. Later, the Americans used similar language to define the terms of engagement with the Lakotas, a nation that Jefferson saw as an "immense power" that should be approached with caution. The Corps of Discovery's interactions with Black Buffalo in 1804 demonstrated that Americans were skeptical that Lakota overtures of friendship were really treacherous ploys to catch the newcomers unawares. These assumptions governed interactions between the United States and the Lakotas throughout the nineteenth century that culminated at Wounded Knee.

The journalists' and Forsyth's accounts of Wounded Knee would set the terms of the debate over what exactly happened at the creek on December 29, 1890. These accounts, drafted by journalists who witnessed the fight and by Colonel Forsyth, told a remarkably consistent story of treacherous Ghost Dancers opening fire on unsuspecting troops. These statements presumed that the soldiers were innocent victims of savage fanatics who violated a white flag of truce. The cavalrymen showed great forbearance, in accordance with the rules of civilized warfare, only returning fire after sustaining heavy casualties. The authors of these statements were conspicuously silent on whether women and children were among the dead when the fighting subsided. These accounts, however, would not remain unchallenged for long, with the Seventh Cavalry's foremost critic coming from within the ranks of the army itself.

2

Exonerating the Seventh Cavalry

ON FEBRUARY 12, 1891, Secretary of War Redfield Proctor issued an official statement on the US Seventh Cavalry's engagement at Wounded Knee Creek, South Dakota. The secretary argued that the fight had started on December 29, 1890, when Minneconjou Lakota Chief Big Foot's "band of savage fanatics," incited by a Ghost Dance medicine man, attacked Colonel James W. Forsyth's unsuspecting troops. The cavalrymen responded to this "treachery" with coolness and discretion, and they had protected the Lakota women and children endangered by the warriors' attack. Proctor conceded that a large number of women and children were among the dead. He insisted, however, that the soldiers were not responsible for their deaths, for various reasons. First, when the Lakota men opened fire on the troops, the bullets missed the soldiers and hit fleeing women and children. Additionally, after the warriors escaped from the surprised troops, they mixed with their families, further endangering the women and children. Finally, Proctor argued that at a distance, the soldiers could not discern the difference between Lakota men and women due to their similar clothing, hair length, and appearance. Proctor concluded by commending Forsyth for his leadership at Wounded Knee and praising the cavalrymen for their gallantry in action.[1]

The Secretary of War's statement was intended as an authoritative intervention in the intense controversy over what exactly had happened at Wounded Knee on December 29, 1890. In this Gilded Age saga, a cacophony of voices competed for primacy. The earliest written accounts, produced by journalists and army officers, heralded the Seventh Cavalry for a heroic triumph over "treacherous savages," while omitting any reference to noncombatant deaths. Reports quickly surfaced, however, of the cavalrymen hunting down and killing fleeing women and children. Major General Nelson A. Miles, a longtime critic of "exterminationist" rhetoric and associated army policies, condemned

Wounded Knee as "the most abominable military blunder and a horrible massacre of women and children," relieved Forsyth of command, and instituted a court of inquiry to investigate the colonel's conduct. Ironically, rather than compiling a record of Forsyth's incompetence, the inquiry based its report on Forsyth's own officers' testimonies, who unanimously supported their commander.[2] The Lakota survivors of Wounded Knee, although peripheral in public discourse, also found ways to participate in the struggles over how the event would be remembered and critique the Seventh Cavalry's narrative. However, it was the power of Proctor's office that allowed him to elevate a particular interpretation of Wounded Knee—one that, like the age in which the secretary operated, glossed over charges of corruption—to official status while marginalizing competing memories of the killings.[3]

"A Sioux Squaw is as Bad an Enemy as a Buck"

Even before the ink had fully dried on Forsyth's official account of Wounded Knee, observers were raising questions about the major gap in his story—namely, the fate of women and children in Big Foot's band. As Lakota scouts and injured survivors of Wounded Knee made their way back to the agency, they shared chilling stories of soldiers hunting down fleeing noncombatants. Reporters quickly published these stories in newspapers.[4] Such allegations would not have been considered news a few decades earlier, since "collateral damage" had long been part of Indian-white warfare. During the Civil War, however, a burgeoning reform movement began applying the word "massacre" to such killings as part of a broader critique of the government's poor treatment of Native peoples. Reformers knowingly shocked their audiences with this language, since most whites associated massacres with bloodthirsty "savages" who delighted in cruelty and indiscriminate murder of innocents. The rhetoric aggravated anxieties that Anglo-Americans—purportedly the most advanced race with the most advanced nation in world history—were regressing into "barbarism." By condemning soldiers' mass killings, reformers sought to preserve their own views of America's greatness by casting atrocities as aberrations incidental to the nation's progress.[5]

Journalists and army officials vigorously disputed these charges, arguing that women and children were not harmless, innocent bystanders. Americans and Indians, after all, were in a race war for control of the continent. Many absolved the troops by arguing that warfare with Indians did not necessitate compliance with the laws of civilized warfare, which required otherwise honorable soldiers to use the savage's methods to effectively combat their enemies. Others insisted that the nation's soldiers actually obeyed the rules of enlightened warfare—even when women and children died—since when fighting Indians, there were no noncombatants. Native women and children, it was contended, fought alongside the warriors. It should be noted that while it was acceptable in Native American societies for women to participate in warfare, such "manly-hearted women" were rare.[6] In the face of reformers' accusations, army officials drew on these stock justifications to defend their men in the field. In some cases, when evidence glaringly undermined their arguments, the army scapegoated middling officers, with the most famous example being the official investigation and condemnation of Colonel John Milton Chivington in the wake of the Sand Creek Massacre of 1864, although Chivington ultimately left the army before receiving formal censure. But in most instances, army officials closed ranks against the reformers' accusations. It was generally assumed that commanding officers would not accuse their subordinates of committing massacre. Scapegoating middling officers and closing ranks effectively constructed massacres of Indian women and children as isolated events, rather than a structural result of the logic of race war.[7]

This context shaped Forsyth's and his media allies' subsequent attempt to control the memory of Wounded Knee in the face of alternative accounts of the fight.[8] *Omaha World-Herald* reporter Thomas H. Tibbles, in an article entitled "All Murdered in a Mass," reported that "the Indian scouts who have come in say that but few of Big Foot's band are left."[9] Tibbles's use of the word "murder" to describe the killings signaled his deep sympathy for the plight of Native peoples and his previous work in publicizing government wrongs against Indians.[10] With his wife, Susette "Bright Eyes" LaFlesche, Tibbles visited wounded Lakota survivors being treated in an Episcopal Chapel-turned-hospital at Pine Ridge. Bright Eyes, a mixed-race Omaha woman, was, like her husband, a journalist and a staunch advocate of Indian rights. The survivors described to the Tibbles how the soldiers killed their families. Additionally, survivors claimed that the Seventh Cavalry had left dead and dying Lakotas on the ground, some of whom may have still been alive.[11]

Heavy snows had fallen on the night of December 29, delaying burial of the bodies for several days. Charles A. Eastman, a Dakota doctor practicing at Pine Ridge, led a team in search of survivors on January 1, 1891. Eastman later described finding "the body of a woman completely covered with a blanket of snow" three miles from Wounded Knee. As they approached the killing field, they "found [more bodies] scattered along as they had been relentlessly

FIGURE 2.1 Big Foot lying dead in the snow at Wounded Knee, 1891, by George Trager, Wounded Knee Massacre Collection, RG2845-13-8. Photo courtesy of Nebraska State Historical Society.

hunted down and slaughtered while fleeing for their lives."[12] Many of his Lakota companions, seeing dead relatives, began singing death songs.[13] The party discovered nine Lakotas, including infants, who had remarkably survived the subfreezing temperatures.[14]

When a burial party finally visited the killing field on January 3, its members saw bloodied bodies strewn across the ground, in a ravine, and even in the distant hills.[15] Photographers captured images of the dead—including the Ghost Dance medicine man and Big Foot—and the bodies piled in the mass grave on a nearby hill, which newspapers and illustrated magazines published over the coming days and weeks across the nation.[16] To augment the appeal of the pictures, the photographers rearranged the bodies in grotesque positions to portray the Lakotas as "treacherous" even in death. One picture showed Big Foot "shot through and through"—as the *Omaha World-Herald* described him—lying "in a sort of solitary dignity" for his photograph.

Another image showed the dead medicine man propped up against another body with a gun placed next to him. Smith stated that the medicine man

had a face which was hideous to view. It gave you a shiver just to glance at it. It was the face of an old man, sharp drawn and wrinkled. The look of a demon was there, but it was not that which caused the remarks of fear and horror, but the face was painted a horrible green. It looked like blue mold and like poison. You could imagine all sorts of supreme villainy and make the head which bore that face its temple. Blood was mingled with the paint and washed red rivers in the coating. He had originally fallen on his face, and he must have lain in that position for sometime, as it was flattened on one side. His hands were clenched, and his body seemed to have a tense appearance. One hand was raised in the air.[17]

Evidence at the scene indicated that friends and relatives of the deceased had removed or already buried as many as fifty additional bodies, increasing the total number of dead to more than two hundred. The burial party interred one hundred and forty-six bodies in a mass grave on a nearby hill, including eighty-two men and sixty-four women and children.[18] Ethnographer James Mooney later described the interment:

FIGURE 2.2 Medicine Man lying dead in the snow at Wounded Knee, 1891, by George Trager, Eli S. Ricker Collection, RG1227-22-21. Photo courtesy of Nebraska State Historical Society.

A long trench was dug and into it were thrown all the bodies, piled up one upon another like so much cordwood, until the pit was full, when the earth was heaped over them and the funeral was complete. Many of the bodies were stripped by the whites, who went out in order to get the "ghost shirts," and the frozen bodies were thrown into the trench stiff and naked.

In contrast to the honorable treatment accorded the bodies of Euro-American soldiers, no one, at least in the English-speaking world, deemed it appropriate to record the Lakotas' names, respect their bodies and clothing, notify their grieving families, bury them in single plots with headstones, or provide a fitting funeral. In Mooney's words, "They were only dead Indians."[19]

How those Indians died, however, demanded some explanation. Although Cressey, Allen, and Forsyth had hoped to obscure any reference to dead non-combatants, others drew on stock justifications to defend the soldiers. The *Lincoln State Journal*'s William F. Kelley, who was present during the fight,

FIGURE 2.3 Burying the dead in the Wounded Knee mass grave, 1891, by George Trager, Eli S. Ricker Collection, RG1227-22-17. Photo courtesy of Nebraska State Historical Society.

explicitly acknowledged that the cavalrymen pursued "men, women, and children," as the Hotchkiss cannon shelled the fleeing people. The soldiers were "shooting them down wherever found, no quarter given by anyone." Kelley justified the killings as the consequence of the warriors' treachery: "It is doubted that if before night either a buck or a squaw out of all of Big Foot's band will be left to tell the tale of this day's treachery. The members of the Seventh cavalry have once more shown themselves to be heroes in deeds of daring."[20] The *Bee* reporter Cressey, making up for his initial avoidance of the subject, argued on December 31 that women and children "were not killed with particular intent, notwithstanding that they had been running around with scalping knives trying to stab the soldiers. They were killed principally by reason of being so mixed with squads of bucks that made dashes to the ravines and were mowed down by the battery."[21] The Indianapolis *Journal* deemed the noncombatant deaths "deplorable" yet justified, since the Lakotas' "sudden attack in this case was in keeping with many others in which they have violated flags of truce or assassinated those who were trying to befriend them."[22]

Even within the army's ranks, Forsyth's official report rang hollow. The public charges and countercharges concerned Major General Nelson A. Miles, who, with only limited information, had initially praised the Seventh Cavalry's conduct at Wounded Knee. Moving his headquarters from Rapid City to the Pine Ridge Agency had delayed his response to Commanding General of the Army John M. Schofield's December 30 congratulatory telegram to the Seventh Cavalry, but on New Year's Day Miles relayed to his superior that "the action of the Col. Commanding [Forsyth] will be a matter of serious consideration and will undoubtedly be the subject of investigation [and] I thought it proper to advise you in view of above facts." Due to Forsyth's "fatally defective" disposition or arrangement of the troops, Miles believed that at least some of the colonel's men had died from friendly fire. Furthermore, contrary to the colonel's official report, "a very large number of women and children were killed in addition to the Indian men."[23] Schofield responded that President Benjamin Harrison "hope[d] that the report of the killing of women and children in the affair at Wounded Knee [was] unfounded." He authorized Miles to conduct "an immediate inquiry and report the result to the Department," and if he found evidence of "unsoldierly conduct," he was to relieve the "responsible officer" of his command.[24]

At first blush, it appears deeply ironic that Miles took this approach. As Jeffrey Ostler has shown, the major general's rhetoric in the months leading to Wounded Knee created a tinderbox waiting to be ignited. Miles indicated to the press that he believed that the Ghost Dance was a vast conspiracy that could lead to the greatest Indian war in the nation's history. It was partly due to Miles's rhetoric that the Harrison administration amassed the largest number of troops in the West since the Civil War.[25] Miles also portrayed Big Foot as "desperate" and "treacherous," and he authorized the Seventh Cavalry to "destroy" the chief's followers if they resisted.[26] And yet, when Miles learned details of the engagement that Forsyth had neglected to report, the major general became the colonel's foremost critic. This could reasonably be seen as Miles seeking to distance himself from the carnage of December 29, 1890.

However, the major general's strong reaction against the deaths of women and children was consistent with his previous opposition to excessive violence and massacres against Native peoples. Miles's decision to pursue an investigation placed him at odds with his mentor, Civil War hero William Tecumseh Sherman. In early January the retired general wrote to his niece, Mary Sherman Miles, suggesting that her husband kill all Lakotas who "dare[d] disturb the progress of this country." The more he killed now, the fewer he would have to kill later.[27] Sherman's counsel reflected race war logic, which in essence was a war of extermination.[28] He disapproved of Miles's decision to relieve Forsyth of command just "because some squaws were killed." Sherman argued that "squaws have been killed in every Indian war," invoking the common claim that even the best soldiers could not distinguish Indian men from women in a fight.[29]

Miles ignored Sherman's advice and selected his close ally Captain Frank Baldwin, acting assistant inspector general, as well as Jacob Ford Kent, division inspector general, to head the inquiry.[30] The major general charged the two men with investigating three issues: first, whether Forsyth's placement of Troops B and K between the warriors and the women and children had caused friendly fire casualties; second, whether any noncombatants "were unnecessarily injured or destroyed"; and third, whether Forsyth had complied with three orders Miles issued in late November and early December—weeks before Wounded Knee—that instructed field officers to forbid their men to mix with Indians and to guard against surprise or treachery. Had Forsyth obeyed these orders, Miles contended, Wounded Knee would have been avoided.[31] Miles hoped to replace the emerging view that Wounded Knee was a heroic battle with a competing interpretation of incompetent leadership that produced unnecessary deaths of soldiers and noncombatants.

Miles's investigation of Forsyth violated the unwritten army rule that commanders support their officers against accusations of killing

noncombatants. After the Marias (or Piegan) Massacre, where Colonel
Eugene M. Baker's Second Cavalry destroyed a peaceful Piegan village on
the Marias River in Montana Territory on January 23, 1870, allegations
quickly spread that of the one hundred and seventy-three Piegans killed
only fifteen had been able-bodied warriors, with the rest being elderly
men, women, and children.[32] Baker's commanding officer, Major General
Philip H. Sheridan, commander of the Division of the Missouri, vigorously
defended his subordinate from Eastern humanitarians who argued that as
civilized and Christian soldiers, the US Army should not target innocent
noncombatants.[33] Sheridan did not deny that the army sometimes killed
women and children, but he excused the deaths as accidental and utilized
well-worn stereotypes of Indian women combatants. He explained that
the army's most successful tactic was the surprise attack on Native villages
during the winter months, when tribes were hampered by limited mobility.
These attacks punished the guilty for thefts, murders, and rapes. If women
and children died, Sheridan contended, it was not the fault of soldiers, but
of the warriors who had committed these crimes against whites. In addition,
Sheridan argued that Indian females fought as aggressively as men, which
rendered them combatants.[34] In the midst of public outrage over killing
women and children, Sheridan and other high-ranking army officials such
as Commanding General of the Army William T. Sherman assured Baker
"that no amount of clamor [had] shaken [their] confidence" in him and his
officers.[35] Baker's career survived, although he did not get promoted before
his 1884 death.[36]

Miles was not cut of the same cloth as Sheridan or Sherman. A successful
commander during the Civil War, Miles was transferred to the West in 1868.
Although he employed the winter campaign tactics advocated by Sheridan,
Miles rejected the notion that Indians required violent subjugation before
submitting to treaties and reservation life. In Miles's view, Indians fought
whites not because indigenes were inherently warlike but because the government too often failed to uphold treaty obligations. The army's role was
to clean up the government's messes, convince the Natives that resistance
was useless, and clear the way for civilization. But he rejected the idea that
excessive violence was necessary to do this, arguing that he did "not believe
in the old army theory of destroying the whole [Indian] race." He instead
advocated diplomacy to end Indian campaigns, which contributed to the
successful conclusions of the Red River War of 1874, the Great Sioux War
of 1876–1877, the Nez Percé War of 1877, and the Geronimo Campaign of
1886.[37] Like most of his contemporaries, he sometimes described Indians as

"treacherous" and "fanatical" (as he had Big Foot prior to Wounded Knee), and he could occasionally resort to violence, but he also believed that competent military leaders could nonetheless reason with Natives. Miles may have preferred diplomacy against indigenous enemies, but he was not averse to criticizing junior officers or even superiors when it was to his advantage. The major general's dislike of Forsyth stretched back several years, suggesting personal animosity informed the investigation.[38] Miles, confident the court would ultimately condemn Forsyth, relieved the colonel of his command on January 5.[39]

The War Department, upon realizing the full extent of Miles's plans, attempted to rein in the major general. Schofield telegraphed Miles on January 6 that "it was not the intention of the President to appoint a court of inquiry. . . You were expected yourself first to inquire into the facts and in the event of its being disclosed that there had been disorderly conduct, to relieve the responsible officer."[40] Despite explicit disapproval from his superiors, Miles moved forward with the investigation, arguing that the inquiry was authorized under army regulations.[41] Several unnamed officials complained to the press that Miles's move was unnecessary and unfair to his men. Although the quoted individuals were not at Wounded Knee, they relied on time-tested army defenses of killing Indian women and children: "Women and men look very much alike in their blanket costume, and the former are quite as fierce fighters as the men. A Sioux squaw is as bad an enemy as a buck at times. Little boys, too, can shoot quite as well as their fathers." Miles's prosecution of Forsyth, another officer complained, would force field commanders to justify the deaths of every Indian killed in battle.[42]

The Inquiry

When Baldwin and Kent opened the inquiry on January 7, 1891, Forsyth's omission of noncombatant deaths in his official Wounded Knee report was no longer defensible. Since it was at that point indisputable that the Seventh Cavalry had killed women and children, the inquiry's primary objective was to determine whether the Seventh Cavalry had "unnecessarily injured or destroyed" noncombatants. However, the principal witnesses were men who held an important stake in the outcome: Forsyth's own subordinates. From January 7 to 10, Baldwin and Kent, with Forsyth present but mostly silent, interviewed eighteen army witnesses—fifteen Seventh Cavalry officers, one First Artillery officer, and two assistant surgeons. Incriminating their commanding officer ran not only counter to the army's unwritten rules of loyalty,

but also placed the witnesses in the precarious position of potentially impli-
cating themselves and their fellow soldiers.

The officers evidently coordinated their testimonies in advance. Meded
Swigert, a civilian who witnessed Wounded Knee, later alleged that "this
affair on the W. K. was hushed up" in order "to shield" Forsyth during the
inquiry: "There was anxiety to keep a part of the truth from the public; this
was evident from the uneasiness manifested by some in authority." Although
Swigert did not specify what exactly had been hushed up, he personally witnessed soldiers falling to friendly fire, cavalrymen shooting running men,
women, and children, and the artillery targeting fleeing Lakotas. The court
of inquiry had been charged to investigate these very allegations, and the witnesses, by and large, denied that they had occurred.[43] Ironically, Miles had
provided Forsyth's allies with a forum where their memories, perceived as
subjective, ephemeral, and unreliable on their own, were transformed into
written evidence—authoritative and objective. Government archivists would
preserve that evidence as the official record of the Forsyth Inquiry, available
for subsequent guardians of the army's reputation to retrieve it and defend
against any further accusations.[44]

Unsurprisingly, the officers stood with their commander and showed little disagreement in their testimonies over what had happened at Wounded
Knee. Given Forsyth's twin objectives to disarm the Indians peacefully
and to guard against escape, the witnesses argued that Forsyth's troop disposition was admirable. No one expected the Indians to fight, and the colonel intended the arrangement "to overawe the Indians."[45] Major Samuel
Whitside, Forsyth's second-in-command, explained: "I would place [the
troops] there myself under similar circumstances."[46] While some witnesses
conceded that the arrangement could have resulted in friendly fire casualties, none would state that such had occurred.[47] Other witnesses flatly denied
friendly fire casualties.[48]

The witnesses agreed that Lakota treachery had precipitated the fight.[49]
Whitside's interpretation was representative. His testimony shared elements
with the account offered by Cressey, the *Omaha Bee* correspondent, suggesting at least a common vocabulary and shared worldview, but also a possible
collaboration. The major was confident that the Lakotas had a "preconcerted
idea of treachery" when they surrendered.[50] During the disarmament, "a medicine man suddenly rose, spoke in a loud tone of voice, [and] threw some dirt
in the air." Subsequently, "one shot was fired by an Indian." The other warriors jumped to their feet, withdrew guns they had been hiding under their
blanket clothing, and "commenced firing at the Troops." Whitside argued

that "at least 50 shots were fired by the Indians before the troops returned fire." Violence therefore resulted when fanatical Indians, acting on the medicine man's signal, attacked unsuspecting soldiers.[51]

When questioned about the large number of noncombatant casualties, the witnesses repeated stock explanations for the deaths. When the warriors fired the initial volley at the troops, they shot in the direction of their own women and children, killing several in the process. Whitside remarked that "the first fire of the Indians themselves could not, but by a miracle, have resulted in anything else than a loss of life to women and children."[52] Furthermore, when the warriors escaped from the soldiers, they mixed with their families in the village. The pursuing soldiers, firing into a crowd, accidentally killed women and children.[53] Drawing on the generalization that female Lakotas were essentially warriors, the witnesses argued that women shot at the soldiers, forcing the troops to return fire in self-defense.[54] The witnesses also testified that the soldiers could not distinguish Indian men from women, because of similar clothing and appearance, resulting in unintentional noncombatant deaths.[55] Captain H. J. Nowlan reported that "it was the cry all over the field, both on the part of officers and enlisted men, not to kill the women and children."[56] No one stopped to question how the officers could discern the differences between the sexes, while their men were completely unable to so do.

Preferring to invoke time-tested justifications for noncombatant deaths meant the witnesses spoke primarily in generalities rather than describe specific instances of soldiers accidentally killing women and children. Only one witness provided a concrete example. Captain Edwin S. Godfrey related that his men had pursued Indians down the ravine and spotted some Lakotas hiding in the creek bottom. Godfrey described giving the obligatory order "not to shoot if they were squaws or children" and "called out 'How [hau] cola [khola],' which means friend." With no Lakota reply, Godfrey's men, against his explicit command, fired six quick shots, which were greeted by "the wailing of a child." According to his testimony, Godfrey immediately ordered his men to stop shooting. The dead included a woman, a teenage boy, and two small children, none of whom had weapons or had made any threatening gestures toward the troops.[57]

Baldwin and Kent concluded their inquiry by inviting two civilians—interpreter Philip Wells and Catholic missionary Francis M. J. Craft—to submit statements. Both men had Indian ancestry, knew the Lakota language, and had lived and worked among the people. Presumably they could provide additional insight into the Indians' actions and motivations in the moments leading to Wounded Knee. However, their credibility was compromised by allegations that Forsyth's officers had tried to exert influence over the civilians present at Wounded Knee. Meded Swigert, for example, later claimed that the "officers had at least one conference with the civilians asking what they knew and warning them not to say too much."[58] Another civilian, George E. Bartlett, indicated that during the inquiry he was reticent to talk about what he had seen, because his "feelings were with the Seventh," but within a few years he felt compelled to speak about the cavalrymen shooting into each other and killing the Lakotas indiscriminately.[59]

Questions arose specifically regarding Wells's and Craft's partiality toward the soldiers. Wells was one quarter Dakota and had worked for several years for the Indian Office as a translator and a "boss farmer" (a supervisor over a reservation district), as well as for the US Army as a scout and interpreter. Wells later recalled that during the inquiry, he was accused of siding with Forsyth in the "bitter feud" with Miles and being "ready to lie for the Seventh Cavalry."[60] Craft had Mohawk ancestry, had worked as a messenger boy in the Civil War, and had served as a Catholic missionary on various Lakota reservations in the 1880s.[61] As a missionary, Craft was highly critical of the Ghost Dance, portraying it as uncivilized.[62] In mid-January 1891 the *Omaha Daily Bee* reported that the Lakotas considered Craft "too good a friend of the soldiers," and that he was a "traitor" to the Lakotas.[63]

Wells, identified as a "half-breed" in the official record, testified on January 11. Up to this point, no one could testify to the content of the medicine man's words or the reaction of the Lakota warriors. Wells explained that during the disarmament the medicine man was telling the young warriors not to be afraid of the soldiers, since he "had received assurance that their bullets [would] not penetrate [them]":[64] "These young bucks answered 'How' [Hau] with great earnestness, this meaning that they were with him or would stand by him." Wells then watched "five or six young bucks throw off their blankets and pull out their arms from under them, [and] brandish them in the air." A single shot rang out and started the melee.[65] The interpreter was injured not long after the fighting began and so could not see subsequent events.[66] While Wells's account undercut claims that the Lakotas went into Wounded Knee with a premeditated plan to attack the soldiers, it supported the argument that the medicine man's "fanaticism" had caused the young warriors to fire at the soldiers.

Craft followed Wells in testifying on January 11. He explained he had gone to Wounded Knee hoping to use his language skills and relationship with the Lakotas to ensure a peaceful outcome. Craft feared that "malicious whites" had "caused such a state of alarm and suspicion" among the Lakotas by telling them that the soldiers would confiscate the warriors' guns and then slaughter the band.[67] The missionary described the medicine man "going through various ceremonies" and telling the warriors "that the soldiers' bullets might not hurt them."[68] Despite Craft's efforts to calm the Lakotas, a young warrior "suddenly fired," which "was followed by many others from the Indians. The soldiers did not fire until they were actually being compelled, and after the Indians had fired many shots."[69] Craft's account contained new details regarding the Lakotas' state of mind prior to the outbreak of shooting, yet like Wells, he was injured early in the fighting. After being stabbed, he was busy tending the wounded, precluding him from observing subsequent events.[70] Despite this, Craft claimed to have seen the warriors mixing with the women and children in the camp. He could provide no specific examples of women and children dying, but he nonetheless assured the court that such deaths were unavoidable, since the soldiers could not distinguish men from women.[71] In Craft's view, the warriors had violated the white flag and that "if women and children were killed in the shelling of this camp, the Indians who caused it [were] to blame."[72]

Even before Kent and Baldwin issued their report on January 13, an anonymous correspondent telegraphed the *New York Tribune* that "it is thoroughly understood that the Colonel will be exonerated. The testimony of the officers and soldiers of the 7th Cavalry leaves no other course open."[73] If Miles believed he could control how Kent and Baldwin interpreted the evidence, he was mistaken. Kent believed that the troop formation "was not judicious in all respects"; however, he found no evidence of friendly fire casualties.[74] As for women and children, he argued that "all care was taken after the Indians made their first break to preserve the lives of noncombatants." Furthermore, "the fact that several women and children were killed or wounded could be ascribed only to the fault of the Indians themselves and the force of unavoidable and unfortunate circumstances."[75] Only the "discipline and coolness" of the soldiers had avoided more noncombatant casualties.[76] Baldwin mostly concurred, but argued that Forsyth should have taken additional precautions to ensure the troops' safety. However, Baldwin concluded that the troops had performed commendably "throughout the engagement."[77]

Miles found the report unacceptable. He believed that unnamed enemies had supported Forsyth out of spite and had unduly influenced the witnesses in the investigation. The major general, however, remained committed to exposing Wounded Knee as a horrid massacre.[78] A friend noted that Miles was indignant over Forsyth's incompetence and "disgusted at the butchery" at Wounded Knee.[79] Unimpressed by the testimony, the major general ordered Kent and Baldwin to interrogate Brigadier General John R. Brooke,

commander of the Department of the Platte and Forsyth's immediate superior. At issue was whether Brooke had delivered three orders Miles had sent
in late November and early December, each of which cautioned the field commanders to guard against treachery and to prohibit their men from mixing
with the Lakotas.[80] In his January 16 testimony, Brooke acknowledged forwarding the orders to Forsyth.[81] Asked whether the colonel had disobeyed
Miles's earlier orders, Brooke replied that Forsyth's men did "not appear to
be 'mixed,'" although he was less sure that the colonel had "guard[ed] against
surprise or treachery." The brigadier general quickly backtracked, however,
stating that his "opinion" was not evidence.[82]

Rather than supply support for Miles's emerging narrative—that Forsyth
had disobeyed explicit orders that would have averted the violence—Brooke
presented a new interpretation of what had happened at Wounded Knee. The
brigadier general argued that the killings had resulted not from Forsyth dis-
regarding orders issued nearly a month before December 29, but rather from
the colonel's careful observance of orders Miles gave just prior to Wounded
Knee. The major general's late December communications indicated Miles
was "exceedingly anxious" for word of Big Foot's capture and disarmament,
since the chief was "cunning and his Indians [were] very bad."[83] On December
27, Miles had explicitly authorized the use of violence against Big Foot in case
the chief resisted capture, stating that "if he fights, destroy him."[84] Reiterating
this order following Big Foot's capture on December 28, Brooke commanded
Forsyth to disarm the warriors, prevent them from escaping, and "if they
fought to destroy them." Brooke wryly stated that "to the best of my knowledge . . . these instructions were obeyed."[85] The orders therefore rationalized
the destruction of Big Foot's band, since the warriors had allegedly resisted
disarmament and the people had attempted to escape.[86]

On January 17 and 18, Baldwin and Kent issued second opinions. Neither
endorsed Brooke's more radical justification of the deaths, but focused on
the brigadier general's statements regarding Miles's late November and early
December warnings against "mixing" with "treacherous" Indians. Baldwin
concluded that Forsyth had "entirely disregarded and lost sight of" Miles's
command to guard against treachery or deception by keeping his troops at a
safe distance.[87] Kent conceded that in light of the new information, Forsyth
did not sufficiently distance his troops from the Lakotas. But Kent defended
Forsyth's troop arrangement:

"Treachery" was practiced by the Indians, whether by a preconcerted
plan, or by the actions of the Indian who fired the first shot cannot be

fully determined from the evidence. I do regard that Colonel Forsyth's command was "surprised" in a measure, but that he took *in his judgment* measures to bring about a peaceful solution of the question at issue, which, however, proved futile.[88]

Even with the Brooke's additional information, Kent was unwilling to second-guess Forsyth's leadership. The two men forwarded their reports to Miles, who began writing his own interpretation of the evidence in an effort to control how it would be received up the government chain of command.

The Indian View of Wounded Knee

While Baldwin and Kent were conducting their official investigation, efforts were being made to record and disseminate the Lakota survivors' memories of Wounded Knee. Philip Wells was the first person to record a translated version of the survivors' words. The interpreter desired statements from wounded survivors in the hospital to counter accusations that he was "ready to lie for the Seventh Cavalry."[89] Accompanying him was Reverend Charles Smith Cook, a Yankton Sioux Episcopalian missionary on Pine Ridge, who assisted Wells with translating and recording statements for three survivors: Elks Saw Him, a thirty-eight-year-old Oglala who had been living with Hump's band on the Cheyenne River Reservation; Frog, Big Foot's forty-eight-year-old Minneconjou brother; and Help Them, an Oglala who had visited Big Foot's camp and was returning home to Pine Ridge. Remarkably, Frog's and Help Them's statements were eventually incorporated into the official record.[90]

Wells left no indication of what questions he asked or his process of translation and transcription. He recorded all three statements in polished first person prose. Each emphasized similar themes, which provides some sense of what Wells wanted them to discuss.[91] Both Elks Saw Him and Frog indicated that Big Foot's band had headed south, not to join the "hostile" Ghost Dancers, but because Red Cloud, Little Wound, and other Oglala leaders had invited the Minneconjous to come to Pine Ridge.[92] All three informants stated that, after the soldiers had moved Big Foot's people to Wounded Knee Creek, the troops and the Lakotas interacted in a friendly manner, although Help Them wondered why the soldiers "kept their guns in readiness for action . . . [and] they placed two cannons on a hill" to cover the camp. All three insisted that Big Foot's Lakotas had no intentions of attacking the soldiers.[93]

On the morning of December 29, the soldiers separated the men from the women and children and Forsyth demanded that the warriors give up their weapons, with the promise that if they complied, the troops would provide food and the whole group would proceed to Pine Ridge.[94] Since only some of the men had guns, Frog believed that all had been given up.[95] Elks Saw Him "heard an officer saying something. He must have given orders, because the soldiers began loading their guns and holding them in readiness for firing."[96] During the disarmament, a medicine man performed the Ghost Dance ceremony and then addressed a group of young warriors, who "were standing together with their guns concealed under their blankets." Help Them could not hear what he said, but he supposed that the medicine man told the young warriors that "the soldiers' bullets could not reach them (the Indians) no matter how the soldiers would shoot at them."[97] At this point, Help Them "heard a white man saying something in excited tones, which [he] could not understand, and looking around, [he] saw some of the Indians throw off their blankets, and raise their guns, and one of the Indians fired a shot."[98] The soldiers answered this single bullet with a volley, injuring Wells's three informants and precluding them from seeing more.[99]

Although the statements of Frog, Help Them, and Elks Saw Him aligned with some points of the Seventh Cavalry's explanations, their accounts departed from the official version in important ways, suggesting that Wells was somewhat restrained in his editing. The informants clearly stated that Big Foot had gone south for peaceful reasons and was therefore not a "hostile." They also explained that the warriors had no intention of fighting beforehand, which undermined the army's claim that the Lakotas had "treacherously" plotted to attack the soldiers. Elks Saw Him stated that the soldiers, with guns loaded and positioned, were ready for a fight even before trouble emerged, raising the possibility that the soldiers were looking for any provocation. In addition, the informants indicated that it was only young men who hid guns under the blankets and fired the first fateful shot, whereas the soldiers had implied that all the warriors were complicit. In Lakota society, in order for young men to prove their manhood, they often had to perform feats of bravery, which mature leaders and parents often considered foolhardy and dangerous.[100] With this context in place, Wells's informants reinforced their argument that there was no premeditated attack sanctioned by Big Foot and other leaders. Finally, Help Them suggested that the young man had fired during a heated exchange with a soldier, not when the medicine man signaled, contrary to the soldiers' claims.

Most striking, however, was what Wells's informants' did not say, which provides some evidence that he shaped the written accounts. At least in Wells's transcription, there was almost no discussion how the women and children died. Elks Saw Him recalled being surrounded by the dead and wounded. He also noted his relief upon hearing that his wife and youngest child survived, but he was concerned that his older daughter was still missing. Neither Frog nor Help Them mentioned losing family members or seeing the dead around them.[101] Wells had a certain purpose in procuring the statements: to defend himself and, by implication, the Seventh Cavalry against accusations of lying to avoid responsibility for noncombatant deaths. In this regard, it was noteworthy that the wounded Lakotas did not blame the soldiers for their injuries or for the deaths of relatives. Instead, Frog blamed the medicine man for "caus[ing] the death of all our people," and Elks Saw Him blamed "the young man who fired the first gun" for the deaths.[102] Certainly, this anger toward the medicine man and young warrior was very plausible in immediate aftermath of Wounded Knee, but it was highly unlikely that Wells's informants completely absolved the soldiers of fault.

While Wells was recording his interviews on January 7, 1891, the Commissioner of Indian Affairs Thomas Jefferson Morgan requested that his Supervisor of Education for North and South Dakota, Elaine Goodale, investigate Wounded Knee. As an advocate of assimilation and soon-to-be spouse of Charles Eastman—a Dakota physician who would become perhaps the best-known Native American in the United States—Goodale saw herself as a "friend of the Indian" whose educational work would help Indians abandon tribalism and embrace modern life. Despite her approach, Goodale admired much in Lakota culture and was critical of the army's "civilizing" methods, which often relied on excessive force.[103] Although Goodale did not identify her sources by name, as Wells did, she interviewed "Indian prisoners who engaged in it [Wounded Knee] and half breeds [that is, multiracial scouts] who were present." In addition, she interviewed "parties who visited the battle field several days after the encounter." This would have included her fiancé Eastman, who had led the search party to Wounded Knee on January 1, 1891, to look for survivors.[104] Goodale believed that knowing where the bodies were located on the field would help her either to verify or challenge the Seventh Cavalry's official story.[105]

In some respects, Goodale's report on her interviews paralleled the statements of Wells's informants. Big Foot was going to Pine Ridge at Red Cloud's invitation and had had no intention of joining the "hostile" Ghost Dancers.

The Minneconjou chief and his warriors had only peaceful intentions when they met the soldiers: "There was constant friendly intercourse between the soldiers and the Indians, even the women shaking hands with the officers and men." The troops surprised the Lakotas with the demand to surrender their weapons, but only some of the men had guns to give up. Showing greater interest in women's experiences during the disarmament than Wells, Goodale emphasized that "the women say they too were searched and their knives (which they allayed [always] carried with them for domestic purposes) taken from them." As the search ended, "one young man, who is described by the Indians as a good for nothing young fellow, fired a single shot," which the troops answered with a volley.[106]

Goodale's informants had heard the Seventh Cavalry's claim that armed women were active participants in the fight. "The weight of the testimony is overwhelmingly against this supposition," Goodale concluded. While allowing that one or two women may have had weapons, the educator argued that the vast majority of men, women, and children were unarmed and were killed while fleeing for their lives: "They were pursued up the ravines and shot down indiscriminately by the soldiers." In some cases, she conceded, killing women and children may have been unavoidable, but "there is no doubt it was in many instances deliberate and intentional." She also argued against the army's claim that the warriors had broken through the cavalry's ranks and mixed with the women, making it impossible for the soldiers not to shoot noncombatants. Eastman and others who had seen the bodies on the field reported to Goodale that the troops' initial volleys had killed the vast majority of the warriors. "The women and children," on the other hand, "were scattered along a distance of two miles from the scene of the encounter."[107]

Doubtless, the striking differences between Wells's interviews and Goodale's report were a product of their differing objectives. Wells wanted to exonerate Forsyth and the troops, while Goodale believed that the soldiers were ultimately avenging their fallen commander, Colonel George Armstrong Custer. She reluctantly accepted that the officers may have warned their men not to shoot at women and children, but contended that in all the excitement, few obeyed their commanders. Goodale concluded her report by arguing that "the irresponsible action of one hot-headed youth should not be the signal for a general and indiscriminate slaughter of the unarmed and helpless." By overemphasizing a single ill-advised shot from the young man, the Seventh Cavalry was blaming the Lakotas for starting the engagement and, in the process, disavowing culpability for everything that followed. In addition to sending her report to Commissioner Morgan, Goodale's statement was published in newspapers across the country, widely disseminating the "Indian Version of the Fight at Wounded Knee."[108]

Settling the Wounded Knee Controversy

The men who ultimately held the power to define Wounded Knee in the government's official records essentially ignored these early Lakota interpretations. After Miles received Baldwin's and Kent's final reports on January 18, he waited another two and a half weeks before forwarding the inquiry record to Washington, DC. In part, the delay was due to the fact that Miles was unwilling to cede to Kent and Baldwin the important task of interpreting the testimonies. Miles therefore composed a substantial cover letter to preface the record, which he sent to the capital on January 31. He sought to shape how the department read the testimony by highlighting certain points against Forsyth and downplaying evidence that supported the colonel. Miles noted that just "as it is important to the best interest of the service that skill and heroism should be rewarded, so also it is important that incompetency and neglect, when found, should not pass unnoticed." Unspecified "injurious reports [that] were current" after the termination of the fighting that had caused Miles to order the investigation so as to assemble all the known facts necessary to fully evaluate Forsyth's conduct.[109]

Miles contended that in spite of several warnings, Forsyth had gone into the disarmament assuming that the warriors would not treacherously resist. In making this point, the general relied primarily on Brigadier General Brooke's testimony regarding Miles's orders to guard against treachery and to avoid mixing soldiers with the Lakotas. Miles argued that Forsyth's assumption that the Lakotas would not resist was untenable given past military encounters with the Natives:

> The disasters that have occurred to our troops in the past from the desperation of the Indian nature are known to all who are familiar with our history. In addition to this it was well known and Colonel Forsyth had been warned that this particular band contained many of the most desperate and deceitful characters in the Sioux nation, and that a religious excitement nearly approaching frenzy had made them peculiarly dangerous.[110]

Like the press and Forsyth's defenders, Miles believed that Ghost Dance was dangerous and defined by fanaticism. Where Miles differed was in his contention that competent military leadership could have controlled that fanaticism and avoided a massacre.

Miles's critique concentrated on Forsyth's troop arrangement and whether the disposition could feasibly have guarded against Indian attack. Miles argued that "it is in fact difficult to conceive how a worse disposition of the troops could have been made." Rather than placing Troops B and K between the warriors and the women and children during the disarmament, Forsyth should have placed the entire command of four hundred and fifty soldiers to separate the Lakota warriors from their families. As it was, Troops B and K were forced to bear "the brunt of the affair," as their comrades withheld fire so as not to hit the men of B and K. Combined with the fact that most of the warriors were unarmed suggested to Miles that the majority of the soldiers who died were killed by friendly fire.[111]

With regard to the deaths of noncombatants, Miles rejected as self-serving the officers' own explanations for the killings and instead, he attached Captain Frank Baldwin's report of January 21, 1891. Baldwin described visiting a spot three miles west of the Wounded Knee site, where he found the Lakotas who had been killed by Captain Godfrey's men on December 29. Contrary to Godfrey's assertion that his men shot from a distance and therefore could not have known who they were killing, "each person had been shot once, the character of which was necessarily fatal in each case. The bodies had not been plundered or molested. The shooting was done at so close a range that the person or clothing of each was powder-burned." Baldwin's report conveyed a potent image of the Seventh Cavalry riding miles away from the original camp to hunt down and execute escaping noncombatants. The brutal description undermined the claims of Godfrey and other officers that they had strenuously ordered their men not to fire upon fleeing women and children.[112] Miles concluded that Baldwin's report exemplified "the results of that unfortunate affair," which the major general "viewed with the strongest disapproval." For Miles, only two options were available for assessing Forsyth's conduct: either the colonel had willfully ignored Miles's repeated warnings against treachery or Forsyth was incompetent to command troops.[113]

In Washington, army officials were equally zealous to control how the evidence would be interpreted, but they developed a starkly different view from Miles. Army Commanding General Schofield, who had previously telegraphed Miles to congratulate the troops, attached a cover letter to the record recommending that Forsyth be restored to his command: "The evidence in these papers show that great care was taken by the officers and generally by the enlisted men to avoid unnecessary killing of Indian women and children." In his "judgment the conduct of the regiment was well worthy of [his initial] commendation."[114]

On February 12, Secretary of War Redfield Proctor wrote his own interpretation of the record, using the power of his office to settle the ongoing controversy over Wounded Knee. Although Proctor evidently accepted a minor point argued by Wells's Lakota informants, the secretary based the majority of his report on Whitside and other officers who testified before the inquiry. In Proctor's view Big Foot's band, which included some of Sitting Bull's followers, "embraced the most fanatical and desperate element among the Sioux." Their surrender to Whitside on December 28 was insincere and simply the "sullen and unwilling yielding of a band of savage fanatics" who lacked food and recognized the troops' superior numbers. Proctor admitted, however, that resistance was concentrated primarily among the "younger braves." The secretary further acknowledged, contrary to Whitside's claim, that Big Foot's warriors lacked "any prearranged plan of treachery." Although implicit, this last point was likely a remarkable concession to Wells's Lakota informants, Frog and Help Them, whose statements on the early part of the fight had been incorporated into the official record.[115]

Forsyth had been tasked with disarming the warriors peacefully, while also ensuring that the "desperadoes" did not escape. Although Proctor had accepted Frog's and Help Them's qualifications on the young men, the secretary rejected their claim that Big Foot had gone south at the invitation of Red Cloud and other chiefs. Rather, Proctor believed that the band intended to raid neighboring settlements, creating the "imperative necessity to prevent escape." The secretary opined that "the troops appear to have been well disposed to prevent an outbreak which was not and could hardly have been anticipated by any one, under the circumstances, even in dealing with Indians," a subtle jab at Miles's argument that Forsyth, had he understood history, should have expected treachery. When the Lakotas seemed reticent to surrender their weapons, Forsyth dispatched men to search the camp, where they found "the squaws making every effort to conceal" weapons.[116] Proctor contended that the Ghost Dance medicine man then incited the warriors, who had been hiding guns under their blankets, to open fire on the soldiers. Following Whitside's testimony, the secretary argued that the warriors fired "at least fifty shots" before the cavalrymen returned fire.[117]

Proctor contended that the warriors, driven by "insane desperation," were to blame for the deaths of their women and children: "Nothing illustrates the madness of their outbreak more forcibly than the fact that their first fire was so directed that every shot that did not hit a soldier must have gone through their own village. There is little doubt that the first killings of women and children was by this first fire of the Indians themselves." The warriors then broke through the soldiers' ranks, retrieved the weapons ostensibly hidden in the camp, and continued firing at the troops. Thereafter, the soldiers had no choice but to fire into groups that included men, women, and children. Repeating a stock justification for killing noncombatants, Proctor argued that the troops could not "distinguish buck from squaw at a little distance when mounted." Despite the enlisted men's apparent inability to discern men from women, the officers were sufficiently clairvoyant to warn their men not to fire on noncombatants. Proctor summarily dismissed Baldwin's claim that Seventh Cavalrymen had executed the woman and children found three miles from Wounded Knee. He concluded that those killings were not connected to the fight, thereby absolving the Seventh Cavalry of any responsibility for the deaths.[118]

Proctor closed his report by exhonerating the Seventh Cavalry for Wounded Knee. There was no evidence that friendly fire had caused the deaths of any of the troops, which reflected "an exceedingly satisfactory state of discipline." Forsyth's men had conducted themselves with "skill, coolness, discretion and forbearance." Although the circumstances of the fight were out of the ordinary, Proctor concluded that neither Forsyth nor his troops had done anything worthy of condemnation. Citing President Harrison's approval, the secretary reinstated the colonel to his command.[119]

With that, the investigation of the conduct of Forsyth and his men at Wounded Knee Creek, South Dakota, on December 29, 1890, was closed. Miles took Proctor's decision personally. When asked for his reaction, he replied: "I do not care to make any statement in regard to it, nor do I care to review the case. What I did, I would do again under the same circumstances."[120] Subsequently, however, he privately argued that Proctor's statement was a "suppression of the truth," which Miles interpreted as a "personal assault."[121] The *Army and Navy Journal* noted in mid-February 1891 that Miles had violated "a rule of exemption," which protected both individual soldiers as well as the army as an institution "against calumny and recrimination." The rule ensured that "reputations honestly and previously established" would remain intact, even if mistakes were made during an otherwise "gallant and faithful discharge of duty."[122] It was later speculated that Proctor had punished the major general for his public indiscretion by substantially reducing the size of Miles's Division of the Missouri.[123]

The major general had also lost the struggle over memory, as Proctor marginalized Miles's interpretation of Wounded Knee as a massacre in the official report. As he exonerated the Seventh Cavalry, the secretary established an authoritative interpretation of the inquiry record, portraying Wounded Knee as a heroic victory over "hostile," "fanatical," and "treacherous savages" who had killed their own women and children. Forsyth and his allies would subsequently sear this image of Wounded Knee into national memory, in the form of twenty Medals of Honor for his men and a monument for those soldiers who gave their lives while subduing Big Foot's band.

3

Honoring Gallant Soldiers

AS NEWS OF Wounded Knee reached Fort Riley, Kansas, the community around the fort showed its eagerness to defend the Seventh Cavalry against charges of killing unarmed Lakota women and children. Reverend D. R. Lowell, post chaplain of Fort Riley, Kansas, was angry. Reports had recently reached the post that "cowardly" newspapers had portrayed the Seventh Cavalry, which was stationed at Fort Riley, "as the bloodiest of butchers, the most unfeeling and cruel of men, [and] as fiends unparalleled by darkest barbarism." In his sermon on January 4, Lowell praised the cavalrymen for honoring their "responsibility to thousands of defenseless families on the frontier; responsibility to their comrades in arms; [and] responsibility to the whole country." The chaplain was certain that Colonel James W. Forsyth's men had met the Lakotas' "unexpected treachery" with bravery, nobility, and heroism. The chaplain also extolled the soldiers' "brave" wives, many of whom were living with their husbands at Fort Riley. The women were "not less heroic than their husbands and suffering not less, with hearts already broken," being forced "to endure the additional pain of seeing their honored husbands" slandered in the press. Lowell spoke for the Fort Riley community when he argued that the troops' "fair names" and "reputations" should be defended against such calumny.[1]

When Colonel Forsyth and the Seventh Cavalry returned to Fort Riley in mid-January 1891, they, like Lowell, were determined to defend their reputations by controlling the public memory of Wounded Knee. Although Fort Riley was located five hundred and fifty miles southeast of the Pine Ridge Reservation—where the majority of the soldiers killed on December 29, 1890, were buried—Forsyth and his allies nonetheless worked to integrate Wounded Knee into the post's strong memorial traditions that celebrated George Armstrong Custer's and the Seventh Cavalry's role in the "winning of the West." The colonel understood that public commemorations could promote consensus and elide controversy by enshrining an authoritative narrative in public memory. Forsyth labored vigorously to shape how Wounded Knee would be remembered through commemorations, funerals, public conferrals of twenty Medals of Honor, and the erection of a monument to his fallen soldiers. In the process, Forsyth and his allies interpreted Wounded Knee as the "last battle" between "civilization" and "savagery" for the continent.[2] Although memorialization of the "Battle of Wounded Knee" was most concentrated at Fort Riley, gradually the event was incorporated into popular representations of civilization's final conquest of savagery.

Honoring the Wounded Knee Dead

For much of human history only the ruling classes marked their burial places and commemorated their actions. The elite reserved to themselves the right to a "written death," in scholar Armando Petrucci's phrase, meaning the practice of recording in writing the names of the deceased and inscribing those names on stone markers. Industrialization and urbanization in the late eighteenth and early nineteenth centuries, however, dramatically democratized burial practices and accompanying funereal markers. Ordinary people began claiming the right to a "written death," with individual burial plots and semipermanent headstones that marked the site of internment with a name.[3] The staggering death toll of the Civil War—more than six hundred thousand dead—radically accelerated these practices and led the federal government to enter the death business by formalizing the process of registering and marking the graves of Union soldiers. Congress created the first permanent National Cemeteries during the war to protect and maintain the troops' final resting places. These cemeteries symbolized the country's gratitude and commitment to those men who sacrificed their lives in defense of the nation against those who sought its disunion.[4]

These memorial practices extended to sites of federal power in the American West. After the Mexican Cession of 1848 and the discovery of gold in California a year later, violence erupted in the 1850s as white settlers encroached on Native lands. The US Army established dozens of new forts throughout the West to protect the overland trails, the growing agricultural settlements, mining operations, and railroads. Custer National Cemetery in Montana, Fort Leavenworth, and Fort Riley (the home of the Seventh Cavalry) in Kansas, and other western posts in the post-Civil War era served as army sites of memory, stakes that firmly anchored the tent of American sovereignty and authority in the American West.[5] When soldiers died in the region they would receive individual burials, their names would be preserved in government records, and headstones would be inscribed with their names. Memorial traditions in these places applied the religious language of sacrifice and martyrdom to a race war context, with headstones celebrating brave men who gave their lives in the struggle of civilization against savagery.[6]

The press heralded the soldiers killed at Wounded Knee as heroes whose deaths advanced the cause of white civilization. The *Junction City Republican*, the hometown newspaper of the Seventh Cavalry at Fort Riley, reported that their "battle cry was 'Remember Custer!' and they slaughtered the Indians in all directions."[7] The paper noted that "the twenty-five white soldiers killed on Monday [December 29, 1890] were worth to the country all the savage red bucks in the United States." Captain George D. Wallace, the paper explained, "sold his life dearly and bravely. One such hero is worth all the Indians in Dakota."[8] Consolingly, the *Republican* noted:

> Although many of the brave soldiers who left Fort Riley a short time ago will never return, the slaughter is on the other foot this time, and Custer and his boys are avenged after an interval of fourteen years. Be it remembered that the Indians were the first to start firing, and they are responsible for the result. If the wiping out of a few hundred of these inhuman and bloodthirsty brutes will bring peace, safety and prosperity to thousands of industrious families in the northwest, then the sacrifice of the lives of our officers and privates will not be in vain.[9]

Comments such as these forged a memory of Wounded Knee that intimately tied the sanctifying deaths of the troops to the United States' race war against savagery. Twenty-five troops were killed on December 29, 1890, along with Oscar Pollack of the Hospital Corps.[10] Another four members of the Seventh Cavalry died of their wounds by the new year.[11] Lists of their names were printed in newspapers across the country. Family members anxiously scanned the newspaper columns identifying the dead, fearing that their son or husband had made the list.[12] Under normal circumstances, these soldiers would have been transported to Fort Riley or to the nearest military fort and interred in the post cemetery, where the graves would be protected and the headstones maintained by federal authorities. However, due to the ongoing military campaign, on New Year's Eve thirty of "the brave boys who fell with face to the foe in the bloody encounter at Wounded Knee" were buried in a cemetery at the Pine Ridge Agency, thereby expanding the network of federal cemeteries in the West that protected the remains of troops killed in action.[13]

GRAVES OF SEVENTH CAVALRY
KILLED AT WOUNDED KNEE,
DEC. 29,1890.

OGLALA SIOUX

FIGURE 3.1 Graves of Seventh Cavalrymen killed at Wounded Knee buried at Pine Ridge, ca. 1905, photographer unknown, Wounded Knee Massacre Collection, RG2845-19-3. Photo courtesy of Nebraska State Historical Society.

Colonel James W. Forsyth and Major Samuel M. Whitside led a procession of fifteen wagons bearing the men's coffins "away from the camp up to the little cemetery situated at the crest of the hill southwest of the agency." The ceremony, administered by the local Episcopalian clergy, took place in a "wild, blinding and bitter . . . wintry storm," requiring that the traditional salute of guns be omitted so as not to alarm the Lakotas. However, "soft notes of the bugle and the wail of the storm whispered the last loving good-by."[14] In subsequent weeks, other wounded soldiers died on Pine Ridge. On January 12, 1891, Private Harry B. Stone succumbed, and Private George Elliott passed the following day. Both were buried with their comrades.[15] The standard issue headstones listed each man's name, rank, company, and regiment, inscribing in stone the soldier's "written deaths."[16]

Although most of the soldiers killed at Wounded Knee were buried with their comrades in the Pine Ridge cemetery, a few were not. War Department bureaucrats gave special consideration to the only officer killed at Wounded Knee, Captain George D. Wallace, by transporting his remains to the nearest post or national cemetery.[17] Wallace was well known nationally, due to his having narrowly missed George Armstrong Custer's and other Seventh Cavalrymen's fate at the Battle of the Little Bighorn in 1876.[18] Initially the department planned to bury the captain's remains at Fort Riley, Wallace's final post and the home of his widow, Carrie Otis Wallace.[19] Although this was not the nearest post to Pine Ridge, it was close enough to justify the expense of transporting the remains. Although he would ultimately be buried in the Wallace family cemetery in Yorkville, South Carolina, his body did stop at Fort Riley to allow a grieving community to see him a final time. "Every available man in the post was drawn up in line at the depot and upon the arrival of the train presented arms while the Seventh cavalry band played a beautiful dirge. The captain's gray horse was draped in mourning."[20]

Following the Fort Riley ceremony, Wallace's corpse continued its journey to South Carolina, where the formal funeral was held on January 7, 1891. The *Harper's Weekly* obituary described the scene:

> The body of the gallant officer, which had been sent to his home in Yorkville, South Carolina, draped in the flag of his troop, was buried with solemn ceremonies at that place. The schools of the town and many of the people joined in the funeral procession; and when the well-deserved eulogies had been pronounced, the local military body fired a salute over his grave.

"His memory," *Harper's* concluded, "will be dear not only to his regiment, but to the whole army."[21]

Aside from Wallace, six other cavalrymen whose deaths stemmed from Wounded Knee were buried away from Pine Ridge. Four troops had their bodies disinterred from the Pine Ridge cemetery by family members and reburied in family plots, demonstrating that far-flung localities participated in the memorialization of Wounded Knee. First Sergeant Dora S. Coffey's family had him transferred to Bloomington, Indiana, where he was reburied. His obituary noted that "he is no longer a soldier of earth, but has joined the great army of the eternal shore."[22] Private James E. Kelley's relations had him removed and reinterred in Chicago, Illinois.[23] Private William J. McClintock's father recovered his son's body and held a funeral for him in Freedom, Ohio. The local newspaper noted that "the flag was at halfmast. The casket was draped with the stars and stripes in honor to the Soldier whom in the flush of youth had gone out to bear arms against the foes of the country."[24] Private Philip Schwenky's body was reburied in Orange, New Jersey.[25] Finally, two wounded soldiers, Sergeants Henry Howard and Alvin H. Haselwood, both subsequently died from their wounds and were buried as "heroes of Wounded Knee" in Fort Riley's post cemetery.[26]

In all, thirty-four Seventh Cavalrymen, plus one member of the Hospital Corps, either died at Wounded Knee or subsequently succumbed to injuries received there. The bodies of most of these men remained buried in the Pine Ridge Agency cemetery, not far from the place they made famous on December 29, 1890. Here their headstones would be protected from vandalism and decay, but would also serve to remind the Lakotas of the military wing of federal power. Five men, including Captain Wallace, were transported for burial near their families. Only two soldiers were interred at Fort Riley, the place where the Seventh Cavalry would return to memorialize what they argued was a heroic victory over savagery at Wounded Knee.

Recognizing Gallant and Meritorious Conduct

Fort Riley was founded in present-day Kansas in 1853 to protect immigrants traveling west along the Oregon, California, and Santa Fe overland trails. In 1866, the Seventh Cavalry was organized at Fort Riley, and for a time served as George Armstrong Custer's home and regimental headquarters.[27] The fort therefore already had storied memorial traditions, to which Forsyth hoped to graft Wounded Knee following his return in early 1891. Commemorating the event would serve two related purposes for the commander. First, it would

allow him to promote the careers of his subordinates—through public recognition by awarding them such encomiums as the Medal of Honor—in
a post-Civil War environment where advancement was a slow and tedious
process. Second, to counter Major General Nelson A. Miles's attempt to portray Wounded Knee as a massacre, Forsyth and his supporters sought to use
commemorative events at Fort Riley to establish a unifying interpretation of
Wounded Knee as a heroic victory.

The *Junction City Republican* declared that Forsyth's "numerous friends
in this city" believed that Miles's "jealousy and hate" had led to an "unmili-
tary and ungentlemanly attack on a brother officer." The paper declared that
the evidence assembled by the January 1891 court of inquiry proved Forsyth
"to be a thorough commanding officer, well posted in Indian warfare, and
the result at Wounded Knee without parallel in military movements against
the Indians."[28] When word reached the post in mid-February that the War
Department had exonerated Forsyth and restored him to his command, the
troops in the post's mess hall rejoiced for their commander. An eyewitness
noted that "for a few seconds you could hear a pin drop." The four hundred
and thirty seven men present then exploded with three cheers "for their gallant colonel," followed by a "tiger," or a howl that intensified the applause.
The cheers "were given with such vim as to make the immense trusses which
span the building fairly shake."[29]

Subsequently, "the whole command marched in company front" to the colonel's residence, "where the cheers were again renewed with redoubled vigor."
Forsyth appeared before his men and thanked them for their conduct on
the field and "for the manly way in which they endorsed the [Department's]
decision."[30] Over the next week congratulatory telegrams flooded into
Forsyth's mailbox from Philadelphia, Fort Leavenworth, Omaha, Chicago,
Washington, DC, and elsewhere, as friends expressed their approval and
congratulations for the exoneration. Brigadier General John R. Brooke, who
had testified before the army inquiry in January, sent his "congratulations on
action taken at Washington regarding [Forsyth's] course at Wounded Knee."
The *Junction City Republican* published excerpts of the telegrams in order to
publicize the broad range of prominent people who supported the colonel.[31]

In April 1891 the Seventh Cavalry band honored Forsyth and his men
with a "Grand Star" concert, which was "the grandest musical event of the
season" at Fort Riley. Prominent European musicians and singers who were
visiting Kansas joined the band onstage.[32] A *Junction City Republican*'s correspondent who attended the concert reported that "the music throughout
was of a very high order, and the execution faultless." Furthermore, "the

description of the Battle of Wounded Knee was thrilling in the extreme" and the portrayal of "the death of Capt. Wallace . . . produced a visible effect on the audience." The reception was so positive that an encore performance was held two weeks later in Junction City.[33]

To strengthen the growing public consensus that the men who fought at Wounded Knee were gallant heroes who the press and Miles had unfairly slandered, Forsyth and his officers petitioned the War Department to recognize several members of the Seventh Cavalry and the First and Second Artillery with the nation's highest military encomium, the Medal of Honor.[34] Congress created the Medal of Honor during the Civil War, which became the nation's highest recognition of valor, bravery, and other soldier-like qualities on the battlefield. Officers observed the conduct of their men in the field, and in cases of extraordinary valor, recommended that deserving individuals receive a medal. Whereas during the Civil War promotion in rank was frequently a rapid process, in the postwar decades advancement was often deliberately slow, and the Medal of Honor was the most visible means for the government to reward gallantry.[35] In an era defined by the public veneration of soldiers who had sacrificed so much for the national cause, such medals were coveted symbols of official recognition.[36]

Prior to reforms in the late nineteenth and early twentieth centuries, the standards for awarding Medals of Honor were vague and unstandardized, which produced a highly politicized system. In one early example of Medal of Honor profligacy, Secretary of War Edwin Stanton in June 1863 promised every man of the 27th Maine Infantry a Medal of Honor if they would voluntarily remain beyond their enlistments to protect Washington, DC. About three hundred soldiers remained in the nation's capital for four additional yet uneventful days. Due to clerical errors, the government issued all eight hundred and sixty-four Maine infantrymen Medals of Honor.[37] In other cases, leaders of factions within the army sought to extend their influence by obtaining medals first for themselves and then for as many of their friends and protégés as possible.[38]

In the wake of the controversy surrounding noncombatant deaths at Wounded Knee, the War Department issued twenty Medals of Honor to soldiers who fought in the engagement. Sixteen of the twenty medals went to the Seventh Cavalry; three went to the First Artillery; and one to the Second Artillery.[39] Wounded Knee therefore ranked second only to the Battle of the Little Bighorn—for which twenty-four members of the Seventh Cavalry received medals—among the most decorated engagements of the Indian Wars.[40] Even allowing for the era's lax standards, historian Jerry Green has raised significant questions regarding the legitimacy of these medals. In no other instance had the War Department been so generous with Medals of Honor after critics charged troopers of perpetrating a massacre. At Wounded Knee the troops outnumbered the warriors almost five to one, and a majority of the Lakota men had been disarmed prior to the outbreak of shooting. The actual fighting lasted less than an hour, whereas prior engagements deemed heroic had lasted several hours and even days. Some of the men who received medals for their conduct at Wounded Knee had questionable characters, including artilleryman John Clancy, who was court-martialed eight times during his career, twice in 1891 alone. Additionally, most of the citations for the Wounded Knee medals only vaguely heralded the "gallantry," "distinguished conduct," and "bravery" of the recipients—with few identifying specific acts of heroism—thereby reinforcing the impression that the medals were awarded to grant favors to subordinates and to bolster the Seventh Cavalry in the midst of the Miles controversy.[41]

The medals played a key role in subsequent commemorations of Wounded Knee at Fort Riley, demonstrating that the past can be remembered as readily with objects as with words.[42] Historically, federal officials had mailed medals to recipients without pomp or circumstance.[43] However, Forsyth's officers departed from this policy and used public parades and ceremonies—time-honored military traditions—to confer medals on their men. This allowed the Seventh Cavalry implicitly to counter accusations of unsoldierly conduct at Wounded Knee as well as to hold up the troops who fought in South Dakota as models of honorable conduct. At a gala day parade for Fort Riley's artillery units held on April 24, 1891, Second Lieutenant Harry L. Hawthorne of the Second US Artillery—who had been seriously injured himself in the fighting—pinned medals on Corporal Paul H. Weinert and Private Joshua B. Hartzog, both of Company E of the First US Artillery. The *Omaha Bee* had recounted in mid-January that the Hotchkiss Cannon-firing corporal had launched "shell after shell" at fleeing Lakotas. "They went down like grain before the reaper—not by ones, twos or threes, but by dozens."[44] One officer noted that "it is our duty as officers to encourage the enlisted men by every means in our power and to show our appreciation for gallant and meritorious conduct when occasion requires." The Seventh Cavalry therefore proudly celebrated the government's official recognition of bravery at Wounded Knee.[45]

During a Decoration Day (later known as Memorial Day) parade on May 30, 1891, Captain W. S. Edgerly, commander of G Troop, pinned a medal on Private Matthew H. Hamilton in front of "hundreds of citizens," which comprised "the largest and most orderly crowd of people ever assembled in [Junction City]." Decoration Day had emerged after the Civil War as an occasion to honor the dead and decorate graves. Americans built monuments to their dead in ever increasing numbers after the war. Revering the dead allowed mourning communities to give meaning to the loss of their departed loved ones. Decoration Day orators in the North frequently invoked religious language of sacrifice and martyrdom to argue that soldiers had shed their blood for a unified and democratic nation.[46]

After decorating veterans' graves in the Fort Riley post cemetery, Captain J. R. McClure reminded the crowd of the great debt owed to the army for preserving the Union during the Civil War. Extending the same logic to the Indian Wars, McClure explained that the Seventh Cavalry had "lost more men in campaigns against the Indians than any other regiment in the service." He interpreted Wounded Knee as justified revenge for the Lakotas' previous "annihilation" of Colonel George Armstrong Custer and the Seventh Cavalry at the Little Bighorn in 1876. Just as the Lakotas had extended no mercy to Custer, Forsyth's men had granted no quarter after Big Foot's warriors had "treacherously" attacked the troops. Although "a few over sensitive Christians charged [the Seventh Cavalry] with killing women," McClure contended that the noncombatants were themselves to blame for getting "in the way" of the troops administering "a fitting punishment for [the Lakotas'] rebellious and barbarous conduct and cruelty."[47] In subsequent weeks, E Troop's Thomas Sullivan, Moshen Feaster, Herman Ziegner, and William G. Austin were all publicly presented Medals of Honor "for conspicuous bravery upon the field of battle."[48]

Although the War Department willingly awarded Medals of Honor to Forsyth's men for Wounded Knee, Miles still retained significant power and respect in the department. When Forsyth sought honorable mentions for some of his officers, the major general dismissed the recommendations as "an insult to the memory of the dead as well as to the brave men living."[49] Some speculated in 1891 that Forsyth, "who won additional laurels by his gallant action in fighting the bloodthirsty Sioux, [would] soon be promoted" to brigadier general. However, the promotion went to someone else, which some observers concluded was due to Miles's influence.[50] Not until November 9, 1894, would Forsyth be advanced in rank.[51] Others saw evidence of persistent fallout for Forsyth from the Miles controversy when the Honor Roll, an annual list of soldiers officially recognized for meritorious conduct, was announced in December 1891. Although the roll included thirty-two men who fought at Wounded Knee, the *Omaha Daily Bee* argued

FIGURE 3.2 Band at Fort Riley, Kansas, ca. 1896, photographer unknown, Pennell Photograph Collection, Pennell 66. Photo courtesy of the Spencer Research Library, University of Kansas.

that it was a "lamentable farce" that Forsyth and Major Samuel M. Whitside had been excluded from the list, since their "intrepidity [had] prevented further slaughter of the soldiers at Wounded Knee."[52] Forsyth may have survived the court of inquiry with considerable clout, but government officials in Washington, DC were more willing to honor the colonel's men than their commander.

In spite of the limits imposed by Miles and his allies on Forsyth's commemorative activities, the Medal of Honor's design had symbolized the post-Wounded Knee situation at Fort Riley well. Under an eagle and American flag, the medal's face portrayed the Greek goddess Minerva, who represented both war and Athenian democracy. She employed a shield marked by stars and stripes for defense while attacking with a fasces, or bound sticks, which represented for the Romans both unity and authority. The medals also portrayed Minerva's nemesis, Discord, who attacked with serpents.[53] While the symbolism most readily applied to the Civil War, Forsyth's officers had stood united behind their commander in the face of divisive accusations. Fort Riley had seen a rising crescendo of public commemorative activities—Reverend Lowell's defensive yet laudatory sermon, the funerals of Wallace, Howard, and Haselwood, the celebration for Forsyth's exoneration, and the series of public conferrals of Medals of Honor—that upheld a certain narrative of Wounded Knee as a heroic battle that should be honored, respected, and remembered, while discouraging open dissent from that view.

Engraving Martyrs' Names in Polished Granite

As the first anniversary of Wounded Knee approached, Forsyth proposed that the Seventh Cavalry weld Wounded Knee into Fort Riley's permanent landscape by building a monument "in memory of the men who lost their lives on the fields of battle." The monument would commemorate both Wounded Knee and a skirmish that occurred nearby at the Drexel Mission on December 30, 1890, where two Seventh Cavalrymen were killed. In keeping with nineteenth-century American custom, the donations of enlisted men, officers, and private citizens—rather than tax dollars—would fund its construction.[54] A century earlier, erecting an obelisk to ordinary soldiers would have been a novel idea. As early as 1799 Americans had erected a shaft to commemorate the "martyrs" killed in the Battle of Lexington, whose blood was shed "in the cause of God & their Country." However, prior to the Civil War most memorials in the United States remembered great generals, not ordinary soldiers.[55]

After 1865, monuments to common soldiers proliferated on the American memorial landscape. More than six hundred thousand dead—an effectively incomprehensible number for most Americans—combined with the shared experience of a mass army of volunteer soldiers, led both Northerners and Southerners to memorialize the names of those who died heroic deaths defending the nation, whether that was imagined as the Union or the South's Lost Cause.[56] By inscribing the names of the dead, monument sponsors sought to solidify particular interpretations of the soldiers' deaths and bind future generations emotionally to the cause and the community for which they died. Their goal was to curtail debate and discord by establishing a single authoritative narrative of the community's past in the apparent permanence of an obelisk. In spite of the opportunity in the postwar years to imagine a racially unified nation, most of the monuments in both the North and the South depicted common soldiers as heroic white males, with blacks only appearing as slaves receiving freedom from great white men or faithful slaves of a bygone era.[57]

In the West, federal troops erected monuments to the heroic sacrifices of martyrs who paid the ultimate price for the establishment of civilization. Placed at sites of federal power, these fixtures cemented in public memory the martial consolidation of American sovereignty and control of western lands. For example, Colonel P. Edward Connor and his California Volunteers dedicated a shaft in 1864 in the post cemetery at Camp Douglas, Utah, to the soldiers killed in an engagement with Shoshone Indians at Bear River, Idaho Territory, the year before. Although subsequent commentators would brand the Bear River engagement a massacre of hundreds of men, women, and children, Connor lauded the fight as a heroic victory that brought peace and civilization to the region, and as such, those soldiers who died should be honored for their service to the nation.[58] Three years later in the post cemetery at Fort Wallace, Kansas, the Seventh Cavalry erected an obelisk "in memory of the soldiers killed in action" against Indians.[59] In 1879, the Department of War created a National Cemetery in Montana Territory to protect the bodies of the Seventh Cavalrymen killed in the Battle of the Little Bighorn. Two years later, mourners erected an eighteen-ton granite monument to honor Colonel George Armstrong Custer and the two hundred and sixty men killed by Sioux, Cheyenne, and Arapaho warriors on June 25, 1876. Observers saw the obelisk as a "landmark of the conflict between civilization and barbarism."[60]

Unlike the memorial traditions surrounding the Battle of the Little Bighorn, which emerged at the actual site of Custer's death and defeat, Forsyth believed that Fort Riley was the best location for his monument to the soldiers killed at Wounded Knee. Although only two of his men were buried in the fort's post cemetery—the majority of those killed at Wounded Knee remained interred at the Pine Ridge Agency in South Dakota—maintaining and protecting a memorial to the Seventh Cavalry on the reservation would have been expensive and laborious in that unreceptive climate. In contrast, as Forsyth had found in early 1891, Fort Riley and its surrounding community provided a natural constituency to sustain the colonel's commemorative efforts. Discussing the proposed memorial, the Chicago *Daily Inter Ocean* noted that "these brave men, whose battle cry was 'Remember Custer,' lived [at Fort Riley], and it was from that place that they went off into the Dakota hills to fight the redskins in the snow of a December evening. Fitting it is that under the shade of Fort Riley should be a shaft to the memory of those brave Indian fighters."[61]

After a year and a half of fundraising, designing, and constructing the monument, the dedication was scheduled for July 24, 1893. A local poet heightened anticipation by portraying Wounded Knee as the Seventh Cavalry's heroic stand against a vast Indian conspiracy "that had sworn death to all." The confederacy had gathered "from North and West," while "the Seventh responded to the country's will/ And met them at Wounded Knee." The poet invoked the notion that the troops killed at Wounded Knee had sacrificed their lives for the good of the nation: "And now the Seventh, with grateful sense/ Of highest service paid,/ Erects her lofty monument,/ Where martyred sons are laid."[62] More than ten thousand people from all over Kansas assembled at Fort Riley for the dedication on a sunny July morning. The *Junction City Union* claimed it was "the largest crowd that ever visited Fort Riley, the largest military reservation in the world." Farmers from surrounding areas suspended their work to attend, the Union Pacific Railroad provided discounted rates for visitors, and local businesses agreed to close their doors during the proceedings. The Seventh Cavalry marched in a mounted dress parade, the cavalry band played the "Star-Spangled Banner" and "America," the artillery performed various drills, and the cavalrymen staged a sham battle to entertain the crowd.[63]

In his dedicatory oration, Kansas state legislator and attorney J. R. Burton argued that "treacherous" Lakota warriors had opened fire on unsuspecting troops:[64] "A wily and savage foe armed with the best weapons at arms' length and without warning opened a deadly fire upon our soldiers." In spite of the surprise, "not a man wavered in the presence of death. They grappled with the treacherous foe and destroyed him and next day at Drexel Mission this regiment won another victory."[65] Reflecting the notion that commemoration served to promote consensus rather than discord, Burton acknowledged that "for a short time" after Wounded Knee, "the spirit of criticism lifted its head claiming the battles were unnecessary and that the killing of the Indians was brutal, reflecting for a moment on the gallant colonel and his regiment." However, a "hot wave of indignation" spread to "every lover of courage and honor in this country," which dissipated the controversy. Real Americans, motivated by a sound understanding of the stakes of the nation's Manifest Destiny, honored rather than reviled the Seventh Cavalry. Burton conveniently omitted that Forsyth's principal critic was Major General Nelson A. Miles, an omission that facilitated the orator's marginalization of the colonel's critics.[66]

Burton interpreted Wounded Knee in the context of the race war between Anglo-Saxon civilization and savagery.[67] For one thousand years before the arrival of Europeans, the orator claimed, the Indians had not progressed in material, civic, or religious matters. Burton was confident that the Natives would not have advanced if given another millennium. They therefore had no claim on the land. Dismissing critics who argued that "the Anglo-Saxon race obtained it unjustly, by force," the orator contended "that no land belongs to any people or race when the claims of a better civilization are asserted." Rather, "virtue and intelligence have the superior rights to ignorance and barbarism. It has ever been so and so it will continue until the end of time." This "law of civilized progress," as scholar Brian Dippie has termed it, was irrevocable. Burton drew on his audience's memories of the Civil War, reiterating Republican arguments that free schools, free homes, and free labor ultimately permitted the North to develop a civilization superior to the South's "slave labor, ignorance, idleness and crime." Union troops thereby "combatted and destroyed savage ideas championed by civilized men." Although brave and committed to its cause, in final analysis the South was ultimately wrong and had to give way to the higher civilization. So it was with Indians and Euro-Americans.[68]

In making his argument, Burton echoed earlier commentators who framed their remembrances around pivotal "last battles," where heroic fighters suppressed indigenous marauders, brought peace to a region, and laid a foundation for subsequent progress and prosperity. The Great Basin's settlers remembered 1863 as the year that Colonel P. Edward Connor's troops ended the Shoshones' supposed reign of terror at Bear River, Idaho Territory.[69] Colonel John Milton Chivington argued that the Sand Creek Massacre of 1864 had pacified the plains of eastern Colorado, allowing Denver and other cities to thrive.[70] When challenging allegations that in 1871 the "old

settlers" had massacred peaceful Apache women and children at Camp
Grant, Arizona Territory, William Oury contended that violent suppression
of Native peoples was an unfortunate yet necessary precursor to the civilized
society that his critics hypocritically enjoyed.[71] Promoters similarly argued
that the Modoc War of 1872–1873, California's "last Indian War," had made
the state safe for civilization.[72]

Burton adapted these ideas, but rather than claiming that Wounded
Knee was essential solely for the northern Great Plains' subsequent prosperity, the legislator contended that the Seventh Cavalry's 1890 victory concluded the race war for North America as a whole. It was the soldiers' role to
enforce the United States' superior claims to the land: "From the landings of
the Pilgrims to the battles of Wounded Knee and Drexel Mission, the soldier
has been the frontiersman, clearing the way for the coming of our civilization." Soldiers made possible all the United States' historic advances in civil
government. In addition, the troops protected and preserved "the lives, liberties and properties of this people," creating a civic duty to honor and respect
the men who sacrificed so much for the nation.[73]

Burton placed the Seventh Cavalry within this history, arguing that the
regiment deserved special recognition in the country's advancement. Since
its founding at Fort Riley in 1866, the cavalry had lost more men to death
and injury than any other unit in the army. "It has fought the savage from the
Rio Grande to the British possessions and has won renown in every department of the great west," Burton related. The regiment's fame began with "the
bloody battle of the Washita," where Custer led his troops against Cheyenne
and Arapaho men, women, and children in 1868. The Seventh Cavalry's
heroics continued "with the signal victories at Wounded Knee and Drexel
Mission" in 1890. The legislator praised the conduct of the "gallant Colonel
Forsyth" and his men, who "performed acts of daring well nigh unparalleled
in the history of warfare." For Burton, the Seventh Cavalry deserved all the
accolades bestowed upon it.[74]

The names of the Seventh Cavalrymen killed at Wounded Knee and
Drexel Mission were therefore worth preserving for the ages. By inscribing
names on presumably permanent monuments, Americans after the Civil
War remembered the common soldiers who died for the nation. Names represented something more than just individual men; they symbolized the virtues and characteristics of ideal American citizen-soldiers. Years later, after
all those who knew the deceased personally had passed on, the names would
instill in subsequent viewers of the monument gratitude and emotional ties
to the nation.[75] The still-veiled monument behind Burton listed the names

of thirty-four Seventh Cavalrymen and one member of the Hospital Corps "killed in the battle with Sioux Indians at Wounded Knee," along with two cavalrymen who succumbed at Drexel Mission.[76] As the local *Junction City Union* noted, "the people who visit Fort Riley in the future will see in this memorial to the dead something grand and magnificent. They will see the names of those brave fellows who succumbed at Wounded Knee . . . engraved upon the polished granite that stands a tribute of honor and of brotherly love to the departed few."[77] The *Omaha Daily Bee* commented that, just as the "clannish" Seventh Cavalrymen "were never known to go back on a comrade in distress, or to forget those who fell fighting by their side," the obelisk would be "a standing reminder of the Seventh cavalry" well into the future at Fort Riley.[78] Burton echoed these remarks by arguing that the listed names would be "cherished as heroes who died for their country," indicating his belief that future Americans—aided by the permanence of the monument—would continue to see Wounded Knee as a heroic victory over the nation's treacherous foes.[79]

At the conclusion of Burton's address, four soldiers stepped forward and grasped the American flag that enveloped the obelisk that towered twenty-five feet in the air. Simultaneously, the artillery fired three salvos while "the band struck up the lively strains of 'Garry Owen,'" which had been Custer's favorite song. The *Abilene Weekly Reflector* noted it was "a tune of peculiar significance, because of it having been played when the Seventh cavalry charged at the Washita and upon similar occasions." The men who unveiled the monument included Saddler Sergeant Otto Voit, who had been with the Seventh Cavalry since its founding and had won a Medal of Honor at the Little Bighorn; Sergeant Adam Neder, who had received a Medal of Honor for gallantry at Wounded Knee; Private Daniel McMahon, who had been injured at Wounded Knee; and Private Frank Lohmiller of the Hospital Corps, who had likewise been with the Seventh Cavalry on December 29, 1890.[80] Captain John C. Gresham, a Medal of Honor recipient who fought at Wounded Knee, wrote for *Harper's Weekly* that once the flags fell, "a mighty shout, deafening and prolonged, went up from the vast multitude," concluding the proceedings.[81]

Captain Gresham noted the somber absence of his comrades who died at Wounded Knee: "The remains of most of our dead still rest in the treeless, homely little Indian cemetery at Pine Ridge, where we laid them on a stormy day of biting winds and rapidly falling snow."[82] Although there had been discussion in the early 1890s of removing the bodies and reinterring them at Fort Riley, the army delayed doing so for fifteen years, apparently waiting for the

FIGURE 3.3 Wounded Knee Monument at Fort Riley, Kansas, ca. 1895, photographer unknown, Wounded Knee Massacre Collection, RG2845-20-1. Photo courtesy of Nebraska State Historical Society.

bodies to decay sufficiently for easy transfer.[83] On August 8 and 9, 1906, contractors disinterred the "heroes of Wounded Knee," including twenty-eight members of the Seventh Cavalry, and Oscar Pollack, of the Hospital Corps. In addition, the body of one Seventh Cavalryman who had died at Drexel Mission on December 30, 1890, was removed. The time had finally come to return the bodies to their Kansas regimental home.[84] The fort's newspaper noted that it was "fitting that this should be their last resting place," since "the history of the regiment has been identified with that of Fort Riley," in particular with the famous campaigns led by George Armstrong Custer.[85]

The bodies would be arranged in the post cemetery in an honorific half-circle around the base of a hill.[86] Nearby stood the Seventh Cavalry Monument, which commemorated "the death of these who died at their duty to the last." Fort Riley would be the resting place "of those who were once members of the famous 7th and who fell in the last Indian fight in which our troops will probably ever be engaged."[87] The transfer of the bodies completed Forsyth's work of transforming Fort Riley into a place of memory—supported by physical objects such as Medals of Honor, the buried soldiers' headstones, and the monument—where the Seventh Cavalry's conduct at Wounded Knee would be honored and revered.[88]

In 1907, the War Department reinforced this designation when it authorized campaign badges for the Indian Wars. Like the Civil War Campaign Badge, the Indian Wars Campaign Badges broadly honored all soldiers who had participated in Indian warfare. The War Department identified by name twelve major campaigns since 1865. The face of the bronze badge displayed "INDIAN WARS" above a mounted Indian, wearing a war bonnet and carrying a spear. The bottom edge was trimmed with arrowheads and a buffalo skull. The reverse side stated "UNITED STATES ARMY" and "FOR SERVICE," showed an eagle with outstretched wings—the symbol of United States sovereignty—with its talons piercing a pile of spears, arrows, a cannon, and a rifle.[89] Regiments were also authorized to display banners with their flags to commemorate those campaigns. The Pine Ridge Campaign of 1890–1891, with Wounded Knee as its most significant engagement, rounded out the twelve, reinforcing the narrative that the Indian Wars had effectively ended at Wounded Knee Creek, South Dakota, on December 29, 1890.[90] The creation of the badge validated the sustained efforts of Forsyth and his allies at Fort Riley to commemorate Wounded Knee as the United States' last heroic victory over Indians.

Buffalo Bill and the Indian Wars

Although memorialization of Wounded Knee was concentrated at Fort Riley in the 1890s, gradually the event made its way into popular representations of the American West. Since the early 1870s, William "Buffalo Bill" Cody had transfixed audiences in the United States and in Europe with gripping portrayals of treacherous Indians, distressed white settlers, and heroic Cavalry rescues. The Wild West, Cody's own show founded in 1883, took the audience through the so-called epochs of human history, from savagery to barbarism to civilization, highlighting the role of the frontier army in the transitions.

The exhibition frequently reenacted the Battle of the Little Bighorn, show-ing Colonel George Armstrong Custer and the Seventh Cavalry as martyrs who shed their blood for the advance of civilization. Each show reinscribed Euro-American innocence and reconfirmed race war assumptions that civili-zation was destined to triumph over savagery. Cody also reenacted the Battle of Summit Springs (1869) and the Battle of Warbonnet Creek (1876), two engagements in which Cody himself participated as an army scout.[91] In the latter fight, Cody scalped Cheyenne warrior Yellow Hair, a moment that the showman commemorated as the first scalp taken to avenge Custer.[92] The pop-ularity of the scene revealed the deep hunger that many Americans felt in the wake of Custer's defeat for vindication.

Over the years, Cody developed close ties with many Lakotas who had toured with the Wild West. During the 1885 season Sitting Bull himself joined the show, and was advertised as the mastermind behind Custer's defeat at the Little Bighorn. During the 1890 Ghost Dance crisis, Major General Nelson A. Miles believed that Cody could utilize his relationship with the medicine man to convince Sitting Bull to surrender himself to authorities. On November 28, 1890, Cody arrived at the Standing Rock Agency, intent on fulfilling his mission and perhaps adding another heroic scene to his rep-ertoire. Agent James McLaughlin, however, contended that he had the situ-ation under control and that the showman was interfering where he was not wanted. McLaughlin asked Indian Office bureaucrats to intercede with the War Department and rescind Cody's orders. The agent successfully delayed Cody until the new orders came through, and the showman left the reserva-tion, only to hear of Sitting Bull's violent death at the hands of the Standing Rock Indian policemen on December 15, 1890.[93]

Cody subsequently added a coda to the 1890–1891 Ghost Dance crisis. Following the surrender and arrest of the leading Ghost Dancers in early 1891, the showman proposed that, rather than punish them, the government should permit the leaders to join his upcoming Wild West tour in Great Britain. The plan was approved. The 1891–1892 tour's promotional materi-als depicted the Ghost Dance as the "hostile" and "fanatical" rebellion that sought, yet failed, to challenge "civilization" in the American West. Like previous tours, Buffalo Bill promised historically accurate exhibitions, with actual Ghost Dancers and even a Lakota survivor of the Battle of Wounded Knee appearing on stage. However, for reasons that remain unclear, Cody opted not to reenact either the Ghost Dance or Wounded Knee during the tour. Historian Sam Maddra has argued that the showman's reluc-tance resulted from his sensitivity to his Lakota employees, many of whom retained belief in the sacred nature of the dance and who had relatives killed at Wounded Knee. Buffalo Bill may have also feared bad publicity from the American press. Finally, Cody saw the Ghost Dance as a form of "fanaticism" that he did not want to encourage through reenactment.[94]

Buffalo Bill's hesitancy to reenact the Ghost Dance and Wounded Knee was ultimately short-lived, as he added both to the Wild West program by the mid-1890s. A new cast, one not as directly tied emotionally to the events of late 1890, might have brought about this change in direction. Historian Jerome Greene suggests, however, that the showman's reversal stemmed from competitors incorporating the Ghost Dance and Wounded Knee into their Wild West shows. Never one to be outdone, Buffalo Bill may have seen other shows successfully reenacting the events of the 1890–1891 Ghost Dance crisis and decided to include similar aspects in his show.[95]

In 1913, Cody decided to produce a feature-length film to the Ghost Dance and Wounded Knee. It would begin with Wovoka, follow the spread of the Ghost Dance on the Lakota reservations, trace the arrival of the army to suppress the feared rebellion, culminate at Wounded Knee, and conclude with the January 1891 peace council. By 1913, Cody was in financial straits. He had recently declared bankruptcy, and revenues from ticket sales from a movie offered the promise of financial recovery. Simultaneously releasing a Western in theaters and other venues had the potential to reach far more fans than Buffalo Bill's traditional tour schedule.[96]

As one of the most entrepreneurial Americans of his generation, Cody was eager to incorporate new technologies into his exhibitions whenever possible. He adopted electrical lights soon after their invention by Thomas Edison in the 1890s. Similarly, Cody quickly seized upon Edison's development of moving picture technology, and the inventor and the showman collaborated on several short films. It was therefore natural for Cody to produce a full-length Western as a summation of a long and successful career marked by innovation. Westerns were barely a decade old in 1913 and they had quickly grown in popularity, drawing on many of the techniques and themes that Cody had first developed in his Wild West.[97]

Cody's choice of subject may have been influenced by Kit Carson's Buffalo Ranch Wild West, a traveling circus that claimed to be "the largest Wild West show on earth." The 1913 tour prominently featured a reenactment of "the Battle of Wounded Knee," the "last brave stand and hopeless struggle of the noble redskin for his freedom and rights." Advertisements also promised that unnamed participants in the fight would appear in the show.[98] Although it remains unclear whether Cody was influenced by Carson's tour, the Buffalo Ranch Wild West's reenactment of Wounded Knee would have raised public awareness of the 1890 massacre in the months prior to the release of Cody's film.

Cody sought and obtained permission from the War Department to use actual soldiers in the film. The department agreed, on the condition that the film would positively portray the army and its contributions to the "Winning of the West." Washington officials even agreed to allow members of the Twelfth Cavalry, stationed at Fort Robinson, Nebraska, to participate as actors in the film. Cody also asked General Nelson A. Miles and other retired army officers, many of whom had been in South Dakota in 1890–1891, to serve as historical consultants. Whereas advertisements for Kit Carson's Wounded Knee reenactment only referenced unnamed participants in the fight, Buffalo Bill would be able to claim that major figures in the 1890–1891 campaign had consulted on his film.[99] The completed film was to be deposited in the War Department's official archive. According to the Chicago *Inter-Ocean*, it would "be the first moving pictorial record of warfare ever preserved by the government."[100] With Miles and other veterans from the campaign acting as historical consultants, expectations were high that the reenactment would be so authentic and accurate that the film itself would become part of the official government record, preserved in an official government archive, and thereby provide an objective source that future historians could use to reconstruct what had happened at Wounded Knee.

The Interior Department also approved Cody's request to shoot the film on the Pine Ridge Reservation in South Dakota. The department granted him permission to hire Lakotas, many of whom had previously toured with Buffalo Bill's Wild West, to perform as actors in the film. The department insisted, however, that Cody conclude the film not with the bloodbath of Wounded Knee, but with scenes of Indians entering modern life. He would need to represent the Lakotas attending school, using farming equipment, and driving cars, reinforcing the assumption that the violence of Wounded Knee was a necessary and effective tool that led to the Indians' adoption of "civilization."[101] As Pine Ridge Superintendent John Brennan summarized, the film would "present historical events which paved the way to racial peace between red and white."[102]

The filming took place on Pine Ridge from late September to early November 1913. Cody hired the Essanay Film Manufacturing Company, which had pioneered the production of Westerns, to handle the technical side of the filming. Theodore Wharton was brought in to direct the movie. Although no copy of the film itself has survived, stills, promotional materials, and a scene list permit a partial reconstruction of its contents and narrative. Although initially Cody had wanted to focus entirely on the 1890–1891 Ghost Dance crisis, he ultimately decided to expand the film chronologically to include the Battle of Summit Creek (1869) and the Battle of War Bonnet Creek (1876), both of which had been regular features of the Wild West for many years.[103]

In an interview given prior to filming, Miles, Cody's chief historical consultant, provided insights into how the film would interpret the Ghost Dance crisis. His comments demonstrated that many of his opinions had not changed since 1890 when he cast the Ghost Dance as "fanatical" threat to American sovereignty that required an overwhelming military response. "The uprising," he explained, "was one of the few in the history of the North American Indian that was caused by religious fanaticism." Wovoka, the Paiute "false Messiah" and "imposter," convinced sixteen tribes to join the uprising.[104] Surviving stills and scene lists suggest that Cody incorporated Miles's interpretation into the film, framing the Ghost Dance crisis as the "Rebellion of 1890–1891."[105] Lakota warriors were shown performing "hostile demonstrations" against whites, and a "charge of the mounted Indians" against the US Cavalry. The scenes then moved to the failed arrest and killing of Sitting Bull in mid-December and the flight of his people south toward Big Foot's camp on the Cheyenne River Reservation.[106]

Cody, however, experienced some difficulties with Miles with the representation of Wounded Knee itself. Miles was the foremost critic of the Seventh Cavalry's conduct at Wounded Knee in the event's aftermath, and his criticisms had not softened in subsequent years. "I have always considered that tragedy as unwarranted and unjustifiable," the retired general explained to Pine Ridge Agent Brennan on October 13, 1913, the day Cody filmed the Wounded Knee reenactment. "I desire to inform you that I have not nor will I take part in the affair, and I am decidedly of the opinion that it is not in the public interest, or for the welfare of the Indians, to have such exhibition presented."[107] Miles's opposition posed a significant dilemma for Cody, given the retired general's prominent role in shaping the film's direction to that point.

Although Miles insisted on remaining at the Pine Ridge Agency while Cody filmed the reenactment, the showman had another historical advisor who had been present at Wounded Knee on December 29, 1890: former army scout and interpreter Philip Wells. Forsyth himself had died in 1906, but he could not have had a better advocate on the field when the filming started.[108] In the January 1891 court of inquiry, the interpreter testified that the Ghost Dance medicine man gave the signal for Big Foot's fanatical warriors, who

FIGURE 3.4 Wounded Knee scene in Buffalo Bill's *The Indian Wars* movie, 1913, photographer unknown. 1913, FB 108, John R. Brennan Collection. Photo courtesy of South Dakota State Historical Society.

were hiding rifles under their Ghost Shirts, to fire on the Seventh Cavalry. Wells's testimony provided a key piece of evidence in support of Forsyth's contention that the warriors, deluded by the Ghost Dance, had treacherously plotted to attack the Seventh Cavalry.[109] According to one reporter, at the reenactment "the Copper Indians, in their bright blankets and strange war paint, sat AGAIN in the basin of the Wounded Knee in their council of war! The war dance of the medicine man was repeated again with all its weird incantations and strange movements!"[110] Surviving stills from the film show armed Lakota warriors attacking the cavalrymen.[111] As a concession to Miles, however, the showman opted not to portray soldiers killing Lakota women and children.[112] Ironically, Miles's opposition forced Cody to represent

Wounded Knee as a heroic victory over "treacherous savages"—the Forsyth interpretation—rather than, as Miles had long insisted, as a massacre of innocent women and children.

After about six weeks of editing, the film opened in theaters and other venues early in 1914.[113] Promotional materials suggest that the two-and-a-half-hour movie was advertised under several names, including *The Last Indian Wars in America*, *Wars for Civilization*, *Last Indian Battles*, *Indian Wars*, *Buffalo Bill's War Pictures*, *Indian War Pictures*, and *Indian Wars Refought by United States Army*. In compliance with his agreement with the Interior Department, the film concluded by showing Native students in school. "The TRANSITION OF THE RED MAN," one surviving scene list states, "from the WARPATH TO PEACE PURSUITS, under the American flag—'The Star Spangled Banner.'"[114] The movie was shown in several cities across the United States, bringing the "Battle of Wounded Knee" to tens of thousands of Americans.[115]

FOLLOWING JAMES FORSYTH'S exoneration in the January 1891 court of inquiry, the colonel returned to Fort Riley, Kansas, intent on rejuvenating his reputation by honoring his gallant soldiers. The War Department rewarded twenty of his men the coveted Medal of Honor, while the Fort Riley community remembered the soldiers slain at Wounded Knee through honorific funerals and the erection of a large monument. Throughout these activities, Forsyth and his allies commemorated Wounded Knee as the final victory in the four-hundred-year struggle between civilization and savagery for the continent. Eventually, this interpretation spread to popular representations of Wounded Knee and was the climax of Buffalo Bill's 1913 movie, *The Indian Wars*.

Forsyth, Buffalo Bill, and other whites therefore created the framework in which Wounded Knee would be memorialized in the years following 1890. Although General Nelson A. Miles contested this interpretation in 1891 and then again in 1913, the most sustained challenge to the Forsyth consensus came from the most unlikely of people: the Lakota survivors of Wounded Knee. Although traumatized and marginalized on South Dakota's reservations, the Lakotas nevertheless found ways to subvert the official version of Wounded Knee in subsequent years, most notably in a monument erected in 1903 at the mass grave in memory of "the Chief Big Foot Massacre."

PART II

Lakota Countermemory

4

"In Memory of the Chief Big Foot Massacre"

ON MAY 28, 1903, five thousand Lakotas assembled near a mass grave on the Pine Ridge Reservation in South Dakota. They had come to dedicate a monument to honor Minneconjou Lakota Chief Big Foot and more than two hundred of his followers killed by the US Seventh Cavalry at Wounded Knee Creek. The Lakotas erected the monument to protest the "Chief Big Foot Massacre," as the obelisk's inscription would call the killings.

The Lakotas' monument was a rare intervention by indigenous peoples in a Western memorial landscape that Euro-Americans largely controlled. Throughout the West, Americans erected monuments to honor George Armstrong Custer and other white soldiers killed in the Indian Wars.[1] Even when whites killed large number of Indians, Americans found ways to memorialize massacres as necessary acts that ostensibly brought peace and progress to the nation.[2] Although there was some disagreement among army officials over what exactly happened at Wounded Knee, the War Department ultimately upheld the Seventh Cavalry's claim that "treacherous" and "fanatical" Ghost Dancers had attacked unsuspecting troops. The official explanation disavowed any responsibility for the deaths of women and children and furthered this narrative by awarding Medals of Honor to twenty soldiers and erecting a monument to soldiers killed. These memorial acts reinforced the emerging national consensus that the "Battle of Wounded Knee" was "civilization's" final triumph over "savagery" for North America.[3]

Confined to reservations, few Natives could challenge these narratives publicly.[4] As historian Ari Kelman explains, during the "so-called era of assimilation" the Indian Office and boarding schools created "institutionalized pressure to forget," imposing policies "that included violent and coercive suppression of the Sun Dance and other tribal practices."[5] Some Natives, however, used education they acquired in American schools to "talk back to civilization."[6] A notable example was George Bent, a Cheyenne survivor of the 1864 Sand Creek Massacre who publicly challenged in writing prevalent explanations that the slaughter of more than one hundred and fifty Cheyennes and Arapahoes was necessary to protect white settlements from hostile Indians and that the killings ultimately brought peace to the region. Instead of pacifying the Great Plains and bringing civilization, Bent concluded that the massacre actually caused previously peaceful Natives to turn against the United States, triggering the Indian Wars that culminated with the Lakota and Cheyenne victory over Custer's Seventh Cavalry at the Little Bighorn in 1876.[7]

Like Bent, the Lakotas employed writing and other tools to challenge the official justifications for the deaths of December 29, 1890. This chapter examines the Wounded Knee survivors' intervention in western public memory during the decade and half following the killings. The survivors were led by Joseph Horn Cloud, a teenager in 1890 who lost his parents and several siblings at Wounded Knee. Horn Cloud used his knowledge of the English language to spearhead the survivors' campaign for justice, filing compensation claims and erecting the obelisk in 1903. The Lakotas' monument challenged not only the dominant memory of Wounded Knee itself, but also the broader narrative that the killings of December 29, 1890, represented the final triumph of civilization over savagery.

Compensation and Its Discontents

Word of the Wounded Knee killings spread like prairie fire through the Lakota reservations. News quickly reached the Cheyenne River Reservation, where Big Foot's band had lived prior to their fateful move south to Wounded Knee Creek on Pine Ridge. "Big Foot's people were massacred by the soldiers after giving up their arms," a Pine Ridge policeman wrote his sister on January 4, noting that "but few escaped." As a result, "there [was] intense feeling among the people against the soldiers."[8] This policeman's account demonstrates that the Lakotas were using the word "massacre" almost immediately to describe what the soldiers had done to Big Foot's band.

The intense feeling described by the policeman had even spread to the Santee Dakotas, cousins to the Lakotas living nearly three hundred miles to the east of Pine Ridge in eastern Nebraska. On January 14, 1891, an anonymous missionary wrote Secretary of War Redfield Proctor, explaining that "the web of inter-relationship among the various tribes of the Sioux Nation is very intricate and extensive." The missionary explained: "The fact that at the recent engagement at Wounded Knee a number were killed has deeply affected all the tribes, as they consider the killing of women and children an unpardonable offense." The missionary found that the killings appalled even "progressive" Santees—those who had previously advocated accommodation to the United States—and that these accommodationists demanded justice.[9] This was not an isolated reaction. Charles Eastman, a Dakota physician serving on Pine Ridge, was among the first people to visit Wounded Knee after the killings. "Fully three miles from the scene of the massacre," he found bodies "as they had been relentlessly hunted down and slaughtered while fleeing for their lives." Eastman later recorded: "All this was a severe ordeal for one who had so lately put all his faith in the Christian love and lofty ordeals of the white man."[10]

Alarmed that Wounded Knee was causing previously loyal Natives to turn on the United States, government officials arranged for a Lakota delegation to express their grievances in the nation's capital.[11] No one from Big Foot's band was selected, but the delegates had interviewed the survivors and were intent on representing their interests. On February 9 Secretary of the Interior John W. Noble met with the delegates, including Minneconjou leader Hump, who was related to many of the victims at Wounded Knee. Hump asked if there would "be some consideration shown the survivors," perhaps the first call on the government to compensate the remaining members of Big Foot's band for their losses.[12]

Noble did not answer Hump directly, but two days later Commissioner of Indian Affairs Thomas J. Morgan met with Chief American Horse, Turning Hawk, and other delegates to discuss Wounded Knee further. Reverend Charles S. Cook of the Pine Ridge Episcopal Church acted as translator. American Horse had interviewed the survivors and had seen "where the bodies were from the track of the blood" on the killing field. What he saw affected him deeply, since the Seventh Cavalry's actions undermined the chief's long-standing advocacy of accommodation to the United States.[13] American Horse "harangued his comrades" for their timidity "and advised them to [speak plainly], no matter how harsh the truth may be."[14] Emboldened by his entreaties, the delegates rejected the Seventh Cavalry's official account of Wounded Knee. Turning Hawk argued that Big Foot's band had no preconceived or treacherous plan to attack the soldiers. The trouble instead started when "a crazy man, a young man of very bad influence, and in fact a nobody among that bunch of Indians, fired his gun." The young warrior was simply

FIGURE 4.1 Full Delegation of Sioux Indians, including American Horse (front row, fifth from left), Hump (third row, fifth from left), and Turning Hawk (fourth row, third from left), 1891, by C. W. Bell, Lakota Indians Collection, RG2063-4-3. Photo courtesy of Nebraska State Historical Society.

trying to prove his bravery and manhood by shooting his weapon in the air. Big Foot and other leaders therefore had disapproved the warrior's actions. For Turning Hawk, the army was using the young warrior's mistake to disavow responsibility for the subsequent killings. Although most of the Lakota men had died from this volley, a few escaped into the nearby ravine, where they were pursued and shot down.[15]

The commissioner then asked about the army's explanations for noncombatant deaths. On whether the women had fired on the soldiers—a key component of the Seventh Cavalry's story—Turning Hawk replied that the women were unarmed. When questioned if Lakota clothing made men indistinguishable from women, the delegate stated wryly that "a man would be very blind if he could not tell the difference between a man and a woman." On whether the fleeing warriors had mixed with women and children, thereby requiring the soldiers to fire at noncombatants, the delegates responded that the men had run in a different direction than their families. Wherever they fled, Lakotas, regardless of gender or age, shared the same fate: death at the hands of pursuing soldiers and Hotchkiss guns.[16] The delegates also reported that the cavalrymen yelled "Remember Custer!" as they shot down the fleeing Lakotas.[17] When the shooting stopped, a soldier announced that hiding Lakotas could safely emerge: "Little boys who were not wounded came out of their places of refuge, and as soon as they came in sight a number of soldiers surrounded them and butchered them there."[18]

Commissioner Morgan replied that "these are very serious charges to make against the United States army" and asked if there were any dissenting views. "Of course we all feel very sad about this affair," American Horse replied, confirming the delegation's unanimity. The chief's long history of loyalty to the government magnified his sorrow. Had the soldiers only killed Big Foot's men, the delegates would have felt relatively little anger toward the United States. Their angst resulted from "the killing of the women, and more especially the killing of the young boys and girls who are to go to make up the future strength of the Indian people." American Horse had come to the nation's capital with "a very great blame against the Government on [his] heart." Turning Hawk confirmed that all the Lakotas were distressed by Wounded Knee.[19]

Commissioner Morgan promised to do what he could to address their grievances.[20] The next day, however, Secretary of War Redfield Proctor publically exonerated the Seventh Cavalry, which perhaps discouraged Morgan from taking any action.[21] Although the delegates left Washington without any explicit assurances of justice for Wounded Knee, their statements were widely reproduced in newspapers, Morgan's annual report, and subsequent publications. For many readers, the delegates' statements were the principal source for understanding the "Lakota view" of Wounded Knee.[22]

Concerned by reports that Wounded Knee had alienated loyal Lakotas like American Horse, on April 3 Congress appropriated $100,000 out of the Treasury to compensate "friendly" Lakotas who had lost property at the hands of "roving bands of disaffected Indians" during the "recent Sioux trouble."[23] Specifically, the act fulfilled Article 1 of the 1868 Treaty of Fort Laramie, which established peace between the Lakota nation and the United States. The article specified that if a white person wronged a Lakota's person or property, or, conversely, if a Lakota wronged the person or property of "any one, white, black, or Indian, subject to the authority of the United States," the federal government would compensate the wronged party.[24]

The Interior Department charged Special Agent James A. Cooper with evaluating the Lakotas' petitions. Beginning in April 1891, more than seven hundred and fifty Lakotas filled out claims, recording their name, residence, lost property and its value, and date of loss. They attached brief narratives describing how "disaffected" Lakotas had destroyed their property while the claimants were away from home, in obedience to the government's 1890 order that all "friendlies" report to the agency. In addition, claims included the signatures (or "X marks") of supporting witnesses and the interpreter.[25]

Cooper reported to his superiors "that as long as the investigation [of] claims continues that there will be no trouble as all the Indians of this tribe seem more interested in filing claims for losses than they are in stirring up strife."[26] Implementing the act seemed to have the desired effect. Successful applicants for compensation had to affirm "that at no time during the late trouble among the Indians, has he been hostile, either by word or action, to the government of the United States." Cooper frequently, although inconsistently, defined "hostility" as participation in the Ghost Dance.[27] The legislation therefore excluded those who had undoubtedly suffered the most during the "Sioux troubles" of 1890–1891—the survivors of Big Foot's band—since they were known Ghost Dancers.

We Lost Our Properties and Whole Families in That Massacre

Although the survivors were scattered, traumatized, and impoverished after Wounded Knee, they nevertheless were cognizant of the government's decision to exclude Big Foot's band from compensation. In the mid-1890s, a literate Lakota named Joseph Horn Cloud and other survivors began artic-ulating their grievances in compensation claims. Patterned after the claims submitted to Special Agent Cooper, these documents were constrained by the legal framework of the 1891 act, which limited compensation to stolen or damaged property. The claimants could not, therefore, demand retribution for the deaths of their relatives under that law. In these early written accounts of Wounded Knee, Horn Cloud and the other survivors demonstrated a keen awareness of the language and memory politics that framed public discussions of the engagement in the early 1890s. By explicitly interpreting Wounded Knee as killings perpetrated by white soldiers against unarmed Lakota men, women, and children, the claimants reinvented and reapplied the English word *massacre*, which whites commonly used to differentiate their "civilized" mode of warfare from indiscriminate killings of noncomba-tants that ostensibly defined how "savages" waged war.

In the immediate aftermath of Wounded Knee, the survivors of Big Foot's band struggled simply to rebuild their lives. The Pine Ridge Reservation's Holy Rosary Catholic Mission School permitted several orphans to live in its boarding school.[28] Other survivors, with the help of Minneconjou leaders Iron Lightning and Hump, returned to their homes on the Cheyenne River reservation.[29] Some white families adopted infants found on the killing field, most notably Nebraska National Guard commander Leonard Colby and his wife Clara Bewick Colby, who adopted a young girl named Lost Bird (*Zintkala Nuni*).[30] In June 1891, Cheyenne River Agent Peraine P. Palmer conducted a "Census of the Sioux Indians Belonging to the Cheyenne River reservation who were in the battle of Wounded Knee and are yet at Pine Ridge Agency, S.D." Palmer listed the names, ages, and sex of about one hun-dred and forty survivors and eighty-six deceased Lakotas. Since the army had interred at least one hundred and fifty bodies in the mass grave, the agent substantially undercounted the number of the dead.[31] A month after Palmer recorded his census, the Pine Ridge Oglalas adopted the remaining orphans of Big Foot's band into their tribal structure.[32]

Number eighty-two on Palmer's census was a young Minneconjou male, identified simply as "Joseph."[33] In his late teens in 1890, Joseph had lost his parents, Mr. and Mrs. Horn Cloud (listed on the census as "dead"), two brothers, and a niece at Wounded Knee. While living at the Holy Rosary Mission School on Pine Ridge, Joseph assumed his father's name, Horn Cloud (what Lakotas called tornadoes), as his surname. He learned carpen-try and periodically worked in several western states as a day laborer and cow-boy. He also converted to Catholicism, eventually becoming, like his better known contemporary Black Elk, a catechist or lay teacher. Horn Cloud had acquired sporadic education as a child and at the mission school, qualifying him to work as a translator and as the Oglala Tribal Council secretary.[34] Horn Cloud used his familiarity with the "enemy's language" to lead the survivors' campaign to seek compensation for their losses at Wounded Knee. He represented a new generation of Natives who had received some education in the early reservation period and embraced the new technology of literacy to improve their peoples' situation under American rule.[35]

Horn Cloud's pursuit of compensation was rooted in both the government's exclusion of Big Foot's band during the 1891 investigation and in Lakota expectations of proper responses to murders. In a remarkable letter penned in his own hand in 1903 to Nebraska newspaper editor and erstwhile judge, Eli S. Ricker, Horn Cloud described his frustration that "friendly" Lakotas in 1891 claimed compensation for items as insignificant as rusty spoons. As for Big Foot's band, "we lost our Properties and whole families" in the "massacree [sic]" at Wounded Knee. Only a few people—"most of younger ones"—had escaped, yet "nobody help[ed] us and look[ed] into this matter for us." The "children's of Big Foot," Horn Cloud argued, had "lost [the] most properties but Government do not look at us he must be sham [ashamed?] because he feed old ones and kill them. That ain't right."[36] Additionally, Horn Cloud's views were probably shaped by traditional Lakota approaches to conflict resolution, which provided that the family of a murdered individual could reasonably expect compensation from the killer who sought in good faith to cover the family's losses.[37]

Five years after Special Agent Cooper's investigation, Horn Cloud drafted a claim for his father's lost property.[38] Following the format of the 1891 claims, he wrote the date, April 15, 1896, and his place of residence, the Holy Rosary Catholic Mission on Pine Ridge. Horn provided a short narrative explaining the circumstances surrounding his family's "losses during the trouble of 1890 and 91. My father's name was Horn Cloud we lived in Cheyenne River at the time and come to Pine Ridge S.D. during the trouble and when we return home the following property belonging to my father who was kill[ed] at Wounded Knee was missing." He listed its worth at $2,045.50. The claim was for restitution for lost property, not lives, but Horn Cloud concluded the document by stating that "Mr. Horn Cloud and his wife and 2 boys was kill[ed] in Wounded Knee Massacre in Dec 29, 1890." Daniel White Lance, Horn Cloud's older brother, also signed the claim.[39] Another brother, Dewey Beard, likewise drafted a claim that listed property, valued at $2,481, that was stolen while he was away from his Cheyenne River home. Beard concluded

FIGURE 4.2 From left, Brothers Dewey Beard, Joseph Horn Cloud, and Daniel White Lance, 1907, by Edward Truman, Eli S. Ricker Collection, RG1227-25-4. Photo courtesy of Nebraska State Historical Society.

the claim by stating that he had "lost his family in massacre, Dec. 29, 1890," including his parents, brothers, niece, wife, and infant son.⁴⁰

The brothers' use of the English word "massacre" in these claims to describe Wounded Knee was not incidental, but rather was central to their linguistic engagement in memory politics. When Ricker interviewed Horn Cloud in 1906, the newspaper editor noted that the Lakotas "always called" Wounded Knee a "massacre," or *Wichakasotapi*, meaning an engagement "where all were wiped out."⁴¹ By insisting on this word, the Lakotas participated in the ongoing debates over distinctions between battles and massacres within the discourse of "race war" between "civilization" and "savagery." These distinctions undergirded and rationalized the United States' Manifest Destiny to displace the Natives of North America. Honor and forbearance defined civilized battles; cruelty and bloodlust characterized savage massacres. Battles were supposedly legitimate engagements between equally matched foes and were governed by universally accepted rules. Civilized forces, in this view, honored white flags, respected the bodies of slain foes, and protected prisoners of war and noncombatants. In contrast, savages ostensibly recognized no rules of warfare, deceived their enemies, and indiscriminately massacred defenseless women and children.⁴²

The Lakotas' insistence that Wounded Knee was a massacre was therefore grounded in the broader linguistic politics that governed remembrance of the consolidation of American sovereignty in the West after the Civil War. Eastern reformers criticized the government's postwar Indian policies and the army's treatment of Indians in the West. These reformers rejected the notion that Natives were inherently warlike, arguing instead that violence in the West resulted from the government's unwillingness to honor treaties. Reformers labeled the 1864 slaughter of Cheyenne and Arapaho noncombatants at Sand Creek in Colorado Territory a "massacre," which marked a significant rhetorical shift since it reversed the categories of "civilized" and "savage" and bemoaned the United States' alleged descent into barbarism.⁴³ Reformers later condemned as massacres the high numbers of Indian noncombatant casualties at Washita, Oklahoma Territory in 1868, at Marias, Montana Territory in 1870, and at Camp Grant, Arizona Territory in 1871.⁴⁴ In addition, reform-minded whites such as Major General Nelson A. Miles argued that the Seventh Cavalry's conduct at Wounded Knee constituted the most "brutal, coldblooded massacre" in American history. The major general condemned his own subordinates' actions because he believed that negotiation was more efficient than violent suppression in campaigns against Indians.⁴⁵

The Lakotas' growing familiarity with English therefore allowed them to inject themselves into these debates. As Ricker recorded, "the Indians sneer at the whiteman's conventional reference to the Custer massacre and the battle of Wounded Knee." The reason, he noted, was "the lack of impartiality of the whites in speaking of the two events—when the whites got the worst of it was a massacre; when the Indians got the worst of it was a *battle*." For the Lakotas, in both cases they were defending themselves against invaders: "The Indians understand that on the Little Big Horn they were defending themselves—their village—their property—their lives—their women and children." At Wounded Knee, "they were attacked, wantonly, cruelly, brutally, and that what little fighting they did was in self-defense."[46] The Lakotas believed that their conduct at the Little Bighorn was legitimate because Custer and his men had invaded their territory. At Wounded Knee, the army had again invaded Lakota lands and slaughtered innocent people. In both scenarios, it was the United States—the ostensibly civilized nation—that had invaded Indian country. By insisting that Wounded Knee was a massacre, the Lakotas rhetorically reversed the categories of "savage" and "civilized."

The brothers twice sent their claims—marked by the English word massacre—to the Commissioner of Indian Affairs in the late 1890s. Just as Thomas Jefferson Morgan had initially been shocked by American Horse's "serious charges" against the army—only to brush the allegations aside—the Indian Office in the 1890s rejected the survivors' claims. Horn Cloud concluded that "this trouble comes from whites but [they] did not tell [the] truth," suggesting that in his mind those who had power to define the official memory of Wounded Knee were consciously suppressing knowledge of the killings.[47]

Wounded Knee as a Place of Memory

Even as Horn Cloud and other survivors were pursuing compensation, the Lakotas were endowing Wounded Knee with profound memorial significance. This marked a second development in the 1890s that contributed to the construction of the Wounded Knee obelisk in 1903. Despite the fact that the Pine Ridge Reservation was government-controlled space, the Lakotas had some power to define how the event would be remembered at the site. The fact that the Wounded Knee killings occurred on a reservation ensured that the survivors and others would have continual access to the site.[48]

By the late nineteenth century, the Lakotas had been confined to reservations for almost two decades.[49] Reservations enabled the government not only to control the Lakotas' movements, but also to initiate the process of turning former enemies into loyal subjects. Both Office of Indian Affairs bureaucrats and church missionaries invested a great deal of time and paper to quantify and record the names of individual Indians, where they lived, how much they ate, their marital status, how much education they had received, and whether they had accepted Christian baptism. Fences marked the boundaries of this space, and travel outside of those limits required special passes. With these bureaucratic and physical restraints in place, the government believed it could remake its Native charges into docile denizens of the American state.[50]

These constraints shaped Lakota mourning practices at Wounded Knee. In April 1891 Pine Ridge officials complained of Lakotas from Standing Rock, Cheyenne River, and other reservations visiting Wounded Knee to mourn. "They cry and howl and work themselves and [the Pine Ridge Oglalas] into a sad state of mind," potentially causing trouble. Although Acting Commissioner of Indian Affairs R. V. Belt conceded that "visiting graves of their dead is perhaps some consolation," he urged the agents of surrounding reservations to "counsel Indians under [their] charge to cease such visits and remain on their reservation."[51]

Such restrictions did not, however, stop the Lakotas living on Pine Ridge from visiting Wounded Knee and remembering their dead. Joseph Horn Cloud's grandson, Leonard Little Finger, recalled that his grandfather "felt a very strong connection, a very strong bond" with the site. Horn Cloud "made it a point to camp there, and he actually slept on the grave. . . . He looked at it as much as another home because that's where the remains of his family [were], and so he held that in very, very high reverence."[52] In this sense, the fact that Wounded Knee happened on a reservation provided advantages to the Lakotas not afforded the survivors of previous massacres in the West. After US troops slaughtered Shoshones at Bear River in Idaho Territory in 1863, Cheyennes and Arapahos at Sand Creek in Colorado Territory in 1864, and Piegans at the Marias River in Montana Territory in 1870, the survivors had only limited access to the killing fields and burial grounds during subsequent years and decades. It was not until the twenty-first century that the Shoshones would gain legal control of the Bear River site and the Cheyennes and Arapahos would acquire the Sand Creek killing field.[53] The site of the Marias Massacre remains outside of tribal control, which has constrained the descendants from holding regular commemorations and performing mourning rituals.[54] In marked contrast, because Wounded Knee took place on Pine Ridge, the Lakotas were able to develop and sustain memorial traditions at the site in spite of the government's attempts to restrict them.

Nearly a year after Wounded Knee, Bureau of American Ethnology scholar James Mooney visited Pine Ridge to research the Ghost Dance. The son of Irish Catholic immigrants, Mooney had developed a reputation as a sympathetic interpreter of the indigenous cultures of North America.[55] Prior to Wounded Knee, Mooney had commenced a detailed ethnographic study of the Ghost Dance's Great Basin origins and subsequent spread throughout the Rocky Mountain and Plains tribes, which he later published as *The Ghost Dance Religion and the Sioux Outbreak of 1890*. This work would become the most influential scholarly interpretation of the Ghost Dance and Wounded Knee for much of the twentieth century. After conducting intense research in army and Indian Office archives, as well as ethnographic research in the field, Mooney concluded that although Big Foot's band was not blameless in the events leading to Wounded Knee, "there can be no question that the pursuit was simply a massacre, where fleeing women, with infants in their arms, were shot down after resistance had ceased and when almost every warrior was stretched dead or dying on the ground."[56]

During his visit to Pine Ridge the ethnographer visited the killing field, where he observed various Lakota mourning practices. He noted that the Lakotas had marked with stakes where the bodies of each member of Big Foot's band fell.[57] These temporary markers aided in the grieving process, as survivors and others transformed the otherwise ordinary stakes into mnemonic devices.[58] Another visitor to the site, Lieutenant Augustus W. Corliss, likewise described "seeing the entire field covered with short sticks flying flags. The Indians had gone there and located the places where their relatives had been killed and marked them with flags."[59] These were likely prayer sticks, which grieving Lakotas would place near burial places, with special markings that aided the dead on their journey to the spirit world.[60]

Mooney also recorded ways that the Lakotas had inscribed meaning at the mass grave on the hill overlooking the killing field. On January 3, 1891, civilian contractors had interred one hundred and forty-six bodies in a sixty-foot long and six-foot wide trench on what was later named "Cemetery Hill," a name reminiscent of Civil War hilltop mass graves.[61] Mooney observed that "the Indians had put up a wire fence around the trench and smeared the posts with sacred red medicine paint" used in the Ghost Dance, belief in which persisted even after Wounded Knee.[62] The religion provided hope that covert performance of the dance's rituals would hasten the Messiah's coming and the return of deceased Indians, including those killed at Wounded Knee.[63]

FIGURE 4.3 Memory sticks at Wounded Knee, 1891, by Mary I. Wright (Gill), Bureau of American Ethnology Records, Illustrations Annual Report 14, National Anthropological Report 14, National Anthropological Archives, Smithsonian Institution.

FIGURE 4.4 Fence at Wounded Knee mass grave, ca. 1891, by James Mooney, Glass Negatives of Indians (Collected by the Bureau of American Ethnology, 1850s–1930s), GN 0320a4. Photo courtesy of National Anthropological Archives, Smithsonian Institution.

Protesting the Chief Big Foot Massacre in Granite

In the late 1890s, the survivors' efforts to obtain redress merged with their memorial traditions when the Lakotas petitioned permission to raise a monument to their dead at the mass grave. The *Omaha World-Herald* reported that the "fitting monuments" that marked the burial places of US troops had inspired the Lakotas' idea for an obelisk.[64] In spite of their confinement to reservations in the late nineteenth century, the Lakotas could obtain passes to visit other agencies or find work, where they doubtless encountered other monuments.[65] For example, in 1886, the great chief Sitting Bull visited the Crow Agency—which encompassed the Little Bighorn battlefield and Custer National Cemetery in Montana Territory—where he observed the granite obelisk that had been raised in 1881 to honor George Armstrong Custer and the Seventh Cavalry. A reporter described Sitting Bull reinscribing the meaning of the Last Stand Hill obelisk as a monument to his warriors' victory over the Seventh Cavalry rather than to Custer's sacrifice.[66] Through this and other experiences, the Lakotas learned the significance of such memorials in American culture and desired their own monument.

For the press, the Lakotas' monument proposal was evidence that the government's assimilation programs were working. From the perspective of social evolutionary thought, acquiring writing and creating permanent monuments to the dead were key components in the transition from barbarism to civilization.[67] In the New York *World*'s opinion, the monument proposal "was a novel request. Usually Indians prefer to recite the tribal deeds of valor orally to their children and leave to posterity unwritten stories of their fame."[68] For the *Omaha World-Herald*, erecting the memorial was "another step from their barbaric life and shows a desire to be more like the white people."[69] After interviewing Indian Office bureaucrats, the *New York Times* stated that "no similar issue has been raised before so far as the authorities here can recall." Erecting such a monument was "an idea new in Indian history, and [was] taken to indicate greater civilization among the Indians than was looked for."[70]

Reporters also believed that the Lakotas were adopting white ways of interpreting Wounded Knee's place in the history of the Indian Wars. In an intriguing parallel to narratives that cast Wounded Knee as the final battle of four centuries of Indian warfare, the text of the Lakotas' planned monument would reportedly "proclaim Wounded Knee to be the last battlefield in which the Indian shall show hostility to his white brother."[71] The proposed inscription would therefore serve the paradoxical purpose of heralding

Lakota bravery while also discrediting the cause that motivated them: resistance against American expansion. In this schema, Wounded Knee would serve as the dividing marker in Indian memory for the moment when Natives abandoned militaristic resistance and laid the foundation for subsequent progress and prosperity.

However, the newspapers overstated the novelty of such memorials among allegedly barbaric Indians. Over time, indigenous peoples had developed complex ways of memorializing their dead. The *New York Times* conceded that Native peoples had long employed "such marks of commemoration as stones . . . to represent the marches of some of the Indian leaders."[72] Although these "memory piles" lacked interpretive texts with alphabetic writing, they nonetheless memorialized heroic deeds in a manner similar to obelisks.[73] Furthermore, before they adopted the Euro-American burial practices, Lakotas and other Plains tribes had placed their dead in trees or on scaffolds. Mourners regularly painted black bands on the scaffold standards to commemorate a warrior's heroics.[74] Lakotas such as Joseph Horn Cloud, who ultimately wrote the Wounded Knee monument's final text, likely saw obelisks as a new technological vehicle to articulate already-established memorial practices.

Additionally, there was substantial evidence even in the 1897 press reports that far from proving a "desire to be more like the white people," the Lakotas envisioned the memorial as a protest against the army's conduct at Wounded Knee. The *Omaha World-Herald* reported that a portion of the inscription would be in Lakota.[75] In the late nineteenth century, written Lakota was only a few decades old. Missionaries had transliterated oral Lakota words into Roman script as a proselytizing tool, adding diacritical marks and devising new characters to express Lakota sounds that lacked English equivalents. Yet once invented, written Lakota was also used to preserve rather than eliminate Lakota culture. Choosing a Lakota inscription was therefore an odd component for a monument to Indian assimilation.[76] Additionally, the New York *World* related that "the Indian Agent at Pine Ridge [was] opposed to the idea," since "the presence of a monument dedicated to Big Foot's band [would] be a constant menace to the peace of the reservation, for the Sioux of South Dakota [were] still bitter over the terrible calamity that wiped [Big Foot's people] out of existence."[77] This article cast significant doubt on the reliability of the report that the monument text would interpret Wounded Knee as the end of resistance against American expansion. Rather, the New York *Sun* explained in 1902 that "the Indians hold [Wounded Knee] to be a massacre, and the monument they are about to erect is intended as a protest against what they regard as the wanton slaughter of people of their race."[78]

When finally dedicated during a three-day ceremony held from May 28 to 30, 1903, the monument permanently rooted Lakota memories at the mass grave, shaping how future visitors to the site would remember Wounded Knee.[79] Standing just over six feet tall, the $350 monument was four-sided, with a gabled summit crowned by a protruding acorn-like zenith.[80] Horn Cloud—the principal proponent for government compensation—designed and funded the monument, although others donated from as little as a dime to as much as five dollars.[81] Five thousand Lakotas from the surrounding reservations assembled at Wounded Knee for the dedication.[82] A reporter described the attendees as "gaudily-dressed" and "gayly bedecked."[83] Most of the Lakota men wore wide-brimmed hats, white shirts, vests, and coats, while the women came in dresses and sat under umbrellas to escape the South Dakota heat. Although there were clouds in the sky, the sun was shining and the wind was stout.[84] Older men passed around a peace pipe, while young Lakotas smoked "city-made cigarets [*sic*]," as they ritually and spiritually prepared with tobacco for the solemnity that followed.[85]

The dedication services demonstrated ways that the Lakotas had selectively appropriated mainstream practices to support their engagement with

FIGURE 4.5 Dedication of the survivors' monument at the Wounded Knee mass grave, 1903, by H. R. Mossman (?), Eli S. Ricker Collection, RG1227-20-16. Photo courtesy of Nebraska State Historical Society.

memory politics. The dedication was held on Memorial Day weekend, a holiday laden with nationalistic symbols and closely associated with remembering the United States' war dead.[86] Furthermore, the speakers emphasized friendship and loyalty to the United States, simultaneously reflecting both the importance of treaties for Lakotas, as well as more than two decades of reservation and government school officials' intense pressures to assimilate.[87] Episcopalian Reverend William J. Cleveland, for example, spoke on the unity of humankind and preached that "God made of men one nation," alluding to Acts 17:26. This was an important verse for those who believed that God had created a single human race, rather than separately creating a privileged white race and inferior dark races.[88] Horn Cloud followed Cleveland: "Standing by the grave wherein lies my father and my brother, and gazing upon the battlefield where they died as did many of my people, I have only good feelings toward the whites and hope we will always be friendly." Oglala Chief Fire Lightning, who lived at Wounded Knee and tended the burial grounds, then spoke: "For many, many years I have been friends with the white people; I helped make the treaty with them; I have never broken that treaty and I wish to end my days a friend to them." Fire Lightning's comments emphasized the centrality of treaties in marking time and shaping indigenous memories of relations with the United States. The crowd also sang in Lakota patriotic songs, including "America" and "My Country 'Tis of Thee," as an American flag waved in the wind.[89]

The Lakotas, however, tempered this pro-American sentiment with traditional Lakota practices. In the late nineteenth century, government officials banned indigenous rituals and practices deemed repugnant to assimilation, including the Sun Dance, which in some iterations included self-mutilation; the Giveaway, which allegedly encouraged "socialism" as community members gave away their possessions to the poor; and the Ghost-Keeping ritual, which helped families mourn the death of loved ones and help the deceased on their journey to the Spirit World. By the turn of the century, however, many Native groups had become adept at holding large gatherings on major patriotic holidays; these celebrations were often little more than screens for the clandestine continuation of banned practices.[90] As recently as 1900, missionaries on the Lakota reservations had complained to the Indian Office that their charges were holding celebrations on July Fourth and other holidays as a means of reviving "old time pernicious practices" such as the Ghost Dance, the Sun Dance, and the Giveaway.[91]

Similarly, dedicating the Wounded Knee monument on Memorial Day weekend allowed the Lakotas to invoke patriotic symbols while covertly performing banned or disapproved rituals and protesting the Seventh Cavalry's actions on December 29, 1890. The services contained elements of the memorial feast, a Lakota ceremony that grieved the dead, aided the deceased in their journey to the spirit world, and strengthened community ties through gift giving. Government officials disliked the feast, since it played much the same role as the banned Ghost-Keeping ritual.[92] For example, the survivors had leaned a framed photograph, a regular element in modern memorial feasts, against the monument.[93] Additionally, a wreath adorned the apex of the obelisk and flowers were arranged at its base.[94] From the nearby ravine, a death trap for many Lakotas on December 29, 1890, an aged Lakota woman emerged singing a death song, as she slowly ascended the hill to the mass grave. Other women joined her song, covered their heads with blankets, and expressed their grief by tossing brightly colored strips of cloth onto the mass grave. The men, likewise, grieved and sought healing by chanting death songs.[95] It is conceivable that the cloth, which could easily be converted to clothing, was afterward given away to poor Lakotas in need of clothing—in other words, a covert Giveaway.[96]

It was the monument itself, though, which embodied the Lakota protest of Wounded Knee. Two sides of the obelisk listed the warriors killed. Under the date of December 29, 1890, a Lakota inscription stated: *Cankpi Opi Eltona Wicakte Picun He Cajepi Kin*—"These are the Names of those Killed at Wounded Knee."[97] Rather than implying assimilation, including Lakota-language text on the monument suggested the creative use of writing to further Lakota objectives. Beginning with Big Foot, the south side—which faced the mass grave—listed twenty-two names of warriors, including Horn Cloud's brothers, William and Sherman.[98] The north side identified an additional twenty-one names.[99] The west side listed only three names, including Horn Cloud, Joseph's father. Inscribed in English beneath his father's name was the phrase: "The peacemaker died here innocent."[100] Family tradition describes Horn Cloud Senior telling one of his sons to raise the white flag after the Seventh Cavalry intercepted Big Foot's people on December 28, 1890.[101] Rather than memorialize the senior Horn Cloud as a warrior, the monument text instead portrayed him as a peacemaker—an important and respected figure in traditional Lakota culture.

Instead of describing the "Battle of Wounded Knee," the inscription defined the conflict as "the Chief Big Foot Massacre." Horn Cloud and other survivors had been calling Wounded Knee a massacre years before the dedication of the monument. Unlike the vast majority of obelisks that dotted the postbellum memorial landscape, the Lakotas' monument protested, rather than celebrated, the soldiers' conduct. The text specifically named Colonel James Forsyth as commander of the United States troops who committed the killings. The inscription defined Big Foot not as a great military leader who opposed Forsyth, but as a peacemaker who "did many good and brave deeds for the white man and the red man."[102] Future visitors to the mass grave would read that "many innocent women and children who knew no wrong died here." In the monument's text, Wounded Knee was not the final battle between civilization and savagery, but rather a wholesale slaughter of innocent people led by a chief who had long sought peaceful coexistence with whites.

The Lakota survivors of Wounded Knee monument protesting the massacre of Big Foot's band just over a decade earlier was a significant intervention in a memorial landscape that was dominated by memorials that celebrated American nationalism, the expansion of civilization, and the inevitable defeat of savagery. The Lakotas' obelisk was the product of two related developments in Lakota culture in the 1890s. In spite of the fact that the survivors had lost more in both human and property than anyone else during the 1890–1891 conflict, Special Agent Cooper's 1891 investigation had excluded them from compensation, due to the pre-Wounded Knee classification of Big Foot's band as "hostile." In 1896, Joseph Horn Cloud filed the first of many compensation claims with the government for the massacre at Wounded Knee. He chose his words carefully as a challenge to the dominant memory that cast the event as a heroic battle. Additionally, the fact that Wounded Knee occurred on a reservation ensured the Lakotas would have continual access to the site and afforded them opportunities to develop memorial traditions rooted in the killing field and at the mass grave. These parallel themes converged in 1903 when the Lakotas inscribed their protest of the Chief Big Foot Massacre in granite. In hindsight, the survivors' memorial was the most visible monument built prior to the 1960s that protested the violence of American expansion.[103]

The government official quoted by New York *World* in 1897 proved prophetic when he claimed "the presence of a monument dedicated to Big Foot's band [would] be a constant menace to the peace of the reservation."[104] Indeed, the mass grave and the obelisk that interpreted the meaning of the deaths that occurred at Wounded Knee would remain the symbolic center of the survivors' (and their descendants') universe in the succeeding years and decades. The successful completion of the monument in 1903 motivated Horn Cloud and other survivors to renew their pursuit of justice and government compensation. Within six months of the monument dedication, they would resubmit their claims, leading to an official Indian Office investigation of the massacre. The survivors would also seek out sympathetic whites who would record and disseminate translated accounts of the Lakota side of Wounded Knee—emphasizing the peaceful nature of Big Foot and his band—and in the process obtain justice and recognition for the wrongs committed against them in 1890.

5

We Never Thought of Fighting

NEARLY SEVEN MONTHS after the dedication of the Lakotas' monument in May 1903, Joseph Horn Cloud wrote to Nebraska newspaper editor Eli S. Ricker about Wounded Knee. Ricker was writing a book on the subject, had attended the dedication ceremony, and had previously sought out Horn Cloud for an interview. Now the Lakota survivor was seeking out Ricker. "I want [to] tell you lot's about this trouble," Horn Cloud explained. "I could explain how this trouble Commence[d]. I knew everything's how this started." In the letter, he described the moments leading up the killings. Colonel James Forsyth demanded to know whether Chief Big Foot wanted to fight or have peace. Stricken with pneumonia, the chief answered that his ancestors had "all [been] friends to the whites or Government ever since [the] treaty" of Fort Laramie was signed in 1868. They had "died in peace," and Big Foot wanted to "do the same." Forsyth's men then "treat[ed] us like some kind of creatures." The warriors were forced to surrender their weapons and soldiers ransacked the camp, emptying the women's bags and scattering cooking equipment. The troops then began to shoot into the defenseless Lakotas. "It is not right to kill [a] sick person laying in bed, don't you [think] Mr. Ricker [?]"[1]

Horn Cloud also raised the issue of compensation in the letter, explaining that he had twice sent claims to the Commissioner of Indian Affairs, but had received no response. "This trouble comes from whites but [they] did not tell [the] truth," Horn Cloud noted, referring to the Seventh Cavalry's official account of the killings. The government had even awarded compensation to "friendly" Lakotas for their losses during the conflict, but had denied justice to the survivors of Big Foot's band. "Nobody help[ed] us and look[ed] into this matter for us," Horn Cloud explained. "Mr. Ricker I wished a good man [would] help us see about this matter." Although not stated explicitly, Horn

Cloud doubtless hoped that Ricker would be that "good man" who would assist the survivors as they renewed their efforts to obtain compensation.[2]

Ultimately, neither Ricker nor anyone else would help the survivors as their claim progressed in 1904 and 1905 through Indian Office channels, where it failed on the basis that government officials had classified Big Foot's band as "hostile" in 1890. In spite of the claim's failure, Horn Cloud maintained a belief that Ricker and other good men could help the Lakotas by recording their memories on paper, a medium that could be transmitted, preserved, and, ideally, shape how others remembered Wounded Knee. Horn Cloud's insistence that Big Foot had been peaceful in 1890 reflected the survivors' ongoing engagement with memory politics. Just as the Lakotas favored the English word "massacre" over "battle" to describe Wounded Knee, the survivors objected to the army's use of the term "hostile" to represent Big Foot's band in 1890. In a series of statements given to Ricker and other sympathetic interlocutors in the early twentieth century, the survivors pitted their memories against official explanations that cast Wounded Knee as the result of "hostile" Ghost Dancers attacking unsuspecting soldiers. Rather, the Seventh Cavalry had massacred the peaceful followers of a peacemaking chief.

1904–1905 Investigation

The investigation that resulted from Horn Cloud's 1904 petition was ultimately an inquiry into memory, as the Lakotas and Indian Office bureaucrats struggled to establish the basic facts leading to Wounded Knee and determine whether the survivors had a valid claim on the government for losses suffered in late 1890. The investigation, however, was not an open query into the truth of what had happened, but rather was constrained by the parameters of the government's indemnity system generally and the 1891 compensation act specifically. The survivors were therefore forced to limit their claim to property losses rather than issues of deeper significance such as ultimate culpability for the fight and the deaths that followed. Although the investigators spent some time verifying the substance of the survivors' property claims, the examinations focused primarily on whether Big Foot's band had been hostile toward the government in 1890, which, if proven, would have automatically disqualified the claim. The inquiry therefore unfolded on unfavorable epistemological grounds for the Lakota claimants, since the investigators operated within a worldview that favored contemporary official records over oral testimony recorded after the fact.

Several factors combined in the early twentieth century to convince Horn Cloud to resubmit his claim. His pursuit of compensation reflected Lakota kinship obligations to pursue justice in the wake of a murder. Traditionally Lakotas punished murderers by ostracizing them, but the victim's relatives had the right to kill the offender in retribution. In many cases, however, the family of the dead demanded compensation from the murderer, which if granted could lead to forgiveness, symbolic cleansing of the offender, and reintegration into Lakota society. Often relatives of a murdered individual would mourn for years until the perpetrator answered the demand for reparations. This compensation could not replace the family member, but it could heal the societal rift created by the murder. In short, the initial failure to obtain compensation did not deter Horn Cloud and other survivors, since they were culturally obligated to pursue justice until it was found.[3]

The 1903 dedication of the monument to the Wounded Knee dead doubtless served as a second catalyst for the remnant of Big Foot's band to organize self-consciously as survivors. The process of raising funds for the monument's construction and planning the dedication program would have put Horn Cloud in touch with other survivors on Pine Ridge, Cheyenne River, and elsewhere. In this context Horn Cloud began drafting two lists: one that identified by name those killed at Wounded Knee and a second that catalogued the names of one hundred and six survivors. The latter list included names of individuals who had returned to the Cheyenne River Reservation after Wounded Knee—such as Fast Boat (also known as Edward Owl King) and Peter One Skunk—as well as Pine Ridge survivors, including Horn Cloud's older brothers, Dewey Beard and Daniel White Lance. The creation of the list suggested that as early as 1903 the survivors of Wounded Knee were not thinking of themselves as isolated individuals, grieving either alone or with those immediately around them, but as part of a group bound together by their memories of a world shattered by the trauma of a massacre.[4]

Additionally, the difficult transition to reservation life in the late nineteenth century had created a culture of claiming compensation among indigenous peoples throughout the United States. While no Lakota would have chosen dependency over self-sufficiency, the economic realities of the reservation forced many Native peoples to pursue any option to increase the flow of cash into their communities. Seeking compensation for treaty violations and other past wrongs provided one means to accomplish this goal. As Jeffrey Ostler has noted, "It was also important that the United States make amends for past injustices so that proper relations between the two nations could be restored."[5] Already by the late nineteenth century, the Lakotas had successfully claimed reparations for horses, guns, and other property seized by the US Army from "friendly" Indians during the so-called Great Sioux War of 1876.[6] In addition, the Lakotas sought compensation for revenues lost from gold and other minerals extracted from the Black Hills, which the United States seized in 1876 under questionable circumstances. Although the Lakotas saw the Black Hills as the cosmological equivalent of the biblical Garden of Eden—their place of origin—they reluctantly conceded that repossession of the land was all but impossible and instead focused on monetary compensation.[7] In 1902 and again in 1903, Lakota leaders met with South Dakota Congressman Eben W. Martin on Pine Ridge to discuss the Black Hills claim. Since Joseph Horn Cloud was then serving as Oglala tribal council secretary, he was probably present at these discussions.[8]

The government's claims system, as defined in treaties and statutes, was framed by the "friendly"/"hostile" binary, which Euro-Americans used to classify Indians according to their orientation toward the United States. Euro-Americans labeled as "hostile" those Natives deemed primitive, inherently warlike, cruel, and inexorably opposed to the "advance of civilization." "Friendlies," on the other hand, were loyal allies to whites. They frequently advocated strategies of accommodation rather than resistance. During periods of war, US troops used these terms as shorthand to categorize Natives as either peaceful or warlike.[9] After the government confined tribes to reservations, however, the meaning of these terms shifted. Indian Office employees adopted the binary to distinguish between those Indians who accepted or resisted the government's assimilation programs. "Friendlies" (also known as progressives) accepted the authority of the agent, sent their children willingly to government schools, embraced Christianity, and wore Euro-American clothing. "Hostiles" (sometimes called traditionalists or nonprogressives), while not militarily opposed to the United States, actively resisted the government's assimilation project. As with any binary, these neat categories never reflected reality. Native leaders may have disagreed over the most effective strategies against the United States' consolidation of power over Indian lands—with some advocating accommodation and others promoting resistance—but all did what they thought necessary to protect their peoples' interests.[10]

This friendly/hostile dichotomy framed the compensation provisions embedded in most treaties between the United States and Indian nations. These provisions, along with congressional statutes that regulated the government's claims process, were designed to prevent parties wronged by isolated instances of theft and property destruction—popularly known as depredations—from resorting to retaliation and ultimately full-scale war.[11] Article 1 of the 1868 Treaty of Fort Laramie, which established peace between the Lakota nation and the United States, stated that if a white individual wronged a Lakota's person or property, or, conversely, if a Lakota wronged the person or property of "any one, white, black, or Indian, subject to the authority of the United States," the federal government would compensate the wronged party out of Treasury funds.[12]

Only friendly Indians had access to the claims system in the wake of conflict, while hostiles were barred from it, regardless of their own personal losses. The Lakotas' 1868 treaty specified that "no one sustaining loss while violating the provisions of this treaty, or the laws of the United States, shall be reimbursed therefor."[13] When Congress appropriated $100,000 to compensate friendly Lakotas for property stolen or damaged by "roving bands of disaffected Indians" during the "recent Sioux trouble," Special Agent James A. Cooper was charged with determining who had been "hostile, either by word or action, to the government of the United States" in 1890.[14] Since Cooper had served as a special advisor for the Indian Office on Pine Ridge during the crisis, he drew on his memory of how civil and military officials had classified certain bands. At times, Cooper deemed participation in the Ghost Dance as sufficient evidence that a Lakota was "disaffected" or "hostile." For example, the agent rejected the claim of an ordinary Oglala applicant, Afraid of Hawk, for admitting in his petition that he had lost some property while visiting Short Bull, a prominent leader of the Ghost Dance movement, in the "hostile" camp in the Badlands.[15] However, Cooper also granted the claims of prominent Lakota leaders No Water, Jack Red Cloud, Big Road, and Hump, and even Short Bull, the very leader Afraid of Hawk had visited. Each of these men had been leading Ghost Dancers at some point during the crisis, but had subsequently advocated for peace. Cooper's inconsistent definition of "friendly" and "hostile" labels demonstrated the instability of such concepts. Cooper excluded the Wounded Knee survivors, since government officials had designated Big Foot's band as hostile in 1890.[16]

As in the 1896 claim, Horn Cloud explained that in the midst of the troubles of 1890, the Oglala Chief Red Cloud had asked Big Foot to come to Pine Ridge in hopes that the Minneconjou chief would use his well-known diplomatic skills to diffuse the tense situation between US troops and the Ghost Dancers who had fled to the Stronghold, a natural enclosure some distance from the agency. Joseph's father, Horn Cloud Senior, was related to Big Foot and an advisor to the chief, and therefore went south with the band. The family left a great deal of property at Cheyenne River in order to move quickly.

After losing his parents, brothers, and other relatives at Wounded Knee, Joseph Horn Cloud discovered that all of his father's property had been stolen. Although he could not identify the culprits, Horn Cloud suspected that neighboring Lakotas, white ranchers, and soldiers had divided the family's horses, cattle, shelter, tools, and even eighteen schoolbooks. Notably, Horn Cloud did not address his family's involvement with the Ghost Dance, likely because he was aware that many government officials equated participation in the dance with "fanaticism" and "hostility" toward the government, although he did emphasize that the family had moved south for peaceful reasons.[17] Horn Cloud's older brother, Dewey Beard, also resubmitted his claim for property stolen from his Cheyenne River home and noted that his family had been killed at Wounded Knee. Other Lakotas Frank Feather, John Shell Necklace, and Tall Woman likewise submitted claims.[18]

Horn Cloud, remembering that the government had previously ignored his claims, also petitioned the Indian Office for the right to hire an attorney to assist in navigating the system.[19] In the early twentieth century it was nearly impossible for Indians to hire lawyers and file suit against the United States. The Indian Office regulated all attorney contracts, ostensibly to protect Natives from unscrupulous lawyers. Even with an attorney, Congress needed to pass special acts granting tribes the right to bring suits against the United States, a process that often took years to complete.[20]

Rather than authorize Horn Cloud to hire counsel, the Indian Office in February 1904 instructed Pine Ridge Agent John R. Brennan to investigate the claim and advise the office whether it had merit.[21] Brennan had cofounded Rapid City, South Dakota, in 1876 and had been active in local and state politics prior to his 1901 appointment as the first civilian agent of Pine Ridge after a decade of military control.[22] Brennan delegated the investigation to James Smalley, the "boss farmer" who resided near the claimants in Kyle, South Dakota.[23] Boss farmers were Indian Office employees who supervised individual farms, arranged leases, distributed rations, assisted reservation law enforcement and, at least in theory, protected tribal members from encroaching white settlers. They also heard complaints, which is probably why Brennan tapped Smalley to evaluate the survivors' claims.[24]

After meeting with Horn Cloud, Smalley recommended against the claim, arguing that Horn Cloud Senior had been hostile in 1890. The farmer reported to Brennan that the Minneconjous, having been "invited by Red Cloud and others to visit Pine Ridge," had left their property behind. Smalley explained that "it seems as soon as they received the invitation to come to Pine Ridge, they left everything and started. As is well known nearly the

whole band were killed at Wd Knee. [Horn Cloud] does not know what
became of the property but thinks it was divided among the Indians whites
and halfbreeds who staid [sic] behind." It remains unclear whether Smalley
conducted additional research in contemporary government documents;
however, he operated under the assumption—promoted by the army and
other non-Natives—that Big Foot and his followers had hostile intentions in
1890. Smalley argued "that Old Man Horn Cloud abandoned his place and
property to come to Pine Ridge and mix into trouble, and now his children
want the Government to pay them for it."[25] The boss farmer therefore rejected
Horn Cloud's historical argument that his father had been peaceful in 1890.

Brennan likewise opposed the claim, asserting for reasons that remain
unclear that the claimants had provided insufficient evidence in their petitions.
On May 4, 1905, Brennan reported to his superiors that "Horn Cloud is unable
to produce evidence or proofs of a tangible nature to substantiate his claim. His
own statement of the loss was about all we were able to secure."[26] Brennan's
assessment is puzzling. A comparison between the claims submitted by friendly
Lakotas in 1891 and Dewey Beard's 1903 claim, for example, demonstrates that
the survivors attempted to follow the format of the earlier petitions. The 1891
claims contained a short narrative describing the losses, a list tabulating the
monetary value of the property, and witnesses who attested the truth of the
petition. Beard's 1903 claim included all of these elements, including the signature of his older cousin, Long Bull, who had also survived Wounded Knee and
would have been familiar with the family's property in 1890. Shell Necklace,
another survivor claimant, had also attested to Beard's petition.[27] Following
Brennan's reasoning, however, the Indian Office rejected the claims.[28]

The government also denied Horn Cloud's request to hire an attorney,
contending that without additional evidence presented under oath, "it
[would be] useless for them to waste time and money employing lawyers to
prosecute their claims. If there [was] valid evidence, they [could] prepare it as
well, or better, under [Brennan's] supervision, than by the aid of any lawyer
that they may be able to procure."[29] This was likely a standardized response.
The government regularly argued that, as the guardian of the Indians' interests, the Indian Office could deal with Native claims better than attorneys.[30]
Brennan, who disdainfully dismissed Lakotas who spent their time pursuing
"will-o'-wisp proposition[s]," was hardly a better advocate than an attorney.[31]
That the claims followed the format of those submitted in compliance with
the 1891 act suggests that there was more going on here than was apparent
on the surface, since an older relative serving as a witness should have been
sufficient for their claims. The survivors learned that as long as the Indian

Office denied them the right to counsel, they were on their own against a bureaucracy that was hostile to their claims.

Good Men to Help Us See About This Matter

Following the failed claim in 1905, Horn Cloud and other survivors channeled their efforts into telling their stories to sympathetic whites. And in the early twentieth century, there were willing listeners associated with two groups—academic ethnographers and amateur historians of the Indian Wars—who wanted to hear and record the survivors' stories.[32] The resulting interviews provided the survivors a means to contest the government's classification of Big Foot's band as hostile in 1890.

The appearance of white interlocutors on the Lakota reservations illustrated the remarkable changes that had occurred in white society since the 1860s, when the Indian reform movement began incorporating indigenous perspectives into their broader critiques of the government's conduct of national expansion. Arguing that killing Indian noncombatants was incompatible with the United States' highest ideals of fairness and justice, reformers such as Helen Hunt Jackson traced the nation's "dishonorable" treatment of indigenous peoples during the nineteenth century. Rather than interpret the violence at Sand Creek in 1864, Marias in 1870, and Camp Grant in 1871 as prerequisites for the establishment of civilization, the reformers argued that these events were horrid massacres that portended the United States' descent into barbarism. Epistemologically, the reformers relied primarily on government documents, some of which summarized the viewpoints of Native victims, as reported by Indian Office agents.[33] However, after the reformers' calls for investigations receded, few whites were interested in asking Indian eyewitnesses to these atrocities to record their memories formally. The majority of the Sand Creek survivors, for example, settled together on the Cheyenne-Arapaho Reservation in Indian Territory (in current-day Oklahoma), yet few reporters or ethnologists sought them out to record their statements.[34] The Cheyennes and Arapahos, for their own part, distrusted whites and had no realistic expectations of justice after the abrogation of the 1865 Treaty of Little Arkansas, which had promised reparations to the survivors.[35] Only in the early twentieth century would survivor George Bent, the educated son of trader William Bent and his Cheyenne wife, Owl Woman, challenge in writing the dominant interpretations of the event.[36] Other survivors preserved and transmitted their memories orally, which were recorded on paper only later in the twentieth century.[37]

The professionalization of ethnography as an academic field in the late nineteenth century marked an important milestone in the changing views toward the reliability of Indian perspectives on the past. Previously, anthropology had been the domain of a few privately funded amateurs, but during the 1880s and 1890s trained research teams operating within the Smithsonian's Bureau of Ethnology, museums, and universities asserted control over the field. It was no coincidence that this professionalization occurred after most Native groups had been militarily subdued and confined to reservations, as anthropologists saw American Indians as accessible, diverse, and exotic specimens of "less-advanced" peoples.[38] Anthropologists, animated by the sense that "authentic" Natives were rapidly disappearing in the face of industrialization and modernization, left their comfortable offices to interview elderly Indians and collect artifacts for preservation. The practitioners of "salvage anthropology" believed that their efforts could capture the elements of Native cultures worth saving before Indians succumbed to the government's assimilation programs.[39] These investigators were primarily concerned with conserving "timeless" Native cultures; however, in the process of interviewing their Indian subjects, ethnologists ineluctably recorded their subjects' historical perspectives on the past.[40]

Professional ethnographers employed an army of bilingual whites and Natives living on reservations to conduct interviews and gather information, which were then forwarded to learned centers for analysis and publication. One such local informant was Pine Ridge physician James R. Walker. When Walker arrived on Pine Ridge in 1896, he brought with him a wealth of experience practicing medicine among Native peoples in the West. Although he espoused the common belief in the superiority of Euro-American medicine, Walker worked with traditional medicine men in his fight against tuberculosis. He thereby gained both their trust and an abiding fascination with indigenous cultures. Walker later explained that he was "determined to know the Indian from the Indian point of view."[41] In 1902, Franz Boas's protégé Clark Wissler, of the American Museum of Natural History in New York, hired Walker to conduct field research on Oglala culture and religion.[42]

As part of his research, Walker interviewed Dewey Beard about Wounded Knee. In addition to his parents, two brothers, and a niece, Beard lost his wife, White Face, and a newborn child on December 29, 1890.[43] Like his brother Joseph Horn Cloud, Beard remained on Pine Ridge, settling not far from the mass grave in Kyle, South Dakota. In the mid-1890s Beard traveled with Buffalo Bill's Wild West show. By 1896 Beard had added "Dewey" to his name, reportedly in honor of Admiral George Dewey.[44] Walker later recalled

FIGURE 5.1 James R. Walker, ca. 1890–1900, photographer unknown, PH.00460 (Scan #10037570), James Walker Collection. Photo courtesy of History Colorado, Denver, Colo.

that Beard's statement was "in his own words as near as could be," although Beard, who never learned English, must have first dictated in Lakota, which was then translated into English by Walker and his assistants.[45] Sensing a compelling story, Western novelist Rex E. Beach obtained a copy of Walker's interview with Beard, which Beach published with minor editorial revisions in 1906 in *Appleby's Booklover's Magazine*.[46] Eventually, Walker's transcription of the Beard interview was preserved with Walker's papers at the Colorado Historical Society.[47]

Western history buffs comprised the second group dedicated to recovering indigenous voices in the late nineteenth and early twentieth centuries. The Lakotas' and Cheyennes' total victory over Colonel George Armstrong Custer and the Seventh Cavalry in the Battle of the Little Bighorn, Montana Territory, on June 25, 1876, presented an intriguing mystery to white enthusiasts: how exactly did Custer die?[48] Since none of Custer's men survived that day, amateur investigators "scoured the reservations for Indian informants to interview," as they hoped to find missing clues on how the Seventh Cavalry met its fate.[49] These inquirers were interested primarily in Custer and the Little Bighorn; however, they often stopped to ask their informants about other fights, recording for the first time in writing the "Indian View" of several engagements.[50]

Around the time Walker interviewed Beard, Nebraska newspaper editor and erstwhile county judge Eli S. Ricker began a lifelong investigation of Wounded Knee and the Indian Wars. During the 1890 excitement over the Ghost Dance, Ricker shared many of the prejudices of whites living on the northern Great Plains, as demonstrated by his signature on a petition by Nebraska citizens demanding that the government disarm the "savages" who threatened white settlers on the Great Plains.[51] By 1903, however, Ricker's attitudes toward indigenous peoples had dramatically shifted, in part due to his reporting on a white sheriff who killed members of a Lakota hunting party in Wyoming, an event Ricker called the "paleface outbreak." Throughout that year, he wrote several articles on Pine Ridge issues that incorporated information from Lakota informants. In addition, he probably attended the dedication of the Wounded Knee monument in May 1903. Convinced that the history of the West had been told primarily from the white perspective, Ricker decided to write a book that privileged indigenous voices and whites sympathetic to Natives.[52] On November 30, 1903, Ricker interviewed George E. Bartlett, the owner of a trading store and a post office at Wounded Knee who had witnessed from a distance the events of December 29, 1890. Bartlett was the first of dozens of people—whites, multiracial individuals, and Lakotas—Ricker interviewed over the next several years for the project.[53]

Ricker quickly identified Joseph Horn Cloud as a valuable informant. After hearing that the journalist was looking for him, in late 1903 the survivor wrote Ricker expressing a desire to discuss Wounded Knee. Not until October 23, 1906, however, did Ricker and Horn Cloud sit down to discuss Wounded Knee.[54] After reading Beach's publication of Walker's Dewey Beard interview, Ricker sought Beard out as well. In February 1907, Ricker interviewed Beard and Daniel White Lance over several sessions totaling eleven and a half hours, with their brother Horn Cloud acting as translator. The resulting interview remains the most detailed and longest account of Wounded Knee from a Lakota survivor ever recorded.[55]

As Ricker compiled his interviews, he tentatively entitled his proposed four-volume work *The Final Conflict Between the Red Men and the Pale Faces*, which would examine indigenous culture, religion, and oratory as well as the Indian Wars and Wounded Knee. He eschewed the use of the word "savage" and rejected the notion that "civilized" Euro-Americans—whom he

FIGURE 5.2 Judge Eli Seavey Ricker, 1916, photographer unknown, Eli S. Ricker Collection, RG1227-1-1. Photo courtesy of Nebraska State Historical Society.

designated "foreigners"—were inherently more advanced and less prone to "barbaric" violence. Whites, in Ricker's estimation, claimed superiority to assuage their guilt over seizing a continent and committing endless wrongs against the indigenous inhabitants. Ricker was certainly not free from anti-Indian stereotypes, occasionally calling Natives lazy and uneducated, but he foreshadowed the New Western History movement of the 1980s by honestly seeking to understand the settlement of America from the viewpoint of its displaced indigenous inhabitants.[56]

As for Wounded Knee, Ricker dismissed explanations, offered by the army and its sympathizers, that "treacherous" Indians had fired on the soldiers or that it was simply an unavoidable accident of war.[57] Rather, he believed the Seventh Cavalry wanted to avenge Custer. Although open to the idea that the soldiers had been drunk, he saw this as a poor excuse for what he considered wanton slaughter.[58] "The disposition to wipe out the band can hardly be questioned," he concluded in his notes. "The cannon which stood at the north west [sic] angle was discharged at an Indian woman escaping with her child over the ridge ... and was killed. This was simply murder."[59] Speaking ironically, Ricker concluded that it could "never be denied that the superior race first opened living veins of blood and made corpses for unmerited graves. ... It was not battle. Nay. It was butchery, it was a crime."[60] Unfortunately, Ricker died before completing his magnum opus, but after his death his family donated his priceless collection of interviews—including Horn Cloud's and Beard's accounts—to the Nebraska State Historical Society.[61]

Another western history enthusiast who interviewed Wounded Knee survivors in the early twentieth century was Walter Mason Camp, a Chicago-based railroad engineer and editor of the *Railway and Engineering Review*. Beginning in 1903, Camp spent twenty summers interviewing nearly two hundred Native and soldier veterans of the Battle of the Little Bighorn and other important engagements. He also mapped the memorial landscape of the Indian Wars, visiting over forty sites of significant conflicts and cataloguing which places had commemorative markers and which did not.[62]

Nearly every summer in the 1910s, Camp sought out new eyewitnesses to interview about Wounded Knee. Unlike the meticulous Ricker, Camp never developed a systematic method for taking notes. The engineer employed whatever paper he had at hand, sometimes using the backs of envelopes or old telegrams to scribble down his informants' statements. Camp developed a rudimentary faculty with the Lakota language during his life, although he relied on interpreters for his fieldwork.[63] In 1912, Camp corresponded with Joseph Horn Cloud about Wounded Knee.[64]

In spite of Camp's willingness to hear the "Indian Side" of Wounded Knee, the engineer's sympathies remained with the Seventh Cavalry throughout his life. In a speech given to the Order of the Indian Wars on January 17, 1920, Camp provided an overview of his research to the assembled veterans, an audience that included soldiers who fought at Wounded Knee. Although he acknowledged that neither the soldiers nor the Indians expected a fight and that the Lakotas interpreted the event as the "Chief Big Foot Massacre" (rather than a battle), he argued that "the blunder that started the firing was committed by one of the Sioux, so they admit themselves." By blaming the fight on the Lakotas, Camp essentially absolved the Seventh Cavalry of responsibility for the carnage that followed.[65] Within five years of delivering this address, Camp's health had failed and he died before completing his final book. Recognizing the value of his massive collection, Camp's fellow "Custerologists" preserved and utilized his papers for their own work. Eventually, Brigham Young University, Indiana University, the Denver Public Library, and the Little Bighorn Battlefield National Monument acquired and preserved portions of the collection—including the interviews with the Wounded Knee survivors—for future researchers.[66]

The final interlocutor was ethnologist Melvin R. Gilmore, who recorded the survivors' statements in the wake of Buffalo Bill Cody's filmed reenactment of Wounded Knee in late 1913.[67] Surprisingly, Joseph Horn Cloud, Dewey Beard, and other survivors participated as actors in the reenactment, in spite of the deep trauma that visiting the site in that context doubtless caused. There is, however, evidence to suggest that they only did so after attempting to stop the filming from proceeding. Horn Cloud reportedly argued that the reenactment "would disturb the spirit of his departed relatives and retard their progress in the happy hunting ground."[68] Cody, however, insisted that the event be included in the film.

When it became apparent that the reenactment would proceed, the survivors agreed to participate, apparently believing that they could influence how Wounded Knee was portrayed on screen. Horn Cloud even served as an interpreter. Perhaps Beard's previous experience touring with Cody convinced the brothers that they could work with the showman.[69] "The Indian survivors were willing to go through with the details of that event," one newspaper noted, "as they were anxious to have a record made of it."[70] On the day of the reenactment, hundreds of Lakotas—eight hundred, by one estimate—gathered in the valley of Wounded Knee.[71] As they had done a decade earlier at the dedication of the monument at the mass grave, the survivors and their relatives reinscribed meaning and memory at the site through grieving rituals.[72] One observer described "grief stricken" Lakotas "pointing out the places where their relatives had fallen and setting up their piteous wails."[73] A correspondent for the *Denver Post* similarly noted that the mourners sang "the ghost song as those who had lost the ones they loved sought again the death place and mourned. Again as the wailing cry mounted higher and higher, again as the sobs came one by one the warriors stalked forward to lay their heads on the shoulder of some weeping Indian woman and then stalk on again." The correspondent concluded that "memory and grief can live long in the heart of an Indian."[74]

FIGURE 5.3 From left, Charles Knife Chief, Melvin R. Gilmore, and White Eagle, 1914, by Melvin Gilmore, Pawnee Indians Collection, RG2065-8-6. Photo courtesy of Nebraska State Historical Society.

As the filmmakers began to enact their own rituals at the site, setting up equipment and directing the soldiers and Lakotas to take their positions, it became apparent that Cody was not interested in the Lakotas' perspectives on how the reenactment should proceed. When the survivors "ventured opinions as to their remembrance of the ways things had happened, they were silenced," one observer noted. The Lakotas were simply "hustled into line by the picture manipulators."[75] Horn Cloud's plan had apparently failed. Rather than using the film to promote their own interests, they witnessed with frustration as the Battle, rather than Massacre, of Wounded Knee unfolded before their eyes.

Ethnographer Melvin R. Gilmore also witnessed the reenactment. As he had previously conducted numerous interviews with indigenous peoples in his capacity as curator of the Nebraska State Historical Society and a doctoral candidate at the University of Nebraska, Gilmore was known on Pine Ridge.[76] According to Gilmore, the Indians held him in such high esteem that they called him "the man who writes things as we tell him."[77] When filming was completed, Gilmore met with the survivors, who described their complaints about Cody's interpretation. The filmmakers had put guns in the Lakotas' hands, when in reality the vast majority of the warriors had been disarmed when the shooting commenced. Furthermore, when the filming began, the number of warriors was made equal to the number of soldiers, when in reality the Lakota men had been significantly outnumbered. Additionally, "No woman [*sic*] or children were killed in the picture making, but in reality, the field after the battle in 1890 was strewn with dead women and children."[78] The survivors wanted Cody to live up to his rhetoric and represent Wounded Knee as accurately as possible, showing an ugly massacre rather than the Seventh Cavalry's narrative of a heroic victory of gallant troops over savage fanatics, with few if any noncombatant casualties.

Gilmore formally interviewed survivors Horn Cloud, Beard, and Mary Mousseau in late October 1913.[79] After taking their statements, Gilmore caused a firestorm when he reported the Lakotas' complaints to the press.[80] In a paper delivered to the Nebraska State Historical Society's annual meeting held from January 20 to 22, 1914, Gilmore discussed his interviews.[81] He argued "that the Indians were greatly wronged in this massacre and the least that can be done in reparation is to tell the truth in history," a not-so-subtle reference to the film's skewed representation of Wounded Knee.[82] He published his paper and the survivors' statements in the *Lincoln Daily Star*.[83] Inspired by Gilmore's activism, Horn Cloud and Beard sought permission to lead a delegation to the nation's capital to protest the film.[84]

However, no evidence has been found to suggest that the delegation actually visited Washington, DC. If it did, the protest had no discernable impact. Versions of the film continued to be shown in theaters through 1917.[85] Once the survivors realized that Buffalo Bill had ignored their memories of Wounded Knee, their principal objective was to stop the film from being deposited in the government's official archives. In early 1916, Cody donated copies of the movie to the War and Interior Departments.[86] Although the *Indian Wars* became part of official government records, the film would ultimately have no long-term impact on how Americans would remember Wounded Knee. Preserved on nitrate film, the extant copies of the movie disintegrated within just a few years. By 1919, the Interior Department's archival catalog did not include the film.[87] Presumably, the War Department's copy disintegrated within a similar period of time. Like the vast majority of films created prior to the 1930s, Buffalo Bill's *Indian Wars* disappeared, never to be recovered.[88]

In contrast, the Lakotas' statements to Gilmore did survive. In 1917, the Society of the American Indians—an early twentieth-century political group that advocated, among other objectives, that the government redress past wrongs against Indians—published the interviews and portions of Gilmore's

1913 presentation in their periodical *The American Indian Magazine*.[89] In addition, the ethnographer deposited his interview notes in the Nebraska State Historical Society. The survivors' 1913 accounts of the massacre therefore weathered the influence of time far better than Buffalo Bill's *The Indian Wars*.[90]

Recounting Wounded Knee

The written accounts produced by the survivors and their interlocutors—Walker, Ricker, Camp, and Gilmore—all shared a central preoccupation: denying that Big Foot and his followers had been hostile against the government in 1890. The prominence of this theme was hardly coincidental, given the Lakotas' pursuit of compensation within a system that explicitly favored friendlies and excluded hostiles. The survivors therefore had a clear motivation to counter the army's official explanations for Wounded Knee. On the other side of the equation, Walker, Ricker, Camp, and Gilmore were aware of the official version and asked the Lakotas what Walker called the "critical" questions regarding the events leading to the killings.[91] Did believing in the Ghost Dance—especially Wovoka's teaching that performing in the dance would transform North America by supernaturally removing white Europeans from it—automatically translate into an actual military conspiracy? Had Big Foot and his followers gone south to Pine Ridge to join Short Bull and the hostiles in the Stronghold? Did the warriors resist the disarmament and then treacherously attack the unsuspecting Seventh Cavalrymen? Were the Lakota men responsible for the deaths of their own women and children? Of course, the official version of Wounded Knee answered these questions affirmatively. The interviews provided a platform for the survivors to respond point by point to these critical questions.

When compared and contrasted across time, the Lakotas' accounts provide a window into the survivors' attempts to recount the terror that doubtless still haunted their memories, as they searched for the best words to articulate Wounded Knee to their auditors. When Walker, Ricker, Camp, and Gilmore entered the Lakota reservations to interview the survivors, they therefore injected themselves into a process of recounting that had been underway since the immediate aftermath of Wounded Knee, as the survivors shared their grief with friends, relatives, and outsiders. As psychologist Henry Greenspan argues in regard to Holocaust survivors, the "testimonies" of victims of atrocities should not be seen as fixed and stable accounts, but rather as "provisional and processual . . . retellings" of traumatic events.[92]

One way of answering the "critical questions" may have made sense in 1891, but not in 1906, especially as the Lakotas acquired greater awareness of ways that the army's version of Wounded Knee carried material ramifications for the survivors' pursuit of compensation.

When Walker interviewed Beard in the early twentieth century, white Americans had blunt tools for interpreting and categorizing groups that fell outside of traditionally accepted definitions of religious expression. Most Euro-Americans believed that God had providentially founded the United States as a "Christian Nation," and although the First Amendment protected the diversity of Protestant churches from state oppression, groups outside of the mainstream could not expect much in the way of toleration. In a new republic marked by an expanding economy and a transient population, Americans were constantly guarding against charlatans peddling counterfeit goods and fake religion. Individuals claiming new revelations presented an especially potent challenge to watchmen on the Protestant tower, who quickly condemned "impostors" and sought to undermine "pretended prophets." Flabbergasted when Americans—ostensibly a smart and discerning people—accepted the claims of alleged deceivers, Protestant defenders claimed that their fellow citizens had been "duped" and suffered from "delusion." Followers of new prophets were even judged to be mentally ill, or at least "monomaniacs," insane in their religious choices but otherwise normal.[93] "Imposters" and "dupes" could be tolerated reluctantly, but "fanatics" posed a sufficient threat to American civil society that violence was often deemed an acceptable response. Protestants used these same blunt tools to describe those considered indigenous imposters such as Wovoka, who posed a substantial threat to white settlers and United States sovereignty. Civil and military authorities argued that the fanatical Lakotas, ostensibly confined to reservations, were plotting the greatest indigenous conspiracy against government authority in American history.[94]

In his interview with Walker, Beard sought to undermine the assumption that all Lakotas were fanatical adherents of the Ghost Dance. According to Walker's translation, a messenger taught Beard's father, Horn Cloud Senior, that "a Savior for the Indians had appeared to an Indian in the far land of the setting sun" and had promised to "bring again the buffalo and antelope and send the white man from all the land where the Indians hunted in the old times." To bring this about, the Indians needed to "dance and pray to this Savior." Upon investigating the Ghost Dance, Beard witnessed some participants falling into trances and claiming to see the Savior in vision: "But I observed that it was bad Indians and Indians that no one used to pay any attention [to] and the medicine men who saw these things."[95] None of Beard's family experienced these manifestations: "Nothing mysterious [*wakan*] would come to any of my father's family."[96] Walker concluded that "the father of the Horn Clouds was a doubting Thomas in the matter of the new Messiah worship."[97] Beard also contended that belief in the Ghost Dance did not automatically render a participant hostile to the United States. When soldiers attempted to force Big Foot and his people to cease dancing in early December 1890, Beard quoted the Minneconjou chief as saying that simply dancing harmed no one. Although Big Foot initially defended his people's right to dance, news of trouble in Sitting Bull's camp caused the chief to reconsider. "We will go back to our camp," Beard remembered Big Foot telling his followers, "so the Great Father [that is, the US government] will know we do not belong to the bad Indians." When troops demanded that Big Foot surrender, the chief complied and insisted that his people were not hostiles.[98]

The second critical question addressed by the survivors was why Big Foot's band had left their Cheyenne River homes and moved south to Pine Ridge in late December 1890. Army officials argued at the time that Big Foot intended to join the other hostiles in the Badlands, likely to consolidate forces for the alleged conspiracy.[99] Horn Cloud and Beard countered this argument in their interviews with Walker and Ricker. They explained that Red Cloud and other Oglala leaders had invited Big Foot—who was known as a peacemaker and skilled negotiator—to visit Pine Ridge in hopes the Minneconjou chief could use his influence to convince the Ghost Dancers in the Badlands to surrender. If successful, the Oglalas would give Big Foot one hundred horses.[100] The earliest Lakota accounts of Wounded Knee, dating to early 1891, referenced this invitation.[101] According to Horn Cloud, Big Foot was initially reluctant to leave his home or to make any movement that would alarm the soldiers. However, a local rancher named John Dunn, known to the Lakotas as Red Beard or Red Whiskers, warned Big Foot on December 23 that troops intended to arrest his warriors and remove them from the reservation. With his warriors intent on fleeing to Pine Ridge, the chief conceded. The Lakotas slipped away from the soldiers and commenced their fateful journey south.[102]

In their interviews, the survivors argued that their conduct between Cheyenne River and Pine Ridge had been peaceful. Beard explained to Ricker that Big Foot had instructed the people to take their cattle with them: "We never thought of fighting or war, therefore [we] had brought our cattle along." Soon after leaving Cheyenne River, Big Foot contracted pneumonia, which slowed their movement. As they approached Pine Ridge, the chief sent messengers to inform the agency that the band "came not secretly, but openly and peaceably." The messengers returned with the news that the Ghost Dancers had abandoned the Badlands and were slowly coming in to the agency. Red Cloud wanted Big Foot to hurry in order to participate in the final negotiations.[103] On December 28, the Lakotas saw soldiers approaching and raised a white flag to signal their peaceful intentions.[104] Major Samuel M. Whitside of the Seventh Cavalry parlayed with Big Foot, who was bleeding from his nose. Whitside explained that he had heard the Minneconjous were a war party, but that Big Foot had convinced him they were peaceful. Horn Cloud quoted the chief: "My great fathers were all friendly to the white people and died in peace, and I want to do the same." Big Foot also explained that Red Cloud had invited him to help broker a peace deal. When Whitside demanded that the Lakotas surrender twenty-five guns, Big Foot stated his willingness to cooperate, but asked that they wait until they arrived at the agency to give up their weapons. The people feared the soldiers might kill them once they were disarmed and defenseless. Whitside, unsure how to proceed, ordered the Lakotas to camp near Wounded Knee for the night. Colonel James W. Forsyth subsequently arrived and assumed command of the Seventh Cavalry.[105]

The next morning, Forsyth commanded the Lakota warriors to assemble a short distance away from the main camp and he repeated the demand that they surrender their weapons. At Big Foot's urging, most of the warriors readily complied. Forsyth, dissatisfied with the number of guns produced, ordered his men to search the camp and the women for any hidden weapons. To Walker, Beard admitted that he had buried his gun with the intention of retrieving it later, while four or five young warriors, reluctant to give up their expensive hunting rifles, concealed them under blankets.[106] Forsyth then stated that he would punish the warriors for not complying with the initial order to disarm the day previous by having his men point rifles at the warriors, without revealing that the guns were unloaded. This unexpected declaration, coupled with interpreter Philip Wells's poor translation, caused considerable excitement among the Lakotas. Beard told Ricker that the warriors "reasoned among themselves and said they were human beings and not cattle to be used that way. They said they did not want to be killed like dogs. 'We are people in this world.'"[107]

For Walker, the most important critical question was how the shooting began—"the spark from which the flame arose."[108] The survivors were likewise anxious to clarify this controversial point. Major Whitside had testified in the January 1891 court of inquiry that Lakota warriors had fired fifty shots before the unsuspecting troops could respond.[109] The earliest Lakota accounts of Wounded Knee conceded that "a crazy man, a young man of very bad influence, and in fact a nobody among that bunch of Indians" had fired the first shot. They insisted that the soldiers answered this single shot with an overwhelming volley that killed the majority of the unarmed Lakota men.[110] Mature Lakota leaders often branded young warriors as "crazy" or "bad," when they, desiring to prove their bravery and manhood, acted imprudently and without the approval of their elders.[111] By invoking this image, Lakotas in the aftermath of Wounded Knee argued that Big Foot and other leaders had not approved the warrior's decision to fire his gun.

Anticipating white interpreters who would seize upon these early accounts as evidence that the Lakotas accepted the blame for starting the fight, the survivors attempted to soften their depiction of the young warrior in their later interviews. Beard acknowledged to Walker that two young men—Black Fox and Yellow Turtle—did not want to surrender their weapons. Beard indicated that, although they initially hid their guns, during the disarmament the two young warriors displayed them openly. Furthermore, Black Fox and Yellow Turtle offered to "give up all their cartridges" and "carry their guns empty." When soldiers approached them to confiscate the rifles forcibly, Yellow Turtle warned them: "My friends, do not come to me in that way for I do not want to hurt you." Black Fox declared that he would die before giving up his gun. During the confrontation, a rifle went off, which the soldiers answered by shooting into the Lakota men.[112]

In their interviews with Ricker and Gilmore, Horn Cloud and Beard added another important detail—Black Fox (or Black Coyote, as Ricker recorded the name) was apparently hearing impaired. "This man who was deaf," Horn Cloud explained, "had been holding up his own gun, [saying] that it had cost him a good deal of money, that if anybody wanted it he must pay for it, for he would not give it up without pay." When soldiers attempted to wrestle the gun away, it went off, precipitating the troops' volley.[113]

At first blush, it would appear that Horn Cloud and Beard had conveniently "remembered" a detail that substantially undermined the official account of "treacherous" warriors attacking troops unawares. None of the Lakotas who gave prior statements had mentioned that the warrior was deaf. However, Seventh Cavalryman Theodore Ragnar, who fought at Wounded Knee, confirmed Horn Cloud's and Beard's claim. After being injured during the Drexel Mission fight of December 30, 1890, Ragnar returned to his native Sweden. In 1894, he recorded his memories of Wounded Knee.[114] Ragnar harbored no sympathies for the Lakotas, describing them as "the most satanic, hang-dog physiognomies I ever was unlucky enough to meet." He recalled seeing "a selection of the worst characters in the Sioux nation ... masters of deceit and cunning who regarded death as an offering at the altar of their hatred of the whites."[115] Despite this invective, Ragnar described the disarmament scene in much the same way as Horn Cloud and Beard: "A deaf warrior was on his way to the pile of weapons in front of the colonel when two soldiers intervened and brutally wrenched the loaded weapon from the young man's hands." An unexpected discharge ensued, followed by the soldiers' "destroying and appalling ... bullet rain" that struck "the Indian mob."[116] Portraying the young warrior as deaf and confused, rather than "treacherous," substantially altered how the lead up to Wounded Knee would be remembered.

The survivors also addressed the soldiers' allegation that a Ghost Dance medicine man had promised the warriors that their Ghost Shirts would protect them from the troop's bullets and had thrown dirt into the air as a signal for the Lakotas to fire on the troops.[117] A few survivors acknowledged in 1891 that during the disarmament the medicine man had performed a Ghost Dance ceremony and addressed a group of young warriors, although these Lakotas could not hear what the man had said.[118] Beard told Walker that his skeptical father, Horn Cloud Senior, had challenged the Ghost Dancer to plead with the Messiah to protect them from the soldiers. The medicine man reluctantly "began to cry to the Great Spirit, and gathered up a handful of dust and threw it towards the sky, and waved his blanket under the dust, as they did in the ghost dance when they call for the Messiah." This happened simultaneously with the soldiers' attempted seizure of the young warriors' guns, but in Beard's recounting to Walker, the two events were unconnected.[119] Horn Cloud told Ricker essentially the same story.[120]

The survivors' interviews affirmed that the soldiers hunted down and killed Lakota men, women, and children, negating the Seventh Cavalry's claim that the deaths were accidental. The troops' initial volley killed most of the Lakota men, followed by a brief but fierce fight at close quarters. Beard in particular showed great valor, receiving multiple wounds and killing four soldiers.[121] Horn Cloud also showed Gilmore a picture of the snow-blanketed dead on the Wounded Knee field and identified a prone figure as his slain brother.[122] The troops then pursued the fleeing Lakotas. Horn Cloud explained to Ricker that "women were killed in the beginning of the fight just the same as the men were killed. Women who were wounded and had babies digged hollow places in the bank and placed the little things in them for safety ... some women were found lying dead with dead infants on their breasts; one mother lay dead; her breast covered with blood from her wound, and her little child was standing by her and nursing."[123] Beard told Ricker that some Lakotas had found refuge in a nearby ravine, but the soldiers stood on the banks and fired into crowds of women and children. Hotchkiss guns stationed on an accompanying hill rained shells onto the helpless people.[124] Remarkably, Horn Cloud escaped unscathed, although Beard and White Lance were badly wounded. Their parents, two brothers, female cousin, and Beard's wife were all killed, while Beard's newborn son died the following March.[125]

Mary Mousseau provided a female survivor's perspective to Gilmore. On the night before the massacre, the soldiers initially refused the women's requests to obtain water, but finally allowed them to go in pairs with a soldier escort. The next morning, after the men were called to the circle and soldiers demanded their weapons, "the women brought some guns to the place where the officers stood." She then described the soldiers' search for weapons in the camp and their behavior toward the women, relating that "a soldier lifted me up and felt all over me in the search," implying that she experienced a form of sexual assault. Her husband was killed in the soldiers' initial volley, and Mousseau's little girl was shot soon thereafter. As she fled with the other women, a soldier's bullet broke her arm above the elbow. Her baby boy, who was strapped to her back, was killed by another bullet. Mousseau and her wounded mother remained near the field until mid-January 1891, surviving only on water. When Indian scouts found them, Mousseau was "very weak and thin" and her clothes were "caked with dried blood."[126]

In seeking to explain the soldiers' actions, Horn Cloud argued that the troops had been drinking. However, the survivor did not condemn all the cavalrymen. Captain George D. Wallace, according to Horn Cloud's interview with Ricker, learned that the young Lakota spoke English and pulled him aside during the disarmament. "Joseph, you better go over to the women and tell them to let the wagons go and saddle up their horses and be ready to skip, for there is going to be trouble; for that officer [either Forsyth or Whitside] is half shot"—a common nineteenth-century euphemism for intoxication.[127] Walker, based on his interview with Beard, was likewise convinced that "intoxicants had an undue effect in producing the result of the disarmament."[128] As Ricker listened to the survivors describe the events leading to the carnage, he scrawled: "Forsyth must have been drunk!"[129] In addition to alcohol, Horn Cloud argued that the friendly fire had killed many of the troops.[130]

A CENTRAL PREOCCUPATION in the survivors' accounts was contesting the notion that Big Foot and his band had been "hostile" in 1890. At the conclusion of his interview with Walker, Beard noted a bitter irony: "When Big

Foot was in the badlands we were very much closer to the camp of the hostile Indians than we were to the agency," he explained. "I sometimes think that if we had all gone and joined the hostiles instead of trying to go to the agency, my people would not have been shot down like wolves."[131] In short, their decision *not* to join the "hostiles" had led to Wounded Knee.

Although they were unable to change the past, the survivors in their interviews attempted to alter how whites remembered that past, and perhaps, in the process, improve their chances of obtaining justice for their losses at Wounded Knee. When taken together, the interviews with sympathetic interlocutors formed a corpus of written accounts that served as a potent challenge to the government's Wounded Knee records. Although the survivors' statements would not achieve "official" status, as had the Seventh Cavalry's reports and the January 1891 court of inquiry record, the Lakotas' statements ultimately were preserved in western archives, where they would subsequently be retrieved and used to undermine the official interpretation of the "Battle of Wounded Knee." That, however, would be in the future. After finding a reprieve with sympathetic interlocutors, the Lakota survivors would renew their pursuit of justice in the 1910s within the government's claims system that was hostile to their memories.

6

Irreconcilable Memories

ON APRIL 12, 1920, retired General Nelson A. Miles met with Commissioner of Indian Affairs Cato Sells in Washington, DC. Accompanying the octogenarian general were Lakotas Joseph Horn Cloud and Dewey Beard, who had come to the nation's capital to file a compensation claim for the Seventh Cavalry's massacre of their relatives at Wounded Knee nearly three decades before. Miles, who had long been critical of the Seventh Cavalry's actions on December 29, 1890, argued that the time had come for the government to "atone" for the massacre and compensate the survivors for their losses. The survivors hoped that with Miles's advocacy, the Office of Indian Affairs would finally give them the justice that they had sought for so long.

This was not the first time that survivors had petitioned for redress within the government's claims system. The brothers had drafted their first claims in 1896 asking for compensation for property lost during the 1890-1891 crisis, and their repeated submissions eventually resulted in an official Indian Office inquiry in 1904–1905. After the failure of that claim, Horn Cloud and other survivors turned their attention to corroborating with sympathetic whites to create written accounts of Wounded Knee. During the second decade of the twentieth century, the survivors renewed their efforts to obtain compensation, resulting in a series of official government investigations that culminated in 1920. The records of the Wounded Knee inquiries, preserved in the Office of Indian Affairs archives, provide an important window into ways that the Progressive era United States government responded to claims by indigenous peoples to correct wrongs committed during the nineteenth-century Indian Wars. Specifically, the inquiries demonstrated the degree to which race war and the "friendly"/"hostile" binary continued to shape remembrance of past violence against Indians. The Wounded Knee investigations in the 1910s forced government bureaucrats to decide between irreconcilable memories, those embedded in official records and those of the Lakota survivors.

1909–1910 Investigation

In late 1909, the remnant of Big Foot's band that had returned to the Cheyenne River Reservation following the massacre filed their own claim for compensation for property that had been destroyed or stolen after they left their Cherry Creek homes on the Cheyenne River Reservation. On September 6, 1909, seventy-six survivors and heirs wrote claims for "household goods, horses, cattle, saddles, hay, etc." that were lost in 1890 while the band was away from their homes.[1] The claimants included survivors who had remained on Pine Ridge, such as Peter Stands, as well as Daniel Blue Hair and Jackson Kills White Man, who had returned to Cheyenne River in the aftermath of Wounded Knee.[2] After Pine Ridge officials rejected Horn Cloud's claim in 1905, the survivors opted to try the Cheyenne River Superintendent, L. F. Michaels, who submitted their affidavits with a letter of explanation to his superiors on January 10, 1910.[3] The cooperation between the survivors on both reservations foreshadowed later collaborations to obtain compensation.

On January 29, 1910, the Department of the Interior tasked Inspector James McLaughlin with evaluating the claims.[4] A career Indian Office employee, McLaughlin had spent nineteen years as an Indian agent, including fourteen on the Standing Rock Agency with the Hunkpapa Lakotas in Dakota Territory. McLaughlin's worldview embodied the "Vanishing Policy" that dominated Indian affairs during the late nineteenth and early twentieth century. He firmly believed that "the immutable law of the survival of the fittest" would result in whites displacing North America's Native population. However, he also held that Indians—with the help of "benevolent" whites such as himself—could make the painful transition from "savagery to civilization" by adopting white ways and assimilating into the American body politic. Although generally considered honest and above corruption, McLaughlin's worldview precluded a sympathetic approach to his charges.[5]

In 1895 McLaughlin was promoted to inspector, rendering him the face of the government in Indian Country as he assessed schools, farms, and agency headquarters, resolved disputes, and negotiated the land deals that opened up reservations to white settlers in the late nineteenth and early twentieth centuries. During the first decade of the new century McLaughlin conducted two investigations of compensation claims, both of which stemmed from Civil War-era conflicts. To guarantee that treasury dollars did not go to former enemies of the United States, McLaughlin scoured government archives to ensure that alleged hostiles did not file illegitimate petitions, and he tended to favor the judgments of previous government officials over the applicants' own word. In the first investigation, pro-Confederacy Creeks destroyed or stole a substantial amount of property from the so-called Loyal Creeks, who allied with the Union. In 1866 the government partially rewarded Loyal Creeks' fidelity by compensating them for their losses, although the tribe's attorneys pressed the government for additional compensation money. In 1903 Congress appropriated an additional $600,000, and McLaughlin analyzed 4,000 claims of survivors and heirs to establish their validity and ensure that no hostiles filed petitions.[6] In the second case, McLaughlin investigated claims from the US-Dakota War of 1862. The government's failure to honor treaty provisions spurred Santee Dakota bands to wage war against federal troops and white settlers in Minnesota. In response to the conflict, Congress abrogated the Dakotas' 1851 treaty and withdrew promised rations from all Santees, regardless of actual participation in the fighting. After the US Court of Claims upheld the Santees' legal challenge, Congress allocated nearly $800,000 to restore suspended annuities, with a condition that former hostiles be excluded from this money. In 1908 and 1909 McLaughlin examined thousands of claims, looking for any evidence of a claimant's alleged hostility toward the government.[7]

McLaughlin brought the same scrutiny to the Lakotas' petitions. He was partially chosen to evaluate the Cherry Creek claims because of his role in the Pine Ridge Campaign of 1890–1891. Secretary of the Interior Franklin Pierce told McLaughlin: "As you were on the ground at the time and are well acquainted with the facts, you are no doubt in a better position to advise the Department regarding the matter than anyone else. In your report will you kindly say whether any of the Indians who have signed statements were responsible for the trouble or if they were all innocent sufferers."[8] As Standing Rock Agent, McLaughlin had opposed the Ghost Dance, which he considered a fanatical and dangerous movement that impeded the Lakotas' progress toward civilization and that challenged the Indian Office's authority on the reservation. His order to arrest Sitting Bull—in McLaughlin's mind the "chief priest and leading apostle" of the Ghost Dance—resulted in the chief's death at the hands of the agency police on December 15, 1890. Many of Sitting Bull's followers, who McLaughlin considered "the more worthless, ignorant, obstinate and non-progressive of the Sioux" had relatives on Cherry Creek, which doubtless colored the inspector's views of the Lakotas' 1909 claims.[9] Although McLaughlin believed that he "was personally acquainted with most of the Indians then residing in the Cherry Creek District of the Cheyenne River Reservation," he recruited E. J. Warner, a trader and former financial agent assigned to Cherry Creek who was acquainted with many of the claimants, to help with the evaluation.[10]

McLaughlin found the claims to be "ridiculously absurd" for multiple reasons. Most of McLaughlin's points reflected his assumption that Big Foot's followers were "backward" in 1890 and that adherence to the Ghost Dance automatically made the Minneconjous hostile to the government. First, he argued that the Cheyenne River Lakotas' losses during the Pine Ridge Campaign had been "insignificant" compared those of other reservations, implying that the Cherry Creek claims had been inflated.[11] Second, he reminded the Interior Department that Congress had appropriated $100,000 to compensate friendly Indians in 1891, which had been distributed in full, and that hostile Natives were ineligible for compensation. He was nearly certain that most, if not all, of the claimants were members of Big Foot's band, and were therefore not "entitled to compensation [for lost property] under the said act of March 3, 1891."[12] Third, even if the Cherry Creek claimants had been friendly in 1890, their claims to the number of tons of hay lost were exaggerated, since average Lakotas at the time did not produce hay in such quantities. Lastly, McLaughlin argued that during periods of unrest, Lakotas would not have left behind items such as "buckskin clothes, tanned-deer skins, and guns."[13] Arguing that the claimants' historical assertions were fabricated, McLaughlin recommended against compensation. On April 22, 1910, the Interior Department notified Superintendent Michaels that the claims had been rejected.[14] Twice during the first decade of the twentieth century, the Office of Indian Affairs had rejected the survivors' compensation claims based largely on the assumption that Big Foot's band had been hostile in 1890 and therefore ineligible for compensation.

The Big Foot Survivors Association

Rather than accept the outcome of this investigation, the Cheyenne River survivors in 1912 turned their sights on the US Court of Claims, the primary avenue for wronged citizens to file claims against the United States. Native peoples were barred from filing claims with the court for most of the entity's first three decades of existence, but in the 1880s this ban was lifted. Thereafter, indigenous peoples increasingly looked to the court to redress treaty violations. Progress for these suits was painfully slow and only a small number of claims were granted awards during the next several decades. The

Court of Claims, however, presented Native peoples an arena in which they could engage in the politics of memory by contesting official narratives of the past. After the difficult experience with the 1909–1910 Indian Office investigation, the survivors were willing to try their luck in the Court of Claims.[15]

These efforts were initiated by the Cheyenne River survivors, who formed the Big Foot Survivors Association as a lobbying organization. In early 1912, the association's primary spokesman, John Makes Long, drafted a legal brief intended for the US Court of Claims.[16] Long was a Minneconjou Lakota whose parents had been killed by the US Seventh Cavalry at Wounded Knee.[17] His brief reflected an explicit awareness that army officers in 1890 had categorized Big Foot and his band as hostiles, a classification that had lasting consequences, since government policy prohibited hostiles from subsequently claiming redress. Long argued that "the records of the government in connection with [Wounded Knee] do not set forth the actual conditions relating thereto." Rather than rely on faulty government records, Long insisted that the court should instead trust "those who have intimate personal knowledge of the history of Big Foot and his band."[18]

Long contended that his relatives' adoption of the Ghost Dance was "not in any way as an indulgence in any hostile movement."[19] The Minneconjous only fled the Cheyenne River Reservation after being warned that the soldiers intended to arrest and remove the band. After the Seventh Cavalry detained them on the Pine Ridge Reservation and demanded their weapons on December 29, the Lakotas complied "in the same spirit of peace" that had marked their conduct since leaving Cheyenne River. Once disarmed, Long alleged, the cavalrymen opened fire on the defenseless Lakotas, killing hundreds of men, women, and children. The survivors, having suffered emotionally and materially for twenty-two years after 1890, demanded that the government redress their grievances.[20]

On April 22, 1912, Long mailed the brief to Commissioner of Indian Affairs Robert G. Valentine. "Without going into the details of evidence," Long explained, "this brief sets forth the case of the [Big Foot Survivors] Association which we believe to be a most meritorious one." Long concluded by expressing his hope that Valentine would "give [the survivors] all possible assistance in [their] efforts to get [their] case before the Court of Claims for a hearing."[21] Valentine's assistant commissioner, T. H. Abbot, responded to Long that bills were pending before Congress that would, if passed, give the Survivors Association access to the Court of Claims.[22] There is evidence that Long even visited Washington, DC, in 1912. Little is known about Long's trip, although it was later remembered that he "presented [the survivors'] claim to different high officials" with the hope of getting compensation "for the wrong done by the United States Army" when it "killed [the survivors'] brothers, sisters, mothers and fathers."[23] These bills, however, did not become laws. Ultimately, the Lakotas' efforts during the second decade of the twentieth century to bring their claims before the Court of Claims were unsuccessful. However, Long's arguments in his brief demonstrate that the survivors were keenly aware of the challenges posed by the friendly/hostile binary in the government's claims system.

Three years later, engineer and amateur historian of the Indian Wars Walter Mason Camp visited the Cheyenne River Reservation, where, using Joseph Horn Cloud as a reference, he located survivors. He found a reliable translator among them—Jim Long, also known as James E. High Hawk, who in the 1930s would become a leader of the Cheyenne River remnant of Big Foot's band.[24] Six survivors—Peter One Skunk, Jessie Swift Dog, Alex High Hawk, Charles Blue Arm, Solomon Afraid of Enemy, and Daniel Blue Hair—provided a joint statement written in Lakota to Camp. The engineer included in his notes that Swift Dog desired a translated version of the account sent to him.[25]

Perhaps realizing that whites would continue to blame the outbreak of fighting on the young warrior who fired the first shot, Camp's informants on the Cheyenne River Reservation went even further to undermine the official version of the disarmament. Evidently, the Cheyenne River-based Big Foot Survivors Association had developed a tradition for narrating Wounded Knee that was distinct from that of Horn Cloud and the Pine Ridge group. In their 1915 Lakota-language statement, One Skunk, Swift Dog, High Hawk, Blue Arm, Afraid of Enemy, and Blue Hair omitted the story of the young warrior altogether. These Lakotas argued that all of the warriors had surrendered their weapons: "As soon as they had done this a whistle blew and all the soldiers loaded their guns. Immediately an officer mounted on a bay horse ordered them to shoot. They shot their guns."[26] John Makes Long, the Survivors Association delegate, presented a similar scenario. The "men had laid down everything they had in the nature of arms, even to their awls," Long argued. "The officer on the knoll was heard to give an order at which the soldiers dropped their guns on their arms and threw in a shell... The soldiers fired, killing many of the men, women and children of Big Foot's band." Long referenced Horn Cloud as "an English speaking Indian" who had understood the officer's command for his men to fire.[27] It is possible that these Cheyenne River survivors omitted the deaf Indian because they believed whites simply used the story to justify the soldiers' subsequent actions.

On the backside of the document, Camp wrote "Big Foot Survivor's [*sic*] Association." Camp's inclusion of this note suggests that One Skunk and the others saw Camp as a potential ally in their pursuit of compensation and justice.[28] Along these lines, Daniel Blue Hair told the engineer that soldiers "looking for trouble" had ransacked his home and stolen his property while he was away at Pine Ridge in late 1890. Such information would have been included in a compensation claim, indicating that the members of the Big Foot Survivors Association were actively considering their options for compensation in 1915.[29]

Marias Massacre Survivors and Compensation Claims

The Lakota survivors of Wounded Knee were not the only Natives in the 1910s who pursued justice from the government for wrongs committed by the US Army during the nineteenth century. In 1913 the Piegan survivors of the Marias Massacre, perpetrated by the US Second Cavalry under the command of Colonel Eugene Baker near the Marias River in Montana Territory on January 23, 1870, began laying the foundation for their own compensation claim. The Indian Office's response to the Piegans' petition paralleled in significant ways the government's reaction to the Wounded Knee survivors' claims.

In August 1869, Piegan Owl Child had murdered prominent white trader Malcolm Clarke as vengeance for an earlier altercation. Colonel Baker received orders to launch a punitive strike on the camp of "hostile" Piegan leader Mountain Chief, who was reportedly harboring Owl Child. Following the attack, surviving Piegans reported to sympathetic Indian Office agents that the Second Cavalry had attacked the wrong camp. Baker's men had instead targeted a known "friendly" leader, Chief Heavy Runner, slaughtering mostly women and children, as the men had been away hunting. Baker released his official reports in response to the public outcry, claiming the cavalrymen had attacked the correct band and had killed one hundred twenty warriors. In spite of his men's best efforts to spare noncombatants, Baker explained, fifty three women and children were accidently killed. War Department officials subsequently exonerated the colonel and his men.[30]

It remains unclear why the Piegan survivors decided in 1913 to pursue compensation from the government for their losses in 1870. However, in February of that year Joseph (Heavy Runner) Kipp, a son of the chief and a scout who had accompanied the Second Cavalry on the day of the massacre, recorded a statement in which he claimed that Baker's men had attacked the wrong camp, in spite of the scout's failed attempt to avert the disaster. Kipp recalled counting two hundred and seventeen bodies, mostly women and children. He also alleged that after shooting Heavy Runner, the soldiers found a letter of recommendation on the chief's person that confirmed the cavalry had attacked the wrong camp. The troops also stole five thousand horses.[31] Other survivors made similar affidavits. Blackfeet Agency Superintendent Arthur E. McFatridge wrote to the Indian Office in support of the survivors' claim, suggesting that Congress appropriate $75,000 as compensation.[32] After a year passed without any decision from Washington, McFatridge wrote again, stating: "I am thoroughly convinced that these people have a just claim, and that their claim should receive some consideration."[33]

Although the Indian Office made some effort to investigate the Piegans' claims in 1914, no actual movement occurred on the issue until Oregon Senator Harry Lane agreed to support the Marias survivors' claim in Congress.[34] Lane introduced a bill on February 2, 1915, "to reimburse the heirs of Chief Heavy Runner on account of his death and property taken from him at the time of the Baker massacre."[35] The Senate Committee on Indian Affairs agreed to consider the bill, but approval from the Department of the Interior was required before the committee could convene a hearing. The department's report found that Baker's official statements "differ very materially" from the Piegan survivors' statements: "It is impossible to reconcile the statements of Joseph Kipp with reports which the military authorities made shortly after the events transpired." The Department of the Interior therefore privileged Baker's contemporary written reports over the Piegan survivors' memories.[36] The Interior Department's report on the bill showed remarkable parallels with Inspector McLaughlin's conclusions in the 1909–1910 Wounded Knee investigation, suggesting common assumptions regarding the reliability of Native memories when compared with official government reports. In spite of this initial failure, the Piegan survivors continued to convince congressmen to sponsor compensation bills for the remainder of the 1910s and even into the 1920s. The Interior Department repeatedly refused to report favorably on the bill.[37]

Looking for Some Relief and Redress from the Government

The Wounded Knee survivors were just as persistent in presenting their claims to the Indian Office during the second half of the 1910s, despite receiving reactions similar to those given the Piegan survivors. Deteriorating economic conditions of the Lakota survivors on Pine Ridge led Joseph Horn Cloud and Dewey Beard to renew their efforts to claim compensation for Wounded Knee in 1917. Perhaps discouraged by the Indian Office's rejection of their previous claims for lost property under the 1891 act, the Lakotas in the late 1910s argued that the government had an obligation to support the survivors financially, especially those with lingering injuries incurred at Wounded Knee. In 1917 and in 1920 Horn Cloud and Beard led delegations to Washington, DC, where they presented their claims in person to government officials. They also recruited retired Lieutenant General Nelson A. Miles, who finally fulfilled Horn Cloud's ideal of a powerful white ally who would support their claims. Despite pursuing alternate arguments, Indian Office bureaucrats continued to interpret the survivors' claims within the confines of the 1891 act and the friendly/hostile binary.

During the 1910s, the economic situation for the survivors worsened, stemming from unintended consequences of the government's assimilation program of allotment. The General Allotment Act of 1887 had divided reservations into one hundred and sixty acre plots, which were then assigned to Indian household heads. During a twenty-five-year trust period, the Indian Office would teach the Indians how to farm in preparation for eventual ownership of the land, self-sufficiency, and productive citizenship. "Surplus" reservation land would then be sold off.[38] Policymakers, under pressure to expedite the opening of surplus lands to white speculators, passed the Burke Act of 1906, which empowered the Secretary of the Interior to truncate the trust period for those Natives deemed "competent" to manage their own affairs. In theory, this mechanism would allow educated Indians to bypass the twenty-five year waiting period, obtain fee-simple title, and develop or sell their allotments as they saw fit.[39] In the 1910s, however, the Indian Office defined "competency" loosely and declared thousands of unprepared Indians "competent," and abandoned the new citizens to market vicissitudes, with intense pressure to sell their land. The one-time profit from a land sale provided temporary relief, but did little to alleviate grinding poverty on the reservations.[40]

Obtaining citizenship also meant the revocation of wardship status, which many reformers saw as a victory over paternalism, but it also meant that the newly christened Indian citizen no longer received treaty-guaranteed rations. These changes to allotment policies adversely impacted the Wounded Knee survivors, many of whom had been crippled in the massacre and were unable to find regular employment. In 1916, Daniel

White Lance received fee-simple title to his allotment, was granted citizenship and cut off from receiving rations. The forty-eight-year-old survivor was the primary means of support for his wife, Julia, and their three children, Susie (fifteen), Lucy (twelve), and John (nine).[41] At Wounded Knee, White Lance received three bullet-wounds in his right leg and another wound on his head. Although he lived, White Lance's wounds never properly healed, causing him to rely on crutches thereafter.[42] In order to pay mounting medical bills, White Lance reluctantly obtained a patent-in-fee for his allotment in 1916, which he promptly sold. The decision relieved some of the debt, but rendered the recently naturalized White Lance ineligible to draw rations for his family. In dire straits, White Lance sought help from his younger brother, Joseph Horn Cloud. Horn Cloud spoke with Indian Office farmer Leonard L. Smith, who controlled the distribution of rations, but local officials would do nothing.[43]

Recognizing that other Wounded Knee survivors were suffering under similar conditions, Horn Cloud and his brother, Dewey Beard, visited the nation's capital in March 1917 at their own expense and lobbied Indian Office bureaucrats directly.[44] While there, Horn Cloud and Beard filed official affidavits recounting Wounded Knee, which paralleled the accounts given to Walker, Ricker, Camp, and Gilmore. Whereas the brothers had previously represented their family as skeptical of the Ghost Dance, their 1917 affidavits omitted discussion of the dance altogether, perhaps because they saw it as ultimately irrelevant to the events preceding Wounded Knee. The survivors argued that without provocation troops had invaded the Lakotas' "peaceful territory," leading Big Foot to leave his Cheyenne River home in hopes of negotiating a peace settlement. On Pine Ridge, the band had surrendered to the Seventh Cavalry under a white flag. The shooting began when intoxicated troops wrestled a gun away from a confused (yet compliant) warrior, resulting in the wanton slaughter of men, women, and children. "Every time I recall this history," Beard stated, "the matter is so vivid in my mind, that it seems to me as though it had happened just yesterday." Horn Cloud explained that "a great many survivors of this band, demoralized by what had happened to them were poor for a long time and unable to get a state of living comfortably, and in fact, many of them ever since live in need." The brothers had come to Washington, DC, to plead the survivors' cause.[45]

Rather than claim compensation for lost property, as they had done in the early 1900s, Horn Cloud and Beard instead petitioned the government to recognize the survivors as a special class that was eligible for continued rations, regardless of citizenship status, due to the army's negligence at Wounded Knee. Although they articulated their proposal as a remedy for disabled Lakotas such as White Lance, Horn Cloud and Beard ultimately envisioned a scenario in which all survivors, as well as dependents and heirs, would be included within that special class.[46] Their idea was therefore roughly analogous to pensions for war veterans and their widows—the primary recipients of government social security prior to the New Deal—with the obvious difference that veterans received support for their service to the army, while the Lakotas would receive compensation for having been wronged by the military.[47] Horn Cloud and Beard also presented a secondary proposal, in which they asked the government to restore treaty-guaranteed annuities Big Foot's band had missed in the chaos of 1890–1891.[48]

While in the capital, Horn Cloud and Beard recruited retired Lieutenant General Nelson A. Miles. In 1903, Horn Cloud had stated his intention to seek out a "good man" to "help us see about this matter" of compensation. In 1917, he reiterated this desire to find "good white people" who would use their influence to convince government officials to grant "relief and redress" to the survivors.[49] Miles and Beard had apparently met in 1891, not long after Wounded Knee, when the general provided the survivor a certificate of good character. During the 1913 filming of *The Indian Wars* on Pine Ridge, Miles issued a second certificate reaffirming Beard's character as "one of the survivors of the Wounded Knee Massacre, in which he was twice seriously wounded and lost his father, mother, two brothers, sister, wife, and child."[50] Miles had long opposed the use of excessive violence against Native peoples, preferring negotiation rather than repression to end conflicts. In 1891 he was the foremost critic of the Seventh Cavalry's conduct at Wounded Knee, and his association with Beard had only reinforced his views on the matter. In support of the survivors' 1917 claim, Miles wrote Commissioner of Indian Affairs Cato Sells that he "regarded the whole affair as most unjustifiable and worthy of the severest condemnation." The general urged the Indian Office and Congress "to make a suitable recompense to the survivors who are still living for the great injustice that was done them and the serious loss of their relatives and property."[51]

Upon receiving Miles's letter the Indian Office ordered Pine Ridge Superintendent John Brennan, who had overseen the 1904–1905 investigation and had cooperated in the filming of *The Indian Wars*, to look into the matter.[52] Rather than investigate the broad proposals for justice advocated by Horn Cloud, Beard, and Miles, Brennan had his staff examine in detail White Lance's personal financial records. On May 22, 1917, the superintendent

FIGURE 6.1 Nelson A. Miles, date unknown, by N. H. Rose, 1195, Main Photograph Collection. Photo courtesy of Arizona State Historical Society-Tucson.

reported that the Indian Office had given White Lance twenty head of heifers and $50 in 1909, that he had received a $129.07 pro rata share of trust funds in 1914, and aside from the money and horses he received in exchange for his allotment, he was paid $119.52 per year in lease money. Brennan also concluded that White Lance was "not totally disabled and could take care of a garden, if so inclined." As for the other Wounded Knee survivors, the army had classified them as hostiles in 1890, rendering them ineligible to receive the annuities they had missed in 1891.[53] Despite Miles's endorsement of the survivors' memories of Wounded Knee, the official version had ultimately guided the government's response to the survivors.

Major Brennan and Buffalo Bill on the Wounded Knee battle field © Miller

FIGURE 6.2 John R. Brennan and William Cody, 1913, photographer unknown, FB 107, John R. Brennan Collection. Photo courtesy of South Dakota State Historical Society.

A Thorough Investigation

The failure of the 1917 claim disappointed the Lakotas, yet three years later the survivors renewed their demands for compensation for the wrongs committed against them. With Miles again supporting the survivors, the Indian Office launched the most extensive government investigation into Wounded Knee since the Forsyth court of inquiry. Whereas the 1891 examination had been based almost entirely on the testimony of the Seventh Cavalry's officers, fifty living Lakota survivors testified for the 1920 investigation. The Lakotas believed that this evidence would finally convince the government to administer justice for the massive loss of life and property at Wounded Knee. However, the official assigned to evaluate the claims, Inspector James McLaughlin, had conducted similar investigations in the past, including the Lakotas' 1909–1910 claim. As a former Standing Rock agent, McLaughlin held strong opinions regarding the Lakotas' history with the United States and the Ghost Dance, which he deemed a fanatical movement that undermined the government's civilization program.

In April 1920, Horn Cloud and Beard once more presented the Wounded Knee survivors' claims in Washington, DC. They again recruited the help of Nelson A. Miles, who accompanied them to the office of Commissioner of Indian Affairs Cato Sells on April 12. According to Sells, the delegates "invited special attention to their request for those Indians who suffered in the battle of Wounded Knee."[54] To support their proposal that the government recognize a special class eligible for government support, Horn Cloud and Beard submitted lists naming sixty-seven survivors then living on the Pine Ridge, Cheyenne River, and Standing Rock Reservations. The lists also identified one hundred and seventy-four individuals who were killed at Wounded Knee, survivors who had subsequently died, and heirs of the victims.[55] Miles reminded the commissioner of his 1917 letter and stated that the present was a favorable time "to atone in part for the cruel and unjustifiable massacre of Indian men and innocent women and children at Wounded Knee." Strengthening the categorical similarities between the survivors and veterans, Miles also urged the Indian Office to award pensions to Indian scouts and soldiers. He asked that the Indian Office present the measures to Congress for action.[56]

Commissioner Sells, interpreting the survivors' claims within the framework of the 1891 compensation act, initially favored rejecting the petitions. Sells informed Miles in a letter that after giving "careful consideration to these claims of the survivors of Wounded Knee," the Indian Office did "not at the

FIGURE 6.3   James McLaughlin, 1915, by D. F. Barry, B-540, Western History Collection.
Photo courtesy of The Denver Public Library.

present time believe that the matter should be presented to Congress." The
commissioner explained that in 1891, Congress had appropriated $100,000
to compensate friendly Indians for losses during the Pine Ridge Campaign
of 1890–1891. Sells believed that "all of the friendly Sioux Indians who had
lost property at the time mentioned were fully compensated." Furthermore,
many Wounded Knee survivors had already tried to obtain compensation,
referring specifically to the 1909 Cherry Creek claims discussed above, which
Indian Office Inspector James McLaughlin had found "ridiculously absurd."
Sells suggested that the survivors file a suit before the Court of Claims "to
have their claims properly adjudicated."[57]

     For reasons that remain obscure, however, Sells changed his mind and
did not send the letter. Perhaps Sells's shift was motivated by his belief that
acknowledging Indians' past grievances could further the government's
assimilationist project. The commissioner believed that allowing the memories of wrongs to fester "made poor soil for good citizenship to take root,"
as scholar Edward Lazarus has explained.[58] Sells shared his predecessor

Francis E. Leupp's concern that allowing the many "wildly absurd" claims promoted by Indians and their attorneys to fester unaddressed "only serve[d] to keep a multitude of Indians in a state of feverish expectancy of getting something for nothing, which is fatal to their steady industry and peace of mind."[59] Leupp's suggestion was to create a special court to adjudicate within three years all outstanding Indian claims, effectively "clear[ing] the atmosphere" by addressing legitimate suits and eliminating the "wildly absurd" ones.[60] As Lazarus suggests, "Sells and his contemporaries wanted to settle the Indian claims, but that did not mean they wanted them settled in favor of the Indians. No nation could serve effectively both as guardian of the claimant and as prospective defendant in the claimant's litigation."[61] Sells perhaps believed that simply investigating the survivors' claims would satisfy the Lakotas and their advocate Miles.

In any case, on May 4, 1920 Sells explained to Secretary of the Interior Barton Payne that "a thorough investigation" was needed, "in order that whatever action may be hereafter decided upon Congress can be informed that it is the result of a complete knowledge of the situation as seems to be practicable at the present time." Despite his apparent open-mindedness, Sells saw Wounded Knee as a "battle" that had resulted from "the so-called 'Messiah Craze,'" suggesting he had not been fully swayed by the survivors' and Miles's arguments.[62] Demonstrating a willingness—no matter how halfhearted—to address past grievances, however, would further Sells's broader assimilationist agenda.

Sells selected Inspector James McLaughlin to conduct the investigation, explaining he was "thoroughly familiar with general conditions pertaining to the troubles referred to by General Miles."[63] Sells also knew that McLaughlin had evaluated—and rejected—the Cherry Creek claims in 1910.[64] McLaughlin's understanding of the "general conditions" leading to Wounded Knee differed sharply from that presented by the survivors to Commissioner Sells, however. "During the Indian 'Messiah Craze,'" McLaughlin explained in a memorandum dated May 5, 1920, Big Foot's band had "abandoned their homes and fled to the Pine Ridge reservation where a large number of Sioux Indians, of the so-called Ghost dancers [*sic*], had congregated." McLaughlin did not use the word "battle" to describe Wounded Knee, preferring terms such as "affair," "disaster," and "melee" to steer a more neutral course between "battle," the army's official label, and "massacre," the Lakota survivors' preferred term.[65] Sells also selected McLaughlin because he was "well-known for his sympathetic interest in the Indians."[66] McLaughlin's "sympathetic interest," however, was contingent on whether Natives abandoned their "losing struggle for an existence according to [their] own ideals" and accepted the road to civilization.[67] After assigning McLaughlin the task, Sells retrieved the letter he had written to Miles and scrawled in the left hand margin: "Hold for Maj. McLaughlin report—5/6/20."[68]

From May through July 1920, McLaughlin interviewed fifty survivors and twenty-nine heirs of the victims living on the Standing Rock, Cheyenne River, and Pine Ridge Reservations, depending heavily on the lists prepared by Horn Cloud and Beard.[69] Relying on his own knowledge of Lakota, the inspector asked each interviewee to discuss personal injuries sustained at Wounded Knee (if applicable), the names of relatives killed, and property stolen following the killings.[70] McLaughlin later stated that "their respective statements . . . were made in a straight forward manner in the presence of quite a number of Indians, and impressed me as reasonably probable as remembered by the relators."[71] McLaughlin was observing a key Lakota strategy for ensuring accuracy in recounting of the past. When sharing their histories orally, others served as witnesses who either confirmed or challenged the reliability of their recollections, making their memories truly collective.[72] This mechanism also protected the survivors against interlopers who would falsely join their ranks, to serve either self-aggrandizing or nefarious ends. For example, McLaughlin interviewed a man named Pain on Hip at Pine Ridge, who claimed to have been at Wounded Knee. McLaughlin was subsequently informed by a number of Indians, including Dewey Beard, that "this man Pain on Hip was not at Wounded Knee, but had frequently claimed in talking with people, who did not know him, that he was in the Wounded Knee conflict and sustained great loss of property in the affair, which assertion is untrue and entirely without foundation."[73]

McLaughlin did not encourage his interviewees to interpret Wounded Knee itself, although a few slipped subtle hints of their views into McLaughlin's record. For example, on May 18 the inspector interviewed Bear Gone on Standing Rock, a sixty-year-old survivor who had lost her husband, Ashes, at Wounded Knee. She showed McLaughlin where she had been shot in the neck, with the inspector noting that "the lacerated scar [was] still showing very plainly." For Bear Gone, the scar was evidence of the physical trauma inflicted by the troops on December 29, 1890. She had lost several horses and other property, including "a rifle which her husband delivered to the US troops at Wounded Knee," a muted suggestion that her husband had been unarmed when killed.[74]

Horn Cloud provided the clearest Lakota perspective on Wounded Knee to McLaughlin. The inspector noted on July 22, 1920, that Horn Cloud "has taken an active interest in this Wounded Knee matter and who has heretofore submitted written statements thereon."[75] Observing Horn Cloud's literacy, the inspector asked the survivor to draft a detailed description of the family's human and material losses. In the resulting statement, Horn Cloud contended that Big Foot's people had died "innocent" at Wounded Knee, language that echoed the 1903 monument inscriptions: "Many innocent women and children who knew no wrong died here" and "the peace maker [Horn Cloud Senior] died here innocent."[76] In addition, Horn Cloud placed his family within the Lakotas' long history with the United States, as illustrated by his father's dedicated service as an army scout. For Horn Cloud, this fact undermined the contention that his family had been hostile in 1890, and instead suggested that the Seventh Cavalry had massacred peaceful Lakotas at Wounded Knee. In a 1915 letter, the survivor articulated this argument more fully and extended the chronology. For one hundred years, Horn Cloud's family had done "many good works ... for sake of Good Government of United States." Horn Cloud first discussed the Lakota Chief Black Buffalo who had signed a "treaty of friendship" with the United States and, after his death, had received full military honors at his funeral.[77] Many of Horn Cloud's male relatives had served as army scouts and each had received letters of recommendation and honorable discharge papers. Horn Cloud Senior was carrying his discharge papers on his person when killed at Wounded Knee. Notably, Horn Cloud's brothers who lost their lives at Wounded Knee, William and Sherman, shared the first and last names of the American general under whom Horn Cloud Senior had served.[78]

McLaughlin also met with Dewey Beard and Daniel White Lance. The inspector noted that Beard "bears a good reputation and impressed me very favorably, but as he don't [*sic*] speak English he desired to await the arrival of his brother Joseph Horned Cloud ... [before making] a detailed statement," which signaled Beard's implicit trust in his brother and unstated distrust of McLaughlin. During the interview Beard presented General Miles's 1913 endorsement, which illustrated the cultural significance of such documents in shaping white-Native interactions. Beard confirmed Horn Cloud's description of the family's losses, but added that he himself had received two serious wounds and his wife and newborn child had been killed.[79] White Lance showed McLaughlin scars from his three wounds, and the inspector recorded that "he has never fully recovered from his wound in the right ankle which is still superating [*sic*] and causes him to walk with a decided limp."[80]

Yet there were limits to McLaughlin's trust in the survivors' memories. Whereas the inspector believed the interviewees could adequately describe their own wounds, identify killed relatives and friends, and list their lost property, the inspector doubted their ability to accurately reconstruct the broader conditions leading to Wounded Knee. For that he turned to Philip Wells, a seventy-year-old "intelligent Sioux mixed-blood" who had served as the Seventh Cavalry's official interpreter during the Pine Ridge Campaign of 1890–1891. Wells had also worked many years for the Indian Office, had advised Buffalo Bill in the 1913 filming of the *Indian Wars* film, and shared McLaughlin's assumptions regarding the backwardness of traditional Lakota culture and the necessity of Indian assimilation into American life.[81] On September 3, 1920, Wells sent the inspector a detailed statement.[82] Wells argued that unrest over broken treaties caused the Lakotas to accept the Ghost Dance.[83] "The Indians," he explained, "being in such a hostile state of mind, and the ghost dance taking possession of them became fanatics."[84] Although Wells acknowledged that the Lakotas believed whites would disappear through supernatural means, rather than an armed insurrection, he nonetheless insisted that Big Foot was treacherous and needed to be disarmed before he reached the other hostiles in the Bad Lands.[85]

Wells defended the conduct of Colonel Forsyth and the Seventh Cavalry at Wounded Knee. Repeating many of the justifications offered by Forsyth's officers during the 1891 inquiry into the colonel's leadership, the interpreter argued that the Lakotas themselves were responsible for the deaths of noncombatants. The warriors themselves, as they fired into the ranks of the soldiers, killed the first women and children. As the fleeing Lakota men mixed with their families in the black-powder-induced fog, the soldiers—many of whom had never seen actual Indians before—inadvertently fired at men and women, since both sexes allegedly wore indistinguishable Ghost Shirts. Even three wounded warriors, who Wells had interviewed in January 1891, confirmed that the soldiers had been kind to the Lakotas. Wells also condemned as false newspaper reports that accused the soldiers of being drunk and goading the Lakotas into fighting. Despite the fact that Wells had been injured early on, and therefore missed much of what he claimed to have seen, McLaughlin deemed the interpreter a more reliable narrator than his survivor interviewees.[86]

Aside from seeking out Wells, McLaughlin conducted research in the archives of the Indian Office, where he located the 1890 reports of Cheyenne River Reservation Agent Perain P. Palmer. Palmer owed his 1890 appointment more to his loyalty to the Republican Party than any special competency with Native peoples.[87] Although the agent described Big Foot as "appear[ing] friendly," Palmer saw the chief's protection of the Ghost Dancers on the reservation as a sign of hostile intentions.[88] He also interpreted the band's acquisition of arms and ammunition as proof of a planned uprising.[89] Palmer's reports painted a picture of Big Foot as the leader of fanatics who defied Indian Office authority by refusing to stop dancing. Despite the agent's initial impression that Big Foot was friendly, he nonetheless recommended that the chief be arrested and removed from the reservation.[90]

After reviewing Palmer's reports and other Indian Office papers, McLaughlin drafted his final report on January 12, 1921. In contrast to Horn Cloud's portrayal of a long history of cooperation between the Lakota nation and the United States, McLaughlin began by situating Big Foot's followers within a broader story of resistance to the government's assimilation programs. These were the people, he explained, who "fled with Sitting Bull after the Battle of the Little Big Horn June 25, 1876."[91] Sitting Bull was the last militant leader to surrender after the Little Big Horn, with cold and hunger forcing him and his followers to abandon their Canadian refuge in 1881. In his autobiography, McLaughlin described the Lakota medicine man as "crafty, avaricious, mendacious, and ambitious," a man who "possessed all of the faults of an Indian and none of the nobler attributes which have gone far to redeem some of his people from their deeds of guilt."[92] To the former Standing Rock agent's consternation, Sitting Bull stubbornly resisted the government's assimilation programs and used his influence to encourage passive resistance elsewhere.[93] As Big Foot's Minneconjous maintained close ties with Sitting Bull, McLaughlin argued that the Cherry Creek Lakotas were "among the least advanced in civilization of any of the Sioux bands" in 1890.[94]

For the inspector, this refusal to accept civilization created fertile ground for adherence to the "Messiah Craze," which he had described in 1890 as "an absurd nonsense" that spread like an "infection" from the southern Lakota reservations northward. Despite the survivors' attempts to downplay the significance of the Ghost Dance, McLaughlin placed it at the center of his analysis. Above all else, the Ghost Dance was "fanaticism." McLaughlin described Sitting Bull—the Ghost Dance's "false prophet"—as the "high priest and leading apostle of this latest Indian absurdity" and as "the Chief Mischief Maker at [Standing Rock] Agency." Aside from deceiving the ignorant classes, he had even swayed "some of the Indians who were formerly numbered with the progressive and more intelligent and many of our very best Indians appear 'dazed' and undecided when talking of it, their inherited superstition having been thoroughly aroused."[95] In 1921, McLaughlin "still retain[ed] a distinct recollection of the dazed condition of the fanatical Ghost Dancing Indians involved in [Wounded Knee]."[96] As for Big Foot's "deluded" followers, they had "been engaged in the wild revelry of the so called Ghost Dance Craze. . . . [They were] the more firm believers in that absurd doctrine from which, through long periods of fasting and exhaustive dancing, they became emaciated and dazed in appearance and heedless to the advice of persons interested in their welfare."[97] They were, therefore, threats to themselves and others.

McLaughlin recounted in his 1921 report that after Sitting Bull's death on December 15, 1890, "the Ghost Dancing fanatics" on Standing Rock "joined Big Foot and his disaffected followers of the Cheyenne River Agency in their stampede from Cherry Creek to Pine Ridge reservation and were therefore of the Big Foot party in the disastrous affair at Wounded Knee."[98] In final analysis, it was this history of stubborn resistance and "Messiah-crazed fanaticism" that created the conditions for Wounded Knee. "The crazed condition and heedlessness of the Indians involved in the Wounded Knee affair," McLaughlin concluded, "was largely responsible for the unfortunate occurrence."[99]

The bulk of McLaughlin's 1921 report comprised of transcribed notes from his interviews on the three reservations, noting each person's wounds, killed relatives, and property lost.[100] The survivors' assertions that the soldiers had attacked largely unarmed Lakotas, who had surrendered their weapons, apparently had no effect on McLaughlin's thinking. Neither did Horn Cloud's explicit affirmation of innocence and discussion of his father's prior service as a scout for the US Army. Furthermore, General Miles's 1917 and 1920 letters, which the inspector had in his possession, did not alter McLaughlin's apparent belief that the Seventh Cavalry bore no responsibility for Wounded Knee. He also had copies of Horn Cloud's and Beard's 1917 affidavits, which portrayed Big Foot as a peaceful chief who was going to Pine Ridge to negotiate peace.[101] These were, apparently, not reliable sources.

Most perplexing was McLaughlin's contention that, three decades following 1890, "the Indians now seldom refer" to Wounded Knee, perhaps forgetting momentarily his own key role in two investigations of the survivors' claims. If anything, the remnant of Big Foot's band had more actively pursued their demands in the 1910s than during the two decades following 1890. McLaughlin was "therefore strongly of the opinion that the peace of mind of the Sioux and interests of the government would best be subserved by not agitating the matter further at this late date." If the first part of this statement was patently false, the second reflected McLaughlin's view that addressing claims for past wrongs simply served to "agitate" the Lakotas and impede their progress toward civilization. As an afterthought, the inspector stated that "as a matter of justice" the government could set aside a paltry sum of

$20,000 to compensate the survivors—not for the deaths of their kin—but for horses and other property lost after Wounded Knee, since the military controlled the field. To that degree, the inspector was willing to admit some fault on the government's part after the killings had already occurred.[102] Commissioner Sells declined McLaughlin's recommendation for Congress to appropriate funds to compensate the survivors for lost horses, preferring to allow the matter to die. Perhaps Sells was simply interested in portraying the government as willing to hear the survivors' claims, but not serious about actually addressing them.

JOSEPH HORN CLOUD, who had spent much of his adult life pursuing justice for the survivors of Wounded Knee, would not live to learn the commissioner's decision. On September 18, 1920, he died of a heart attack at his home in Kyle, South Dakota, not far from the mass grave where his family and his people were buried.[103] As the most active and persistent survivor during the three decades following Wounded Knee, Horn Cloud had pursued compensation within a system that was not ready to listen to indigenous persectives on the past. Government officials in 1890 had defined Big Foot and his people as hostiles because the Messiah Craze was deemed a fanatical threat to the American social order. The survivors worked tirelessly to establish that although they may have participated in the Ghost Dance, they had not been hostile to the government. Horn Cloud and other Lakotas attempted to rework official narratives by portraying Big Foot as a peace-seeking chief who was killed by drunk and vengeful Seventh Cavalrymen. Although the survivors had a prominent advocate in Miles, government bureaucrats repeatedly concluded that the Lakotas' memories were irreconcilable with narratives embedded in official government records.

The death of Horn Cloud, while devastating, did not completely demoralize the remaining members of Big Foot's band. In 1923 Paul Bull Eagle, president of the Big Foot Survivors Association, announced plans to hold a "day of lament" at the mass grave to "honor, and decorate over the graves of innocent children, women and men that are resting under their own soil awaiting for judgment day." They would remember "where Big Foot and his band were disarmed and massacred by the United States Army," since "a third of a century has passed since that un-excusable [*sic*] action occurred."[104] In the 1930s, the remaining survivors, recognizing a shift in white attitudes toward Native claims for justice, would honor Horn Cloud's legacy by bringing their claims before the Congress of the United States.

7

Liquidating the Liability of the United States

"THE WOUNDED KNEE massacre survivors have come," Commissioner of Indian Affairs John Collier noted in April 1938, referring to the recent appearance of two Lakota delegates before Congress. "What a beam of light they . . . shed upon a mournful phase of Indian history, now forty-six years in the past."[1] The witnesses testified in support of a bill that would "liquidate the liability of the United States for the massacre of Sioux Indian men, women, and children at Wounded Knee on December 29, 1890," by granting $1,000 per victim to the survivors and heirs, as well as $1,000 for Lakotas injured in the fighting. This sudden entrance onto the national stage provided a platform for the survivors' ongoing engagement with the politics of memory, centered on such English words as "massacre" and "hostility." In the 1930s the survivors framed their memories of Wounded Knee as a violation of treaty rights, and that just compensation was necessary to heal the rift between the Lakota nation and the United States.

That the Commissioner of Indian Affairs was championing, rather than dismissing, the survivors' claims in the 1930s reflected the changes that had occurred in the government's relationship with Native nations since the Progressive Era. In 1920 Congress passed legislation opening the US Court of Claims to several tribes for the first time, including the Lakotas. A decade later, the Court of Claims had a backlog of over one hundred Indian suits, some brought by the Lakotas, claiming nearly three billion in principal and interest.[2] Partially as a reward for Native American military service in World War I, in 1924 Congress granted citizenship to all Indians born in the United States. In states such as South Dakota with substantial indigenous populations, this act encouraged congressional representatives to advocate for their new Indian constituents' causes.[3] Finally, Franklin Delano Roosevelt and John Collier's Indian New Deal, passed in 1934, upended federal Indian policies first implemented in the 1880s, as the Indian Office abandoned allotment and assimilation in favor of supporting tribal land bases, encouraging cultural pluralism, and establishing limited self-government.[4] All of these factors combined to make the Office of Indian Affairs, the Department of the Interior, and congressmen assigned to the House Committee on Indian Affairs sympathetic to legislation recognizing an obligation to "liquidate" the nation's "liability" incurred at Wounded Knee in 1890.

However, the same forces that created a more favorable atmosphere in the 1930s for the Lakotas' claims created opposition to the very idea of compensating those formerly considered enemies of the United States. The US Army vigorously defended the official version of Wounded Knee established in 1890–1891, arguing before Congress that hostile and fanatical Ghost Dancers had treacherously attacked the Seventh Cavalry, rendering the Lakotas responsible for the deaths of their own women and children. Representatives from states without significant Indian constituencies had little incentive to support controversial legislation to correct an "ancient wrong." Others, concerned with rising government spending, cited fiscal responsibility in their opposition to the bill. Even congressmen sympathetic to the survivors' cause feared that successful passage of the bill would open the floodgates to claims for other massacres. Although World War II ultimately forced the survivors and their advocates to abandon temporarily the legislation, the preceding decade witnessed a substantial debate over the "legacies" and "liabilities" of the nineteenth-century conquest of the North American West.[5]

Tell the Good White People What Happened at Wounded Knee

In the early 1930s, the survivors laid a foundation for this debate by dictating accounts of Wounded Knee to Pine Ridge Superintendent James H. McGregor. The survivors had previously sought out sympathetic whites such as Eli S. Ricker and retired Lieutenant General Nelson A. Miles who not only recorded and publicized their memories, but also spoke out in favor of their compensation claims. The statements given to McGregor supported the Lakotas' subsequent efforts to claim compensation before Congress later in the decade. The survivors' statements emphasized many of the same themes first addressed by Joseph Horn Cloud, Dewey Beard, and other survivors who previously dictated formal accounts: Big Foot's band was peaceful in 1890, they cooperated with the Seventh Cavalry during the disarmament, and the soldiers had massacred the defenseless Indians. Moreover, the Lakotas' growing awareness of treaty rights in the 1930s provided a new narrative structure for their memories of Wounded Knee.

Other than the Lakotas' advanced age, several factors influenced their decision to commit their memories to paper in the early 1930s. First, in 1928 Congress had authorized a major investigation of claims for horses and other property the US Army had seized during the so-called Great Sioux War of 1876 under the compensation provision in the 1868 Treaty of Fort Laramie. Drafting these "Pony Claims" doubtless reminded the survivors of their previous attempts to obtain compensation for Wounded Knee.[6] Second, the onset of the Great Depression in 1929 further impoverished an already poor people, and the growing awareness of Roosevelt's proposals for using government resources to alleviate suffering likely influenced the survivors' thinking.[7] Finally, in 1931 Nebraska poet laureate John G. Neihardt interviewed Catholic catechist and Lakota holy man Nicholas Black Elk on Pine Ridge. Neihardt was particularly interested in Black Elk's memories of Wounded Knee. Although he was not present when the firing started, the holy man and other Oglalas rescued some of Big Foot's band from the soldiers. The excitement surrounding Neihardt's visit, which included the poet's adoption into the Oglala tribe, likely drew the attention of the Wounded Knee survivors and Superintendent McGregor.[8]

Within a few months of Neihardt's 1931 visit, McGregor began conducting his own research for a book on Wounded Knee.[9] He was a sympathetic non-Native who genuinely sought to understand the event from a Lakota perspective. He would later argue that "about the only thing that has been written [on Wounded Knee], is from the pens of white people, who have often been prejudiced writers and made heroes of the soldiers, and blood-thirsty savages of the Indians. The Sioux have said but little and written less." He believed he had "a duty toward the survivors" to record and disseminate their memories to a broader audience.[10]

McGregor interviewed the survivors during their annual reunions at the Wounded Knee mass grave.[11] At a Memorial Day service held on May 25, 1932, the remnant of Big Foot's band gathered to remember those killed at the site four decades earlier. They sang "America, the Beautiful," prayed, listened to speeches, and decorated the mass grave with flowers. Although they previously had held group meetings at the site—such as a "day of lament" in 1923—this 1932 meeting was later remembered as the first annual survivors' reunion.[12] On this occasion, McGregor interviewed

Afraid of Enemy, a seventy-eight-year-old Lakota from the Cheyenne River Reservation.[13] At another meeting held just under a year later, at least twenty-one individuals—seventeen men and five women—gave statements to McGregor.[14] The youngest survivors were in their late forties in 1933, while the oldest were in their late seventies.[15] Nearly two-thirds were from the Pine Ridge Reservation, although a decent-sized delegation represented the Cheyenne River survivors.[16]

The Lakotas contrasted McGregor favorably with previous interlocutors. Some survivors retained vivid memories of Buffalo Bill's 1913 filming of *The Indian Wars* on Pine Ridge, which brought Wounded Knee to moving pictures.[17] Edward Owl King recalled that "some years ago they had a moving picture taken of this Massacre. The Indians without thinking went ahead and performed in the ways that were directed by some white people, not truthfully but just the way they wanted it presented in pictures. That tells the wrong story. . . [The old men] all agree that the presentation of the Massacre was all wrong."[18] Afraid of Enemy stated that "I want my good friends to tell the good white people what they did to us here at Wounded Knee. We know [McGregor] is our friend and we know that some white people are good friends of the Indians, but most of them do not like us and not have sympathy for us poor Indians."[19] Daniel White Lance opined that prior to McGregor, "there had never been an Agent that has taken [such] interest in us. . . What he has done for us is the same as wiping away our tears," a reference to a Lakota mourning ritual.[20] White Lance, who in the early twentieth century had seen several unsympathetic officials reject the compensation petitions of his brother, Joseph Horn Cloud, spoke from experience.

The survivors were well aware that in white society, the army's contemporary written records carried greater cultural weight than the Lakotas' orally recounted memories. Joseph Black Hair, for example, argued that soldiers "are required to carry on warfare under certain laws and regulations and they know that they must not go beyond these laws and regulations and have to give an account of their actions, therefore their reports must show that they were right and could not be blamed in no way, so they make reports without opposition in their favor." This explained not only why the army had written accounts, but also why those reports took the form they did. The survivors, on the other hand, were "not compelled to make a report, nor to following any legal instruction so they have not on record anywhere an account of what really happened."[21] Nevertheless, Lakotas had found ways to record their memories in dictated accounts, compensation claims, and even a monument at the mass grave. Even when recounting orally, as McGregor observed, they did so in a group setting. This allowed them to substantiate each other's memories, a common verification technique in oral recitation.[22]

As they had in earlier accounts, the survivors defended Big Foot and his band by emphasizing the peaceful nature of their visit, thereby implicitly challenging the army's argument that the Lakotas had been "hostile" in 1890. Nellie Knife argued that "we were going to Pine Ridge to see our relations and Big Foot was to be in a Big Council."[23] James Pipe on Head, Big Foot's grandson, remembered that when they saw the soldiers approaching, "Big Foot told these people to raise the white flag; that means peace. So on a stick they fixed a white flag and they carry it. The old man advised these people that if the soldiers meet them they must not be disturbed, [and] the Indians must not start anything."[24] Dewey Beard, who McGregor portrayed as "well preserved and very active," despite his seventy-seven years, described Major Samuel Whitside's demand for the Lakotas' weapons on December 28, 1890. Big Foot replied that "he was a peaceful man" and that they would willingly surrender their weapons at Pine Ridge. The chief, however, was fearful that "something crooked" would happen and children would be endangered if the disarmament occurred away from the agency.[25]

The Seventh Cavalry responded to the white flag by surrounding the Lakotas, stationing cannons on a nearby hill, and repeating the demand that they surrender their weapons. Dog Chief remembered that "the soldiers just came on like they were going to run over us and then they spread out like they were going to fire on us. . . . Well we had the white flag but the soldiers did not but took the cannon off from the mules and was working at them like they was going to fight."[26] On the night of December 28, Peter Stand recalled hearing a "metallic sound as though the soldiers were moving. . . . The women went for water, came back and reported that the infantry and the cavalry had surrounded us. We didn't know what to think, after hearing all of that, we were kind of a little bit afraid and it bothered us a little through the night."[27] The next morning an interpreter told the warriors to deposit their weapons a short distance away from the women and children, and the soldiers promised that as soon as the guns were surrendered, they would proceed to Pine Ridge.[28] Most of the men placed their guns in a pile, while the soldiers searched some Lakotas individually for hidden weapons.[29] Bertha Kills Close to Lodge remembered that "soldiers came over to where I was and searched the wagon, throwing down our dishes that we had packed in the wagon and took our knives, axes and awls and anything that could be used for a weapon."[30] The cavalrymen also entered tents, pushing women out of the way in the process. Survivor Mary Mousseau remembered that "one white man with a Roman nose seemed to have a whole lot to do with me. Every now and then he felt me around the waist to see if I had any knives. I threw my blanket back and showed them I didn't have anything." Her statement hinted that some soldiers used inappropriate tactics bordering on sexual assault during the search.[31]

The survivors' accounts reflected the divergent narrative traditions developed in the various survivor communities with regard to how the shooting started. Dewey Beard, consistent with ways that he and other Pine Ridge survivors had told the story previously, described troops grabbing a young warrior who was willingly setting his rifle down: "They came on and grabbed the gun that he was going to put down. Right after they spun him around there was the report of a gun, [which] was quite loud. I couldn't say that anybody shot but following that was a crash."[32] In contrast, Cheyenne River Lakotas recalled hearing an officer giving orders that they could not comprehend, followed by the soldiers firing at the warriors.[33] Charley Blue Arm did not recall hearing a gunshot before the soldiers opened fire.[34] Joseph Black Hair argued against "the reports of the soldiers [that] state that we the Indians that participated in this affair fired the first shot, and caused injury." The official version claimed that "all at once [a warrior] pulled out from under his blanket a gun which he kept concealed and with it killed a soldier, [and] for this reason they fired on those that were gathered in the center." Black Hair rejected this explanation, contending that all of the warriors' weapons had been confiscated prior to the soldiers opening fire.[35]

Strikingly, none of the survivors mentioned the Ghost Dance or a medicine man in their accounts. As psychologist Henry Greenspan has shown, survivor accounts of atrocities should not be seen as fixed or stable. Rather, they should be interpreted as fluid and part of the ongoing process of finding the best words and methods to represent the horrors of their experience.[36] The earliest Lakota accounts of Wounded Knee said essentially nothing about the role of Ghost Dance in the lead-up to the killings. Some of these statements, however, acknowledged that a medicine man addressed the young warriors just prior to the outbreak of fighting, although none of the relators could hear what he was saying. As the survivors began dictating extended accounts to sympathetic whites in the early twentieth century, they addressed the Ghost Dance directly. Beard, for example, recognizing that many whites interpreted the dance as a fanatical movement that cultivated hostility toward the United States, represented his family as skeptical Ghost Dancers and Big Foot as peaceful despite his advocacy of the dance. He and other Pine Ridge survivors acknowledged the presence of the medicine man, but insisted that the holy man's actions played no role in the outbreak of shooting.[37] On the other hand, the Cheyenne River survivors omitted the Ghost Dance and the medicine man altogether in their accounts, a tactic that Beard and Horn Cloud partially adopted in their later affidavits.[38] By the 1930s, this was the survivors' dominant narrative approach to Wounded Knee.

For the warriors standing or sitting in the circle, the soldiers' initial volley brought chaos and death. Peter Stand recalled hearing someone yell in Lakota for everyone to hit the ground.[39] Some lost consciousness and fell, awakening later surrounded by slain relatives.[40] Charlie Blue Arm recalled standing by "the truce flag, or white flag, that we had was stuck in the mud. . . . I noticed that all the Indians were lying about dead under the truce flag."[41] Several commented on the smoke from the soldiers' guns that obscured their vision, as they ran blindly into the fog. George Running Hawk recalled: "I became unconscious, lost my mind. I must have been running, not knowing anything, out of my mind. First thing I became conscious like, I was down here at the creek."[42] White Lance, for example, remembered seeing "Big Foot lying down with blood on his forehead and his head kinda to the right side. I never heard that they take advantage of a sick man." Others described flying bullets, their friends falling dead all around them, and seeing bodies piling up.[43]

When the women and children heard the crash of gunfire, they fled for safety. Nellie Knife, who was about twenty years old in 1890, recounted having to leave behind a young girl, Brown Ear Horse, who was shot. Knife described her helplessness as "the wife of One Skunk . . . screamed and cried" after being shot, "but I could not help her as the bullets were flying thick and I wanted to get to a safe place."[44] Frank Sits Poor, who was too young to be called to the circle with the men, remembered "sitting in a teepee and all at once it sounded to me like a crash of lightening as though wire was falling over the teepee." Upon exiting the tent a soldier pointed his gun at him, but Sits Poor remarkably escaped.[45] James Pipe on Head, who was about ten in 1890, recalled seeing his baby sister shot while she was strapped in a cradle on her mother's back.[46] Henry Jackson, who was perhaps six years old at the time of Wounded Knee, carried traumatic memories of his mother being shot in the head: "I have never said anything about this. I didn't like to on account of my mother who was shot right with me and it appears that it just happened this morning; it makes me feel bad."[47]

Some Lakotas escaped the torrent of bullets and found safety in a nearby ravine. Yet the refuge soon turned into a death trap. The survivors recalled that two cannons on the nearby hill rained exploding shells into their hiding place, while soldiers positioned themselves on both sides of the ditch and fired at the huddled people.[48] John Little Finger remembered that "there was a lot of Indians following up the ravine and I was with them, and on each side of this ravine soldiers were shooting down on us. . . Most of [the people hiding] were women and children and, of course, defenseless and helpless; above them the soldiers just got near them and shot these people down."[49] Peter Stand recalled hiding with about sixty Lakotas in the ravine; only eleven came out alive.[50] Little Finger described hearing a voice call out in Lakota that it was safe to come out. When he emerged, he saw soldiers executing survivors. The soldiers "lost their bravery and started to run" when a group of Pine Ridge Lakotas, including Black Elk, arrived at the scene.[51]

James Hi Hawk interpreted the massacre as a grave wrong committed by the United States against the sovereign Lakota nation. "Did not our forefathers and the United States Government," he queried, "say in that most sacred treaty of April 29, 1868 . . . [that] 'From this day forth all wars between the parties to this agreement, shall cease forever'?" He argued that "this Massacre is absolutely a grave injustice and disgraceful act committed against Big Foot's band by the United States Army. It is the most shameful, cowardly and treacherous killing ever staged by [the] United States Government. In my opinion, it [was not] warfare but a cold blooded murder."[52] Hi Hawk's interpretation reflected the increased consciousness of treaties that emerged among Indian activists in the wake of World War I and in the growing number of claims for treaty violations submitted to the Court of Claims in the 1920s.[53] Rooting his memory of Wounded Knee within the historical obligations of the 1868 Treaty of Fort Laramie, Hi Hawk provided a framework for the Lakotas' claim that the United States was legally liable for Wounded Knee.

Pursuing Congressional Compensation

As early as 1903, the survivors determined to seek out "good men" who would advocate for their compensation claims. A succession of these "good white people"—James R. Walker, Eli S. Ricker, Walter Mason Camp, and Melvin R. Gilmore—had corresponded with and recorded the survivors' statements and expressed sympathy for the Lakotas' sufferings at Wounded Knee.[54] But it wasn't until Joseph Horn Cloud and Dewey Beard recruited retired Lieutenant General Nelson A. Miles that the survivors had found a powerful supporter of their claims. Miles's influence only extended so far, however, as the Indian Office was dubious about the survivors' claims.[55] Prior to McGregor, no reservation agent had supported the Lakotas' arguments so

vigorously.[56] Through McGregor's advocacy the survivors convinced South
Dakota Congressman Theodore Werner, Commissioner of Indian Affairs
John Collier, and Acting Secretary of the Interior Charles A. West to support compensation, in spite of the Department of War's manifest opposition
to the proposal.

McGregor's initial inquiry into the feasibility of compensation was met
with skepticism. On April 3, 1933, McGregor asked his friend Joseph Coursey,
an attorney in Rapid City, South Dakota, for his legal opinion. The superintendent argued "that the Indians were gr[i]eviously wronged and some
amends should be made for them even at this late date" and inquired into the
survivors' chances.[57] Coursey's response was pessimistic. He considered the
likelihood of success for such a claim "beyond [his] wildest dreams," claiming
he had a million (unspecified) reasons why it would fail.[58]

McGregor also sought the Indian Office's support. He explained in a
letter to Washington that the Seventh Cavalry had made "an unwarranted
attack upon [the Lakotas] after they were disarmed. . . . I believe that certain
Indians are entitled to have their case presented in legal form with a view of
being properly re-munerated."[59] Recently appointed Commissioner of Indian
Affairs John Collier, however, was doubtful Congress would consider the
proposal. Collier argued that since "the War Department claims that the Big
Foot band was hostile and that this was a battle instead of a massacre," it
was unlikely that the government would compensate those deemed former
enemies of the United States.[60] This reasoning had stymied the survivors' previous claims for compensation. The superintendent persisted in his efforts to
recruit Commissioner Collier, however, explaining in a letter of December
18, 1933:

> I think I hold a different idea of this unfortunate incident to most
> white people, as I have made a special study of it, and it is my belief that
> a very grave and irreparable wrong was done to Big Foot and his band
> of Sioux Indians on December 29, 1890. I have talked to many of the
> survivors, talked to some that are carrying lead yet that was fired into
> them without provocation, and am convinced that these people have a
> just claim against the Government.

McGregor acknowledged that the army would stand by its official explanations, but he was confident that the survivors' statements could prove that
they were not "hostile" on December 29, 1890: "There is an old Indian woman
living in the district, who has a very badly crippled arm caused by a gun-shot

wound on that memorable day. She has gone through life a cripple, yet she did no Government official any wrong." McGregor remained hopeful the Office would support the survivors' claims.[61]

Even without explicit support in Washington, the survivors pushed ahead with their plans. They met on February 24, 1934, to draft a "Justification of a Relief Bill for the Survivors of the Wounded Knee Massacre," a title that reflected the New Deal "relief" jargon of the decade. Following James Hi Hawk's logic, the document framed the massacre as a violation of the first article of the 1868 Treaty of Fort Laramie, which had declared that war between the United States and the Lakota nation would "forever cease." Like many of the survivors' statements to McGregor, the Justification for a Relief Bill omitted discussion of the Ghost Dance, affirmed Big Foot's peaceful mission, described the Lakotas' cooperation with the Seventh Cavalry's demand for their weapons, and represented the troops as slaughtering defenseless men, women, and children: "From the facts of this massacre the US soldiers representing the Government violated the Government's own agreement when they killed Big Foot and his band, and therefore should pay indemnity or some such consideration to the survivors."[62]

With the Justification of a Relief Bill in hand, McGregor approached South Dakota Representative Theodore Werner (D) as a potential sponsor of a bill. In the early twentieth century, the survivors had been essentially on their own during the Indian Office's investigations of Wounded Knee. The prospect of gaining the support of a congressman was beyond their expectations. Yet with the passage of the Indian Citizenship Act in 1924, South Dakota's representatives found it worthwhile to hear their Lakota constituents' concerns. McGregor informed the congressman that Wounded Knee should be considered a massacre, not a battle, and that the survivors had organized in hopes that they "might be paid something for the wrongs they suffered." The superintendent suggested that the Justification of a Relief Bill could be used to convince Congress to right the wrong the Seventh Cavalry had committed in 1890.[63] On October 18, 1934, the congressman informed McGregor that he had read the survivors' statement and that he would introduce a compensation bill.[64]

Encouraged by Werner's response, Cheyenne River denizens James Hi Hawk and Philip Blackmoon, along with Pine Ridge resident Richard Afraid of Hawk, drafted a sample bill on June 20, 1935. The document described Big Foot's band as a group of Lakotas who were guaranteed protection under the Fort Laramie and subsequent treaties. In violation of the treaties, these Lakotas suffered "the inexcusable and terrible disaster of Chief Big Foot and his Band under the hands of the United States Army, December 29, 1890, known as the Wounded Knee Massacre." The bill called for $50,000 for each Lakota killed, including unborn children, as well as $75 per month, retroactive to 1890, for wounded survivors.[65]

Werner, realizing that such a bill would never pass Congress, drafted H.R. 11778, which framed Wounded Knee as a "liability" that the US government was obligated to "liquidate." He drastically lowered the proposed figures to $1,000 per victim, to be paid to the heirs, and $1,000 per wounded survivor (or heir), and submitted the bill on March 12, 1936. Although Werner reduced the compensation to appease non-Natives, his decision to present a bill that would "liquidate the liability of the United States for the massacre of Sioux Indian men, women, and children at Wounded Knee on December 29, 1890," demonstrated that the Lakotas had succeeded in naming the 1890 engagement a massacre in government records and framing the event as a wrong that the government was obligated to correct. Werner's legislation was therefore a significant departure from the responses of previous government officials to the survivors' claims.[66] Furthermore, the bill also showed that the army was losing its power to control how the deaths at Wounded Knee would be defined in government documents.

The War Department, unsurprisingly, opposed the bill. Acting Secretary of War Malin Craig articulated his opposition to Daniel W. Bell, Roosevelt's head of the Bureau of the Budget (precursor to the Office of Management and Budget), perhaps believing that having Bell oppose the bill on budgetary grounds would effectively kill it. Craig quoted liberally from his predecessor Redfield Proctor's analysis of the January 1891 inquiry into Colonel James W. Forsyth's conduct claiming the report contained all of the "pertinent facts" relating to Wounded Knee. Proctor portrayed Big Foot's band as "savage fanatics" and alleged that the Lakotas had not surrendered sincerely.[67] During the disarmament a Ghost Dance medicine man provoked the warriors into attacking the soldiers, who patiently endured heavy fire before fighting back. Proctor contended that the warriors themselves were responsible for the deaths of women and children, since "their first fire was so directed that every shot that did not hit a soldier must have gone through their own village." Furthermore, Proctor argued, "it is impossible to distinguish buck from squaw at a little distance when mounted," thereby excusing any soldier who might have shot and killed a fleeing woman. In addition, Forsyth's officers repeatedly had instructed their men not to shoot noncombatants. Proctor dismissed claims that friendly fire accounted for army casualties, concluding that the soldiers had acted with "coolness, discretion, and forbearance."[68]

Craig also reproduced portions of Major General Nelson A. Miles's 1891 damning critiques of Forsyth, but then ignored them in favor of Major General John M. Schofield's report, which rejected Miles's conclusions.[69] Based on these documents, Craig concluded that since the War Department had already investigated the matter thoroughly, "There appears to be no reason why the surviving Sioux Indians or their next of kin should be reimbursed by the United States Government for the result of an action for which, insofar as the records of the Department show, they were responsible."[70] Craig's negative assessment of the compensation bill showed that, due to the survivors' growing influence, the army was forced to defend the memory of Wounded Knee encoded in reports written in late 1890 and 1891. Budget director Bell, influenced at least in part by Craig's letter, informed the Committee on Indians Affairs that the bill "would not be in accord with the program of the President."[71] In spite of this opposition, Acting Secretary of the Interior Charles W. West supported the bill in June 1936. The Interior Department's approval was necessary before the bill could advance to committee, so West's support was crucial for the legislation's advancement. However, the support came too late to schedule a hearing, as the Seventy-fourth Congress expired on June 20, 1936. With this foundation in place, however, the survivors had reason to be optimistic of the bill's progress in the next session of congress.[72]

Debating the United States' Liability for Wounded Knee

During the fall 1936 elections, Republican journalist Francis H. Case defeated Werner and replaced him as Representative for South Dakota.[73] Despite his differing party affiliation, Case promoted his predecessor's bill with gusto, successfully guiding it through the first several steps of the complicated legislative process during his first year in office. Progress in Washington, however, paralleled discontent in South Dakota. Although the Lakotas understood that monetary reparations could never replace their deceased relatives, the survivors divided over what dollar amount could satisfy the United States' "liability" for Wounded Knee. The division roughly reflected the survivors' geographic separation, as the Pine Ridge Lakotas supported the existing compensation figure of $1,000 per victim, while the Cheyenne River group opposed the bill, arguing that such a figure was an insult to their relatives killed at Wounded Knee.

The Republican Case had opposed the Indian New Deal of the 1930s, on the grounds that the program's support for cultural pluralism and self-government undermined the United States' long-standing assimilation policy. Ironically, however, it was Case's advocacy of assimilation that led him to support the survivors' compensation claims, since he believed that lingering frustrations over past wrongs impeded entry into the mainstream of American society. Guided by this general philosophy, Case introduced multiple bills in Congress to establish the Indian Claims Commission (ultimately created in 1945), which would settle outstanding suits stemming from treaty violations and other past wrongs. He believed this was essential to legitimate the government in the eyes of Native claimants and, in the process, encourage assimilation and good citizenship.[74]

Case reintroduced Werner's bill as H.R. 2535 early in the first session of the Seventy-Fifth Congress.[75] Before the bill could be presented for a vote on the House floor, it would need to pass through several layers of preliminary examination and approval. First, the Department of the Interior needed again to study and endorse the legislation. Then, the House Committee on Indian Affairs would form a subcommittee to hold hearings. After that, the entire Indian Affairs Committee would need to approve it, at which point the bill would go to the House floor. Completing each phase was a time consuming process, with potential obstacles every step of the way.

FIGURE 7.1 Congressman Francis H. Case, ca. 1930s, photographer unknown, P195, General Photo Collection. Photo courtesy of South Dakota State Historical Society.

Although Case successfully maneuvered his bill through the first stages, the survivors themselves became divided over whether to support H.R. 2535 or demand greater monetary recognition from the government for the wrongs of Wounded Knee. On February 12, 1937, James Hi Hawk, a rancher living on the Cheyenne River Reservation who had played a prominent role in developing the survivors' compensation proposals, sent Case a scathing indictment of the Seventh Cavalry's conduct at Wounded Knee and American society's whitewashing of the event. Hi Hawk condemned the soldiers who "cover[ed] up their cowardly killing and murdering" by calling the event a "battle," as well as "teachers and professors [who] teach it in schools [as] 'The Battle of Wounded Knee.'" Interpreting the slaughter through biblical images, the Congregationalist Lakota contended that "God cannot excuse their awful deed," having "heard the voices of the men, women and children blood's crieth [*sic*] unto him from the ground. He will avenge for those poor innocent peace and home loving people that were inhumanely murdered in 1890."[76] Hi Hawk contended that Wounded Knee was a massacre of historic proportions and the United States needed to be held accountable. However, "the relief bill drafted by Mr. Werner was not in harmony with majority of the living survivors. He worded it to suit himself and, merely to pass the bill in order to stick a feather in his hat... We realized that the Werner Relief Bill was rather insufficient in the amount as liquidated against the United States." Once the government offered reasonable compensation, the remaining survivors "will be consoled, and in our infirm ages will have been comforted thru that benefit we have wished and seeked for, in vain." "An entirely new indemnity bill," one that would be acceptable to the survivors, was necessary.[77]

Case responded with surprise, stating to Hi Hawk that "you are the first one who has written me this way about the previous bill not being satisfactory." The congressman had understood that the survivors' attorneys and representatives had drawn up the bill, and that Werner simply introduced what they gave him. An exasperated Case explained that he had resubmitted the bill early in the session in order to get it on track toward passage, but he nonetheless encouraged Hi Hawk and the other survivors to discuss possible changes and, if necessary, even a whole new bill. The representative cautioned, however, that the other members of Congress would likely find Werner's bill—with its lower price tag—more palatable than the survivors' alternative.[78]

Hi Hawk, despite his confident tone, did not speak for all survivors, especially outside of his sphere of influence on the Cheyenne River Reservation. Even as he was writing Case to oppose the legislation, the Pine Ridge group

began choosing delegates to testify in support of Case's bill, ultimately select-
ing Dewey Beard and James Pipe on Head.[79] Beard had long been active
in the survivors' memory politics and had likely given more interviews on
Wounded Knee than any other survivor. Pipe on Head was Big Foot's grandson and served as president of the Pine Ridge survivors' group.[80] In March,
James Brown Dog, a Lakota nonsurvivor, began recording individual claims
in anticipation of the passage of Case's bill. Since Brown Dog interviewed
Cheyenne River survivors, Case had reason to believe that Hi Hawk's influence did not even completely extend over his own reservation community.[81]

In April 1937, Case received good news. The House Committee on
Indian Affairs, expecting a favorable report from the Interior Department,
appointed a subcommittee to examine the bill, the Brown Dog claims, and
ethnographer James Mooney's account of Wounded Knee.[82] Case also hoped
that the Indian Office would approve and fund a Lakota delegation to testify before the subcommittee in Washington, DC.[83] On April 28 the Interior
Department, as predicted, issued a positive report on the bill. Acting Secretary
Charles West based his assent on General Nelson A. Miles's 1917 letter to
Indian Office officials, in which he argued that "the least the Government can
do is to make a suitable recompense to the survivors . . . for the great injustice
which was done them and the serious loss of their relatives and property."[84]
West also quoted Lakota leaders Turning Hawk's and American Horse's 1891
statements before Commissioner of Indian Affairs Thomas J. Morgan and
Mooney's "authoritative historical work," both of which concluded that the
army had committed a massacre. In addition, West cited the Indian Office's
1920 Wounded Knee investigation, which had recommended that Congress
compensate survivors for property lost after the killings.[85] Based on these
sources, West was convinced that Wounded Knee was a "massacre pure and
simple," which "can be viewed as both an injury to the individuals who were
killed or wounded and as an injury to the entire Sioux tribe."[86] April 1937
therefore saw several important milestones for Case's bill.

Simultaneously, however, Hi Hawk asked Case "to disregard all former
Bills" until the survivors reached agreement.[87] In mid-May, Hi Hawk accused
the Pine Ridge survivors of "being in a state of faction" and singled out James
Pipe on Head as someone who "was doing considerable letter writting [sic]
to Washington without the consent or knowledge of most of the Pine Ridge
Survivors." Hi Hawk also complained that many in the Pine Ridge group
continued to support the Werner bill: "Evidently there is a lack of intelligence amongst our people—any average white or Sioux can swayed [sic] them
as he wanted whether or not it was best for the Sioux. That idea seems to

[have] prevailed especially among the Southern group."[88] This geographic division manifested itself in the different names preferred by each group. The Cheyenne River survivors had previously organized as the Big Foot Survivors Association, a name they continued to use throughout the 1930s. The Pine Ridge survivors, however, preferred the Wounded Knee Survivors Association, possibly to emphasize their proximity to the physical location of the killings.[89] Aside from his accusations against Pipe on Head, Hi Hawk also attempted to delegitimize James Brown Dog, arguing that the Cheyenne River survivors had not authorized him to record claims.[90]

On June 5, 1937, Hi Hawk forwarded a substitute bill to Case. While not demanding the $50,000 per victim as did the survivors' earlier proposal, the new legislation presented figures in excess of the $1,000 in the standing bill. It asked for $20,000 for each pregnant Lakota woman killed, $15,000 for wounded Lakotas shot and killed after the fighting ended, and $10,000 for other victims, paid to the heirs. The bill specified $5,000 for wounded survivors and $500 for survivors who escaped Wounded Knee without injuries.[91] Case thanked Hi Hawk for the new bill, but warned that "a large membership of the House" opposed "any Indian legislation. . . . I would like to get everything that you suggest, but what we want and what we can get from Congress may be two different things, as you understand."[92] Although Case was a committed advocate of the survivors' memories of Wounded Knee, he remained skeptical that their ideas of just compensation would find broad support in Congress.

In early July 1937, Case consulted with the Lakota tribal attorney, Ralph Case (no relation), who for a decade and a half had prosecuted the Lakotas' claim to the Black Hills. The attorney demonstrated, in Jeffrey Ostler's language, "a real passion" for his clients' issues, "one grounded in his personal empathy."[93] After reading the substitute bill, Ralph Case recommended postponing a hearing until the survivors came to an agreement, since the current congressional session would end in August. Personally, the attorney had "no illusions about the recommendations. They will not be in legislative form, nor will they in any way be adoptable."[94] Representative Case informed Hi Hawk that they would wait until the following year, explaining that since so much time had passed since 1890, "we would like to have the bill as nearly right as possible."[95] The two Cases likely hoped that they could appease Hi Hawk while convincing the other survivors that H.R. 2535 was the best available option. Case met with survivors on both reservations that fall (the exact date remains unknown), where he recommended against changing his bill, since the Secretary of the Interior had already approved it and altering

it would likely lessen its chances of passing Congress.[96] Survivor Louis Iron
Hawk later explained that the majority of the survivors preferred Case's bill
over Hi Hawk's, since they were aging and fearful of dying before a compensation bill passed.[97]

Help Us to Forget the Whole Wounded Knee Affair

Five years after giving their statements to McGregor, the remnant of Big
Foot's band would finally have their day in the spotlight. Whereas the compensation bill had stalled in the 1936 and 1937 congressional sessions, in 1938
the Lakotas' delegates would defend their people and their memories before
Congress and demand that the government take responsibility for a massacre. Reflecting traditional Lakota notions of conflict resolution, the witnesses
argued that compensation would help the survivors symbolically "forget" the
trauma of Wounded Knee and begin the healing process. Representative
Case sought to make the Lakotas' petition a reality, in spite of stiff opposition from the US Army and fiscal conservatives. The House Committee on
Indian Affairs approved the bill in mid-1940, potentially setting the stage for
a historic debate on the House floor over the United States' lingering liabilities from the nation's violent dispossession of Native peoples. However, as
Congress's attention shifted away from domestic issues toward international
affairs, Case and the Lakotas were left with a small margin of error to pass
the bill.

In early 1938, as the third session of the Seventy-Fifth Congress commenced, the Indian Affairs Committee appointed John R. Murdock
(D-AZ), Bruce Barton (R-NY), and Anthony J. Dimond (D-AK) to consider
Case's bill.[98] Nearly half a century after witnessing the slaughter at Wounded
Knee, James Pipe on Head and Dewey Beard prepared to testify in the seat
of American power. It is noteworthy that Pipe on Head and Beard were
both Pine Ridge survivors, perhaps indicating that Hi Hawk had succeeded
in convincing his fellow Cheyenne River survivors to boycott the bill, or at
least withdraw active support.[99] Pipe on Head's and Beard's testimonies represented the climax of the survivors' half-century efforts to shape the public
memory of Wounded Knee and would serve as the basis for subsequent committee debate over the bill.

The two Cases—Francis and Ralph—provided introductory remarks.
Representative Case discussed Nelson A. Miles's 1917 argument that the
government should recompense the survivors "for the great injustice" they
suffered on December 29, 1890.[100] Attorney Case anticipated common

allegations that he and his legal colleagues had stirred up the Lakotas' memories of Wounded Knee in order to make money: "This particular slaughter of women and children and unarmed men was, to our mind, so outrageous that we would not under any circumstances accept anything in the way of attorney's fees from this Survivors Association. For that reason, we prefer that the record should show that this is one Indian claim that is not fomented nor engendered by attorneys for the tribe, but solely from the people themselves."[101] The attorney then provided an overview of the history of Lakota relations with the United States, with the resulting land loss, treaty violations, and warfare with the US Army. He also suggested that at Wounded Knee, the Seventh Cavalry sought to avenge their fallen commander, Colonel George Armstrong Custer, who was killed at the Little Bighorn in 1876.[102]

Survivor delegate James Pipe on Head followed with an overview of Wounded Knee. Reflecting the narrative conventions then current in the 1930s, Pipe on Head omitted discussion of the Ghost Dance and began instead with Big Foot's use of the white flag to signal his peaceful intentions.[103] Pipe on Head argued that the Minneconjous had "always maintained a friendly relationship with [whites]."[104] To aid his presentation, he displayed two paintings of Wounded Knee he had made with his brother. The first showed the location of the troops and the Lakotas on December 29, 1890, which demonstrated that the arrangement of the soldiers likely caused some friendly fire deaths.[105] The second image showed snow-covered bodies strewn across the ground.[106] Together, they portrayed before and after images of the killing field.[107] He then described the disarmament, the soldiers' initial volley, and Big Foot's death. "After they had stuck up the flag of truce," Pipe on Head explained, "the people shed their blood. It was a case of slaughtering a bunch of defenseless mothers and some babies in the cradle." When the Lakotas sought refuge in a ravine, "the soldiers came up and told them it was all over and to get up. . . . They sat on top of the hill, in good spirit, and the soldiers surrounded them and shot them down again."[108] Pipe on Head concluded by suggesting that passage of the bill would help alleviate suffering and poverty on the reservation.[109]

Dewey Beard likewise emphasized Big Foot's peaceful intentions and the significance of the white flag. He recalled that his people "always had been told that when the white flag was stuck up there would be no trouble, and the people believed in that white flag."[110] After the soldiers had confiscated the Lakotas' weapons, they began firing on the fleeing men, women, and children. Beard himself was shot in the leg. He explained: "At that time my wife and I had a baby 22 days old, and right at the time when the firing started

I missed my wife, and later I found out that she was shot through the breast. The little 22-day-old baby was nursing from the same side where the mother was wounded and the child was choked with blood. A few days afterwards the little boy died."[111] After hobbling away, Beard fell to the ground. The soldiers "knew that I was wounded and helpless, and they came and shot me all over again, in the breast." He saw soldiers shooting other injured people, who likewise could not defend themselves.[112]

Beard saw compensation as appropriate, considering the fact that Lakota young men had fought in World War I for the United States, the same "Government which some 47 years ago shot down their helpless unarmed grandfathers and grandmothers at Wounded Knee Creek."[113] As Paul C. Rosier has argued, "Serving the interests of the United States as soldiers [in World War I] and as champions of its democratic ideals, Native Americans embraced the obligations of this relationship while demanding obligations in return, a mutually reinforcing set of commitments that animated their hybrid patriotism after the war."[114] Beard's language therefore reflected the complex relationship between the United States and indigenous peoples, as the Lakotas affirmed their loyalty and friendship while insisting the government not only accept their counternarrative of Wounded Knee, but also compensate the survivors for the wrong committed there.

Both Beard and Pipe on Head echoed traditional Lakota ways of conflict resolution when they argued that compensation could symbolically help the Lakotas "forget" Wounded Knee and heal the breach between the United States and the Lakota nation.[115] As Vine Deloria Jr. and Clifford M. Lytle have noted, "Criminal problems [such as murder] were resolved with an eye toward restitution, not retribution. . . . The primary consideration was to provide compensation for the victim's relatives and to return the tribe, insofar as it was possible, to the original state of equilibrium."[116] Beard argued that because the army "has done what we call one of the biggest murders, . . . the United States must be ashamed of it, . . . because they never even offered to reimburse us or settle in any way."[117] Beard pleaded with Congress to approve the bill "and help us to forget the whole Wounded Knee affair."[118]

After the hearing, Pipe on Head and Beard returned to Pine Ridge, with a letter from Case outlining for the Survivors Association what they had accomplished. The representative named the subcommittee members, identified the written materials that they had consulted beforehand (including Mooney's writings and Brown Dog's claims), and described how the court reporter recorded the survivors' testimonies in short hand. "I want to compliment you and the other members of your delegation," Case wrote to Pipe on Head, "on the good showing you made, and especially on the way in which your story as an eyewitness supported the evidence given by other testimony." Case also cautioned the survivors that the bill still had a long road to travel before passage. The subcommittee would allow the army to respond to the survivors' charges, and then the entire Committee on Indian Affairs needed to approve the bill. Case would then bring the legislation to the floor, but he warned that "it is very hard to get special Indian money bills through the Congress." If passed by the House, the bill would then have to go to the Senate and later the president, but Case was pleased with their progress.[119]

Case was also happy that the press had, for the most part, covered the hearing in a positive light. Not long after the survivors' arrival in Washington, Commissioner Collier met with them, and newspapers widely reproduced photographs of their meeting.[120] Collier himself published an editorial describing their visit in the April 1938 edition of *Indians at Work*, copies of which Case forwarded to various interested parties.[121] Incidentally, Collier also quoted from the survivors' testimonies in a 1939 speech to defend his Indian New Deal as a payment of the "nation's debt" for crimes like Wounded Knee.[122] *American Weekly*, newspaper magnate William Randolph Heart's illustrated magazine, published an article detailing the hearings on April 24, 1938, which included reproductions of the two images Pipe on Head displayed to the subcommittee.[123] Case purchased and distributed the last one hundred copies of the article, explaining to recipients that *American Weekly* had the largest circulation in the world, with seven million subscribers.[124] To one correspondent he noted that "we have been able to attract a good deal of attention and with the publicity we have received I am sure we have worked up a sentiment for the bill."[125]

On May 12, the subcommittee held another hearing to allow the War Department to respond, with Lieutenant Colonel R. H. Brennan defending the army's conduct at Wounded Knee. His remarks reflected prevailing assumptions among white Americans that they (and their ancestors) were innocent victims of indigenous aggression.[126] Brennan based his argument on army reports produced soon after Wounded Knee, which alleged that Big Foot's band had been "guilty of great treachery" when they fired on the soldiers. The women, furthermore, had concealed weapons during the disarmament, which they later used to attack the soldiers. He argued that it was not in the government's interests to compensate "people who were killed while under arms fighting against the Government." When asked about General Miles's 1917 characterization of Wounded Knee as a "massacre," Brennan replied that Miles was an elderly man in 1917, suggesting that his memory

FIGURE 7.2 From left, Dewey Beard, Commissioner of Indian Affairs John Collier, and James Pipe-on-Head, 1938, photographer unknown, AP380304143. Photo courtesy of Associated Press.

had become confused over the years.[127] Contrary to Brennan's assertion, as early as 1891 Miles had portrayed Wounded Knee as the most "brutal, cold-blooded massacre" in American history.[128] Representative Case challenged Brennan on whether the government should compensate the Lakotas for the deaths of women and children. Knowing that Brennan had dismissed Miles's 1917 letter as unreliable, Case cited army reports and James Mooney's ethnographic work as contemporary evidence of soldiers pursuing and killing noncombatants. Brennan responded that the army disavowed responsibility for the people found dead miles away. In addition, he contended that the troops were unable to distinguish Indian women from men at a distance.[129]

In spite of Brennan's best efforts to defend the army's official explanation for Wounded Knee, the subcommittee was far more concerned with whether granting compensation would set an unwise precedent for subsequent claims. Brennan himself argued that acquiescing to the survivors' demand for reparations would be "a tremendous reflection on the service to say that action that produces losses means a massacre of the other side," and would open the door for challenges to other controversial incidents involving the troops in the Indian Wars and the Philippine-American War.[130] Subcommittee member John R. Murdock argued that there had been numerous Indian massacres in the West. "If we turn back the pages for 50 years," Murdock asked, "and try to deal justly in these cases, will we be opening the door?"[131] Murdock's question likely reflected the position that most Indian nations had legitimate grievances stemming from the United States' conquest of the West, although there was disagreement over how to address their claims in a responsible way. Case responded that Wounded Knee was recent enough to make an exception, suggesting that he believed that some claims should be given priority. Case contended that the recentness of an atrocity mattered. Some massacres happened so long ago that granting redress to descendants, who may or may not have inherited their ancestors' sufferings, made little sense. Although Wounded Knee happened nearly a half-century before, Case explained that "many of these claimants are living today and bear the marks of their wounds."[132]

Subcommittee members wondered if, in fact, other tribes had already pursued compensation for past massacres. George M. Paulus, representing the Indian Office's Claims Section, testified at the hearing that in the 1910s the heirs of Piegan Chief Heavy Runner had in fact petitioned the government to compensate them for the loss of life and property resulting from the 1870 Marias Massacre in Montana Territory.[133] In 1913 Heavy Runner's children filed claims arguing that the cavalry had confused their father's peaceful Piegan band with a "hostile" one. The Piegan survivors convinced some low-level Indian Office bureaucrats and even Oregon Senator Harry Lane to support their claim, resulting in the introduction of a compensation bill to Congress in 1915. However, the Indian Office and the Department of the Interior opposed the bill, arguing that it was essentially impossible at that late date to reconcile the army's contemporary written reports and the survivors' memories.[134] Although the Heavy Runner legislation was never close to becoming law, the fact that another tribe had sought reparation for a massacre confirmed Murdock's suspicion that "dealing justly" with Wounded Knee would "open the door" for similar claims.

The subcommittee was unable to finish its report on the bill before the session expired on June 16, 1938, but an optimistic Case reintroduced the legislation as H.R. 953 in January 1939, early in the Seventy-sixth Congress.[135] Secretary of the Interior Harold L. Ickes wrote a new statement of support for the Interior Department on the new bill, paving the way for renewed consideration by the Indian Affairs Committee.[136] Based on the testimony taken in the 1938 hearings and accompanying written materials, the Committee on Indian Affairs voted to approve the bill with amendments on July 19, 1939. In spite of Ralph Case's assurances that he would not accept a fee for his services, the committee expressly prohibited attorneys from profiting on the settlement. Additionally, the committee attached the amount awarded to wounded survivors to the Veterans Administration's rating scale, depending on the severity of the injury.[137] Despite the army's attempts to block the Wounded Knee bill, which explicitly recognized the United States' liability for the Seventh Cavalry's conduct on December 29, 1890, the legislation had made it out of committee. Swayed by the survivors' and Case's arguments, the committee members also overcame their concerns that successful passage could set a precedent for subsequent claims.

Despite this historic achievement, Case still faced significant obstacles in his efforts to shepherd the bill to passage in the House. Congress had lost its appetite for reform by the late 1930s. Commissioner Collier no longer held legislative influence, and bills favoring Natives had little chance of passage.[138] Case also feared that anti-Indian racism and fiscal conservatism would kill the bill. "Too many members out of the 435 members make fun of all Indian bills and go home and tell their people how much money they have saved," the South Dakota representative noted in a letter to James Pipe on Head, "without considering whether the bill is just or not."[139] Case singled out Missouri Representative John C. Cochran as a significant opponent. Since he represented a state with a relatively small Indian population, Cochran had little incentive to support any legislation that favored Indians. Furthermore, as the chairman of the Committee on Expenditures in Executive Departments (now called the Committee on Oversight and Government Reform), he was especially wary of what he considered wasteful spending. Cochran was alarmed by the rising costs associated with Indian claims in the 1930s. He believed that the government had already spent too much money on Indians and he regularly opposed or tried to limit bills with monetary payments to tribes.[140] Case wrote to Cochran in hopes of convincing the congressman to consider the merits of the Wounded Knee bill, but to no avail.[141]

Case also suspected that many representatives would vote against the bill solely on the US Army's opposition. In January 1939, just as Case was reintroducing the Wounded Knee act, retired Brigadier General E. D. Scott published "Wounded Knee: A Look at the Record" in *The Field Artillery Journal*.[142] Scott, concerned over Pipe on Head's and Beard's 1938 appearance before Congress, decided "to examine the official records of the engagement" to counter the survivors' memories of a massacre. Based on his analysis of the documents compiled by the 1891 court of inquiry, Scott concluded that the Seventh Cavalry had conducted themselves honorably and had earned their Medals of Honor. The retired general assumed that "the sworn evidence of eye-witnesses, obtained on the spot by a tribunal following the cool and impartial procedure prescribed by law and regulation" was far more "accurate" than "tales" recorded later.[143] In contrast, "under the guidance of a Washington lawyer," the Lakota witnesses had not told the truth in their testimonies, although Scott conceded that "they may believe [that] their recollections of what happened forty-seven years ago are accurate."[144] He could not envision a scenario in which the Seventh Cavalry's officers would close ranks in order to defend their commander, and themselves, from charges of incompetency and murder. According to Scott, the contemporaneous written record was accurate and reliable, while the Lakotas, recounting from memory nearly a half century later, were confused at best by the passage of time.

Given these assumptions, it should not be surprising that Scott found in the record a complete vindication of the Seventh Cavalry and sufficient evidence to refute the survivors' arguments. He dismissed as unsubstantiated rumors claims that the cavalrymen had been drunk or that avenging Custer was their motivation.[145] The retired general ignored Miles's arguments that Forsyth had disobeyed orders and that the colonel's troop arrangement had resulted in friendly fire deaths. Inexplicably, given his insistence on the reliability of the record, Scott ignored testimonies given before the court of inquiry that confirmed Miles's contentions.[146] Instead, he repeated the justifications of the killings embedded in the record. He argued that the warriors' "attack on the troops," sparked by "a strange religious hallucination" was as "treacherous as any in the history of Indian warfare."[147] When firing at the troops, the Lakota men's bullets overreached and killed their own women and children. If any soldiers did kill noncombatants, it was only because Lakota men and women dressed so similarly that it was impossible to distinguish them. Some Lakota women even shot at the cavalrymen, forcing them to return fire.[148] With the exception of one isolated instance of a "hysterical recruit" shooting an injured Lakota, Scott concluded that "there [was] nothing to conceal or apologize for in the Wounded Knee battle."[149] Rather than compensating the Lakotas, who did "not come into court with clean hands," Congress should be helping the "bereaved white families" of the soldiers who lost their lives.[150]

While Scott was composing his article, Case obtained a copy of the court of inquiry record for his own analysis. Through correspondence with historian Frank McNitt, the representative learned that the army had withheld the record from the public.[151] Only at the request of Will Rogers (the politician, not the humorist), who was Chairman of the House Committee on Indian Affairs, did the War Department release the report.[152] In marked contrast to Scott, Case found evidence in the army's own papers that the deaths of both the Indians and the soldiers resulted from the cavalrymen having disobeyed Major General Nelson A. Miles's orders. The representative was optimistic that the new information "that had been kept in the secret files of the War Department all these years" would convince reluctant congressmen to support the bill.[153]

Ultimately, with the United States making preparations to enter World War II, Case and the survivors found their options severely limited as the Seventy-sixth Congress neared its end. With the House concentrating nearly all legislation on national defense, the Committee on Indian Affairs had few chances to present its bills for consideration by the entire body.[154] Case had one last wild card: the Consent Calendar. This option would have allowed the bill to come to the floor, but passage required unanimous support. Despite Case's efforts to resolve concerns about the bill, when it came up for a vote on August 5, 1940, three opponents voted "no," and the bill died with the session.[155]

WITH THE ONSET of World War II, Congress funneled nearly all available money to the war effort and essential services. Case and the survivors decided it would be better to wait until later to reintroduce the compensation legislation.[156] It remains unclear whether Case's bill, had it reached the House floor for a regular vote, would have passed. Equally uncertain is whether the Senate would have passed the legislation or whether Roosevelt would have signed it. Yet the survivors' pursuit of compensation in the 1930s remains significant for what it reveals about the United States' capacity to acknowledge lingering liabilities stemming from the nineteenth-century violent dispossession of Native peoples. To strengthen their argument, the Lakotas reframed Wounded Knee as a violation of the 1868 Treaty of Fort Laramie. The environment of the 1930s allowed the survivors to recruit several powerful "good white people"—McGregor, Werner, Case, Collier, West, and the members of the House Committee on Indian Affairs—who advocated passage of the legislation. The fact that a bill that explicitly recognized the United States' liability for Wounded Knee got out of committee was a historic achievement, regardless of the legislation's ultimate fate.

Conclusion

SURVIVING WOUNDED KNEE

ON NOVEMBER 2, 1955, Dewey Beard passed away quietly in his sleep on the Pine Ridge Reservation, just a few years shy of his one hundredth birthday.[1] He was well enough known at the time of his death that the *New York Times* published his obituary, describing him as "the last surviving Sioux Indian who fought at the Little Big Horn, better known as Custer's Last Stand." The paper also reported that Beard had survived Wounded Knee, "one of the last engagements between whites and Indians in 1890. His family was wiped out and Mr. Beard was wounded."[2] However, the nation's newspaper of record failed to mention the third major struggle for which he had dedicated much of his life: seeking justice for Wounded Knee. Like many victims of traumatic events, the memories of Wounded Knee surfaced on a regular basis during his subsequent years. More than a quarter century after Wounded Knee, Beard stated: "Every time I recall this history, the matter is so vivid in my mind, that it seems to me as though it had happened just yesterday."[3] In 1938, Beard uttered a simple yet profound statement to a congressman asking him about Wounded Knee: "If I was killed at that time [in 1890], I would not be here testifying for my people."[4] For more than half a century, Beard had been a survivor, testifying to anyone who would listen of the sufferings inflicted upon his people at Wounded Knee.

Beard's engagement with the politics of memory played out on a memorial terrain already claimed by the Seventh Cavalry and the Department of War. Immediately after the event, reporters and Colonel James W. Forsyth attempted to control how Wounded Knee would be remembered by publishing articles and writing official reports that blamed the event on "fanatical" Ghost Dancers who attacked unsuspecting troops. Denying this narrative,

Major General Nelson A. Miles launched a full-scale effort to hold Forsyth accountable both for friendly fire deaths of soldiers and the killings of Lakota noncombatants. Miles was representative of several sympathetic whites who in subsequent decades staked a counterclaim to Wounded Knee, arguing that it was a horrific massacre that was a stain on the American nation, rendering the 1890 event a contested site of memory. Forsyth's allies succeeded in steering the January 1891 court of inquiry toward a favorable outcome for the commander of the Seventh Cavalry. Instead of branding Wounded Knee a massacre—which, for Miles, was an accurate descriptor—the witnesses in the inquiry cast the event as the result of "savage," "fanatical," and "hostile" Ghost Dancers who attacked the unsuspecting Seventh Cavalry. The testimonies became the "official record" of Wounded Knee, preserved in government archives and an authoritative source for subsequent discussions of the event.

Following his vindication in early 1891, Forsyth and his defenders sought to incorporate Wounded Knee into the memorial traditions of the Seventh Cavalry and, more broadly, the nation. Upon his return to the cavalry's home at Fort Riley, Kansas, Forsyth publicly commemorated the "Battle of Wounded Knee." Twenty of his men would receive the coveted Medal of Honor for gallantry in the engagement. In 1893, the cavalry erected a towering obelisk at Fort Riley to honor the soldiers who died on December 29, 1890. By 1893 Wounded Knee had achieved the status of the battle that had ended four centuries of "race war" for the continent, marking the moment that civilization had triumphed over savagery. Twenty years later, William Buffalo Bill Cody produced *The Indian Wars*, an epic film that reenacted the "Ghost Dance War of 1890" that culminated at Wounded Knee.

Dewey Beard and his brothers, Joseph Horn Cloud and Daniel White Lance, were well aware of the broad contours of the official memory of Wounded Knee. The survivors claimed a potent stake in how Wounded Knee would be remembered—and contested—as a site of memory in America. In 1896, they drafted the first compensation claims for property losses associated with what they called the "Wounded Knee Massacre." Having observed that the government compensated "friendly" Lakotas for their losses in 1890—while excluding the survivors of Big Foot's band on the grounds that they had been "hostile" Ghost Dancers—the brothers decided to test the system with their claims. Although the Indian Office essentially ignored the 1896 claims, they started what would become for Beard a decades-long engagement with the politics of memory over Wounded Knee. In 1903, Horn Cloud, Beard, and others raised sufficient funds to erect a monument on the hill at the mass grave where their family members were buried. Raising this obelisk "in memory of the Chief Big Foot Massacre" ensured that the site would be interpreted as a massacre—rather than a battle—in the years and decades that would follow.

In 1904, Horn Cloud and Beard renewed their pursuit of justice in the form of compensation by resubmitting their claims, which resulted in an official government inquiry into Wounded Knee in 1904 and 1905. Ultimately, the Indian Office officials assigned to evaluate the survivors' claims would maintain the government's stance that Big Foot's band had been hostile in 1890 and therefore ineligible for compensation. With their claim stalled, Beard and Horn Cloud would instead channel their energies into producing accounts of Wounded Knee with white ethnologists and amateur historians of the Indian Wars. To these individuals, the Lakotas insisted that Big Foot was a peaceful chief, that participation in the Ghost Dance had not rendered them hostile toward the government, and that the soldiers had used an errant shot from a deaf Lakotas' gun as justification for slaughtering the band. Some of these sympathetic whites, such as Eli S. Ricker, went beyond simply recording the Lakotas' statements by incorporating the survivors' perspectives into broader interpretations of the European settlement of the continent. Others, like Melvin R. Gilmore, sought to publicize the survivors' memories and demanded that the government acknowledge the truth about Wounded Knee.

Beard and Horn Cloud likely watched with interest as the survivor community living on the Cheyenne River Reservation submitted property claims in 1909 for their possessions lost during the 1890 crisis, which resulted in another official investigation in 1910. However, as in the earlier inquiry, the government maintained that Big Foot's band had been hostile in 1890, and therefore ineligible for compensation. In 1917 and again in 1920, Beard and Horn Cloud met with senior Indian Office bureaucrats in Washington, DC, when they petitioned the government to provide rations to the survivors of Wounded Knee. In both years, the survivors recruited the assistance of retired general Nelson A. Miles, who obliged by lobbying the Commissioner of Indian Affairs and by arguing that the government had an obligation to "atone" for the massacre at Wounded Knee. Miles's support led to two official inquiries, with the 1920 investigation producing the most detailed catalog of the survivor community's human and property losses ever made. The record created from this inquiry was based largely on the list drafted by Horn Cloud and Beard of every known living survivor and heirs of victims. Inspector James McLaughlin, who conducted the investigation, stated that Beard bore "a good reputation" and that the survivor "impressed [him] very favorably."

The 1920 investigation resulted in the only recommendation for compensation from a government official during the three decades after Wounded Knee. After an extended discussion of the fanatical, savage, and hostile disposition of Big Foot's band in 1890, McLaughlin stated that the government might consider compensating the Lakotas $20,000 for property lost *after* the massacre, when the military permitted relic hunters to pick the field clean. Ultimately, even this paltry recommendation received little consideration in Washington. With Horn Cloud's death in 1920 Beard lost not only a brother, but also his principal ally in seeking compensation.

Beard must have been amazed by the dramatic changes that occurred in American society during the 1930s. The Great Depression and the New Deal had radically shifted how the federal government approached its Indian charges. Beard found that the Bureau of Indian Affairs (the new name for the Indian Office) had significantly changed its stance toward Wounded Knee. Rather than discouraging the survivors' claims, Pine Ridge Superintendent James McGregor became one of the Lakotas' foremost advocates. Commissioner of Indian Affairs John Collier departed from his predecessors' skepticism of the survivors' memories and endorsed their renewed pursuit of compensation. Secretary of the Interior Harold Ickes likewise signed off on the Lakotas' claims, citing Miles's previous support for government action. Beard must have found the transformation of the Indian Bureau's position on Wounded Knee breathtaking.

In addition, in the 1930s Congress became a viable avenue for Beard and the remaining survivors to pursue compensation through legislation. In 1924 Congress had granted citizenship to all Native people born in the United States, which turned Indians into constituents to be courted by politicians. South Dakota Congressman Francis Case introduced legislation intended to compensate the survivors and heirs $1,000 for every Lakota killed or wounded at Wounded Knee. Beard traveled to Washington in 1938 to testify before the nation's governing body about the murders that occurred on December 29, 1890, and to plead with the government to help him "forget" the wrong committed by granting compensation. His testimony demonstrated how traditional Lakota approaches to conflict resolution continued to frame how Beard and other survivors saw their demands for compensation and justice. Based in part on Beard's 1938 statement, the House Committee on Indian Affairs reported favorably on Case's bill in 1940, in spite of strong opposition from the War Department, which held firmly to the accuracy of its official records created in 1890 and 1891. However, anti-Indian racism and fiscal conservatism combined to kill the bill before it was given a full hearing on the House's floor. With the onset of World War II, the survivors decided to withdraw the bill until another opening appeared.

Unfortunately, another window would not come, at least in Beard's lifetime. Case hoped the new Indian Claims Commission (ICC), which had been established in 1945 specifically to assess Indian claims, would accept the survivors' claim.[5] However, the ICC repeatedly barred the survivors on the grounds that they were not a recognizable group according to the commission's definition, which generally meant a federally acknowledged tribe.[6] In 1976, during the United States' bicentennial, the survivors' descendants would return to Congress, and although hearings were held on the Lakotas' compensation legislation, the bill would not make it out of committee.[7] Beard's great-granddaughter, Marie Not Help Him, embodied his lasting legacy by testifying before Congress in 1990 in anticipation of the centennial of the killings. She explained that early in the twentieth century, Beard had sought compensation from the government for his "loss of property, of life, and for injuries sustained," even visiting the nation's capital at his own expense to seek justice.[8] She concluded that "as he has mourned, I will too—until we are given a sincere apology, a fitting memorial and monument and compensation for the losses suffered by the people."[9] Congress did pass a resolution expressing the government's "deep regret" for the Lakotas' human and property losses a century before, but the word "apology" was intentionally omitted from the resolution so as to undercut the survivors' compensation claim. The "regret" resolution was used to promote a national memorial at Wounded Knee, which came close to becoming a reality in 1995, but was ultimately defeated by opposition within the Lakota community.[10]

Beard had dedicated his life as a survivor to testify to what had happened at Wounded Knee, an obligation he no doubt felt toward his wife, newborn son, mother, father, brothers, niece, and other relatives whose lives had been claimed in that massacre. He also felt an obligation to the dozens of survivors who struggled to articulate in words the trauma that had shattered their lives on December 29, 1890. Although Beard never learned to speak or write English, he nevertheless found ways to speak Lakota to individuals who heard, translated, and recorded his words on paper, a medium that could share a form of his memories that could influence others who never met or spoke with him.

And what an impact his accounts of Wounded Knee have had. Beard's statement to James R. Walker was published in 1906, which caught the attention of Eli S. Ricker, who in turn conducted a multi-part interview with Beard in 1907 that produced the longest and most detailed account of the massacre ever recorded from a Lakota survivor's perspective. Although Ricker's interview with Beard was not published during his lifetime, the account has been published three separate times in the second half of the twentieth century and served as a key source for subsequent historical works. Melvin R. Gilmore interviewed Beard in 1913 and subsequently published a transcription of the translated account, which was then republished by the Society of American Indians in 1917. In addition, the Indian Office investigations of Wounded Knee recorded and preserved multiple statements by Beard prior to 1920.

Beard's 1933 statement to James McGregor has probably had the largest circulation of any of the survivor's many accounts. In 1940, McGregor published *The Wounded Knee Massacre from the Viewpoint of the Sioux*. In the short book the retired Pine Ridge Superintendent narrated Lakota history, describing Big Foot's pre-1890 reputation as a peacemaker, the arrival of the Ghost Dance on the Lakota reservations, and the events leading to Wounded Knee. The book explicitly critiqued the army's official explanations, and, despite McGregor's own paternalistic assumptions, sought to represent the Lakotas' perspectives faithfully. Most significantly, the former superintendent included transcriptions of his interviews with the survivors. In subsequent years, the book was reprinted at least sixteen times, dramatically expanding the circulation of their recorded memories and shaping how Wounded Knee would later be remembered.[11]

McGregor's book and its accompanying survivor testimonies particularly impacted writer and historian Dee Brown, whose *Bury My Heart at Wounded Knee: An Indian History of the American West* provided a synthesis of US–Indian relations from 1860 to 1890 for nonspecialists. Rather than relate the familiar tale of heroic white settlers and soldiers "winning the West," Brown recounted "an incredible era of violence, greed, audacity, sentimentality, undirected exuberance, and an almost reverential attitude toward the ideal of personal freedom for those who already had it."[12] In short, it presented "a narrative of the conquest of the American West as the victims experienced it."[13] Brown based his Wounded Knee chapter almost entirely on the survivors' statements published by McGregor, in particular Beard's account.[14] He dismissed the army's interpretation and privileged the survivors' memories of a massacre.

Many Americans found Brown's book captivating, as demonstrated by the work's residence on the *New York Times'* bestseller list for fifty-seven weeks after its publication.[15] Brown was not the first writer to negatively reinterpret the United States' history with Native peoples, but he did have the good fortune to publish his revisionist perspective when a substantial number of

Americans were ready to embrace it. Brown's readers were attracted to *Bury My Heart at Wounded Knee* because of their growing sensitivity to the United States' history of racial injustice and environmental degradation. Many saw parallels between the United States' Indian Wars and the Vietnam War, seeing both as racially driven conflicts that involved American imperialism and massacres. In addition, the book illuminated the history behind Native American activists' demands that the government honor nineteenth-century treaties with Indian nations.[16] As its culminating chapter was based on the Lakotas' statements to McGregor, *Bury My Heart at Wounded Knee* brought Beard's, Louise Weasel Bear's, and other survivors' recorded memories to a national and international audience.[17]

Aside from dictating their memories of sympathetic whites, Beard and the survivors created memorial traditions at Wounded Knee that ensured it would become a place of memory that was recognizable even outside of the Lakota community. Because Wounded Knee occurred within the boundaries of the Pine Ridge Reservation, the survivors had some control over how the site would be interpreted. Joseph Horn Cloud's monument explicitly identified the mass grave as the resting place of innocent men, women, and children massacred by the Seventh Cavalry. The survivors' regular commemorations at the site further signaled to others the importance of the place. Native intellectual Vine Deloria, for example, later recalled that "the most memorable event of [his] early childhood [in the 1930s] was visiting Wounded Knee." He also remembered that the Lakotas revered the survivors, including, undoubtedly, Dewey Beard.[18]

When the American Indian Movement occupied Wounded Knee in 1973, the place therefore already held a deep memorial significance among the Lakotas and others who visited. In retrospect, the Pine Ridge Agent proved prophetic in 1897 when he claimed, "the presence of a monument dedicated to Big Foot's band [would] be a constant menace to the peace of the reservation."[19] Beginning in the late 1960s, Indian activists had made it a practice of occupying significant sites in order to attract media attention, and Wounded Knee would be one, along with Alcatraz Island, Plymouth Rock, Mount Rushmore, and the Bureau of Indian Affairs building in Washington, DC. The American Indian Movement (AIM) had come to Pine Ridge to support a local protest against President Dick Wilson of the Oglala Tribal Council, who was accused of harassing and oppressing traditional tribal members.[20] Drawing on the potent symbolism of Wounded Knee, accrued after years of survivor commemorations and embodied in the survivors' monument, AIM occupied the site for seventy-one days, exchanging gunfire with federal agents

FIGURE 8.1 American Indian Movement Occupation of Wounded Knee, 1973, photographer unknown, AP7303270941. Photo courtesy of Associated Press.

while drawing on imagery of the 1890 massacre to heighten the stakes of the confrontation.[21]

Bury My Heart at Wounded Knee and AIM's occupation of the site thus built upon the Lakota survivors' prolonged engagement in the politics of memory. For decades, the survivors had testified to the suffering inflicted upon their people at Wounded Knee. In accordance with traditional Lakota values, they asked the government to compensate them for the wrongs committed against them that violated solemn treaty obligations. Ultimately, the survivors demonstrated that the Indian Wars had not ended in 1890; rather, the venue of struggle had changed from the battlefield to the landscape of memory. Although the United States never compensated the Lakotas for their losses at Wounded Knee, the survivors' unyielding pursuit of justice left an imprint on the American memorial landscape that continues to reverberate one hundred and twenty-five years later.[22]

Notes

INTRODUCTION

1. Dee Brown, *Bury My Heart at Wounded Knee: An Indian History of the American West* (1970; repr., New York: Henry Holt, 2000), xviii.
2. Brown, *Bury My Heart at Wounded Knee*, xvii.
3. Sherry L. Smith, *Hippies, Indians, and the Fight for Red Power* (Oxford: Oxford University Press, 2012), 149–50.
4. Paul Chaat Smith and Robert Allen Warrior, *Like a Hurricane: The Indian Movement from Alcatraz to Wounded Knee* (New York: New Press, 1996), chaps. 9–12; Elizabeth Rich, "Remember Wounded Knee: AIM's Use of Metonymy in 21st Century Protest," *College Literature* 31, no. 3 (Summer 2004): 70–91; Akim Reinhardt, *Ruling Pine Ridge: Oglala Lakota Politics from the IRA to Wounded Knee* (Lubbock: Texas Tech University Press, 2007).
5. See Robert M. Utley, *Last Days of the Sioux Nation*. 2nd ed. (New Haven, CT: Yale University Press, 2004); Jeffrey Ostler, *The Plains Sioux and US Colonialism from Lewis and Clark to Wounded Knee*, Studies in North American Indian History (Cambridge: Cambridge University Press, 2004); Rani-Henrik Andersson, *The Lakota Ghost Dance of 1890* (Lincoln: University of Nebraska Press, 2008); Heather Cox Richardson, *Wounded Knee: Party Politics and the Road to an American Massacre* (New York: Basic Books, 2010); Jerome A. Greene, *American Carnage: Wounded Knee, 1890* (Norman: University of Oklahoma Press, 2014).
6. See Maurice Halbwachs, *On Collective Memory*, ed. and trans. Lewis A. Coser, the Heritage of Sociology (Chicago: University of Chicago Press, 1992); Maurice Halbwachs, *The Collective Memory*, trans. Francis J. Ditter Jr. and Vida Yazdi Ditter (New York: Harper Colophon Books, 1980); see also Geoffrey Cubitt, *History and Memory*, Historical Approaches (Manchester: Manchester University Press, 2007), 26–65; and Jeffrey K. Olick, Vered Vinitzky-Serouissi, and Daniel Levy, eds., *The Collective Memory Reader* (Oxford: Oxford University Press, 2011), 16–29.

7. Jeffrey K. Olick and Joyce Robbins, "Social Memory Studies: From 'Collective Memory' to the Historical Sociology of Mnemonic Practices," *Annual Review of Sociology* 24 (1998): 122–26.

8. Benedict Anderson, *Imagined Communities: Reflections on the Origins and Spread of Nationalism.* 2nd ed. (New York: Verso, 1991).

9. Pierre Nora, "General Introduction: Between Memory and History," in *Realms of Memory: Rethinking the French Past*, dir. Pierre Nora, vol. 1, *Conflicts and Divisions*, ed. Laurence D. Kritzman, trans. Arthur Goldhammer (New York: Columbia University Press, 1996), 1–23. Pierre Nora, "General Introduction," in *Rethinking France: Les Lieux de Memoire*, dir. Pierre Nora, vol. 1, *The State*, trans. Richard C. Holbrook (Chicago: University of Chicago Press, 2001), vii–xxxiii.

10. Michael Kammen, *Mystic Chords of Memory: The Transformation of Tradition in American Culture* (New York: Knopf, 1991); John Bodnar, *Remaking America: Public Memory, Commemoration, and Patriotism in the Twentieth Century* (Princeton, NJ: Princeton University Press, 1992); David W. Blight, *Race and Reunion: The Civil War in American Memory* (Cambridge, MA: Belknap Press of Harvard University Press, 2001); Cubitt, *History and Memory*, 175–76, 222–23; Karl Jacoby, *Shadows at Dawn: A Borderlands Massacre and the Violence of History* (New York: Penguin, 2008).

11. Michel Foucault, *Language, Counter-Memory, Practice: Selected Essays and Interviews*, ed. Donald F. Bouchard, trans. Donald F. Bouchard and Sherry Simon (Ithaca, NY: Cornell University Press, 1977); Popular Memory Group, "Popular Memory: Theory, Politics, Method," in *Making Histories: Studies in History-Writing and Politics*, ed. Richard Johnson, Gregor McLennan, Bill Schwarz, and David Sutton (Minneapolis: University of Minnesota Press, 1982), 205–52; Michael Kammen, "Commemoration and Contestation in American Culture: Historical Perspectives," *Amerikastudien/American Studies* 48, no. 2 (2003): 185–205; Indra Sengupta, ed., *Memory, History, and Colonialism: Engaging with Pierre Nora in Colonial and Postcolonial Contexts* (London: German Historical Institute London, 2009); Linda Tuhiwai Smith, *Decolonizing Methodologies: Research and Indigenous Peoples*, 2nd ed. (London: Zed Books, 2012), 24–25, 34–36; Ari Kelman, *A Misplaced Massacre: Struggling Over the Memory of Sand Creek* (Cambridge, MA: Harvard University Press, 2013).

12. See Frederick E. Hoxie, *A Final Promise: The Campaign to Assimilate the Indians, 1880–1920* (Lincoln: University of Nebraska Press, 1984).

13. Frederick E. Hoxie, ed., *Talking Back to Civilization: Indian Voices from the Progressive Era*, the Bedford Series in History and Culture (Boston: Bedford/St. Martin's, 2001); Kevin Bruyneel, *The Third Space of Sovereignty: The Postcolonial Politics of US–Indigenous Relations* (Minneapolis: University of Minnesota Press, 2007); Donald L. Fixico, *Indian Resilience and Resistance: Indigenous Nations in the Modern American West*, the Modern American West (Tucson: University of Arizona Press, 2013).

14. See H. D. Rosenthal, *Their Day in Court: A History of the Indian Claims Commission* (New York: Garland Publishing, 1990); Christian W. McMillen, *Making Indian Law: The Hualapai Land Case and the Birth of Ethnohistory* (New Haven, CT: Yale University Press, 2007); Frederick E. Hoxie, *This Indian Country: American Indian Activists and the Place They Made* (New York: Penguin, 2012), chap. 5; David E. Wilkins, *Hollow Justice: A History of Indigenous Claims in the United States*, the Henry Roe Cloud Series on American Indians and Modernity (New Haven, CT: Yale University Press, 2013).

CHAPTER 1

1. Craig Howe, "Lewis and Clark among the Tetons: Smoking out What Really Happened," *Wicazo Sa Review* 19, no. 1, American Indian Encounters with Lewis and Clark (Spring 2004): 47–72, quotes on 48.
2. Howe, "Lewis and Clark among the Tetons."
3. William Clark, journal, September 25–26, 1804; John Ordway, journal, September 26, 1804, *The Journals of the Lewis and Clark Expedition Online*, http://lewisandclarkjournals.unl.edu, accessed November 29, 2014.
4. Clark, journal, September 25, 27–28, 1804; Joseph Whitehouse, journal, September 27–28, 1804, *The Journals of the Lewis and Clark Expedition Online*. On Native treachery in European discourse, see Gary B. Nash, "The Image of the Indian in the Southern Colonial Mind," in *The Wild Man Within: An Image in Western Thought from the Renaissance to Romanticism*, eds. Edward Dudley and Maximilian E. Novak (London: Henry M. Snyder and Co., 1972), 65; Boyd D. Cothran, *Remembering the Modoc War: Redemptive Violence and the Making of American Innocence* (Chapel Hill: University of North Carolina Press, 2014), 29–75; but contrast Karen Ordahl Kupperman, "English Perceptions of Treachery, 1583–1640: The Case of the American 'Savages,'" *The Historical Journal* 20, no. 2 (June 1977): 263–87.
5. On the notion of race war, see Richard Slotkin, *The Fatal Environment: The Myth of the Frontier in the Age of Industrialization, 1800–1860* (1985; repr., Norman: University of Oklahoma Press, 1998), 228–29.
6. Michael Witgen, *An Infinity of Nations: How the Native New World Shaped Early North America*. Early American Studies (Philadelphia: University of Pennsylvania Press), 164–65.
7. Colin Calloway, *One Vast Winter Count: The Native American West before Lewis and Clark*. History of the American West (Lincoln: University of Nebraska Press, 2003), 213–15, 241–42, 263; Sophie White, *Wild Frenchmen and Frenchified Indians: Material Culture and Race in Colonial Louisiana*. Early American Studies (Philadelphia: University of Pennsylvania Press, 2014).
8. Ostler, *The Plains Sioux and U.S. Colonialism*, 21–23; Jerome A. Greene, *American Carnage: Wounded Knee, 1890* (Norman: University of Oklahoma Press, 2014), 9–10; Richard White, "The Winning of the West: The Expansion

of the Western Sioux in the Eighteenth and Nineteenth Centuries," *Journal of American History* 65, no. 2 (September 1978): 319–43; Pekka Hämäläinen, "The Rise and Fall of Plains Horse Cultures," *Journal of American History* 90, no. 3 (December 2003): 8333–62.

9. Elizabeth A. Fenn, *Encounters at the Heart of the World: A History of the Mandan People* (New York: Hill and Wang, 2014).

10. Quoted in David Freeman Hawke, *Those Tremendous Mountains: The Story of the Lewis and Clark Expedition* (New York: Norton, 1980), 75.

11. Ostler, *The Plains Sioux and U.S. Colonialism*, 19, 36–38; Greene, *American Carnage*, 11.

12. Ostler, *The Plains Sioux and U.S. Colonialism*, 40–58; Greene, *American Carnage*, 13–16.

13. Ostler, *The Plains Sioux and U.S. Colonialism*, 58–84; Greene, *American Carnage*, 17–21; Joy S. Kasson, *Buffalo Bill's Wild West: Celebrity, Memory, and Popular History* (New York: Hill and Wang, 2000).

14. Patrick Wolfe, "Settler Colonialism and the Elimination of the Native," *Journal of Genocide Research* 8, no. 4 (December 2006): 387–409.

15. Patrick Wolfe, "After the Frontier: Separation and Absorption in US Indian Policy," *Settler Colonial Studies* 1, no. 1 (2011): 13–14.

16. See Frederick E. Hoxie, *A Final Promise: The Campaign to Assimilate the Indians, 1880–1920* (Lincoln: University of Nebraska Press, 1984).

17. Ostler, *The Plains Sioux and U.S. Colonialism*, 109–48. Jeffrey D. Means, "'Indians Shall Do Things in Common': Oglala Lakota Identity and Cattle-raising on the Pine Ridge Reservation," *Montana: The Magazine of Western History* 61, no. 3 (Autumn 2011): 3–21; Greene, *American Carnage*, 27–28.

18. Ostler, *The Plains Sioux and U.S. Colonialism*, 149–68; David Wallace Adams, *Education for Extinction: American Indians and the Boarding School Experience, 1875–1928* (Lawrence: University Press of Kansas, 1995); Frederick E. Hoxie, "From Prison to Homeland: The Cheyenne River Indian Reservation before WWI," *South Dakota History* 10, no. 1 (Winter 1979): 1–24; Donald L. Fixico, *Indian Resilience and Rebuilding: Indigenous Nations in the Modern American West*, The Modern American West (Tucson: University of Arizona Press, 2013), 46–69.

19. Todd M. Kerstetter, *God's Country, Uncle Sam's Land: Faith and Conflict in the American West* (Urbana: University of Illinois Press, 2006), 84–87; Ostler, *The Plains Sioux and U.S. Colonialism*, 169–93.

20. Ostler, *The Plains Sioux and U.S. Colonialism*, 194–216.

21. Ostler, *The Plains Sioux and U.S. Colonialism*, 217–42; Hoxie, *A Final Promise*, 41–82; Greene, *American Carnage*, 30–53.

22. Ostler, *The Plains Sioux and U.S. Colonialism*, 7. Emphasis in the original.

23. Kerstetter, *God's Country, Uncle Sam's Land*, 88, 90–91; Rani-Henrik Andersson, *The Lakota Ghost Dance of 1890* (Lincoln: University of Nebraska Press, 2008), 31–38.

24. Kerstetter, *God's Country, Uncle Sam's Land*, 82–83; Ostler, *The Plains Sioux and U.S. Colonialism*, 243–63; *New Lakota Dictionary*, 611; Greene, *American Carnage*, 65–71.

25. Dominique Colas, *Civil Society and Fanaticism: Conjoined Histories*, trans. Amy Jacobs. Mestizo Spaces/Espaces Métissés (Redwood City, CA: Stanford University Press, 1997).

26. Susan Juster, *Doomsayers: Anglo-American Prophecy in the Age of Revolution*. Early American Studies (Philadelphia: University of Pennsylvania Press, 2003).

27. Robert Rogers, *A Concise Account of North America* (London: For the Author, 1765), 218.

28. Richard White, *The Middle Ground: Indians, Empires, and Republics in the Great Lakes Region* (Cambridge: Cambridge University Press, 1991), 279; Adam Jortner, *The Gods of Prophetstown: The Battle of Tippecanoe, the Holy War for the American Frontier* (Oxford: Oxford University Press, 2011), 6, 149, 230.

29. "Getting Ready to Fight," *The Daily Critic* (Washington, DC), September 26, 1890.

30. "The Messiah Craze," *The Inter Ocean* (Chicago, Illinois), November 23, 1890.

31. "Probably a Mormon Trick," *New York Times*, November 8, 1890, 5.

32. Patrick Q. Mason, *The Mormon Menace: Violence and Anti-Mormonism in the Postbellum South* (Oxford: Oxford University Press, 2011); Stephen C. Taysom, *Shakers, Mormons, and Religious Worlds: Conflicting Visions, Contested Boundaries*. Religion in North America (Bloomington: Indiana University Press, 2011); J. Spencer Fluhman, *"A Peculiar People": Anti-Mormonism and the Making of Religion in Nineteenth Century America* (Chapel Hill: University of North Carolina Press, 2012).

33. Lawrence Coates, "The Mormons and the Ghost Dance," *Dialogue: A Journal of Mormon Thought* 18 (Winter 1985): 89–111; Todd Kerstetter, "Spin Doctors at Santee: Missionaries and Dakota-Language Reporting of the Ghost Dance and Wounded Knee," *Western Historical Quarterly* 28, no. 1 (Spring 1997): 45–67; Kerstetter, *God's Country, Uncle Sam's Land*, 95–103; Gregory Smoak, *Ghost Dance and Identity: Prophetic Religion and Ethnogensis in the Nineteenth Century* (Berkeley: University of California Press, 2006); W. Paul Reeve, *Religion of a Different Color: Race and the Mormon Struggle for Whiteness* (Oxford: Oxford University Press, 2015).

34. Greene, *American Carnage*, 55–64.

35. Raymond J. DeMallie, "The Lakota Ghost Dance: An Ethnohistorical Account," *Pacific Historical Review* 51, no. 4 (Nov. 1982): 385–405.

36. Andersson, *The Lakota Ghost Dance*, 44, 46, 65, 84.

37. Ostler, *The Plains Sioux and U.S. Colonialism*, 274 n. 32; Andersson, *The Lakota Ghost Dance*, 76.

38. Andersson, *The Lakota Ghost Dance*, 47–48; Ostler, *The Plains Sioux and U.S. Colonialism*, 272.

39. Nelson A. Miles to Adjutant General, November 28, 1890, *Reports And Correspondence Relating To The Army Investigations Of The Battle At Wounded Knee And To The Sioux Campaign Of 1890–1891* (Washington, DC: Government Printing Office, 1975), M-983-1, 1:279, 283; Andersson, *The Lakota Ghost Dance*, 67–73; Ostler, *The Plains Sioux and U.S. Colonialism*, 280–88.

40. Andersson, *The Lakota Ghost Dance*, 60; Ostler, *The Plains Sioux and U.S. Colonialism*, 294–97.

41. DeMallie, "The Lakota Ghost Dance," 392.

42. Heather Cox Richardson, *Wounded Knee: Party Politics and the Road to an American Massacre* (New York: Basic Books, 2010), 170.

43. Richardson, *Wounded Knee*, 170–71, 176–77; Ostler, *The Plains Sioux and U.S. Colonialism*, 291–92; Greene, *American Carnage*, 87–90, 96–102.

44. Ostler, *The Plains Sioux and U.S. Colonialism*, 292; Greene, *American Carnage*, 90–92, 96.

45. Perain P. Palmer to Commissioner of Indian Affairs, October 29, 1890, M983-1, 1:27–29.

46. See also Andersson, *The Lakota Ghost Dance*, 122–23.

47. Ostler, *The Plains Sioux and U.S. Colonialism*, 289–301.

48. Linenthal, "'A Sore from America's Past,'" *Sacred Ground*, 127–71; Jerome A. Greene, *Stricken Field: The Little Bighorn Since 1876* (Norman: University of Oklahoma Press, 2008); "Medal of Honor Recipients: Indian Wars Period," www.history.army.mil/html/moh/indianwars.html, accessed July 3, 2012.

49. See Brian W. Dippie, *Custer's Last Stand: The Anatomy of an American Myth* (1976; repr., Lincoln: Bison Books, 1994); Slotkin, *The Fatal Environment*; Joy S. Kasson, *Buffalo Bill's Wild West: Celebrity, Memory, and Popular History* (New York: Hill and Wang, 2000); Louis A. Warren, *Buffalo Bill's America: William Cody and the Wild West Show* (New York: Knopf, 2005); Elliott, *Custerology*.

50. *The Daily News (Denver, CO)*, November 25, 1890. Such calls for vengeance had first appeared in the press in the wake of the Little Bighorn in 1876. Buffalo Bill's Wild West show had ingrained in American culture the idea of avenging Custer, representations of which continued well into the 1890s (see Kasson, *Buffalo Bill's Wild West*, 244–46).

51. Ostler, *The Plains Sioux and U.S. Colonialism*, 300.

52. Ostler, *The Plains Sioux and U.S. Colonialism*, 311–12, 314.

53. Ostler, *The Plains Sioux and U.S. Colonialism*, 319.

54. Ostler, *The Plains Sioux and U.S. Colonialism*, 316.

55. Ostler, *The Plains Sioux and U.S. Colonialism*, 320–26.

56. Andersson, *The Lakota Ghost Dance*, 151–52; Ostler, *The Plains Sioux and U.S. Colonialism*, 328–29.

57. Frog, statement, January 7, 1891, in "Report of Investigation into the Battle at Wounded Knee Creek, South Dakota, Fought December 29th, 1890," 65, M983-1,

2:717; Joseph Horn Cloud, statement, October 23, 1906, Richard E. Jensen, ed., *Voices of the American West*, vol. 1, *The Indian Interviews of Eli S. Ricker, 1903–1919* (Lincoln: University of Nebraska Press, 2005), 195.

58. Ostler, *The Plains Sioux and U.S. Colonialism*, 330–31.

59. Ostler, *The Plains Sioux and U.S. Colonialism*, 333–37.

60. Ostler, *The Plains Sioux and U.S. Colonialism*, 338–60.

61. Jill A. Edy, "Journalistic Uses of Collective Memory," *Journal of Communication* 49, no. 2 (Spring 1999): 71–85. See also George R. Kolbenschlag, *A Whirlwind Press: News Correspondents and the Sioux Indian Disturbances of 1890–1891* (Vermillion: University of South Dakota Press, 1990).

62. Gary L. Roberts, "Sand Creek: Tragedy and Symbol," (PhD diss., University of Oklahoma, 1984), 13, 17–18.

63. Slotkin, *The Fatal Environment*, 410–11, 476.

64. Tom Pessah, "Violent Representations: Hostile Indians and Civilized Wars in Nineteenth-Century USA," *Ethnic and Racial Studies* 37, no. 9 (July 2014): 1628–45.

65. W. H. Cressey, "A Bloody Battle," *Omaha Daily Bee*, December 30, 1890, 1. On the various papers that picked up Cressey's account, see Kolbenschlag, *A Whirlwind Press*, 72–73.

66. Richard White, "Frederick Jackson Turner and Buffalo Bill," in *The Frontier in American Culture*, ed. James R. Grossman (Berkeley: University of California Press, 1994), 7–66; Patricia Limerick, *The Legacy of Conquest: The Unbroken Past of the American West* (1987; repr., New York: Norton, 2006), 35–54.

67. W. H. Cressey, "A Bloody Battle," *Omaha Daily Bee*, December 30, 1890, 1.

68. Cressey, "A Bloody Battle," *Omaha Daily Bee*, December 30, 1890, 1.

69. Charles W. Allen, "Reckless Braves Slaughtered by the Score," *New York Herald*, December 31, 1890, 3.

70. See Kolbenschlag, *A Whirlwind Press*, 72–73.

71. See Col. James Forsyth to Brig. Gen. John R. Brooke, December 29, 1890, M983-1, 1:758; Brig. Gen. John R. Brooke to Maj. Gen. Nelson A. Miles, December 29, 1890, M983-1, 1:634; Maj. Gen. Nelson A. Miles to Adjutant General (hereafter AG), December 29, 1890, M983-1, 1:633.

72. Maj. Gen. Nelson A. Miles to AG, December 30, 1890, M983-1, 1:635.

73. Commanding General of the Army is the equivalent of today's Army Chief of Staff (Maj. Gen. Nelson A. Miles to Maj. Gen. John M. Schofield, December 30, 1890, in M983-1, 1:641).

74. Col. James Forsyth to Acting Assistant AG (hereafter AAAG), December 31, 1891, M983-1, 2:819.

75. Forsyth to AAAG, December 31, 1891, M983-1, 2:819.

76. Forsyth to AAAG, December 31, 1891, M983-1, 2:820.

77. Forsyth to AAAG, December 31, 1891, M983-1, 2:820.

CHAPTER 2

1. Secretary of War Redfield Proctor to Maj. Gen. Nelson A. Miles, February 12, 1891, 1-3, *Reports And Correspondence Relating To The Army Investigations Of The Battle At Wounded Knee And To The Sioux Campaign Of 1890–1891* (Washington, DC: Government Printing Office, 1975), M983-2, 2: 1130–32.

2. As quoted in Peter R. DeMontravel, *A Hero to His Fighting Men: Nelson A. Miles, 1839–1925* (Kent, OH: Kent State University Press, 1998), 206.

3. On dominant memory, see Popular Memory Group, "Popular Memory: Theory, Politics, Method," in *Making Histories: Studies in History-Writing and Politics*, edited by Richard Johnson, Gregor McLennan, Bill Schwarz, and David Sutton (Minneapolis: University of Minnesota Press, 1982), 207–08; Karl Jacoby, *Shadows at Dawn: A Borderlands Massacre and the Violence of History* (New York: Penguin, 2008).

4. Thomas H. Tibbles, "All Murdered in a Mass," *Omaha World-Herald*, December 30, 1890; Bright Eyes, "Horrors of War," *Omaha World-Herald*, January 2, 1891.

5. Roberts, "Sand Creek," 1–34; Slotkin, *The Fatal Environment*, 476; Jacoby, *Shadows at Dawn*, 223–24; Ari Kelman, *A Misplaced Massacre: Struggling Over the Memory of Sand Creek* (Cambridge, MA: Harvard University Press, 2013), 213–18.

6. Royal B. Hassrick, *The Sioux: Life and Customs of a Warrior Society* (1964; repr., Norman: University of Oklahoma Press, 1967), 32, 39; Beatrice Medicine, "'Warrior Women'—Sex Role Alternatives for Plains Indian Women," in *The Hidden Half: Studies of Plains Indian Women*, eds. Patricia Albers and Beatrice Medicine (Lanham, MD: University Press of America, 1983), 267–80; Laura Jane Moore, "Lozen: An Apache Warrior Woman," in *Sifters: Native American Women's Lives*, ed. Theda Perdue (Oxford: Oxford University Press, 2001), 92–107.

7. Richard Slotkin, "Massacre," *Berkshire Review* 14 (1979): 112–32; Roberts, "Sand Creek," 1–34; Slotkin, *The Fatal Environment*, 476; On army defenses for killing noncombatants, see Sherry L. Smith, *The View from Officers' Row: Army Perceptions of Western Indians* (Tucson: University of Arizona Press, 1991), 68–72; Jacoby, *Shadows at Dawn*, 223–24; Kelman, *A Misplaced Massacre*, 9–18, 41.

8. See Michael Schudson, "The Past in the Present and the Present in the Past," *Communication* 11 (1989): 105–13.

9. Tibbles, "All Murdered in a Mass," *Omaha World-Herald*, December 30, 1890.

10. Frederick E. Hoxie, *A Final Promise: The Campaign to Assimilate the Indians, 1880–1920* (Lincoln: University of Nebraska Press, 1984), 4–9.

11. Bright Eyes, "Horrors of War," *Omaha World-Herald*, January 2, 1891; Dorothy Clarke Wilson, *Bright Eyes: The Story of Susette LaFlesche, an Omaha Indian* (New York: McGraw-Hill, 1974).

12. Charles A. Eastman (*Ohiyesa*), *From the Deep Woods to Civilization: Chapters in the Autobiography of an Indian* (Boston: Little, Brown, 1916), 111.

13. Eastman, *From the Deep Woods*, 111–13.

14. W. H. Cressey, "The Beginning of the End," *Omaha Bee*, January 2, 1891.

15. W. H. Cressey, "Rumors of a Skirmish," *Omaha Daily Bee*, January 3, 1891; "Thirsting for Blood Now," *Omaha World-Herald*, January 4, 1891; Carl Smith, "A Resume of the Horrors Found on the Battle Field by the Burial Corps.," *Omaha World-Herald*, January 5, 1891.

16. Smith, "A Resume of the Horrors," *Omaha World-Herald*, January 5, 1891. See William E. Huntzicker, "The 'Sioux Outbreak' in the Illustrated Press," *South Dakota History* 20, no. 4 (1990): 299–322; Richard E. Jensen, R. Eli Paul, and John E. Carter, *Eyewitness at Wounded Knee*. The Great Plains Photography Series (Lincoln: University of Nebraska Press, 1991), and Christina Klein, " 'Everything of Interest in the Late Pine Ridge War Are Held by Us for Sale': Popular Culture and Wounded Knee," *Western Historical Quarterly* 25, no. 1 (Spring 1994): 45–68.

17. Smith, "A Resume of the Horrors," *Omaha World-Herald*, January 5, 1891.

18. Capt. F. A. Whitney to AAAG, January 3, 1891, M983-1, 2:824; Maj. Gen. Nelson A. Miles to AG, January 5, 1891, M983-1, 2:814; W. H. Cressey, "Omens of Bloodshed," *Omaha Daily Bee*, January 6, 1891.

19. James Mooney, *The Ghost-Dance Religion and Wounded Knee*, in *Fourteenth Annual Report of the Bureau of Ethnology to the Smithsonian Institution, 1892–93* (Washington, DC: Government Printing Office, 1896), 878 and plate C.

20. *Lincoln State Journal (Lincoln, NB)*, December 30, 1890, reprinted in *Omaha World-Herald*, December 30, 1890.

21. W. H. Cressey, "A Deadly Triangle," *Omaha Daily Bee*, December 31, 1890.

22. As quoted in "Lessons of Wounded Knee," *Daily Inter Ocean (Chicago)*, January 2, 1891.

23. Maj. Gen. Miles to Maj. Gen. Schofield, January 1, 1891, M983-1, 2:785.

24. Maj. Gen. Schofield to Maj. Gen. Miles, January 2, 1891, M983-1, 2:777.

25. Ostler, *The Plains Sioux and U.S. Colonialism*, 289–312.

26. Ostler, *The Plains Sioux and U.S. Colonialism*, 313–37.

27. Quoted in DeMontravel, *A Hero to His Fighting Men*, 206.

28. Slotkin, *The Fatal Environment*, 360–61.

29. Quoted in DeMontravel, *A Hero to His Fighting Men*, 206.

30. Robert Wooster, *Nelson A. Miles and the Twilight of the Frontier Army* (Lincoln: University of Nebraska Press, 1993), 188–89.

31. "Report of Investigation Into the Battle at Wounded Knee Creek, South Dakota, December 29, 1890," 1, M983-1, 2:653; Maj. Gen. Nelson A. Miles to AG, January 5, 1891, M983-1, 2:81.

32. On the Marias Massacre and its aftermath, see W. B. Pease to Alfred Sully, February 6, 1870, in US Congress, Piegan Indians, 41st Cong., 2nd sess., 1870, H. Ex. Doc. 185, 7; Paul Hutton, "Phil Sheridan's Pyrrhic Victory: The Piegan Massacre, Army Politics, and the Transfer Debate," *Montana: The Magazine of*

Western History 32, no. 2 (Spring 1982): 32–43; Andrew R. Graybill, *The Red and the White: A Family Saga of the American West* (New York: Liveright, 2013).

33. Hutton, "Phil Sheridan's Pyrrhic Victory," 39.

34. Phil Sheridan to William Sherman, February 28, 1870 and Sheridan to Sherman, March 18, 1870, in US Congress, Piegan Indians, 41st Cong., 2nd sess., 1870, H. Ex. Doc. 269, 9, 70–71.

35. Sheridan to E. D. Townsend, April 19, 1870, in US Congress, Piegan Indians, 41st Cong., 2nd sess., 1870, H. Ex. Doc. 269, 74. See also Sherman to Sheridan, March 28, 1870, in US Congress, Piegan Indians, 41st Cong., 2nd sess., 1870, H. Ex. Doc. 269, 72.

36. Hutton, "Phil Sheridan's Pyrrhic Victory," 42–43.

37. Wooster, *Nelson A. Miles*, 69, 72, quote on 74, 84–85, 89, 91–93, 104, 150–52, 182.

38. Wooster, *Nelson A. Miles*, 72, 82, 85, 89–90, 96–97, 123, 154–55, 188.

39. Maj. Gen. Nelson A. Miles to Maj. Gen. John M. Schofield, January 5, 1891, M983-1, 2:811.

40. Maj. Gen. John M. Schofield to Maj. Gen. Nelson A. Miles, January 6, 1891, M983-1, 2:828.

41. Maj. Gen. Nelson A. Miles to Maj. Gen. John M. Schofield, January 6, 1891, M983-1, 2:826.

42. Carl Smith, "The Forsythe Inquiry," *Omaha World-Herald*, January 10, 1891.

43. Meded Swigert, interview, March 31, 1905, in Richard E. Jensen, ed., *Voices of the American West*, vol. 2, *The Settler and Soldier Interviews of Eli S. Ricker, 1903–1919* (Lincoln: University of Nebraska Press, 2005), 20.

44. Geoffrey Cubitt, *History and Memory*. Historical Approaches (Manchester: Manchester University Press, 2007), 188–89; E. D. Scott, "Wounded Knee: A Look at the Record," *The Field Artillery Journal* 29, no. 1 (January–February 1939): 5–24.

45. Capt. W. S. Edgerly, G Troop, testimony, January 9, 1891, "Report of Investigation," February 4, 1891, 39, M983-1, 2:691.

46. Maj. S. M. Whitside, testimony, January 11, 1891, "Report of Investigation," 57, M983-1, 2:709.

47. Capt. C. S. Ilsley, E Troop, testimony, January 9, 1891, "Report of Investigation," 32, 34, M983-1, 2:684, 686; Capt. Henry Jackson, testimony, C Troop, January 9, 1891, "Report of Investigation," 35, 37, M983-1, 2:687, 689; Edgerly, testimony, January 9, 1891, "Report of Investigation," 39, M983-1, 2:691; Capt. Allyn Capron, 1st Art., testimony, January 10, 1891, "Report of Investigation," 47, M983-1, 2:699; Asst. Surgeon Charles B. Ewing, testimony, January 10, 1891, "Report of Investigation," 54–55, M983-1, 2: 706–07.

48. Capt. M. Moylan, A Troop, testimony, January 7, 1891, "Report of Investigation," 13–14, M983-1, 2: 665–66; Asst. Surgeon J. V. B. Hoff, testimony, January 8, 1891, "Report of Investigation," 20, M983-1, 2:672; Capt. Edwin S. Godfrey, D Troop, testimony, January 8, 1891, "Report of Investigation," 27, M983-1, 2:679; Lt. W. W.

Robinson, Acting Adjutant, testimony, January 9, 1891, "Report of Investigation," 43, M983-1, 2:695; Lt. L.S. McCormick, Adjutant, testimony, January 10, 1891, "Report of Investigation," 50, M983-1, 2:702; Whitside, testimony, January 11, 1891, "Report of Investigation," 56–57, M983-1, 2: 708–09.

49. Capt. Charles A. Varnum, B Troop, testimony, January 7, 1891, "Report of Investigation," 16, M983-1, 2:668; Lt. W. J. Nicholson, I Troop, testimony, January 7, 1891, "Report of Investigation," 18, M983-1, 2:670; Hoff, testimony, January 8, 1891, "Report of Investigation," 23, M983-1, 2:675; Lt. Charles W. Taylor, testimony, A Troop, January 8, 1891, "Report of Investigation," 29, M983-1, 2:681; Robinson, testimony, January 9, 1891, "Report of Investigation," 41-42, M983-1, 2: 693–94.

50. Whitside, testimony, January 7, 1891, "Report of Investigation," 11–12, M983-1, 2:663-64.

51. Whitside, testimony, January 7, 1891, "Report of Investigation," 7–8, M983-1, 2: 659–60.

52. Whitside, testimony, January 7, 1891, "Report of Investigation," 11, M983-1, 2:663. See also Moylan, testimony, January 7, 1891, "Report of Investigation," 14, M983-1, 2:666; Nicholson, testimony, January 7, 1891, "Report of Investigation," 18, 19, M983-1, 2:670, 671; Capron, testimony, January 10, 1891, "Report of Investigation," 47, M983-1, 2:699; Capt. H. J. Nowlan, I Troop, testimony, January 10, 1891, "Report of Investigation," 49, M983-1, 2:701.

53. Moylan, testimony, January 7, 1891, "Report of Investigation," 14, M983-1, 2:666; Nicholson, testimony, January 7, 1891, "Report of Investigation," 19, M983-1, 2:671; Godfrey, testimony, January 8, 1891, "Report of Investigation," 27, M983-1, 2:679; Robinson, testimony, January 9, 1891, "Report of Investigation," 42, M983-1, 2:694; Lt. T. Q. Donaldson Jr., G Troop, testimony, January 9, 1891, "Report of Investigation," 44, M983-1, 2:696; Lt. S. R. H. Tompkins, D Troop, testimony, January 9, 1891, "Report of Investigation," 45, M983-1, 2:697; Capron, testimony, January 10, 1891, "Report of Investigation," 47, M983-1, 2:699.

54. Whitside, testimony, January 7, 1891, "Report of Investigation," 11, M983-1, 2:663; 2nd Lt. Sedgwick Rice, E Troop, January 8, 1891, "Report of Investigation," 28, M983-1, 2:680; Capron, testimony, January 10, 1891, "Report of Investigation," 47, M983-1, 2:699.

55. Godfrey, testimony, January 8, 1891, "Report of Investigation," 27, M983-1, 2:679; Rice, January 8, 1891, "Report of Investigation," 28, M983-1, 2:680; Taylor, testimony, January 8, 1891, "Report of Investigation," 31, M983-1, 2:683; Ilsley, testimony, January 9, 1891, "Report of Investigation," 33, M983-1, 2:685; Robinson, testimony, January 9, 1891, "Report of Investigation," 42–43, M983-1, 2: 694–95; Capron, 1st Art., testimony, January 10, 1891, "Report of Investigation," 46–47, M983-1, 2: 698–99.

56. Nowlan, testimony, January 10, 1891, "Report of Investigation," 49, M983-1, 2:701. See also Whitside, testimony, January 7, 1891, "Report of Investigation,"

11, M983-1, 2:663; Moylan, testimony, January 7, 1891, "Report of Investigation," 14, M983-1, 2:666; Nicholson, testimony, January 7, 1891, "Report of Investigation," 19, M983-1, 2:671; Hoff, testimony, January 8, 1891, "Report of Investigation," 20, 21, M983-1, 2:672, 673; Godfrey, testimony, January 8, 1891, "Report of Investigation," 25, 27, M983-1, 2:677, 679; Rice, testimony, January 8, 1891, "Report of Investigation," 28, M983-1, 2:680; Taylor, testimony, January 8, 1891, "Report of Investigation," 30, M983-1, 2:682; Ilsley, testimony, January 9, 1891, "Report of Investigation," 33, M983-1, 2:685; Jackson, testimony, January 9, 1891, "Report of Investigation," 35, 36, M983-1, 2:687, 688; Robinson, testimony, January 9, 1891, "Report of Investigation," 43, M983-1, 2:695; Donaldson, testimony, January 9, 1891, "Report of Investigation," 44, M983-1, 2:696; Tompkins, testimony, January 9, 1891, "Report of Investigation," 45–46, M983-1, 2: 697–98.

57. Godfrey, testimony, January 8, 1891, "Report of Investigation," 25, M983-1, 2:677. "Hau" is a common Lakota greeting; "khola" is a male friend of a man ("Hau," "khola," *New Lakota Dictionary* [2008; 2nd ed., Bloomington: Lakota Language Consortium, 2011], 151, 307).

58. Swigert, interview, March 31, 1905, in Jensen, ed., *The Settler and Soldier Interviews*, 20.

59. "An Awful Vengeance: The Battle of Wounded Knee," *Cincinnati Times-Star*, undated, copied in George E. Bartlett, statement, November 30, 1903, Jensen, ed., *The Settler and Soldier Interviews*, 37–38.

60. Philip F. Wells, statement, October 2, 1906, in Jensen, ed., *The Indian Interviews*, 122–23, 127; Philip F. Wells, "Ninety-six Years Among the Indians of the Northwest—Adventures of an Indian Scout and Interpreter in the Dakotas," *North Dakota History* 15, no. 4 (1948): 294; Frederick Hoxie, "From Prison to Homeland: The Cheyenne River Indian Reservation before WW I," *South Dakota History* 10, no. 1 (Winter 1979): 21–22; Heather Cox Richardson, *Wounded Knee: Party Politics and the Road to an American Massacre* (New York: Basic Books, 2010), 265.

61. See Thomas W. Foley, ed., *At Standing Rock and Wounded Knee: The Journals and Papers of Father Francis M. Craft, 1888–1890* (Norman, OK: Arthur H. Clark Company, 2009).

62. See Kerstetter, "Spin Doctors at Santee," *Western Historical Quarterly* 28, no. 1 (Spring 1997): 45–67.

63. "Said to be a Peace Disturber," *Omaha Daily Bee*, January 16, 1891.

64. P. F. Wells, testimony, January 11, 1891, "Report of Investigation," 60, M983-1, 2:712.

65. Wells, testimony, January 11, 1891, "Report of Investigation," 61–62, M983-1, 2: 713–14. "Hau" is a common Lakota greeting, but can also be used to signify agreement ("Hau," *New Lakota Dictionary*, 151).

66. Wells, testimony, January 11, 1891, "Report of Investigation," 62, M983-1, 2:714.

67. Reverend Francis M. J. Craft, testimony, January 11, 1891, in "Report of Investigation," 69, M983-1, 2:721.

68. Craft, testimony, January 11, 1891, in "Report of Investigation," 71, M983-1, 2:723.
69. Craft, testimony, January 11, 1891, in "Report of Investigation," 72, M983-1, 2:724.
70. Craft, testimony, January 11, 1891, in "Report of Investigation," 73, M983-1, 2:725.
71. Craft, testimony, January 11, 1891, in "Report of Investigation," 72, M983-1, 2:724.
72. Craft, testimony, January 11, 1891, in "Report of Investigation," 73, M983-1, 2:725.
73. "Col. Forsyth Blameless," *New York Tribune*, January 11, 1891.
74. Maj. J. Ford Kent, Fourth Infantry, statement, January 13, 1891, "Report of Investigation," 74, 75, M983-1, 2:726, 726.
75. Kent, statement, January 13, 1891, "Report of Investigation," 74–75, M983-1, 2: 726–27.
76. Kent, statement, January 13, 1891, "Report of Investigation," 75, M983-1, 2:727.
77. Capt. Frank D. Baldwin, Fifth Infantry, statement, January 13, 1891, "Report of Investigation," 76–77, M983-1, 2: 728–29.
78. DeMontravel, *A Hero to His Fighting Men*, 206.
79. Quoted in Wooster, *Nelson A. Miles*, 190.
80. AAG H. C. Corbin to Major J. F. Kent and Captain F.D. Baldwin, January 16, 1891, "Report of Investigation," 85, M983-1, 2:737.
81. Brig. Gen. John R. Brooke, testimony, January 16, 1891, "Report of Investigation," 88–89, M983-1, 2: 740–41.
82. Brooke, testimony, January 16, 1891, "Report of Investigation," 95, M983-1, 2:747.
83. Brooke, testimony, January 16, 1891, "Report of Investigation," 88, 90, M983-1, 2:740, 742.
84. Brooke, testimony, January 16, 1891, "Report of Investigation," 101, M983-1, 2:753.
85. Brooke, testimony, January 16, 1891, "Report of Investigation," 93, M983-1, 2:745.
86. See also Brig. Gen/James W. Forsyth to Secretary of War, September 1, 1895, 13–15, M983-2.
87. Capt. Frank D. Baldwin, Fifth Infantry, statement, January 17, 1891, "Report of Investigation," 98, M983-1, 2:750.
88. Maj. J. Ford Kent, Fourth Infantry, statement, January 18, 1891, "Report of Investigation," 96–97, M983-1, 2: 748–49. Emphasis in original.
89. Wells, "Ninety-six Years Among the Indians," 290–95.
90. Only Frog's and Help Them's statements were published in the official Forsyth inquiry report (Frog, statement, January 7, 1891, and Help Them, statement, January 7, 1891, in "Report of Investigation," 65–68, M983-1, 2: 717–20). Wells later provided Eli S. Ricker Elks Saw Him's statement (Elks Saw Him [*He-ha-ka-wan-ya-ka-pi*], statement, January 7, 1891, in Philip F. Wells, statement, October 2, 1906, Jensen, ed., *The Indian Interviews*, 131–32). For Frog's age, see "Census of the Sioux Indians Belonging to the Cheyenne River reservation who were in the battle of Wounded Knee and are yet at Pine Ridge Agency, S.D. Taken June 30/91," entry 75, http://oyate1.proboards.com/index.cgi?board=census&action=print&thread=550, accessed April 1, 2013. On Cook, see Jensen, ed., *The Indian Interviews*, 414 n. 201.

91. On editors of dictated Native American accounts, their techniques, and varying degrees of transparency, see H. David Brumble III, *American Indian Autobiography* (Berkeley: University of California Press, 1988), 72–97.

92. Elks Saw Him, statement, January 7, 1891, Jensen, ed., *The Indian Interviews*, 131; Frog, statement, January 7, 1891, "Report of Investigation," 65, M983-1, 2: 717.

93. Frog, statement, January 7, 1891, "Report of Investigation," 65, M983-1, 2:717; Help Them, statement, January 7, 1891, "Report of Investigation," 67, M983-1, 2:719; Elks Saw Him, statement, January 7, 1891, Jensen, ed., *The Indian Interviews*, 131.

94. Frog, statement, January 7, 1891, "Report of Investigation," 65, M983-1, 2:717; Help Them, statement, January 7, 1891, "Report of Investigation," 67, M983-1, 2:719; Elks Saw Him, statement, January 7, 1891, Jensen, ed., *The Indian Interviews*, 131–32.

95. Frog, statement, January 7, 1891, "Report of Investigation," 66, M983-1, 2:718; Elks Saw Him, statement, January 7, 1891, Jensen, ed., *The Indian Interviews*, 131–32.

96. Elks Saw Him, statement, January 7, 1891, Jensen, ed., *The Indian Interviews*, 132.

97. Frog, statement, January 7, 1891, "Report of Investigation," 66, M983-1, 2:718; Help Them, statement, January 7, 1891, "Report of Investigation," 67, M983-1, 2:719; Elks Saw Him, statement, January 7, 1891, Jensen, ed., *The Indian Interviews*, 132.

98. Help Them, statement, January 7, 1891, "Report of Investigation," 67, M983-1, 2:719. See also Frog, statement, January 7, 1891, "Report of Investigation," 66, M983-1, 2:717 and Elks Saw Him, statement, January 7, 1891, Jensen, ed., *The Indian Interviews*, 132.

99. Frog, statement, January 7, 1891, "Report of Investigation," 66, M983-1, 2:718; Help Them, statement, January 7, 1891, "Report of Investigation," 67, M983-1, 2:719; Elks Saw Him, statement, January 7, 1891, Jensen, ed., *The Indian Interviews*, 132.

100. Hassrick, *The Sioux*, 73–74.

101. Frog, statement, January 7, 1891, "Report of Investigation," 66, M983-1, 2:718; Help Them, statement, January 7, 1891, "Report of Investigation," 67, M983-1, 2:719; Elks Saw Him, statement, January 7, 1891, Jensen, ed., *The Indian Interviews*, 132.

102. Frog, statement, January 7, 1891, "Report of Investigation," 66, M983-1, 2:718; Help Them, statement, January 7, 1891, "Report of Investigation," 67, M983-1, 2:719; Elks Saw Him, statement, January 7, 1891, Jensen, ed., *The Indian Interviews*, 132.

103. See Katherine Ellinghaus, "Reading the Personal as Political: The Assimilationist Views of a White Woman Married to a Native American Man, 1880s–1940s,"

Australasian Journal of American Studies 18, no. 2 (December 1999): 23–42 and Margaret D. Jacobs, "The Eastmans and the Luhans: Interracial Marriage between White Women and Native American Men, 1875–1935," *Frontiers: A Journal of Women Studies* 23, no. 3 (2002): 29–54.

104. Eastman (*Ohiyesa*), *From the Deep Woods to Civilization*, 110–13.
105. "The Indian Version of the Fight at Wounded Knee," *Wichita (KS) Daily Eagle*, January 17, 1891.
106. "The Indian Version," *Wichita (KS) Daily Eagle*, January 17, 1891.
107. "The Indian Version," *Wichita (KS) Daily Eagle*, January 17, 1891.
108. "The Indian Version," *Wichita (KS) Daily Eagle*, January 17, 1891; "A Tale of Wounded Knee," *San Francisco Call*, January 17, 1891; "Miss Goodale's Story of the Battle," *(NY) Sun*, January 17, 1891; "How It Happened," *Arizona Republican*, January 17, 1891; "Miss Goodale's Report on Wounded Knee," *Salt Lake Herald*, January 17, 1891; "Severe on the Seventh," *Worthington (MN) Advantage*, January 17, 1891; "How Things Went," *St. Paul (MN) Daily Globe*, January 17, 1891, 4.
109. Maj. Gen. Nelson A. Miles, Endorsement, January 31, 1891, "Report of Investigation," 114, M983-1, 2:766.
110. Miles, Endorsement, January 31, 1891, "Report of Investigation," 114, M983-1, 2:766.
111. Miles, Endorsement, January 31, 1891, "Report of Investigation," 115, M983-1, 2:767.
112. Capt. Frank D. Baldwin, Fifth Infantry, to AAG, January 21, 1891, "Report of Investigation," 81, M983-1, 2:733.
113. Miles, Endorsement, January 31, 1891, "Report of Investigation," 115, M983-1, 2:767.
114. Maj. Gen. J. M. Schofield, Indorsement, February 4, 1891, "Report of Investigation," 116, M983-1, 2:768.
115. Proctor to Miles, February 12, 1891, 1, M983-2, 2:1130.
116. Proctor to Miles, February 12, 1891, 1, M983-2, 2:1130.
117. Proctor to Miles, February 12, 1891, 2, M983-2, 2:1131.
118. Proctor to Miles, February 12, 1891, 2, M983-2, 2:1131.
119. Proctor to Miles, February 12, 1891, 3, M983-2, 2:1132.
120. "General Miles Declines to Talk," *Omaha World-Herald*, February 13, 1891.
121. Quoted in Jerry Green, ed., *After Wounded Knee: Correspondence of Major and Surgeon John Vance Lauderdale while Serving with the Army Occupying the Pine Ridge Indian Reservation, 1890–1891* (East Lansing: Michigan State University Press, 1996), 39.
122. "The Case of General Forsyth," *Army and Navy Journal*, February 14, 1891, 425; see also *Omaha World-Herald*, January 18, 1891, 4.
123. "Plans of the President," *Omaha Daily Bee*, August 10, 1892.

CHAPTER 3

1. "Loyal to the Seventh," *Junction City Republican*, January 9, 1891.

2. Barry Schwartz, "The Social Context of Commemoration: A Study in Collective Memory," *Social Forces* 61, no. 2 (December 1982): 374–402; Michael Kammen, *Mystic Chords of Memory: The Transformation of Tradition in American Culture* (New York: Knopf, 1991).

3. H. W. Janson, *The Rise and Fall of the Public Monument* (New Orleans: The Graduate School Tulane University, 1976), 2; Armando Petrucci, *Writing the Dead: Death and Writing Strategies in the Western Tradition*, trans. Michael Sullivan (Redwood City, CA: Stanford University Press, 1998).

4. G. Kurt Piehler, *Remembering War the American Way* (Washington, DC: Smithsonian Institution Press, 1995), 49–52; Mark Hughes, *Bivouac of the Dead* (Bowie, MD: Heritage Books, 1995), 6; John R. Neff, *Honoring the Civil War Dead: Commemoration and the Problem of Reconciliation*. Modern War Studies (Lawrence: University Press of Kansas, 2005), 103–41.

5. Francis Paul Prucha, "Forts," in *The New Encyclopedia of the American West*, ed. Howard R. Lamar (New Haven, CT: Yale University Press, 1998), 387–90; Anne F. Hyde, *Empires, Nations, and Families: A History of the North American West, 1800–1860*. History of the American West Series (Lincoln: University of Nebraska Press, 2011), 347–514.

6. Richard Slotkin, *The Fatal Environment: The Myth of the Frontier: The Myth of the Frontier in the Age of Industrialization, 1800–1860* (1985; repr., Norman: University of Oklahoma Press, 1994), 228–29; William McKale and William D. Young, *Fort Riley: Citadel of the Frontier West* (Topeka: Kansas State Historical Society, 2000); Hughes, *Bivouac of the Dead*, 37–39, 147–49, 194–95; Jerome A. Greene, *Stricken Field: The Little Bighorn Since 1876* (Norman: University of Oklahoma Press, 2008).

7. "War With the Savages," *Junction City (KS) Republican*, January 1, 1891.

8. "Newspaper Comment," *Junction City (KS) Republican*, January 9, 1891.

9. "The Indian War," *Junction City (KS) Republican*, January 2, 1891.

10. *Seventh Cavalry:* Serg. Maj. Richard W. Corwine. *A Troop*: Serg. Arthur C. Dyer, Pvt. Henry Frey, Pvt. George P. Johnson, Pvt. Michael Regan, and Pvt. James Logan. *B Troop*: Serg. Dora S. Coffey, Pvt. John Costello, Pvt. Ralph L. Cook, Corp. Harry R. Forrest, and Pvt. William S. Mezo. *C Troop*: Pvt. Jan De Vreede. *D Troop*: Pvt. Frank T. Reinecky. *E Troop*: Serg. Robert H. Nettles and Pvt. August Kellner. *I Troop*: Blacksmith Gustav Korn, Pvt. Daniel Twohig, Pvt. James E. Kelley, and Pvt. Pierce Cummings. *K Troop*: Captain George D. Wallace, Serg. William F. Hodges, Pvt. John M. McCue, Pvt. Joseph Murphy, Pvt. William J. McClintock, and Pvt. Philip Schenkey. *Hospital Corps*: Hospital Steward Oscar Pollack. Miles misidentified Pvt. William Adams, K Troop, as wounded, but he was among those killed on December 29, 1890 (Maj. Gen. Nelson A. Miles to AG,

January 3, 1891, M983-1, 2:788; "Book of Interments in the Pine Ridge Agency at Pine Ridge, S.D.," 217–18, *US, Burial Registers, Military Posts and National Cemeteries, 1862–1960,* http://search.ancestry.com/search/db.aspx?dbid=3135, accessed December 2, 2010, Provo, UT: Ancestry.com Operations, Inc., 2012).

11. Three soldiers died during the night march from Wounded Knee to Pine Ridge, including Pvt. Bernard Zehnder and Corp. Albert S. Bone, both I Troop, and Corp. Charles H. Newell, B Troop. Pvt. Herman Granberg, A Troop, died on December 30, 1890 (Maj. Gen. Nelson A. Miles to AG, January 3, 1891, M983-1, 2:788; "Book of Interments in the Pine Ridge Agency at Pine Ridge, S.D.," 217–18.

12. *New York Times,* December 31, 1890, 1; "The Lost at Wounded Knee: List of the Soldiers Killed and Wounded in Monday's Battle," *New York Times,* January 1, 1891, 1; "Killed and Wounded," *Junction City (KS) Republican,* January 2, 1891; "The Indian War," *Junction City (KS) Republican,* January 2, 1891.

13. See Hughes, *Bivouac of the Dead*; C. H. Cressey, "The Soldiers' Funeral," *Omaha Daily Bee,* January 1, 1891, 1.

14. C. H. Cressey, "The Soldiers' Funeral," 1. Initially, the intent was to bury the soldiers by troop, but as wounded soldiers died and others were removed for burial elsewhere, the scheme broke down. Those buried, by lot number, included *Hospital Corps.*: Hospital Steward Oscar Pollack (1). *A Troop:* Serg. Maj. Richard W. Corwine (2), Serg. Arthur C. Dyer (3), Pvt. Henry Frey (4), Pvt. George P. Johnson (5), Pvt. Michael Regan (6), and Pvt. James Logan (7). *B Troop:* Serg. Dora S. Coffey (8), Corp. Harry R. Forrest (9), and Corp. Charles H. Newell (10). *C Troop:* Pvt. Jan De Vreede (11). *D Troop:* Pvt. Frank T. Reinecky (12). *E Troop:* Serg. Robert H. Nettles (13) and Pvt. August Kellner (14). *I Troop:* Corp. Albert S. Bone (15), Blacksmith Gustav Korn (16), Pvt. Daniel Twohig (17), Pvt. James E. Kelley (18), Pvt. Pierce Cummings (19), and Pvt. Bernard Zehlinder (20). *K Troop:* Serg. William F. Hodges (21), Pvt. John M. McCue (22), Pvt. Joseph Murphy (23), Pvt. William J. McClintock (24), Pvt. Philip Schenkey (25), and Pvt. William Adams (26). *B Troop:* Pvt. John Costello (27), Pvt. Ralph L. Cook (28), and Pvt. William S. Mezo (29). *A Troop:* Pvt. Herman Granberg (30). See "Book of Interments," 217–18. Pvt. Dominick Franceschetti (31), G Troop, was killed at the Drexel Mission skirmish on December 30, 1890, and was also buried in the cemetery (Maj. Gen. Nelson A. Miles to AG, January 3, 1891, M983-1, 2:792).

15. Pvt. Harry B. Stone, B Troop, replaced Pvt. James E. Kelley in Lot 18, after Kelley's family members retrieved his body. Pvt. George Elliott, K Troop, was buried in Lot 32 ("Book of Interments," 217–18).

16. See "Graves of Seventh Cavalry Killed at Wounded Knee December 29, 1890," undated photograph, Wounded Knee Massacre Photographs, RG 2845-19-3, Nebraska State Historical Society, Lincoln, Nebraska.

17. Greene, *Stricken Field*, 21.

18. John D. Mackintosh, *Custer's Southern Officer: Captain George D. Wallace, 7th U.S. Cavalry* (Lexington, SC: Cloud Creek Press, 2002).

19. "2nd Lt. George D. Wallace," www.geni.com/people/2nd-Lt-George-D-Wallace-7th-US-Cavalry/6000000018280398055, accessed December 6, 2014.

20. *Democratic Sentinel (Junction City, KS)*, January 8, 1891; "Our Dead at Home," *Junction City (KS) Republican*, January 9, 1891.

21. "Captain G. D. Wallace," *Harper's Weekly* 35 (January 17, 1891), 41–42.

22. *Bloomington (IN) Telegraph*, January 27, 1891, 4.

23. See "He Died Fighting the Indians," *Chicago Daily Tribune*, January 23, 1891, 6.

24. "Freedom," *Garretsville (OH) Journal*, February 5, 1891.

25. *Orange (NJ) Journal*, February 7, 1891. I am indebted to genealogist Marilyn W. Grua for the information regarding the reburials of these four soldiers.

26. "Army News," *Junction City (KS) Republican*, January 9, 1891; *Democratic Sentinel (Junction City, KS)*, January 29, 1891; "Death of Haselwood: One of the Gallant Heroes of Wounded Knee Dies at Fort Riley," *Democratic Sentinel (Junction City, KS)*, March 19, 1891. Howard, I Troop, and Haselwood, A Troop, were buried in lots F:10 and F:13 in the post cemetery, respectively.

27. McKale and Young, *Fort Riley*.

28. "A Complete Vindication," *Junction City (KS) Republican*, February 20, 1891.

29. "How the News Was Received Here," *Junction City (KS) Republican*, February 20, 1891. "In the United States, after three cheers are given, it is usual to add a howl, called 'the *tiger*,' in order to intensify the applause" (Albert Barrere, ed., *A Dictionary of Slang, Jargon, and Cant* [London: George Bell and Sons, 1897], 2:334).

30. "How the News Was Received Here," *Junction City (KS) Republican*, February 20, 1891.

31. "Congratulatory Telegrams," *Junction City (KS) Republican*, February 20, 1891.

32. *Junction City Republican*, April 3, 1891, 7.

33. "Concert at Fort Riley," *Democratic Sentinel (Junction City, KS)*, April 16, 1891.

34. Although bearing similar names, independent historian Jerry Green should not be confused with National Parks scholar Jerome Greene. (Jerry Green, "The Medals of Wounded Knee," originally published in *Nebraska History* (Summer 1994), www.dickshovel.com/GreenIntro.html, accessed April 19, 2012; Brig. Gen. James W. Forsyth to Sec. of War Daniel S. Lamont, September 1, 1895, *Reports And Correspondence Relating To The Army Investigations Of The Battle At Wounded Knee And To The Sioux Campaign Of 1890–1891* (Washington, DC: Government Printing Office, 1975), M983-2.)

35. Allen Mikaelian, *Medal of Honor: Profiles of America's Military Heroes From the Civil War to the Present* (New York: Bill Adler Books, 2002), xviii; Ron Owens, *Medal of Honor: Historical Facts and Figures* (Paduca, KY: Turner Publishing Co., 2004).

36. Robert Wooster, email to the author, June 27, 2012.

37. An official review board in 1917 rescinded the 27th Maine Infantry's medals ("The Purge of 1917," www.homeofheroes.com/moh/corrections/purge_army.html, accessed April 15, 2013).

38. Robert Wooster, email to the author, June 27, 2012

39. *Awarded in 1891: A Troop:* Pvt. George Hobday, and Pvt. Adam Neder; *B Troop:* Serg. James Ward, and Pvt. Marvin C. Hillock; *E Troop:* Serg. Albert W. McMillan, Serg. William G. Austin, Pvt. Mosheim Feaster, Pvt. Thomas Sullivan, and Pvt. Herman Ziegner; *G Troop:* 1st Serg. Frederick E. Toy and Pvt. Matthew Hamilton; *I Troop:* 1st Serg. Jacob Trautman and Serg. George Loyd; *K Troop:* Serg. Bernhard Jetter; *1st Art.:* Corp. Paul Weiner, and Pvt. Jacob B. Hartzog. *Awarded in 1892*: Musician John E. Clancy, 1st Artillery and 1st Lt. Harry L. Hawthorne, 2nd Artillery. *Awarded in 1893*: 1st Lt. Ernest A. Garlington, A Troop. Awarded in 1895: 1st Lt. John C. Gresham, B Troop, www.history.army.mil/html/moh/indianwars.html, accessed July 20, 2012.

40. See Owens, *Medal of Honor*, 49.

41. Green, "The Medals of Wounded Knee"; "Medal of Honor Recipients: Indian Wars Period," www.history.army.mil/html/moh/indianwars.html, accessed July 20, 2012.

42. Alan Radley, "Artefacts, Memory and a Sense of the Past," in *Collective Remembering*, eds. David Middleton and Derek Edwards (London: Sage, 1990), 57.

43. "Decoration of an American Soldier," *Harper's Weekly*, September 19, 1891, 716.

44. "Paul Winert's Bravery," *Omaha Daily Bee*, January 16, 1891.

45. "Presentation of the Medals," *Junction City (KS) Republican*, May 1, 1891, 8.

46. David W. Blight, *Race and Reunion: The Civil War in American Memory* (Cambridge, MA: Belknap Press of Harvard University Press, 2001), 64–97; Kirk Savage, *Standing Soldiers, Kneeling Slaves: Race, War, and Monument in Nineteenth-Century America* (Princeton, NJ: Princeton University Press, 1997).

47. "Decoration Day," *Junction City (KS) Republican*, June 5, 1891, 7.

48. "Fort Riley," *Junction City (KS) Republican*, July 3, 1891, 7; "More Honors for E Troop," *Junction City (KS) Republican*, July 10, 1891, 7.

49. Green, "The Medals of Wounded Knee."

50. *Democratic Sentinel (Junction City, KS)*, April 2, 1891; "He May Be Promoted Now," *Omaha Daily Bee*, August 24, 1891.

51. "They Head the Army," *Washington (DC) Times*, November 10, 1894.

52. "Recent Army Decorations," *Omaha Daily Bee*, December 30, 1891. All of the Medal of Honor recipients noted above, except for Musician John C. Clancy, were included in the Roll of Honor, although Harry L. Hawthorne, Ernest A. Garlington, and John C. Gresham had not yet received their medals. The others named to the roll include: *B Troop:* Capt. Charles A. Varnum and Serg. Harry W. Capron; *E Troop:* 1st Lt. Horatio G. Sickel, and Serg. John F. Trittle; *I Troop:* Capt. Henry K. Nowlan; *K Troop:* Pvt. Frederick George, Trumpeter

James Christianson, and Nathan Follman; *1st Art.*: Capt. Allyn Capron, Priv. George Green, and Priv. John Flood; *Hospital Corps.*: Lt. Col. Dallas Bache, medical director and Maj. John Van R. Hoff, surgeon ("Roll of Honor of the Army," *Omaha World-Herald*, December 27, 1891).

53. Mikaelian, *Medal of Honor*, xviii.

54. "History of Four of the Greatest Wars in the History of Indian Warfare," *Junction City (KS) Union*, July 27, 1893; Piehler, *Remembering War the American Way*.

55. Savage, *Standing Soldiers, Kneeling Slaves*, 166–68; image of monument, http://upload.wikimedia.org/wikipedia/commons/d/d3/Monument_ inscription_-_Lexington%2C_MA.JPG, accessed April 29, 2013.

56. Savage, *Standing Soldiers, Kneeling Slaves*, 166–68.

57. Savage, *Standing Soldiers, Kneeling Slaves*, 4–8; Franciose Choay, *The Invention of the Historic Monument*, trans. Lauren M. O'Connell (Cambridge: Cambridge University Press, 2001); Kenneth E. Foote, *Shadowed Ground: America's Landscapes of Violence and Tragedy*, Rev. ed. (Austin: University of Texas Press, 2003), 111–44.

58. Ephraim D. Dickson III, "Honoring the Fallen: Establishment of the Fort Douglas Cemetery," *Fort Douglas Vedette: Newsletter of the Fort Douglas Museum Association* 34, no. 3 (Fall 2009): 3–6.

59. Image of monument, www.kgs.ku.edu/Publications/Photos/Wallace/WA-Soldiers-monument.jpg, accessed July 16, 2012.

60. Greene, *Stricken Field*, 20–33, quote at 31.

61. "The Battle of Wounded Knee: Review of the Campaign Which a Monument Unveiling Recalls," *Daily Inter Ocean (Chicago)*, July 24, 1893.

62. C.J.C., "A Review: To the Boys of the Seventh," *Junction City (KS) Union*, July 8, 1893.

63. "Dedication Exercises at Fort Riley," *Democratic Sentinel (Junction City, KS)*, July 22, 1893; "Dedication at Fort Riley," *Democratic Sentinel (Junction City, KS)*, July 22, 1893; "History of Four of the Greatest Wars in the History of Indian Warfare," *Junction City (KS) Union*, July 27, 1893.

64. "Joseph Ralph Burton, 1852–1923," *Biographical Register of the United States Congress*, http://bioguide.congress.gov/scripts/biodisplay.pl?index=B001154, accessed September 19, 2011.

65. "Heroes of Wounded Knee," *Abilene (KS) Weekly Reflector*, July 27, 1893.

66. "Heroes of Wounded Knee," *Abilene (KS) Weekly Reflector*, July 27, 1893; Savage, *Standing Soldiers, Kneeling Slaves*, 4. See also Capt. John C. Gresham, "The Wounded Knee Monument," *Harper's Weekly*, August 5, 1893, 752.

67. Roy Harvey Pearce, *Savagism and Civilization: A Study of the Indian and the American Mind*, Rev. ed. (Berkeley: University of California Press, 1988), 155–68; Slotkin, *The Fatal Environment*, 228–29.

68. "Heroes of Wounded Knee," *Abilene (KS) Weekly Reflector*, July 27, 1893; Brian W. Dippie, *The Vanishing American: White Attitudes and U.S. Indian Policy* (Lawrence: University Press of Kansas, 1982), 29–31.

69. Scott R. Christensen, *Sagwitch: Shoshone Chieftain, Mormon Elder, 1822–1887* (Logan, UT: Utah State University Press, 1999), 58; *The Passing of the Redman: Being a Succinct Account of the Last Battle that Wrested Idaho from the Bondage of the Indians* (Preston, ID: Franklin County Historical Society and Monument Committee, 1917), http://archive.org/details/passingofredmanboofranrich, accessed May 15, 2012.

70. Ari Kelman, *A Misplaced Massacre: Struggling Over the Memory of Sand Creek* (Cambridge, MA: Harvard University Press, 2013), 9, 18.

71. Karl Jacoby, *Shadows at Dawn: A Borderlands Massacre and the Violence of History* (New York: Penguin, 2008), 236–37.

72. Boyd D. Cothran, *Remembering the Modoc War: Redemptive Violence and the Making of American Innocence* (Chapel Hill: University of North Carolina Press, 2014), 113–40.

73. "Heroes of Wounded Knee," *Abilene (KS) Weekly Reflector*, July 27, 1893; The Battle of Wounded Knee: Review of the Campaign Which a Monument Unveiling Recalls," *Daily Inter Ocean (Chicago)*, July 24, 1893; Philip J. Deloria, *Indians in Unexpected Places* (Lawrence: University Press of Kansas, 2004), 62.

74. "Heroes of Wounded Knee," *Abilene (KS) Weekly Reflector*, July 27, 1893.

75. Kirk Savage, "Faces of the Dead," www.kirksavage.pitt.edu/?p=209, accessed October 1, 2011.

76. *Seventh Cavalry:* Serg. Maj. Richard W. Corwine; *A Troop:* Serg. Arthur C. Dyer, Serg. Alvin H. Haselwood, Pvt. Henry Frey, Pvt. Herman Granberg, Pvt. George P. Johnson, Pvt. James Logan, and Pvt. Michael Regan; *B Troop:* Serg. Dora S. Coffey, Corp. Harry R. Forrest, Corp. Charles Newell, Pvt. Ralph L. Cook, Pvt. John Costello, Pvt. William S. Mezo, and Pvt. Harry Stone; *C Troop:* Pvt. Jan De Vreede; *D Troop:* Pvt. Frank T. Reinecky; *E Troop:* Serg. Robert H. Nettles and Pvt. August Kellner; *I Troop:* Serg. Henry Howard, Corp. Albert S. Bone, Blacksmith Gustav Korn, Pvt. Pierce Cummings, Pvt. James E. Kelley, Pvt. Daniel Twohig, and Pvt. Bernhard Zehnder; *K Troop:* Captain George D. Wallace, Serg. William F. Hodges, Pvt. William Adams, Pvt. George Elliott, Pvt. William J. McClintock, Pvt. John M. McCue, Pvt. Joseph Murphy and Pvt. Philip Schenkey; *Hospital Corps:* Hospital Steward Oscar Pollack. Pvt. Dominick Francishetti, G Troop, and 1st Lt. James D. Mann, K Troop, were the two Seventh Cavalrymen killed at Drexel Mission.

77. "Fort Riley," *Junction City (KS) Union*, July 1, 1893.

78. "Military Matters," *Omaha Daily Bee*, April 24, 1892.

79. "Heroes of Wounded Knee," *Abilene (KS) Weekly Reflector*, July 27, 1893; Radley, "Artefacts, Memory and a Sense of the Past," 48.

80. "The Battle of Wounded Knee: Review of the Campaign Which a Monument Unveiling Recalls," *Daily Inter Ocean (Chicago, IL)*, July 24, 1893; "Fort Riley's Big Day," *Junction City (KS) Republican*, July 28, 1893.

81. Capt. John C. Gresham, "The Wounded Knee Monument," *Harper's Weekly*, August 5, 1893, 752.

82. Gresham, "The Wounded Knee Monument," *Harper's Weekly*, August 5, 1893, 752.

83. "Military Matters," *Omaha Daily Bee*, April 24, 1892.

84. Elbert Mead, statement, in Richard E. Jensen, ed., *Voices of the American West*, vol. 2, *The Settler and Soldier Interviews of Eli S. Ricker, 1903–1919* (Lincoln: University of Nebraska Press, 2005), 55.

85. "7th Cavalry Dead—Returned Here for Burial in Post Cemetery," *Fort Riley Guidon (KS)*, September 30, 1906, 2.

86. The Pine Ridge cemetery burial order was, with few exceptions, reproduced in the Fort Riley post cemetery. By lot number: *Hospital Corps:* Hospital Steward Oscar Pollack (D:104); *Seventh Cavalry:* Serg. Maj. Richard W. Corwine (D:105); *A Troop:* Serg. Arthur C. Dyer (D:106), Pvt. Henry Frey (D:107), Pvt. George P. Johnson (D:108), Pvt. Michael Regan (D:109), and Pvt. James Logan (D:110); *K Troop:* Pvt. George Elliott (D:111); *B Troop:* Corp. Harry R. Forrest (D:112) and Corp. Charles H. Newell (D:113); *C Troop:* Jan De Vreede (D:114); *D Troop:* Frank T. Reinecky (D:115); *E Troop:* Serg. Robert H. Nettles (D:116) and Pvt. August Kellner (D:117); *I Troop:* Corp. Albert S. Bone (D:118), Blacksmith Gustav Korn (D:119), and Pvt. Daniel Twohig (D:120); *B Troop:* Pvt. Harry B. Stone (D:121); *I Troop:* Pvt. Pierce Cummings (D:122), and Pvt. Bernard Zehnder (D:123); *K Troop:* Serg. William T. Hodges (D:124), Pvt. John M. McCue (D:125), and Pvt. Joseph Murphy (D:126); *G Troop:* Pvt. Dominick Franceshetti (Drexel Mission; D:127). *A Troop:* Herman Grandberg (D:128); *K Troop:* William Adams (D:129); *B Troop:* John Costello (D:130), Ralph L. Cook (D:131), and William S. Mezo (D:132).

87. "7th Cavalry Dead," *Fort Riley (KS) Guidon*, September 30, 1906, 2.

88. Radley, "Artefacts, Memory and a Sense of the Past," 51.

89. See image of badge, www.omsa.org/photopost/showphoto.php?photo=2783& size=big, accessed July 21, 2012.

90. David T. Zabeki, "Decorations, Medals, and Military Honors," in *The Encyclopedia of North American Indian Wars, 1607–1890: A Political, Social, and Military History*, ed. Spencer C. Tucker (Santa Barbara: ABC-Clio, 2011), 2:881.

91. Richard White, "Frederick Jackson Turner and Buffalo Bill," in *The Frontier in American Culture*, ed. James R. Grossman (Berkeley: University of California Press, 1994), 7–66; Richard Slotkin, *Gunfighter Nation: The Myth of the Frontier in Twentieth-Century America* (1992; Norman: University of Oklahoma Press, 1998), 63–87; Joy S. Kasson, *Buffalo Bill's Wild West: Celebrity, Memory, and Popular History* (New York: Hill and Wang, 2000); Louis S. Warren, *Buffalo Bill's America: William Cody and the Wild West Show* (New York: Knopf, 2005).

92. Paul L. Hedren, "The Contradictory Legacies of Buffalo Bill's First Scalp for Custer," *Montana: The Magazine of Western History* 55, no. 1 (Spring 2005): 16–35.

93. Jeffrey Ostler, *The Plains Sioux and U.S. Colonialism from Lewis and Clark to Wounded Knee*. Studies in North American Indian History (Cambridge: Cambridge University Press, 2004), 313–16.

94. Sam A. Maddra, *Hostiles? The Lakota Ghost Dance and Buffalo Bill's Wild West* (Norman: University of Oklahoma Press, 2006).

95. "Daring Feats by Horsemen," *New York Times*, May 10, 1894, 9; Jerome A. Greene, *American Carnage: Wounded Knee, 1890* (Norman: University of Oklahoma Press, 2014), 524 n. 15; Philip Burnham, *Song of Dewey Beard: Last Survivor of the Little Bighorn* (Lincoln: University of Nebraska Press, 2014), 96, 99.

96. Warren, *Buffalo Bill's America*, 536; Kasson, *Buffalo Bill's Wild West*, 255–56.

97. Kasson, *Buffalo Bill's Wild West*, 255–56.

98. *Hopkinsville Kentuckian*, April 3, 1913, 3; *Adams County Free Press (Corning, IA)*, May 14, 1913, 2; *Grand Rapids (WI) Daily Tribune*, July 2, 1913, 5.

99. L. G. Moses, *Wild West Shows and the Images of American Indians, 1883–1933* (Albuquerque: University of New Mexico Press, 1996), 229.

100. "Gen. Miles on Way to 'Fight' Indians," *Inter-Ocean*, October 8, 1913, 12.

101. Moses, *Wild West Shows*, 229.

102. As quoted in Greene, *American Carnage*, 366.

103. Moses, *Wild West Shows*, 231.

104. "Gen. Miles on Way to 'Fight' Indians," *(Chicago) Inter-Ocean*, October 8, 1913, 12.

105. "Gen. Miles on Way to 'Fight' Indians," *(Chicago) Inter-Ocean*, October 8, 1913, 12; Kasson, *Buffalo Bill's Wild West*, 259–61.

106. "Buffalo Bill to Reenact Stirring Indian Fights for Moving Pictures," *Evening Herald (Albuquerque, NM)*, September 13, 1913, 4; Moses, *Wild West Shows*, 231.

107. Lieut. Gen. Nelson A. Miles to John R. Brennan, October 12, 1913, in Brennan Scrapbook, 279, John R. Brennan Collection, SDSHS.

108. "Makers of History Who Died During the Past Year," *Kansas City Globe*, December 31, 1906, 3.

109. On Wells's testimony, see pp. 41–42.

110. Gertrude M. Price, *Tacoma Times*, November 12, 1913, 3; " 'Movies' Portrayal of Wounded Knee is Again Revived," *Rapid City (SD) Daily Journal*, January 10, 1914.

111. See also Andrea I. Paul, "Buffalo Bill and Wounded Knee: the Movie," *Nebraska History* 71, no. 4 (Winter 1990): 187.

112. Mrs. John Brennan to Ruth Hill, October 1913, John R. Brennan Family Papers, SDSHS; "Sioux Indians Go To Washington With a Grievance," *(NY) World*, November 30, 1913.

113. Moses, *Wild West Shows and the Images of American Indians*, 245–56.

114. *Wichita Beacon*, December 31, 1914, 8; *Pioneer (Bemidji, MN)*, November 29, 1914, 3; Kasson, *Buffalo Bill's Wild West*, 261.

115. Burnham, *Song of Dewey Beard*, 105.

CHAPTER 4

1. Edward Tabor Linenthal, *Sacred Ground: Americans and Their Battlefields* (Urbana: University of Illinois Press, 1991) and Michael A. Elliott, *Custerology: The Enduring Legacy of the Indian Wars and George Armstrong Custer* (Chicago: University of Chicago Press, 2007).

2. Karl Jacoby, *Shadows at Dawn: A Borderlands Massacre and the Violence of History* (New York: Penguin, 2008) and Ari Kelman, *A Misplaced Massacre: Struggling Over the Memory of Sand Creek* (Cambridge, MA: Harvard University Press, 2013).

3. "Report of Investigation Into the Battle at Wounded Knee Creek, South Dakota, December 29, 1890," 1–136, *Reports And Correspondence Relating To The Army Investigations Of The Battle At Wounded Knee And To The Sioux Campaign Of 1890–1891* (Washington, DC: Government Printing Office, 1975), M983-1, 2: 651–768; Redfield Proctor to Nelson A. Miles, February 12, 1891, 1–3, M983-2, 2: 1130–32; Jerry Green, "The Medals of Wounded Knee," originally published in *Nebraska History* (Summer 1994), www.dickshovel.com/GreenIntro.html, accessed April 19, 2012; "Heroes of Wounded Knee," *Abilene (KS) Weekly Reflector*, July 27, 1893.

4. On memory as contestation, see "Popular Memory: Theory, Politics, Method," in *Making Histories: Studies in History Writing and Politics*, edited by Richard Johnson, Gregor McLennan, Bill Schwarz, and David Sutton (Minneapolis: University of Minnesota Press, 1982), 205–52; Michael Kammen, "Commemoration and Contestation in American Culture: Historical Perspectives," *Amerikastudien/ American Studies* 48, no. 2 (2003): 185–205.

5. Kelman, *A Misplaced Massacre*, 34.

6. Frederick E. Hoxie, *Talking Back to Civilization: Indian Voices from the Progressive Era*. Bedford Series in History and Culture (Boston: Bedford/St. Martin's, 2001).

7. Kelman, *A Misplaced Massacre*, 34–42, quote on 34.

8. Joseph H. Hurst to H. C. Merriam, January 8, 1891, quoted in H. C. Merriam to Nelson A. Miles, January 11, 1891, in *Report of the Secretary of War; Being Part of the Message and Documents Communicated to the Two Houses of Congress at the Beginning of the First Session of the Fifty-Second Congress* (Washington, DC: Government Printing Office, 1892), 227.

9. Charles R. Stroh to Redfield Proctor, January 14, 1891, M983-2, 2: 1022–23.

10. Charles A. Eastman, *From the Deep Woods to Civilization: Chapters in the Autobiography of an Indian* (Boston: Little, Brown, and Company, 1916), 111, 114.

11. Nelson A. Miles to Adjutant General (AG), January 27, 1891, M983-2, 2:1019; on the delegation, see Richardson, *Wounded Knee*, 297–98.

12. "Mr. Noble Meets the Sioux," *Omaha Sunday Bee*, February 8, 1891.

13. "The Wounded Knee Fight," *(NY) Sun*, February 12, 1891.

14. "Serious Charges Made," *Washington Critic*, February 11, 1891; Steve Potts, "American Horse," *The Encyclopedia of North American Indian Wars, 1607–1890*, 1: 13–14.

15. "The Wounded Knee Fight," (*NY*) *Sun*, February 12, 1891.

16. "The Wounded Knee Fight," (*NY*) *Sun*, February 12, 1891.

17. "The Wounded Knee Fight," (*NY*) *Sun*, February 12, 1891. See also John Shangrau, interview, November 5, 1906, in Richard E. Jensen, ed., *Voices of the American West*, vol. 1, *The Indian Interviews of Eli S. Ricker, 1903–1919* (Lincoln: University of Nebraska Press, 2005), 262.

18. "The Wounded Knee Fight," (*NY*) *Sun*, February 12, 1891.

19. "The Wounded Knee Fight," (*NY*) *Sun*, February 12, 1891.

20. *Sixtieth Annual Report of the Commissioner of Indian Affairs to the Secretary of the Interior, 1891* (Washington, DC: Government Printing Office, 1891), 181.

21. Redfield Proctor to Nelson A. Miles, February 12, 1891, 1–3, M983-2, 2: 1130–32.

22. "Indians Tell Their Story: Pathetic Recital of the Killing of Women and Children," *New York Times*, February 12, 1891, 6; "Was It to Avenge Custer?" *Omaha World-Herald*, February 12, 1891; "Custer's Avengers," *Los Angeles Herald*, February 12, 1891; T. A. Bland, ed., *A Brief History of the Late Military Invasion of the Home of the Sioux* (Washington, DC: National Indian Defence Association, 1891), 15–17; *Sixtieth Annual Report of the Commissioner of Indian Affairs*, 179–81; James Mooney, *The Ghost-Dance Religion and the Sioux Uprising of 1890*, in *Fourteenth Annual Report of the Bureau of Ethnology to the Smithsonian Institution, 1892–93* (Washington, DC: Government Printing Office, 1896), 884–86; Roy L. Brooks, ed., *When Sorry Isn't Enough: The Controversy over Apologies and Reparations for Human Injustice* (New York: New York University Press, 1999), 252–53.

23. Ch. 543, "An act making appropriations for the current and contingent expenses of the Indian Department, and for fulfilling treaty stipulations with various Indian tribes, for the year ending June thirtieth, eighteen hundred and ninety-two, and for other purposes," March 3, 1891, *The Statutes at Large of the United States of America from December, 1889, to March 1891, and Recent Treaties, Conventions, and Executive Proclamations* (Washington, DC: Government Printing Office, 1891), 26:1002. On the federal indemnity system, see Larry C. Skogen, *Indian Depredation Claims, 1796–1920*, Legal History of North America (Norman: University of Oklahoma Press, 1996).

24. Treaty with the Sioux—Brulé, Oglala, Miniconjou, Yanktonai, Hunkpapa, Blackfeet, Cuthead, Two Kettle, Sans Arcs, and Santee—and Arapaho, April 29, 1868, in *Indian Affairs: Laws and Treaties*, comp. and ed. by Charles J. Kappler (Washington, DC: Government Printing Office, 1904), 2:998. See also Skogen, *Indian Depredation Claims*, 188.

25. R. Eli Paul, "The Investigation of Special Agent Cooper and Property Damage Claims in the Winter of 1890 1891," *South Dakota History* 24, no. 3 (Winter 1994): 216–17.

26. Paul, "The Investigation of Special Agent Cooper," 216.

27. Paul, "The Investigation of Special Agent Cooper," 221.

28. Charles Blindman Sr. to Francis Case, March 29, 1937, Wounded Knee Massacre-Indian File, Binder 2, Francis H. Case Collection, University Archives, McGovern Library, Dakota Wesleyan University, Mitchell, South Dakota.

29. Annie Eagle Body, statement, January 15, 1937; Alice Dog Arm (Kills Plenty), statement, April 16, 1937; Nellie Knife, statement, n.d., Wounded Knee Massacre-Indian File, Binder 2, Case Collection, University Archives, McGovern Library, Dakoa Wesleyan University.

30. W. H. Cressey, "Omens of Bloodshed," *Omaha Daily Bee,* January 6, 1891; "Story of Lost Bird," *Omaha Daily Bee,* September 2, 1891; Mooney, *The Ghost-Dance,* 879–81; Renee Sansom Flood, *Lost Bird of Wounded Knee: Spirit of the Lakota* (New York: Scribner, 1995).

31. "Census of the Sioux Indians Belonging to the Cheyenne River Reservation Who Were in the Battle of Wounded Knee and are Yet at Pine Ridge Agency, S.D. Taken June 30/91," http://oyate1.proboards.com/index.cgi?board=census&action=print&thread=550, accessed April 1, 2013; F. A. Whitney to Acting Assistant Adjutant General (AAAG), January 3, 1891, M983-1, 2:824; Nelson A. Miles to AG, January 5, 1891, M983-1, 2:814; W. H. Cressey, "Omens of Bloodshed," *Omaha Daily Bee,* January 6, 1891; Frank D. Baldwin to Assistant Adjutant General (AAG), February 5, 1891, in M983-1, 2: 1075–76.

32. *Letter from the Secretary of the Interior, In Relation to the Affairs of the Indians at the Pine Ridge and Rosebud reservations in South Dakota,* 52nd Cong., 1st sess., Ex. Doc. 58, 46, 49, 70.

33. "Census of the Sioux Indians."

34. Joseph Horn Cloud, statement, October 23, 1906, in Jensen, ed., *The Indian Interviews,* 191; Joseph Kocer, statement, December 11, 1904, in Jensen, ed., *The Settler and Soldier Interviews,* 41; "Joseph Horn Cloud," *The Indian Sentinel* 2, no. 7 (July 1921): 332–34; Raymond J. DeMallie, *The Sixth Grandfather: Black Elk's Teachings Given to John G. Neihart* (Lincoln: University of Nebraska Press, 1984).

35. Joy Harjo and Gloria Bird, eds., *Reinventing the Enemy's Language: Contemporary Native Women's Writings of North America* (New York: Norton, 1997) and Scott Richard Lyons, *X-Marks: Native Signatures of Assent* (Minneapolis: University of Minnesota Press, 2010).

36. Joe Horn Cloud to Eli S. Ricker, December 23, 1903, Eli S. Ricker Collection, Nebraska State Historical Society, Lincoln, Nebraska.

37. See Royal B. Hassrick, *The Sioux: Life and Customs of a Warrior Society* (Norman: University of Oklahoma Press, 1964), 48–51; DeMallie, ed., *The Sixth Grandfather,* 391–94.

38. Joe and Daniel Horn Cloud, claim, April 15, 1896, photocopy, and Dewey Horn Cloud Beard, claim, April 15, 1896, photocopy, both in Box 3563B, H76.1, South Dakota State Historical Society, Pierre, South Dakota and Horn Cloud to Ricker, December 23, 1903, Ricker Collection, NSHS.

39. Joe and Daniel Horn Cloud, claim, April 15, 1896, photocopy in Box 3563B, H76.1, SDSHS.

40. Dewey Horn Cloud Beard, claim, April 15, 1896, photocopy in Box 3563B, H76.1, SDSHS.

41. Joseph Horn Cloud, statement, October 23, 1906, Jensen, ed., *The Indian Interviews*, 191; *New Lakota Dictionary*, 2nd ed. (Bloomington: Lakota Language Consortium, 2011), 1002.

42. Gary L. Roberts, "Sand Creek: Tragedy and Symbol," (PhD diss., University of Oklahoma, 1984), 1–34; Richard Slotkin, *The Fatal Environment: The Myth of the Frontier in the Age of Industrialization, 1800–1890* (1985; repr., Norman: University of Oklahoma Press, 1994), 476; Jacoby, *Shadows at Dawn*, 223–24.

43. Roberts, "Sand Creek," 1–34.

44. Paul A. Hutton, "Phil Sheridan's Pyrrhic Victory: The Piegan Massacre, Army Politics, and the Transfer Debate," *Montana: The Magazine of Western History* 32, no. 2 (Spring: 1982): 32–43; Richard Slotkin, "Massacre," *Berkshire Review* 14 (1979): 112–32; Jacoby, *Shadows at Dawn*, 223–24.

45. Nelson A. Miles to G. W. Baird, November 20, 1891, quoted in Jerry Green, ed., *After Wounded Knee: Correspondence of Major and Surgeon John Vance Lauderdale while Serving with the Army Occupying the Pine Ridge Indian Reservation, 1890–1891* (East Lansing: Michigan State University Press, 1996), 33; Robert Wooster, *Nelson A. Miles and the Twilight of the Frontier Army* (Lincoln: University of Nebraska Press, 1993).

46. Jensen, ed., *The Indian Interviews*, 425 n. 5. Emphasis original.

47. Horn Cloud to Ricker, December 23, 1903, Ricker Collection, NSHS.

48. Walter Johnson, "On Agency," *Journal of Social History* 37, no. 1 (August 2003): 113–24.

49. Frederick E. Hoxie, "From Prison to Homeland: The Cheyenne River Indian Reservation before WWI," *South Dakota History* 10, no. 1 (Winter 1979): 1–24 and Paul C. Rosier, *Serving Their Country: American Indian Politics and Patriotism in the Twentieth Century* (Cambridge, MA: Harvard University Press, 2009).

50. Frederick E. Hoxie, *A Final Promise: The Campaign to Assimilate the Indians, 1880–1920* (Lincoln: University of Nebraska Press, 1984); Richard White, *"It's Your Misfortune and None of My Own": A New History of the American West* (1991; repr., Norman: University of Oklahoma Press, 1993), 439–41; Philip J. Deloria, *Indians in Unexpected Places* (Lawrence: University Press of Kansas, 2004), 26–27.

51. R. V. Belt to John Willock Noble, April 9, 1891, M983-2, 2:1430.

52. Leonard Little Finger, interview, July 24, 1990, in Wounded Knee National Register of Historic Places Continuation Sheet, 38, http://pdfhost.focus.nps.gov/docs/NHLS/Text/66000719.pdf, accessed March 23, 2013.

53. Leo Killsback, "Sand Creek Massacre National Historic Site Dedicated," *Indian Country Today*, May 14, 2007, http://indiancountrytodaymedianetwork.com/ictarchives/2007/05/14/sand-creek-massacrenational-historic-site-dedicated-90781,

accessed May 11, 2013; Kelman, *A Misplaced Massacre*; "Tribe Remembers Nation's Largest Massacre," *Indian Country Today*, March 10, 2008, http://indiancountrytodaymedianetwork.com/ictarchives/2008/03/10/tribe-remembers-nations-largest-massacre79058, accessed May 11, 2013.

54. Mark Ratledge, "Observing the 1870 Baker Massacre," *The Buffalo Post: A News Blog About Native People and the World We Live In*, February 23, 2010, www.buffalopost.net/?p=7108, accessed May 11, 2013.

55. George Ellison, "Introduction: James Mooney and the Eastern Cherokee," in James Mooney, *History, Myths, and Sacred Formulas of the Cherokees* (Fairview, NC: Bright Mountain Books, 1992), 3–4.

56. Mooney, *The Ghost-Dance*, 868–70.

57. Mooney, *The Ghost-Dance*, plate XCIX, between 872 and 873.

58. Alan Radley, "Artefacts, Memory and a Sense of the Past," in *Collective Remembering*, eds. David Middleton and Derek Edwards (London: Sage, 1990), 48.

59. *Denver Post*, November 15, 1903, quoted in Jensen, ed., *The Settler and Soldier Interviews*, 389 n. 78. See also E. C. Swigert, statement, March 31, 1905, in Jensen, ed., *The Settler and Soldier Interviews*, 44; Mooney, *The Ghost Dance*, 869; Greene, *American Carnage*, 350.

60. Marla N. Powers, *Oglala Women: Myth, Ritual, Reality* (1986; repr., Chicago: University of Chicago Press, 1988), 94.

61. F. A. Whitney to AAAG, January 3, 1891, M983-1, 2:824; Nelson A. Miles to AG, January 5, 1891, M983-1, 2:814; W. H. Cressey, "Omens of Bloodshed," *Omaha Daily Bee*, January 6, 1891; Frank D. Baldwin to AAG, February 5, 1891, in M983-1, 2: 1075–76; John R. Neff, *Honoring the Civil War Dead: Commemoration and the Problem of Reconciliation*. Modern War Studies (Lawrence: University Press of Kansas, 2005), 25, 54.

62. Richmond L. Clow, "The Lakota Ghost Dance After 1890," *South Dakota History* 20, no. 4 (Winter 1990): 323 33.

63. Mooney, *The Ghost-Dance*, 779, 878–79; plate CI, between 876 and 877; L. G. Moses, *The Indian Man: A Biography of James Mooney* (1984; repr., Lincoln: Bison Books, 2002), 63–65.

64. "Graves of Dead Sioux," *Omaha World-Herald*, June 16, 1897.

65. "Indians Are Now Working," *Omaha Daily Bee*, August 17, 1903.

66. Hoxie, *Parading Through History*, 148.

67. Dippie, *The Vanishing American*, 95–106; Hoxie, *A Final Promise*, 17–20.

68. "A New Indian War Threatened," *(NY) World*, June 6, 1897.

69. "Graves of Dead Sioux," *Omaha World-Herald*, June 16, 1897.

70. "The Sioux Monument Scheme," *New York Times*, June 18, 1897.

71. "Graves of Dead Sioux," *Omaha World-Herald*, June 16, 1897.

72. "The Sioux Monument Scheme," *New York Times*, June 18, 1897.

73. Jean M. O'Brien, *Firsting and Lasting: Writing Indians Out of Existence in New England* (Minneapolis: University of Minnesota Press, 2010), 58, 88.

74. Hassrick, *The Sioux*, 295–97. Raymond J. Demallie, email to the author, July 31, 2012.

75. "Graves of Dead Sioux," *Omaha World-Herald*, June 16, 1897.

76. Todd Kerstetter, "Spin Doctors at Santee: Missionaries and the Dakota-Language Reporting of the Ghost Dance and Wounded Knee," *Western Historical Quarterly* 28, no. 1 (Spring 1997): 45–67; *New Lakota Dictionary*.

77. "A New Indian War Threatened," *(NY) World*, June 6, 1897.

78. "Indian Protest in Granite," *(NY) Sun*, November 2, 1902.

79. Radley, "Artefacts, Memory and a Sense of the Past," 48.

80. *Rushville (NB) Standard*, May 22, 1903.

81. "Indian Protest in Granite," *(NY) Sun*, November 2, 1902; "Indians Erect a Monument," *Omaha World-Herald*, May 22, 1903; Pine Ridge Agency clerk to Kimball Brothers, March 22, 1904, Misc. Letters and Telegrams, vol. 45, 439, RG 75, National Archives and Records Administration, Kansas City, Missouri.

82. T. R. Porter, "Red Men Erect Monument to Fallen Warriors," *Omaha World Herald* (Nebraska), June 7, 1903, 24.

83. "Sioux Monument to Braves Who Fell at Wounded Knee," *The Cedar Rapids (Iowa) Evening Gazette*, June 13, 1903, 11 and Frances Desmore, *Teton Sioux Music*. Smithsonian Institution, Bureau of American Ethnology, Bulletin 61 (Washington, DC: Government Printing Office, 1918), 81.

84. "Dedication of the Wounded Knee Monument," photograph, Ricker Collection, NSHS.

85. T. R. Porter, "Red Men Erect Monument to Fallen Warriors," *Omaha World Herald* (Nebraska), June 7, 1903, 24; William K. Powers, *Oglala Religion* (1975; repr., Lincoln: University of Nebraska Press, 1982), 132.

86. On the establishment of Memorial Day on May 30, see Blight, *Race and Reunion*, 71.

87. David Wallace Adams, *Education for Extinction: American Indians and the Boarding School Experience, 1875 1928* (Lawrence: University Press of Kansas, 1995).

88. Colin Kidd, *The Forging of Races: Race and Scripture in the Protestant Atlantic World, 1600–2000* (Cambridge: Cambridge University Press, 2006).

89. "Sioux Monument to Braves Who Fell at Wounded Knee," *The Cedar Rapids (IA) Evening Gazette*, June 13, 1903, 11. "Dedication of the Wounded Knee Monument," photograph, Ricker Collection, NSHS. Eli S. Ricker, diary, ca. 1903, in Jensen, ed., *The Settler and Soldier Interviews*, 56.

90. Ostler, *The Plains Sioux and U.S. Colonialism*, 169–93; Tom Holm, *The Great Confusion in Indian Affairs: Native Americans and Whites in the Progressive Era* (Austin: University of Texas Press, 2005), 40.

91. William J. Cleveland and A. J. Johnson to W. H. Clapp, June 22, 1900, box 32, fd. January 9, 1900-August 31, 1900, Misc. Letters Received from the Office of Indian Affairs, RG 75, NARA-KC; W. A. Jones to the US Indian Agents of the Sioux Agencies in South Dakota, November 28, 1900, Land box 22, fd. January 3-December 19, 1900, Misc. Letters Received from the Office of Indian Affairs, RG 75, NARA-KC). Acting Commissioner of Indian Affairs to John Brennan, May 15, 1905, Land box 23, fd. January 6, 1905-December 28, 1905, Misc. Letters Received from the Office of Indian Affairs, RG 75, NARA-KC.

92. Powers, *Oglala Women*, 195.

93. Powers, *Oglala Religion*, 131–34; Powers, *Oglala Women*, 198.

94. "Dedication of the Wounded Knee Monument," photograph, Eli S. Ricker Collection.

95. "Sioux Monument to Braves Who Fell at Wounded Knee," *The Cedar Rapids (IA) Evening Gazette*, June 13, 1903, 11 and T. R. Porter, "Red Men Erect Monument to Fallen Warriors," *Omaha World-Herald*, June 7, 1903, 24.

96. Powers, *Oglala Women*, 185–86. I am indebted to the late Marie Not Help Him for assistance on this point.

97. My thanks to Leonard Little Finger, Mike Her Many Horses, and the late Marie Not Help Him for this translation.

98. Names inscribed on the south side: Chief Big Foot, Mr. High Hawk, Mr. Shading Bear, Long Bull, White American, Black Coyote, Ghost Horse, Living Bear, Afraid of Bear, Young Afraid of Bear, Yellow Robe, Wounded Hand, Red Eagle, Pretty Hawk, Wm. Horn Cloud, Sherman Horn Cloud, Scatters Them, Red Fish, Swift Bear, He Crow, Little Water, and Strong Fox.

99. Names inscribed on the north side: Spotted Thunder, Shoots the Bear, Picked Up Horses, Bear Cuts Body, Chase in Winter, Tooth Its Hole, Red Horn, He Eagle, No Ears, Wolf Skin Necklace, Lodge Skin Knopkin (?), Charge At Them, Weasel Bear, Bird Shakes, Big Skirt, Brown Turtle, Blue American, Pass Water In Horn, Scabbard Knife, Small She Bear, and Kills Seneca.

100. Names inscribed on the west side: Horn Cloud, Courage Bear, and Crazy Bear.

101. Marie Not Help Him, phone interview, June 15, 2011.

102. On Big Foot as a peacemaker, see Ostler, *The Plains Sioux and U.S. Colonialism*, 327.

103. Paul Scolari, "Indian Warriors and Pioneer Mothers: American Identity and the Closing of the Frontier in Public Monuments, 1890–1930," (PhD diss., University of Pittsburgh, 2005), 13, 17.

104. "A New Indian War Threatened," *(NY) World*, June 6, 1897.

CHAPTER 5

1. Joseph Horn Cloud to Eli S. Ricker, December 23, 1903, Eli S. Ricker Collection, Nebraska State Historical Society, Lincoln, Nebraska.

2. Horn Cloud to Ricker, December 23, 1903, Ricker Collection, NSHS.

3. Royal B. Hassrick, *The Sioux: Life and Customs of a Warrior Society* (Norman: University of Oklahoma Press, 1964), 48–51; Raymond J. DeMallie, ed., *The Sixth Grandfather: Black Elk's Teachings Given to John G. Neihardt* (Lincoln: University of Nebraska Press, 1984), 391–94; Larry C. Skogen, *Indian Depredations Claims, 1796–1920*. Legal History of North America (Norman: University of Oklahoma Press, 1996), 9.

4. Joseph Horn Cloud, "List of Survivors of Big Foot's Band," ca. 1903, Richard E. Jensen, ed., *Voices of the American West*, vol. 1, *The Indian Interviews of Eli S. Ricker* (Lincoln: University of Nebraska Press, 2005), 204, 206–08. See also Joseph Horn Cloud, survivors list, July 10, 1917, Cherry Creek, South Dakota, photocopy in Wounded Knee Compensation Papers, 1891–1976, H76-24, South Dakota State Historical Society, Pierre, South Dakota.

5. Jeffrey Ostler, *The Lakotas and the Black Hills: The Struggle for Sacred Ground*. The Penguin Library of American Indian History (New York: Viking, 2010), 128. See also Raymond J. DeMallie, "Pine Ridge Economy: Cultural and Historical Perspectives," in *American Indian Economic Development*, ed. Sam Stanley (The Hague: Mouton Publishers, 1978), 251–57, and Jeffrey D. Means, "'Indians Shall Do Things in Common': Oglala Lakota Identity and Cattle-Raising on the Pine Ridge Reservation," *Montana: The Magazine of Western History* 61, no. 3 (Autumn 2011): 3–21.

6. Mario Gonzalez and Elizabeth Cook-Lynn, *The Politics of Hallowed Ground: Wounded Knee and the Struggle for Indian Sovereignty* (Urbana: University of Illinois Press, 1999), 395 n. 32.

7. Ostler, *The Lakotas and the Black Hills*, 3–27.

8. Ostler, *The Lakotas and the Black Hills*, 129–30; Horn Cloud to Ricker, December 23, 1903, Ricker Collection, NSHS; "Joseph Horn Cloud," *The Indian Sentinel* 2, no. 7 (July 1921): 333.

9. Richard Slotkin, *The Fatal Environment: The Myth of the Frontier in the Age of Industrialization, 1800–1890* (1985; repr., Norman: University of Oklahoma Press, 1994), 100–01.

10. Jeffrey Ostler, *The Plains Sioux and U.S. Colonialism from Lewis and Clark to Wounded Knee* (Cambridge: Cambridge University Press, 2004), 7, 194–216.

11. See Skogen, *Indian Depredation Claims*.

12. Treaty with the Sioux—Brulé, Oglala, Miniconjou, Yanktonai, Hunkpapa, Blackfeet, Cuthead, Two Kettle, Sans Arcs, and Santee—and Arapaho, April 29, 1868, in *Indian Affairs: Laws and Treaties*, compiled and edited by Charles J. Kappler (Washington, DC: Government Printing Office, 1904), 2:998. Initially, Article 1 required the Lakotas themselves to compensate parties wronged by "bad Indians" out of treaty annuities, but after 1870 the Treasury Department assumed all compensation payments in the indemnity system (Skogen, *Indian Depredation Claims*, 188).

13. Treaty with the Sioux, April 29, 1868, in *Indian Affairs*, 2:998.

14. R. Eli Paul, "The Investigation of Special Agent Cooper and Property Damage Claims in the Winter of 1890–1891," *South Dakota History* 24, no. 3 (Winter 1994): 221.

15. Paul, "The Investigation of Special Agent Cooper," 219.

16. Paul, "The Investigation of Special Agent Cooper," 234; Rani-Henrik Andersson, *The Lakota Ghost Dance of 1890* (Lincoln: University of Nebraska Press, 2008), 347 n. 179.

17. James Smalley to John Brennan, no date, Letters Received, 1881–1907, 1905-36010, RG 75, National Archives and Records Administration-Washington, DC. I am indebted to Philip Burnham for documents in this file.

18. John R. Brennan to CIA, [May 4, 1905], Letters Received, 1881–1907, 1905-36010, RG 75, NARA-W. It remains unclear whether these individuals were survivors or heirs of victims.

19. Acting Commissioner of Indian Affairs to John Brennan, February 17, 1904, Finance folder January 2, 1904-July 27, 1904, Finance box July 7, 1903-December 29, 1906, Letters Received from the Office of Indian Affairs, RG 75, National Archives and Records Administration-Kansas City, Missouri.

20. Edward Lazarus, *Black Hills, White Justice: The Sioux Nation versus the United States, 1775 to the Present* (1991; reprint, Lincoln: Bison Books, 1999), 124, 138–40.

21. Acting CIA to Brennan, February 17, 1904, Finance folder January 2, 1904-July 27, 1904, Finance box July 7, 1903-December 29, 1906, Letters Received from the Office of Indian Affairs, RG 75, National Archives and Records Administration-KC.

22. See John C. Borst, "The John R. Brennan Family Papers at the South Dakota Historical Resource Center," *South Dakota History* 14, no. 1 (1984): 68–72.

23. John Brennan to James Smalley, February 23, 1904, Letters Received, 1881–1907, 1905-36010, RG 75, NARA-W.

24. Frederick E. Hoxie, "From Prison to Homeland: The Cheyenne River Indian Reservation before WWI," *South Dakota History* 10, no. 1 (Winter 1979): 21–22.

25. James Smalley to John Brennan, no date, Letters Received, 1881–1907, 1905-36010, RG 75, NARA-W.

26. John R. Brennan to CIA, [May 4, 1905], Letters Received, 1881–1907, 1905-36010, RG 75, NARA-W.

27. Dewey Beard, claim, no date, Letters Received, 1881–1907, 1905-36010, RG 75, NARA-W. See also Horn Cloud, statement, October 23, 1906, in Jensen, ed., *The Indian Interviews*, 201.

28. Acting Commissioner of Indian Affairs to John Brennan, May 17, 1905, Finance folder January 3-December 29, 1905, Finance box 20, July 7, 1903-December 29, 1906, RG 75, NARA-KC.

29. Acting CIA to Brennan, May 17, 1905, Finance folder January 3-December 29, 1905, Finance box 20, July 7, 1903-December 29, 1906, RG 75, NARA-KC.

30. H. D. Rosenthal, *Their Day in Court: A History of the Indian Claims Commission* (New York: Garland Publishing, 1990), 22.

31. Lazarus, *Black Hills, White Justice*, 130.

32. Aside from James R. Walker, Eli S. Ricker, Walter Mason Camp, and Melvin Gilmore, New York artist William Reed interviewed survivor Dewey Beard sometime between 1907 and 1913. Reed's interview notes have not yet been located (Dewey Beard, interview, October 24, 1913, Melvin R. Gilmore Notebook, Melvin R. Gilmore Papers, NSHS).

33. US Congress, *Piegan Indians*, House Executive Documents 49, 185, 197, and 269, 41st Cong., 2nd Sess. (1870); Paul Hutton, "Phil Sheridan's Pyrrhic Victory: The Piegan Massacre, Army Politics, and the Transfer Debate," *Montana: The Magazine of Western History* 32, no. 2 (Spring 1982): 32–43; Ostler, *The Plains Sioux and U.S. Colonialism*, 46–48; Karl Jacoby, *Shadows at Dawn: A Borderlands Massacre and the Violence of History* (New York: Penguin, 2008), 187; Ari Kelman, *A Misplaced Massacre: Struggling Over the Memory of Sand Creek* (Cambridge, MA: Harvard University Press, 2013), 213–18; Andrew R. Graybill, *The Red and the White: A Family Saga of the American West* (New York: Liveright, 2014).

34. Gary Leland Roberts, "Sand Creek: Tragedy and Symbol," (PhD diss., University of Oklahoma, 1984), 701–11.

35. "Roberts, "Sand Creek," 699; Kelman, *A Misplaced Massacre*, 94.

36. Kelman, *A Misplaced Massacre*, 33–42.

37. Roberts, "Sand Creek," 710–11.

38. Hoxie, *A Final Promise*, 16.

39. Hoxie, *Talking Back to Civilization*, 17; Holm, *The Great Confusion in Indian Affairs*, 54.

40. Peter Nabokov, *A Forest of Time: American Indian Ways of History* (Cambridge: Cambridge University Press, 2002), 2–11.

41. Quoted in James R. Walker, *Lakota Belief and Ritual*, eds. Raymond J. DeMallie and Elaine A. Jahner (1980; repr., Lincoln: Bison Books, 1991), 7.

42. Walker, *Lakota Belief and Ritual*, 13–33.

43. Beard, "The Ghost Dance and Wounded Knee Fight," n.d., in Walker, *Lakota Society*, 168. On Beard, see Philip Burnham, *Song of Dewey Beard: Last Survivor of the Little Bighorn* (Lincoln: University of Nebraska Press, 2014).

44. Phillip Burnham, email to author, July 25, 2011; Dewey Horn Cloud Beard, Claim, April 15, 1896, photocopy in Box 3563B, H76.1, SDSHS.

45. James R. Walker, interview, November 21, 1906, in Jensen, ed., *The Settler and Soldier Interviews*, 24.

46. Rex E. Beach, "Wounded Knee," *Appleby's Booklover's Magazine* 7 (January–June 1906): 731–37.

47. Walker, *Lakota Society*, 157.

48. Michael Elliott, *Custerology: The Enduring Legacy of the Indian Wars and George Armstrong Custer* (Chicago: University of Chicago Press, 2007), 191–223.

49. Elliott, *Custerology*, 217.

50. Jerome A. Greene, *Lakota and Cheyenne: Indian Views of the Great Sioux War, 1876–1877* (Norman: University of Oklahoma Press, 1994), xxxiii; Elliott, *Custerology*, 220.

51. Donald F. Danker, "The Wounded Knee Interviews of Eli S. Ricker," *Nebraska History* 62, no. 2 (Summer 1981): 151.

52. Danker, "The Wounded Knee Interviews," 152–53; Jensen, ed., *The Indian Interviews*, xv-xvi, 56.

53. George E. Bartlett, statement, November 30, 1903, in Jensen, ed., *The Settler and Soldier Interviews*, 27–38. See also Danker, "The Wounded Knee Interviews," 151–243; Susan Forsyth, *Representing the Massacre of American Indians at Wounded Knee, 1890–2000* (Lewiston, NY: Edwin Mellon Press, 2003), 61–62, 68, 70–71, 73–75, 82–86; Heather Cox Richardson, *Wounded Knee: Party Politics and the Road to an American Massacre* (New York: Basic Books, 2010), 308–11.

54. Horn Cloud, statement, October 23, 1906, in Jensen, ed., *The Indian Interviews*, 191.

55. Beard, interview, February 20, 1907, in Jensen, ed., *The Indian Interviews*, 226; Eli S. Ricker to wife, November 21, 1907, quoted in Danker, ed., "The Wounded Knee Interviews," 241–42 n. 48.

56. Jensen, ed., *The Indian Interviews*, xvii-xviii. For the seminal New Western History text, see Patricia Nelson Limerick, *The Legacy of Conquest: The Unbroken Past of the American West* (1987; repr., New York: Norton, 2006).

57. Ricker, statement, in Jensen, ed., *The Settler and Soldier Interviews,* 16.

58. Ricker, statement, in Jensen, ed., *The Settler and Soldier Interviews*, 59, 61, 62.

59. Ricker, statement, in Jensen, ed., *The Settler and Soldier Interviews*, 59.

60. Ricker, statement, in Jensen, ed., *The Settler and Soldier Interviews*, 62.

61. Jensen, ed., *The Indian Interviews*, xxiii.

62. W. M. Camp, "Ghost Dance and Battle of Wounded Knee," *Winners of the West* 10, no. 11 (October 30, 1933): 4; Jerome A. Greene, "The Uses of Indian Testimony in the Writing of Indian Wars History," *Journal of the Order of the Indian Wars* 2, no. 1 (Winter 1981): 4; "Register of the Walter Mason Camp Papers, 1905–1925," http://files.lib.byu.edu/ead/XML/MSS57.xml, accessed June 18, 2013.

63. Elliott, *Custerology*, 196–97.

64. Walter Mason Camp to Joseph Horn Cloud, April 12, 1912; and Joseph Horn Cloud to Walter Mason Camp, May 4, 1912, Walter Mason Camp Papers, Little Bighorn Battlefield National Monument, Crow Reservation, Montana. When it was created in the 1970s, the Brigham Young University register of Camp's papers listed all known Camp documents held at BYU, Indiana University, and the Denver Public Library. Although the register lists an interview Camp conducted with Horn Cloud on July 12, 1912, the repository of the interview was not included, and I have been unable to locate it. (See "Register of the Walter Mason Camp Papers, 1905–1925," L. Tom Perry Special Collections, Harold B. Lee Library, Brigham Young University, Provo, Utah).

65. "Wounded Knee Indian Side," Data on Monument and Notes of Battlefield Fight from Indian Side (1910), Camp Collection, Manuscripts Department, Lilly Library, IU; Camp, "Ghost Dance and Wounded Knee," *Winners of the West*, 4.

66. "Register of the Walter Mason Camp Papers, 1905–1925."

67. On the circumstances leading to the film, see p. 73–80.

68. Sandra K. Sagala, *Buffalo Bill on the Silver Screen: The Films of William F. Cody*. The William F. Cody Series on the History and Culture of the American West (Norman: University of Oklahoma Press, 2013), 85.

69. Burnham, *Song of Dewey Beard*, 101–02.

70. "Says Wounded Knee Movies Are Unfair," *Lincoln Daily Star*, November 3, 1913, 1.

71. Ryley Cooper, "Thrill of Actual Battle Leaps Forth From Indian War Films," unidentified clipping, accessed 1/24/2015, *The William F. Cody Archive*.

72. On the dedication, see p. 99–103.

73. Gilmore, "The Truth of the Wounded Knee Massacre," *The American Indian Magazine* 5, no. 4 (October–December 1917): 241.

74. As quoted in Burnham, *Song of Dewey Beard*, 101.

75. Gilmore, "The Truth of the Wounded Knee Massacre," 241.

76. Robert L. Welsch, "Introduction," in Melvin R. Gilmore, *Prairie Smoke* (1929; Repr., St. Paul, MN: Minnesota Historical Society, 1987), xiv, xviii, xxi.

77. Melvin R. Gilmore, "The Truth of the Wounded Knee Massacre," 241.

78. Gilmore, "The Truth of the Wounded Knee Massacre," 241.

79. Joe Horncloud, interview, October 24, 1913, in Gilmore, "The Truth of the Wounded Knee Massacre," 242–48. No manuscript of Horn Cloud's testimony has been located. Dewey Beard, interview, October 27, 1913, Gilmore Notebook, Gilmore Collection, NSHS. The printed version of Beard's testimony is misdated as November 27, 1913, and is given under Beard's Lakota name, Iron Hail (Gilmore, "The Truth of the Wounded Knee Massacre," 248–51); Mary Mousseau, interview, October 29, 1913, Gilmore Notebook, Gilmore Collection, NSHS; Mrs. Mosseau [*sic*], interview, October 29, 1913, in Gilmore, "The Truth of the Wounded Knee Massacre," 251–52.

80. "Maj. Gen. Lee Here; Not in Wounded Knee Sham," *Omaha World-Herald*, October 23, 1913, 4; "Wounded Knee 'Movies' Said to be Defective," *Omaha World-Herald*, November 4, 1913, 2; "Criticizes Battle Films," *Sioux City Journal*, November 4, 1913; "Sioux Indians Go To Washington With a Grievance," *(NY) World*, November 30, 1913; "'Movies' Portrayal of Wounded Knee is Again Revived," *Rapid City (SD) Daily Journal*, January 10, 1914, in Brennan Scrapbook, 309, Brennan Collection, SDSHS. See also Lieut. Gen. Nelson A. Miles to John R. Brennan, October 12, 1913, in Brennan Scrapbook, 279, Brennan Collection, SDSHS; Frank Baldwin to John Brennan, December 6, 1913, Brennan Scrapbook, 31, Brennan Collection, SDSHS; John Brennan to Nelson A. Miles, December 6, 1913, Brennan Scrapbook, 312, Brennan Collection, SDSHS.

81. Gilmore, "The Truth of the Wounded Knee Massacre," 241; *Publications of the Nebraska State Historical Society* 18 (1917): 290; "Lincoln News Notes," *Omaha World-Herald*, January 26, 1914, 3.

82. Gilmore, "The Truth of the Wounded Knee Massacre," 242.

83. Gilmore, "The Truth of the Wounded Knee Massacre," 240–52.

84. John R. Brennan to CIA, March 10, 1914, Letters Sent to the Commissioner of Indian Affairs, January-April 1914, 221, RG 75, NARA-KC; "Claim Movies Misrepresenting," *Red Cloud (NB) Chief*, April 2, 1914, 6.

85. *Wyoming Tribune*, May 24, 1917, in *The William F. Cody Archive: Documenting the Life and Times of an American Icon*, http://codyarchive.org/texts/wfc.adv00922.html, accessed January 24, 2015.

86. D. C. to Ezekiel Ayers, January 28, 1916; Ezekiel Ayers to William F. Cody, April 16, 1916, *The William F. Cody Archive*, http://codyarchive.org/texts/wfc.css00603.html and http://codyarchive.org/texts/wfc.css00612.html, accessed January 24, 2015.

87. Moses, *Wild West Shows and the Images of American Indians*, 245.

88. "Library Reports on America's Endangered Silent-Film Heritage," December 4, 2013, www.loc.gov/today/pr/2013/13-209.html, accessed January 9, 2015.

89. Gilmore, "The Truth of the Wounded Knee Massacre," 240–52.

90. Gilmore, Notebook, Melvin R. Gilmore Papers, NSHS.

91. Walker, statement, November 21, 1906, in Jensen, ed., *The Settler and Soldier Interviews*, 24.

92. Henry Greenspan, *On Listening to Holocaust Survivors: Beyond Testimony*, 2nd Ed. (New York: Paragon House, 2010), 3, 42.

93. J. Spencer Fluhman, *"A Peculiar People": Anti-Mormonism and the Making of Religion in Nineteenth-Century America* (Chapel Hill: University of North Carolina Press, 2012).

94. "Getting Ready to Fight," *The Daily Critic* (Washington, DC), September 26, 1890; "The Messiah Craze," *The Inter Ocean* (Chicago, Illinois), November 23, 1890; "They Are Wild," *Omaha Daily Bee*, November 21, 1890; Nelson A. Miles to Adjutant General, November 28, 1890, M-983, 1:279, 283; Scott L. Pratt, "Wounded Knee and the Prospect of Pluralism," *Journal of Speculative Philosophy* 19, no. 2 (2005): 150–66; Todd M. Kerstetter, *God's Country, Uncle Sam's Land: Faith and Conflict in the American West* (Urbana: University of Illinois Press, 2006), 81–123.

95. Beard, "The Ghost Dance and Wounded Knee Fight," n.d., in Walker, *Lakota Society*, 157.

96. Beard, "The Ghost Dance and Wounded Knee Fight," 158.

97. Walker, statement, November 21, 1906, Jensen, ed., *The Settler and Soldier Interviews*, 24.

98. Beard, "The Ghost Dance and Wounded Knee Fight," 158–59.

99. Ostler, *The Plains Sioux and U.S. Colonialism*, 333.

100. Beard, "The Ghost Dance and Wounded Knee Fight," 160–61; Horn Cloud, statement, October 23, 1906, Jensen, *The Indian Interviews*, 195; Beard, statement, February 20, 1907, Jensen, *The Indian Interviews*, 209.

101. Frog, statement, January 7, 1891, "Report of Investigation into the Battle at Wounded Knee Creek, South Dakota, Fought December 29th, 1890," February 4, 1891, 65, *Reports And Correspondence Relating To The Army Investigations Of The Battle At Wounded Knee And To The Sioux Campaign Of 1890–1891* (Washington, DC: Government Printing Office, 1975), M983-1, 2: 717; Elks Saw Him, statement, January 7, 1891, Jensen, ed., *The Indian Interviews*, 131; "The Indian Version of the Fight at Wounded Knee," *Wichita (KS) Daily Eagle*, January 17, 1891.

102. Beard, "The Ghost Dance and Wounded Knee Fight," 159–60; Horn Cloud, statement, October 23, 1906, Jensen, ed., *The Indian Interviews*, 194–95; Beard, statement, February 20, 1907, Jensen, ed., *The Indian Interviews*, 212–23; Andrew Good Thunder, statement, July 12, 1912, 9–10, Camp Collection, Manuscripts Division, Lilly Library, IU.

103. Beard, statement, February 20, 1907, Jensen, ed., *The Indian Interviews*, 214; Good Thunder, statement, July 12, 1912, 13, Camp Collection, Manuscripts Division, Lilly Library, IU.

104. Horn Cloud, statement, October 23, 1906, Jensen, ed., *The Indian Interviews*, 196; Beard, statement, February 20, 1907, Jensen, ed., *The Indian Interviews*, 216.

105. Horn Cloud, statement, October 23, 1906, Jensen, ed., *The Indian Interviews*, 197–98; Beard, "The Ghost Dance and Wounded Knee Fight," n.d., in Walker, *Lakota Society*, 161; Beard, statement, February 20, 1907, Jensen, ed., *The Indian Interviews*, 216.

106. Beard, "The Ghost Dance and Wounded Knee Fight," 163–64; Good Thunder, statement, February 12, 1912, 25, Camp Collection, Manuscripts Division, Lilly Library, IU; One Skunk, Swift Dog, High Hawk, Blue Arm, Afraid of Enemy, and Blue Hair, statement, September 1915, Camp Collection, Manuscripts Department, Lilly Library, IU.

107. Beard, "The Ghost Dance and Wounded Knee Fight," 164; Horn Cloud, statement, October 23, 1906, Jensen, ed., *The Indian Interviews*, 199; Beard, statement, February 20, 1907, Jensen, ed., *The Indian Interviews*, 218–19.

108. Walker, interview, November 21, 1906, in Jensen, ed., *The Settler and Soldier Interviews*, 24.

109. Maj. Samuel M. Whitside, testimony, January 7, 1891, "Report of Investigation," 11–12, M983-1, 2: 663–64.

110. Frog, statement, January 7, 1891, "Report of Investigation," 65, M983-1, 2: 717; Elks Saw Him, statement, January 7, 1891, Jensen, ed., *The Indian Interviews*, 131; "The Indian Version of the Fight at Wounded Knee," *Wichita (KS) Daily Eagle*, January 17, 1891; quote in "The Wounded Knee Fight," *(NY) Sun*, February 12, 1891.

111. Hassrick, *The Sioux*, 73–74.

112. Beard, "The Ghost Dance and Wounded Knee Fight," 164–65. See also, Good Thunder, statement, February 12, 1912, 27–29, Camp Collection, Manuscripts Division, Lilly Library, IU.

113. Horn Cloud, statement, October 23, 1906, Jensen, ed., *The Indian Interviews*, 200; Beard, statement, February 20, 1907, Jensen, ed., *The Indian Interviews*, 219; Joseph Horn Cloud, statement, October 24, 1913, in Gilmore, "The Truth of the Wounded Knee Massacre," 247; Dewey Beard, statement, October 27, 1913, 5, Gilmore Notebook, Gilmore Collection, NSHS.

114. Christer Lindberg, ed., "Foreigners in Action at Wounded Knee," *Nebraska History* 71, no. 4 (Fall 1990): 171.

115. Lindberg, "Foreigners in Action at Wounded Knee," 174.

116. Lindberg, "Foreigners in Action at Wounded Knee," 176.

117. Whitside, testimony, January 7, 1891, "Report of Investigation," 7–8, M983-1, 2: 659–60; P. F. Wells, testimony, January 11, 1891, "Report of Investigation," 60–62, M983-1, 2: 712–14.

118. Help Them, statement, January 7, 1891, "Report of Investigation," 67, M983-1, 2:719. See also Frog, statement, January 7, 1891, "Report of Investigation," 66, M983-1, 2:717 and Elks Saw Him, statement, January 7, 1891, Jensen, ed., *The Indian Interviews*, 132.

119. Beard, "The Ghost Dance and Wounded Knee Fight," 164–65.

120. Horn Cloud, statement, October 23, 1906, Jensen, ed., *The Indian Interviews*, 200–01.

121. Beard, "The Ghost Dance and Wounded Knee Fight," 165–68; Horn Cloud, statement, October 23, 1906, Jensen, ed., *The Indian Interviews*, 201–02; Beard, statement, February 20, 1907, Jensen, ed., *The Indian Interviews*, 219–25.

122. Joseph Horn Cloud, statement, October 24, 1913, in Gilmore, "The Truth of the Wounded Knee Massacre," 243–48; Dewey Beard, statement, October 27, 1913, 4–8, Gilmore Notebook, Melvin R. Gilmore Collection, Nebraska State Historical Society, Lincoln, Nebraska.

123. Horn Cloud, statement, October 23, 1906, Jensen, ed., *The Indian Interviews*, 201.

124. Beard, statement, February 20, 1907, Jensen, ed., *The Indian Interviews*, 220–25.

125. Beard, "The Ghost Dance and Wounded Knee Fight," 168; Horn Cloud, statement, October 23, 1906, Jensen, ed., *The Indian Interviews*, 203; Beard, statement, February 20, 1907, Jensen, ed., *The Indian Interviews*, 226.

126. Mary Mousseau, interview, October 29, 1913, Gilmore Notebook, Gilmore Collection, NSHS; Mrs. Mosseau [sic], interview, October 29, 1913, in Gilmore, "The Truth of the Wounded Knee Massacre," 251–52. Otto Chief Eagle acted as interpreter for Mousseau's interview.

127. Horn Cloud, statement, October 23, 1906, Jensen, ed., *The Indian Interviews*, 200; Jonathan Green, *Cassell's Dictionary of Slang*, 2nd ed. (London: Weidenfeld & Nicholson, 2005), 670.

128. Walker, statement, November 21, 1906, in Jensen, ed., *The Settler and Soldier Interviews*, 25.

129. Beard, statement, February 20, 1907, Jensen, ed., *The Indian Interviews*, 219.

130. Horn Cloud, statement, October 23, 1906, Jensen, ed., *The Indian Interviews*, 201.

131. Beard, "The Ghost Dance and Wounded Knee Fight," 168.

CHAPTER 6

1. Louis Pfaller, *James McLaughlin: The Man With an Indian Heart* (New York: Vantage Press, 1978), 363, 426 n. 71.

2. Pfaller, *James McLaughlin*, 362.

3. McLaughlin to Secretary of the Interior, April 6, 1910, 3, Wounded Knee Massacre Claims, No. 31678—1920—260, RG 75, NARA-W. I am indebted to Mike Her Many Horses for copies of documents in this file.

4. McLaughlin to Secretary of the Interior, April 6, 1910, 2, Wounded Knee Massacre Claims, No. 31678—1920—260, RG 75, NARA-W.

5. James McLaughlin, *My Friend the Indian* (New York: Houghton Mifflin, 1910), vii. For more on McLaughlin's general worldview and context, see Frederick E. Hoxie, *A Final Promise: The Campaign to Assimilate the Indians* (Lincoln: University of Nebraska Press, 1984) and Tom Holm, *The Great Confusion in Indian Affairs: Native Americans and Whites in the Progressive Era* (Austin: University of Texas Press, 2005), 1–22.

6. Pfaller, *James McLaughlin*, 349–51.

7. Pfaller, *James McLaughlin*, 358–60.

8. Quoted in Pfaller, *James McLaughlin*, 362.

9. Ostler, *The Plains Sioux and U.S. Colonialism*, 212–16, 320–26. See also Pfaller, *James McLaughlin*, 128–31.

10. McLaughlin to Secretary of the Interior, April 6, 1910, 1–2, Wounded Knee Massacre Claims, No. 31678—1920—260, RG 75, NARA-W.

11. McLaughlin to Secretary of the Interior, April 6, 1910, 2, Wounded Knee Massacre Claims, No. 31678—1920—260, RG 75, NARA-W.

12. McLaughlin to Secretary of the Interior, April 6, 1910, 3, Wounded Knee Massacre Claims, No. 31678—1920—260, RG 75, NARA-W.

13. McLaughlin to Secretary of the Interior, April 6, 1910, 2–3, Wounded Knee Massacre Claims, No. 31678—1920—260, RG 75, NARA-W.

14. McLaughlin to Secretary of the Interior, April 6, 1910, 3–4, Wounded Knee Massacre Claims, No. 31678—1920—260, RG 75, NARA-W; Pfaller, *James McLaughlin*, 363.

15. H. D. Rosenthal, *Their Day in Court: A History of the Indian Claims Commission* (New York: Garland Publishing, 1990); Christian W. McMillen, *Making Indian Law: The Hualapai Land Case and the Birth of Ethnohistory* (New Haven, CT: Yale University Press, 2007).

16. John M. Long, brief, 1912, copy in James E. High Hawk to Thomas R. Nelson, Esq., April 2, 1924, 1891–1944 Wounded Knee, Sioux Miscellany Manuscripts, Box 3549B, H 75.321, Fd. 10, South Dakota State Historical Society, Pierre, South Dakota.

17. John M. Long to CIA R. G. Valentine, April 22, [1912], copied in High Hawk to Nelson, Esq., April 2, 1924, Sioux Miscellany Manuscripts, SDSHS; J. E. Hi Hawk to Ralph H. Case, Ralph H. Case Papers, Archives and Special Collections, University Libraries, University of South Dakota, Vermillion, South Dakota. The exact date of the BFSA's founding remains unknown, although it is possible that it was founded in preparation for this attempted suit before the Court of Claims.

18. Long, brief, 1912, copy in High Hawk to Nelson, Esq., April 2, 1924, Sioux Miscellany Manuscripts, SDSHS.

19. Long, brief, 1912, copy in High Hawk to Nelson, April 2, 1924, 3–5, Sioux Miscellany Manuscripts, SDSHS.

20. Long, brief, ca. 1912, copy in High Hawk to Nelson, April 2, 1924, 5–8, quote on 7, Sioux Miscellany Manuscripts, SDSHS. The Indian Office declined to support the BFSA's Court of Claims suit (T. H. Abbot to John M. Long, June 14 [or 18], 1912, copied in High Hawk to Nelson, Esq., April 2, 1924, Sioux Miscellany Manuscripts, SDSHS).

21. John M. Long to Robert G. Valentine, April 22, [1912], copied in James E. Highhawk to Thomas R. Nelson, Esq., April 2, 1924, Box 3549B, H 75.321, Fd. 10, 1891–1944 Wounded Knee, Sioux Miscellany Manuscripts, SHSHS.

22. T. H. Abbot to Long, June 14 [or 18], 1912, copied in James E. Highhawk to Thomas R. Nelson, Esq., April 2, 1924, Box 3549B, H 75.321, Fd. 10, 1891–1944 Wounded Knee, Sioux Miscellany Manuscripts, SHSHS.

23. J. E. Hi Hawk to Ralph H. Case, July 10, 1947, Ralph H. Case Papers, Archives and Special Collections, University Libraries, University of South Dakota, Vermillion, South Dakota.

24. Questions for Horn Cloud, Rosebud Reservation Interviews, Summer of 1912, Walter Mason Camp Collection, Manuscripts Department, Lilly Library, Indiana University, Bloomington, Indiana; Cheyenne River Reservation notes, September 1915, Camp Collection, Manuscripts Department, Lilly Library, IU.

25. Peter One Skunk, Jessie Swift Dog, Alex High Hawk, Charles Blue Arm, Solomon Afraid of Enemy, and Daniel Blue Hair, statement, September 1915, Cheyenne River Reservation notes, September 1915, Camp Collection, Manuscripts Department, Lilly Library, IU. Ray DeMallie graciously translated this document at my request.

26. One Skunk, Swift Dog, High Hawk, Blue Arm, Afraid of Enemy, and Blue Hair, statement, September 1915, Camp Collection, Manuscripts Department, Lilly Library, IU.

27. Long, brief, 1912, copy in High Hawk to Nelson, April 2, 1924, 7, Sioux Miscellany Manuscripts, SDSHS.

28. One Skunk, Swift Dog, High Hawk, Blue Arm, Afraid of Enemy, and Blue Hair, statement, September 1915, Camp Collection, Manuscripts Department, Lilly Library, IU.

29. Cheyenne River Reservation notes, September 1915, Camp Collection, Manuscripts Department, Lilly Library, IU.

30. See US Congress, *Piegan Indians*, House Executive Documents 49, 185, and 269, 41st Cong., 2nd Sess. (1870) Paul Hutton, "Phil Sheridan's Pyrrhic Victory: The Piegan Massacre, Army Politics, and the Transfer Debate," *Montana: The Magazine of Western History* 32, no. 2 (Spring 1982): 32–43; Andrew R. Graybill, *The Red and the White: A Family Saga in the American West* (New York: Liveright, 2014).

31. Joseph Kipp, statement, February 8, 1913, "Claims of the Heirs of Chief Heavy Runner, SB 287, Letters & Affidavit," MF 53a-d, Montana Historical Society, Helena, Montana. I am indebted to Andrew R. Graybill for copies of documents in this file.

32. Arthur E. McFatridge to Commissioner of Indian Affairs, February 8, 1913, "Claims of the Heirs of Chief Heavy Runner, SB 287, Letters & Affidavit," MF 53a-d, MHS.

33. Arthur E. McFatridge to Cato Sells, January 14, 1914, "Claims of the Heirs of Chief Heavy Runner, SB 287, Letters & Affidavit," MF 53a-d, MHS.

34. Assistant Commissioner of Indian Affairs to Secretary of War, April 7, 1914; Henry Breckinridge to Secretary of the Interior, April 10, 1914; Dick Kipp, William Upham, and Emma Miller to Harry Lane, January 18, 1915, "Claims of the Heirs of Chief Heavy Runner, SB 287, Letters & Affidavit," MF 53a-d, MHS.

35. A Bill to reimburse the heirs of Chief Heavy Runner on account of his death and property taken from him at the time of the Baker massacre, S. 7523, February 2, 1915, 63rd Cong., 3rd Sess.

36. First Assistant Secretary of the Interior to Henry F. Ashurst, February 20, 1915, "Claims of the Heirs of Chief Heavy Runner, SB 287, Letters & Affidavit," MF 53a-d, MHS.

37. A Bill to reimburse the heirs of Chief Heavy Runner on account of his death and property taken from him at the time of the Baker massacre, S. 1543, December 10, 1915, 64th Cong., 1st Sess.; A Bill to reimburse the heirs of Chief Heavy Runner on account of his death and property taken from him at the time of the Baker massacre, S. 417, April 4, 1917, 65th Cong., 1st Sess.; A Bill to reimburse the heirs of Chief Heavy Runner on account of his death and property taken from him at the time of the Baker massacre, S. 3775, January 22, 1920, 66th Cong., 1st Sess.; A bill to reimburse the Heirs of Chief Heavy Runner on account of his death and for property taken from him at the time of the Baker massacre, April 12, 1921, S. 287, 67th Cong., 1st Sess.; T. J. Walsh to Dick Kipp, January 16, 1926, "Claims of the Heirs of Chief Heavy Runner, SB 287, Letters & Affidavit," MF 53a-d, MHS.

38. Hoxie, *A Final Promise*, 147–87.

39. Hoxie, *A Final Promise*, 220.

40. Raymond J. DeMallie, "Pine Ridge Economy: Cultural and Historical Perspectives," in *American Indian Economic Development*, edited by Sam Stanley (The Hague: Mouton Publishers, 1978), 257–60; Janet McDonnell, "Competency Commissions and Indian Land Policy, 1913–1920," *South Dakota History* 11 (Winter 1980): 21–34; Lazarus, *Black Hills, White Justice*, 125–27.

41. Indian Census Rolls, Pine Ridge Agency, 1916, 151, M595_370, *U.S., Indian Census Rolls, 1885–1940*, http://search.ancestry.com/search/db.aspx?dbid=1059, accessed December 20, 2012. Provo, UT: Ancestry.com Operations Inc, 2007.

42. Horn Cloud, statement, October 23, 1906, in Jensen, ed., *The Indian Interviews*, 201; Hearing Record, March 10, 1917, 1, photocopy in Application for Rations, Wounded Knee Injury 1917, Archives and Special Collections, University Libraries, USD.

43. Hearing Record, March 10, 1917, 1, photocopy in Application for Rations, Wounded Knee Injury 1917, Archives and Special Collections, University Libraries, USD.

44. Hearing Record, March 10, 1917, 1, photocopy in Application for Rations, Wounded Knee Injury 1917, Archives and Special Collections, University Libraries, USD; Joseph Horn Cloud, affidavit, March 12, 1917, 3, Wounded Knee Massacre Claims, No. 31678—1920—260, RG 75, NARA-W.

45. Joseph Horn Cloud, affidavit, March 12, 1917, Wounded Knee Massacre Claims, No. 31678—1920—260, RG 75, NARA-W; Beard, affidavit, March 12, 1917, Wounded Knee Massacre Claims, No. 31678—1920—260, RG 75, NARA-W. Henry Standing Bear, a Lakota cofounder of the Society of American Indians, helped Horn Cloud translate the affidavits (see Lazarus, *Black Hills, White Justice*, 130–37).

46. Hearing Record, March 10, 1917, 1–3, photocopy in Application for Rations, Wounded Knee Injury 1917, Archives and Special Collections, University Libraries, USD.

47. Theda Skocpol, "America's First Social Security System: The Expansion of Benefits for Civil War Veterans," *Political Science Quarterly* 108, no. 1 (Spring 1993): 85–116.

48. Hearing Record, March 10, 1917, 2–3, photocopy in Application for Rations, Wounded Knee Injury 1917 Archives and Special Collections, University Libraries, USD.

49. Horn Cloud to Ricker, December 23, 1903, Ricker Collection, NSHS; Horn Cloud, affidavit, March 12, 1917, Wounded Knee Massacre Claims, No. 31678—1920—260, RG 75, NARA-W.

50. James McLaughlin to Cato Sells, January 12, 1921, 18–19, photocopy in Wounded Knee Compensation Papers, SDSHS; James H. McGregor, *The Wounded Knee*

Massacre from the Viewpoint of the Sioux (1940; repr., Rapid City, SD: Fenske Printing, 1993), 98.

51. Nelson A. Miles to [Cato Sells], 13 March 1917, photocopy in Wounded Knee Compensation Papers, SDSHS.

52. E. B. Merritt to John R. Brennan, March 13, 1917, photocopy in Application for Rations, Wounded Knee Injury, 1917, Archives and Special Collections, University Libraries, USD.

53. John R. Brennan to [Cato Sells], May 11, 1917, photocopy in Application for Rations, Wounded Knee Injury, 1917, Archives and Special Collections, University Libraries, USD.

54. Cato Sells to John Barton Payne, May 4, 1920, photocopy in Wounded Knee Compensation Papers, SDSHS.

55. Horn Cloud and Beard, Pine Ridge Survivors List, May 28, 1917, photocopy in Wounded Knee Compensation Papers, SDSHS; Joseph Horn Cloud and Dewey Beard, Cheyenne River Survivors List, July 10, 1917, photocopy in Wounded Knee Compensation Papers, SDSHS; Joseph Horn Cloud and Dewey Beard, Standing Rock Survivors List, July 10, 1918, photocopy in Wounded Knee Compensation Papers, SDSHS. The lists contained an additional forty names of Lakotas who cannot definitively shown to be survivors, at least eleven of whom were heirs. Horn Cloud and Beard also identified one hundred and three survivors who had died prior to 1917, as well as one hundred and seventy-four individuals who were killed at Wounded Knee (Deceased Survivors List, July 10, 1918, photocopy in Wounded Knee Compensation Papers, SDSHS; Joseph Horn Cloud, "List of Indians Killed and Wounded in Sioux Massacre," 4, ca. 1920, photocopy in Wounded Knee Compensation Papers, SDSHS).

56. Nelson A. Miles to Cato Sells, April 12, 1920, photocopy in Wounded Knee Compensation Papers, SDSHS.

57. Cato Sells to Nelson A. Miles, May 6, 1920, 3, Wounded Knee Massacre Claims, No. 31678—1920—260, RG 75, NARA-W.

58. Lazarus, *Black Hills, White Justice*, 131.

59. Francis E. Leupp, *The Indian and His Problem* (New York: Scribners and Sons, 1910), 194, 195.

60. Leupp, *The Indian and His Problem*, 196. Leupp's proposal would become reality with the creation of the Indian Claims Commission in 1946 (Rosenthal, *Their Day in Court*).

61. Lazarus, *Black Hills, White Justice*, 135.

62. Sells to Payne, May 4, 1920, photocopy in Wounded Knee Compensation Papers, SDSHS.

63. Sells to Payne, May 4, 1920, photocopy in Wounded Knee Compensation Papers, SDSHS.

64. Sells to Miles, May 6, 1920, No. 31678—1920—260, Wounded Knee Massacre Claims, RG 75, NARA-W.

65. James McLaughlin, memorandum, May 5, 1920, photocopy in Wounded Knee Compensation Papers, SDSHS.

66. Sells to Payne, May 4, 1920, photocopy in Wounded Knee Compensation Papers, SDSHS.

67. McLaughlin, *My Friend the Indian*, vii.

68. Sells to Miles, May 6, 1920, 1, Wounded Knee Massacre Claims, No. 31678—1920—260, RG 75, NARA-W.

69. See marginal notes on Horn Cloud and Beard, Pine Ridge Survivors List, May 28, 1917, photocopy in Wounded Knee Compensation Papers, SDSHS; Horn Cloud and Beard, Cheyenne River Survivors List, July 10, 1917, photocopy in Wounded Knee Compensation Papers, SDSHS; Horn Cloud and Beard, Standing Rock Survivors List, July 10, 1918, photocopy in Wounded Knee Compensation Papers, SDSHS.

70. Notebook 40, MF roll 17, 4–8 (Standing Rock), 9–25 (Cheyenne River), 28–73 (Pine Ridge), James McLaughlin Papers, Assumption Abbey Archives, Richardton, North Dakota; McLaughlin to Sells, January 12, 1921, photocopy in Wounded Knee Compensation Papers, SDSHS; Forsyth, *Representing the Massacre*, 62–63, 69, 75–78, 86–88.

71. McLaughlin to Sells, January 12, 1921, photocopy in Wounded Knee Compensation Papers, SDSHS.

72. H. David Brumble III, *American Indian Autobiography* (Berkeley: University of California Press, 1988), 26–27; David Middleton and Derek Edwards, "Conversational Remembering: A Social Psychological Approach," in *Collective Remembering*, edited by David Middleton and Derek Edwards (London: Sage Publications, 1990), 23–45; Geoffrey Cubitt, *History and Memory* (Manchester: Manchester University Press, 2007), 189–90.

73. Pain on Hip, statement, July 21, 1920, Notebook 20, 60, MF roll 17, McLaughlin Papers, Assumption Abbey Archives.

74. Bear Gone (aka Mrs. High Cat), statement, May 18, 1920, Notebook 40, 2–3, MF roll 17, McLaughlin Papers, Assumption Abbey Archives.

75. Joseph Horn Cloud, statement, July 22, 1920, Notebook 20, 1, 59, MF roll 17, McLaughlin Papers, Assumption Abbey Archives.

76. Joseph Horn Cloud to James McLaughlin, July 23, 1920, Wounded Knee Massacre Claims, No. 31678—1920—260, RG 75, NARA-W.

77. Joseph Horn Cloud to Franklin Lane, May 8, 1915, RG 75, NARA-W. I am indebted to Phillip Burnham for a copy of this document. On Black Buffalo's relations with the United States, see Robert L. Fisher, "The Treaties of Portage Des Sioux," *Mississippi Valley Historical Review* 19, no. 4 (March 1933): 495–508; James P. Ronda, *Lewis and Clark Among the Indians*, Bicentennial Edition (Lincoln: University of Nebraska Press, 2002), 27–41; Craig Howe, "Lewis and Clark among the Tetons: Smoking Out What Really Happened," *Wicazo Sa Review* 19, no. 1, American Indian Encounters with Lewis and Clark (Spring 2004): 131–43.

78. Horn Cloud to Lane, May 8, 1915, RG 75, NARA-W. Horn Cloud to McLaughlin, July 23, 1920, Wounded Knee Massacre Claims, No. 31678—1920—260, RG 75, NARA-W. On William Tecumseh Sherman, see Michael Fellman, *Citizen Sherman: A Life of William Tecumseh Sherman* (Lawrence: University Press of Kansas, 1995).

79. Beard, statement, July 22, 1920, Notebook 20, 59, MF roll 17, McLaughlin Papers, Assumption Abbey Archives.

80. White Lance, statement, July 22, 1920, Notebook 20, 63, MF roll 17, McLaughlin Papers, Assumption Abbey Archives.

81. "Sketch of Philip Faribault Wells," in Jensen, ed., *The Indian Interviews*, 121–23.

82. McLaughlin to Sells, January 12, 1921, 25, photocopy in Wounded Knee Compensation Papers, SDSHS.

83. Philip F. Wells to Hugh L. Scott and James McLaughlin, September 3, 1920, Wounded Knee Massacre Claims, No. 31678—1920—260, RG 75, NARA-W.

84. Philip F. Wells, statement, September 3, 1920, 1, Wounded Knee Massacre Claims, No. 31678—1920—260, RG 75, NARA-W.

85. Wells to Scott and McLaughlin, September 3, 1920, 12, Wounded Knee Massacre Claims, No. 31678—1920—260, RG 75, NARA-W; Wells, statement, September 3, 1920, 6–7, Wounded Knee Massacre Claims, No. 31678—1920—260, RG 75, NARA-W.

86. Wells, statement, January 3, 1920, 7–11, Wounded Knee Massacre Claims, No. 31678—1920—260, RG 75, NARA-W.

87. On the spoils system and Palmer's appointment, see Richardson, *Wounded Knee*, 170–73.

88. Perain P. Palmer to T.J. Morgan, October 29, 1890, M983-1, 1: 27–29.

89. Perain P. Palmer to T.J. Morgan, November 10, 1890, M983-1, 1: 30–32. For an alternative explanation for the arms acquisitions, see Ostler, *The Plains Sioux and U.S. Colonialism*, 294.

90. For an analysis of Palmer's reports, see Rani-Hendrik Andersson, *The Lakota Ghost Dance of 1890* (Lincoln: University of Nebraska Press, 2008), 122–24.

91. McLaughlin to Sells, January 12, 1921, 1, photocopy in Wounded Knee Compensation Papers, SDSHS.

92. McLaughlin, *My Friend the Indian*, 180; Ostler, *The Plains Sioux and U.S. Colonialism*, 213–15.

93. Pfaller, *James McLaughlin*, 92.

94. McLaughlin to Sells, January 12, 1921, 1, photocopy in Wounded Knee Compensation Papers, SDSHS.

95. Pfaller, *James McLaughlin*, 129.

96. McLaughlin to Sells, January 12, 1921, 1, photocopy in Wounded Knee Compensation Papers, SDSHS.

97. McLaughlin to Sells, January 12, 1921, 24, photocopy in Wounded Knee Compensation Papers, SDSHS.

98. McLaughlin to Sells, January 12, 1921, 1, photocopy, Wounded Knee Compensation Papers, SDSHS.

99. McLaughlin to Sells, January 12, 1921, 26, photocopy in Wounded Knee Compensation Papers, SDSHS.

100. McLaughlin to Sells, January 12, 1921, 2–23, photocopy in Wounded Knee Compensation Papers, SDHS.

101. On McLaughlin's possession of these items, see McLaughlin to Sells, January 12, 1921, 26–27, photocopy in Wounded Knee Compensation Papers, SDSHS.

102. McLaughlin to Sells, January 12, 1921, 26, photocopy in Wounded Knee Compensation Papers, SDSHS.

103. "Joseph Horn Cloud," *The Indian Sentinel* 2, no. 7 (July 1921): 332–34.

104. Paul Bull Eagle, James Black Hawk, and James E. High Hawk to H. M. Tidwell, September 23, 1923, Main Decimal File, 053 Historical Data 1915, 1916, 1923, RG 75, NARA-KC.

CHAPTER 7

1. John Collier, editorial, *Indians at Work* 5, no. 8 (April 1938): 1–2.

2. H. D. Rosenthal, *Their Day in Court: A History of the Indian Claims Commission* (New York: Garland Publishing, 1990), 10–19; Edward Lazarus, *Black Hills, White Justice: The Sioux Nation versus the United States, 1775 to the Present* (1991; reprint, Lincoln: Bison Books, 1999), 138; Christian W. McMillen, *Making Indian Law: The Hualapai Land Case and the Birth of Ethnohistory* (New Haven, CT: Yale University Press, 2007), 62.

3. Francis Paul Prucha, *The Great Father: The United States Government and the American Indians* (Lincoln: University of Nebraska Press, 1984), 793–94.

4. Kenneth R. Philp, *John Collier's Crusade for Indian Reform, 1920–1954* (Tucson: University of Arizona Press, 1977).

5. Patricia Nelson Limerick, *The Legacy of Conquest: The Unbroken Past of the American West* (1987; reprint, New York: Norton, 2006).

6. Mario Gonzalez and Elizabeth Cook-Lynn, *The Politics of Hallowed Ground: Wounded Knee and the Struggle for Indian Sovereignty* (Urbana: University of Illinois Press, 1999), 395-405 n. 32.

7. Donald Lee Parman, *Indians and the American West in the Twentieth Century* (Bloomington: Indiana University Press, 1994), 89–106.

8. Raymond J. DeMallie, ed., *The Sixth Grandfather: Black Elk's Teachings Given to John G. Neihardt* (Lincoln: University of Nebraska Press, 1984), 30–47, 271, 275. Black Elk dictated in Lakota to his son, Benjamin, who then translated the words into English, which were then recorded in shorthand by Neihardt's daughter, Enid. Neihardt published a heavily edited account of the interview in 1932 as *Black Elk Speaks*.

9. See James H. McGregor to Grant Wright, October 27, 1931, Main Decimal File, 053 Historical Data 1927–1932, RG 75, National Archives and Records Administration-Kansas City, Missouri.

10. James H. McGregor, *The Wounded Knee Massacre from the Viewpoint of the Sioux* (1940; reprint, Rapid City, SD: Fenske Printing, 1993), 4.

11. On McGregor's editorial method, see Susan Forsyth, *Representing the Massacre of American Indians at Wounded Knee, 1890–2000*. Native American Studies (Lewiston, NY: Edwin Mellon Press, 2003), 63–64, 68–73, 78–82. McGregor employed William Bergen and Henry Standing Bear, a "red progressive" cofounder of the Society of American Indians, as his interpreters, as well as an unnamed stenographer. McGregor, *The Wounded Knee Massacre*, 80; Hazel W. Hertzberg, *The Search for an American Indian Identity* (Syracuse, NY: Syracuse University Press, 1971), 36, 328 n. 12; Lazarus, *Black Hills, White Justice*, 130–37.

12. Memorial Day Program, May 25, 1932, Main Decimal File, 053 Historical Data 1927–1932, RG 75, NARA-KC; "The Ninth Annual Reunion and Memorial of the Survivors and Heirs of Chief Big Foot Band at the Historic Cemetery," June 28–29, 1941, Main Decimal File, fd. 044 Monuments and Memorials, bx 160 042.0-047 1922-28, RG 75, NARA-KC.

13. Afraid of Enemy, statement, May 25, 1932, Wounded Knee Massacre Claims, No. 31678—1920—260, RG 75, National Archives and Records Administration, Washington, DC. I am indebted to Mike Her Many Horses for copies of documents in this file.

14. James Pipe on Head, et al., Resolution, February 14–15, 1933, Main Decimal Files, 036 Departmental Relations War Department, RG 75, NARA-KC. See also White Lance, statement, no date, and George Running Hawk, statement, no date, Wounded Knee Massacre Claims, No. 31678—1920—260, RG 75, NARA-W. At least nine typed manuscript statements—not all of them complete—have survived, including those for Bertha Kills Close to Lodge, Charley Blue Arm, Donald Blue Hair, George Running Hawk, Henry Jackson, James Hi Hawk, Peter Stand, Rough Feather, White Lance (Wounded Knee Massacre Claims, No. 31678—1920—260, RG 75, NARA-W). Along from these, McGregor reproduced twelve additional statements in *The Wounded Knee Massacre*, for which manuscripts have not been located: Dewey Beard (95–97), James Pipe on Head (98–99), Louise Weasel Bear (101), Mary Mousseau (105–06), Edward Owl King (107–09), John Little Finger (111–12), Alice Dog Arm or Kills Plenty (114), Frank Sits Poor (120–21), Richard Afraid of Hawk (121–22), Joseph Black Hair (122–24), Dog Chief (124–26), and Nellie Knife (130). McGregor also identified Charles Blind Man as a survivor who gave an account, but the account does not ultimately appear in McGregor's book, and no manuscript account has been located (McGregor, *The Wounded Knee Massacre*, Table of Contents).

15. 40s: James Hi Hawk (48), Henry Jackson (49). 50s: Edward Owl King (52), James Pipe on Head (53), George Running Hawk (54), Alice Dog Arm (56), Donald

Blue Hair (58), John Little Finger (59), Charles Blue Arm (59). 60s: Bertha Kills Close to Lodge (60), Richard Afraid of Hawk (60), Peter Stand (63), Nellie Knife (63), White Lance (64), Rough Feather (69). 70s: Dog Chief (72), Dewey Beard (77), Mary Mousseau (77), and Joseph Black Hair (77). The ages for Louise Weasel Bear and Frank Sits Poor have not been identified, although Weasel Bear implied to McGregor that she was an adult in 1890, while Sits Poor suggested he was a child (Weasel Bear, statement, McGregor, *The Wounded Knee Massacre*, 101; Sits Poor, statement, McGregor, *The Wounded Knee Massacre*, 120).

16. Pine Ridge: George Running Hawk, Henry Jackson, Peter Stand, Rough Feather, White Lance, Dewey Beard, James Pipe on Head, Mary Mousseau, John Little Finger, Richard Afraid of Hawk, Joseph Black Hair, Frank Sits Poor, and Dog Chief. Cheyenne River: Charles Blue Arm, Donald Blue Hair, James Hi Hawk, Edward Owl King, Alice Dog Arm, and Nellie Knife. Standing Rock: Louise Weasel Bear. Unknown: Bertha Kills Close to Lodge.

17. On the filming of the movie, see pp. 75–79 and 117–19.

18. Edward Owl King, statement, McGregor, *The Wounded Knee Massacre*, 108–09. See also Afraid of Enemy, statement, May 25, 1932, McGregor, *The Wounded Knee Massacre*, 119.

19. Afraid of Enemy, statement, May 25, 1932, McGregor, *The Wounded Knee Massacre*, 118–19.

20. White Lance, statement, McGregor, *The Wounded Knee Massacre*, 110.

21. Joseph Black Hair, statement, McGregor, *The Wounded Knee Massacre*, 123.

22. See statements of Peter Stand and James Hi Hawk, Wounded Knee Massacre Claims, No. 31678—1920—260, RG 75, NARA-W; White Lance, statement, no date, Wounded Knee Massacre Claims, No. 31678—1920—260, RG 75, NARA-W; see also Mary Mousseau and Edward Owl King, statements, McGregor, *The Wounded Knee Massacre*, 4, 105, 108–09. On witnesses affirming memories during oral recitation, see H. David Brumble III, *American Indian Autobiography* (Berkeley: University of California Press, 1988), 26–27 and Geoffrey Cubitt, *History and Memory*, Historical Approaches (Manchester: Manchester University Press, 2007), 189–90.

23. Nellie Knife, statement, McGregor, *The Wounded Knee Massacre*, 130. See also statements of Bertha Kills Close to Lodge and Dog Chief, McGregor, *The Wounded Knee Massacre*, 106, 125.

24. James Pipe on Head, statement, McGregor, *The Wounded Knee Massacre*, 98. See also Charley Blue Arm, statement, no date, Wounded Knee Massacre Claims, No. 31678—1920—260, RG 75, NARA-W; Dewey Beard, statement, McGregor, *The Wounded Knee Massacre*, 95; Louise Weasel Bear, statement, McGregor, *The Wounded Knee Massacre*, 101; Dog Chief, statement, McGregor, *The Wounded Knee Massacre*, 124–25.

25. Dewey Beard, statement, McGregor, *The Wounded Knee Massacre*, 95.

26. Dog Chief, statement, McGregor, *The Wounded Knee Massacre*, 124. See also statements of White Lance and Henry Jackson or Harry Kills White Man, no date, Wounded Knee Massacre Claims, No. 31678—1920—260, RG 75, NARA-W.

27. Peter Stand, statement, McGregor, *The Wounded Knee Massacre*, 116.

28. Betha Kills Close to Lodge, statement, no date, Wounded Knee Massacre Claims, No. 31678—1920—260, RG 75, NARA-W; George Running Hawk, statement, no date, Wounded Knee Massacre Claims, No. 31678—1920—260, RG 75, NARA-W; White Lance, statement, no date, Wounded Knee Massacre Claims, No. 31678—1920—260, RG 75, NARA-W; Dewey Beard, statement, McGregor, *The Wounded Knee Massacre*, 96; Dog Chief, statement, McGregor, *The Wounded Knee Massacre*, 125.

29. Charley Blue Arm, statement, no date, Wounded Knee Massacre Claims, No. 31678—1920—260, RG 75, NARA-W; Donald Blue Hair, statement, no date, Wounded Knee Massacre Claims, No. 31678—1920—260, RG 75, NARA-W; Peter Stand, statement, McGregor, *The Wounded Knee Massacre*, 116; Richard Afraid of Hawk, statement, McGregor, *The Wounded Knee Massacre*, 121.

30. Betha Kills Close to Lodge, statement, no date, Wounded Knee Massacre Claims, No. 31678—1920—260, RG 75, NARA-W; Charley Blue Arm, statement, no date, Wounded Knee Massacre Claims, No. 31678—1920—260, RG 75, NARA-W; George Running Hawk, statement, no date, Wounded Knee Massacre Claims, No. 31678—1920—260, RG 75, NARA-W; Louis Weasel Bear, statement, McGregor, *The Wounded Knee Massacre*, 101; John Little Finger, statement, McGregor, *The Wounded Knee Massacre*, 111; Mrs. Alice Dog Arm or Kills Plenty, statement, McGregor, *The Wounded Knee Massacre*, 114; Nellie Knife, statement, McGregor, *The Wounded Knee Massacre*, 130.

31. Mary Mousseau, statement, McGregor, *The Wounded Knee Massacre*, 105. See also Henry Jackson or Harry Kills White Man, no date, Wounded Knee Massacre Claims, No. 31678—1920—260, RG 75, NARA-W, and Dog Chief, statement, McGregor, *The Wounded Knee Massacre*, 125.

32. Dewey Beard, statement, McGregor, *The Wounded Knee Massacre*, 97. See also White Lance, statement, no date, Wounded Knee Massacre Claims, No. 31678—1920—260, RG 75, NARA-W, and Peter Stand, statement, no date, Wounded Knee Massacre Claims, No. 31678—1920—260, RG 75, NARA-W.

33. Peter One Skunk, Jessie Swift Dog, Alex High Hawk, Charles Blue Arm, Solomon Afraid of Enemy, and Daniel Blue Hair, affidavit, September 1915, Walter Mason Camp Collection, Lilly Library, Indiana University, Bloomington, Indiana; Henry Jackson or Harry Kills White Man, no date, Wounded Knee Massacre Claims, No. 31678—1920—260, RG 75, NARA-W; Rough Feather, statement, McGregor, *The Wounded Knee Massacre*, 99–100; John Little Finger, statement, McGregor, *The Wounded Knee Massacre*, 111; Richard Afraid of Hawk, statement, McGregor, *The Wounded Knee Massacre*, 121–22; Dog Chief, statement, McGregor, *The Wounded Knee Massacre*, 125.

34. Charley Blue Arm, statement, no date, Wounded Knee Massacre Claims, No. 31678—1920—260, RG 75, NARA-W.

35. Black Hair, statement, McGregor, *The Wounded Knee Massacre*, 123. See also Donald Blue Hair, statement, no date, Wounded Knee Massacre Claims, No. 31678—1920—260, RG 75, NARA-W; James Pipe on Head, statement, McGregor, *The Wounded Knee Massacre*, 99; Louis Weasel Bear, statement, McGregor, *The Wounded Knee Massacre*, 101.

36. Henry Greenspan, *On Listening to Holocaust Survivors: Beyond Testimony.* 2nd ed. (New York: Paragon House, 2010).

37. On the earliest survivor accounts, see pp. 45–49. On Beard's extended accounts, see pp. 112–16 and pp. 121–26.

38. On the Cheyenne River narrative traditions, see p. 133.

39. Peter Stand, statement, McGregor, *The Wounded Knee Massacre*, 116.

40. Richard Afraid of Hawk, statement, McGregor, *The Wounded Knee Massacre*, 122; Dog Chief, statement, McGregor, *The Wounded Knee Massacre*, 125.

41. Charley Blue Arm, statement, no date, Wounded Knee Massacre Claims, No. 31678—1920—260, RG 75, NARA-W. See also Dewey Beard, statement, McGregor, *The Wounded Knee Massacre*, 97.

42. George Running Hawk, statement, no date, Wounded Knee Massacre Claims, No. 31678—1920—260, RG 75, NARA-W; Bertha Kills Close to Lodge, statement, no date, Wounded Knee Massacre Claims, No. 31678—1920—260, RG 75, NARA-W; Donald Blue Hair, statement, no date, Wounded Knee Massacre Claims, No. 31678—1920—260, RG 75, NARA-W; Peter Stand, statement, McGregor, *The Wounded Knee Massacre*, 116; Rough Feather, statement, McGregor, *The Wounded Knee Massacre*, 100; White Lance, statement, no date, Wounded Knee Massacre Claims, No. 31678—1920—260, RG 75, NARA-W.

43. Bertha Kills Close to Lodge, statement, no date, Wounded Knee Massacre Claims, No. 31678—1920—260, RG 75, NARA-W; Donald Blue Hair, statement, no date, Wounded Knee Massacre Claims, No. 31678—1920—260, RG 75, NARA-W; George Running Hawk, statement, no date, Wounded Knee Massacre Claims, No. 31678—1920—260, RG 75, NARA-W; Peter Stand, statement, no date, Wounded Knee Massacre Claims, No. 31678—1920—260, RG 75, NARA-W; Rough Feather, statement, McGregor, *The Wounded Knee Massacre*, 100; White Lance, statement, no date, Wounded Knee Massacre Claims, No. 31678—1920—260, RG 75, NARA-W; Dewey Beard, statement, McGregor, *The Wounded Knee Massacre*, 97; Richard Afraid of Hawk, statement, McGregor, *The Wounded Knee Massacre*, 122; Dog Chief, statement, McGregor, *The Wounded Knee Massacre*, 125.

44. Nellie Knife, statement, McGregor, *The Wounded Knee Massacre*, 130. See also Louise Weasel Bear, statement, McGregor, *The Wounded Knee Massacre*, 101 and Mary Mousseau, statement, McGregor, *The Wounded Knee Massacre*, 105–06.

45. Frank Sits Poor, statement, McGregor, *The Wounded Knee Massacre*, 121.

46. James Pipe on Head, statement, McGregor, *The Wounded Knee Massacre*, 99.

47. Henry Jackson or Harry Kills White Man, statement, no date, Wounded Knee Massacre Claims, No. 31678—1920—260, RG 75, NARA-W. See also James Hi Hawk, statement, no date, Wounded Knee Massacre Claims, No. 31678—1920—260, RG 75, NARA-W, and Edward Owl King, statement, McGregor, *The Wounded Knee Massacre*, 108.

48. Charley Blue Arm, statement, no date, Wounded Knee Massacre Claims, No. 31678—1920—260, RG 75, NARA-W; Alice Dog Arm or Kills Plenty, statement, McGregor, *The Wounded Knee Massacre*, 114; Bertha Kills Close to Lodge, statement, no date, Wounded Knee Massacre Claims, No. 31678—1920—260, RG 75, NARA-W; White Lance, statement, no date, Wounded Knee Massacre Claims, No. 31678—1920—260, RG 75, NARA-W; Dewey Beard, statement, McGregor, *The Wounded Knee Massacre*, 97; Edward Owl King, statement, McGregor, *The Wounded Knee Massacre*, 108.

49. John Little Finger, statement, McGregor, *The Wounded Knee Massacre*, 112.

50. Peter Stand, statement, no date, Wounded Knee Massacre Claims, No. 31678—1920—260, RG 75, NARA-W.

51. John Little Finger, statement, McGregor, *The Wounded Knee Massacre*, 112. See also Dog Chief, statement, McGregor, *The Wounded Knee Massacre*, 125.

52. James Hi Hawk, statement, McGregor, *The Wounded Knee Massacre*, 127. See also James Hi Hawk, statement, no date, Wounded Knee Massacre Claims, No. 31678—1920—260, RG 75, NARA-W.

53. Paul C. Rosier, *Serving Their Country: American Indian Politics and Patriotism in the Twentieth Century* (Cambridge, MA: Harvard University Press, 2009), 42–70.

54. On these sympathetic interolocutors and the survivors, see pp. 111–26.

55. On Miles's advocacy of the survivors' claims, see pp. 138–44.

56. For the survivors' authorization of McGregor to pursue their claims, see James Pipe on Head, Charles Blindman Sr., Louis Iron Hawk, Richard Afraid of Hawk, Jackson He Crow, Alfred Frog, Peter Stands, and John Little Finger, Resolution, February 14–15, 1933, Main Decimal Files, 036 Departmental Relations War Department, RG 75, NARA-KC.

57. James H. McGregor to Joseph Coursey, April 3, 1933, Main Decimal File, 053 Historical Data 1932–1938, RG 75, NARA-KC.

58. Joseph Coursey to James H. McGregor, April 11, 1933, Main Decimal File, 053 Historical Data 1932–1938, RG 75, NARA-KC.

59. James H. McGregor to CIA C. J. Rhodes, April 3, 1933, Main Decimal File, 053 Historical Data 1932–1938, RG 75, NARA-KC.

60. John Collier to James H. McGregor, May 8, 1933, Main Decimal File, 053 Historical Data 1932–1938, RG 75, NARA-KC.

61. James H. McGregor to John Collier, December 18, 1933, Main Decimal File, 053 Historical Data 1932–1938, RG 75, NARA-KC. McGregor likely referred to Mary Mousseau (McGregor, *The Wounded Knee Massacre*, 105).

62. Justification of a Relief Bill, ca. February 26, 1934, English translation, Main Decimal File, 053 Historical Data 1932–1938, RG 75, NARA-KC. See also Wounded Knee Survivors Association, minutes, February 26, 1934, Main Decimal File, 053 Historical Data 1932–1938, RG 75, NARA-KC; James H. McGregor to James Pipe on Head, May 10, 1934, Main Decimal File, 053 Historical Data 1932–1938, RG 75, NARA-KC.

63. James H. McGregor to Theodore Werner, May 10, 1934, Main Decimal File, 053 Historical Data 1932–1938, RG 75, NARA-KC.

64. Theodore B. Werner to James H. McGregor, August 28, 1934, Main Decimal File, 053 Historical Data 1932–1938, RG 75, NARA-KC; Theodore B. Werner to James H. McGregor, October 18, 1934, Main Decimal File, 053 Historical Data 1932–1938, RG 75, NARA-KC.

65. James Hi Hawk, Philip Blackmoon, and Richard Afraid of Hawk, Justification for a Relief Bill, draft, June 20, 1935, Main Decimal File, 053 Historical Data 1932–1938, RG 75, NARA-KC.

66. Theodore B. Werner to James H. McGregor, July 18, 1935, Main Decimal File, 053 Historical Data 1932–1938, RG 75, NARA-KC; James H. McGregor to James Pipe on Head, August 2, 1935, Main Decimal File, 053 Historical Data 1932–1938, RG 75, NARA-KC; James H. McGregor to Theodore B. Werner, August 2, 1935, Main Decimal File, 053 Historical Data 1932–1938, RG 75, NARA-KC; Theodore B. Werner to James H. McGregor, August 9, 1935, Main Decimal File, 053 Historical Data 1932–1938, RG 75, NARA-KC; A Bill to Liquidate the Liability of the United States for the Massacre of Sioux Indian Men, Women, and Children at Wounded Knee on December 29, 1890, HR 11778, March 12, 1936, 74th Cong., 2nd sess., copy in Wounded Knee Massacre-Indian File, Francis H. Case Collection, University Archives, McGovern Library, Dakota Wesleyan University, Mitchell, South Dakota.

67. Malin Craig to Daniel W. Bell, June 3, 1936, in *Hearings Before the Subcommittee on Indian Affairs*, HR 2535, To Liquidate the Liability of the United States for the Massacre of Sioux Indian Men, Women, and Children on December 29, 1890, 75th Cong., 3rd sess., March 7, and May 12, 1938 (Washington, DC: Government Printing Office, 1938), 4.

68. Craig to Bell, June 3, 1936, in HR 2535, *Hearings*, 5.

69. Craig to Bell, June 3, 1936, in HR 2535, *Hearings*, 6–7.

70. Craig to Bell, June 3, 1936, in HR 2535, *Hearings*, 7.

71. Charles W. West to Will Rogers, April 28, 1937, HR 2535, *Hearings*, 4. On Roosevelt's (generally negative) views on granting compensation for past wrongs, see Rosenthal, *Their Day in Court*, 75–76.

72. West to Rogers, April 28, 1937, HR 2535, *Hearings*, 3.

73. Francis H. Case, *Biographical Directory of the United States Congress*, http:// bioguide.congress.gov/scripts/biodisplay.pl?index=C000221, accessed October 19, 2012.

74. Nancylee Lamport, "Francis Case: His Pioneer Background, Indian Legislation, and Missouri River Conservation" (MA thesis, University of South Dakota, 1972), 36; Richard R. Chenoweth, "Francis Case: A Political Biography," *South Dakota Historical Collections* 39 (1976–78): 322–25; David E. Wilkins, *Hollow Justice: A History of Indigenous Claims in the United States*. The Henry Roe Cloud Series on American Indians and Modernity (New Haven, CT: Yale University Press, 2013).

75. A bill to liquidate the liability of the United States for the massacre of Sioux Indian men, women, and children at Wounded Knee on December 29, 1890, HR 2535, January 11, 1937, 75th Cong., 1st sess., Wounded Knee Massacre-Indian File, Case Collection, University Archives, McGovern Library, Dakota Wesleyan University (hereafter DWU).

76. J. E. Hi Hawk to Francis Case, February 12, 1937, Wounded Knee Massacre-Indian File, Case Collection, University Archives, McGovern Library, DWU. On Hi Hawk, see *National Council of the Congregational Churches of the United States, 18th Regular Meeting, Grand Rapids, Michigan, October 21–29, 1919* (New York: Office of the National Council, 1919), 67; *South Dakota's Ziebach County, History of the Prairie* (Dupree, SD: Ziebach County Historical Society, 1982), http://files.usgwarchives.net/sd/ziebach/history/z-hst-21.txt, accessed July 9, 2013. At some point, probably in the 1920s, Hi Hawk simplified the spelling of his surname from "High Hawk" to "Hi Hawk."

77. Hi Hawk to Case, February 12, 1937, Wounded Knee Massacre-Indian File, Case Collection, University Archives, McGovern Library, DWU.

78. Francis Case to J. E. Hi Hawk, February 18, 1937, Wounded Knee Massacre-Indian File, Case Collection, University Archives, McGovern Library, DWU.

79. Francis Case to Louis Iron Hawk, February 5, 1937, Wounded Knee Massacre-Indian File, Case Collection, University Archives, McGovern Library, DWU; Henry Standing Bear to Francis Case, March 4, 1937, Wounded Knee Massacre-Indian File, Case Collection, University Archives, McGovern Library, DWU; James Pipe on Head to Francis Case, April 14, 1937, Wounded Knee Massacre-Indian File, Case Collection, University Archives, McGovern Library, DWU.

80. Technically, Pipe on Head was Big Foot's grandnephew, but in Lakota kin terms, he was the chief's grandson (see Mrs. Pipe on Head, statement, in James McLaughlin to Cato Sells, January 12, 1921, 10, photocopy in Wounded Knee Compensation Papers, South Dakota State Historical Society).

81. John Brown Dog to Francis Case, March 25, 1937, Wounded Knee Massacre-Indian File, Case Collection, University Archives, McGovern Library, DWU; Francis Case to James Brown Dog, March 31, 1937, Wounded Knee Massacre-Indian

File, Case Collection, University Archives, McGovern Library, DWU; James Brown Dog, statement, April 9, 1937, Wounded Knee Massacre-Indian File, Case Collection, University Archives, McGovern Library, DWU; James Brown Dog to Francis Case, April 17, 1937, Wounded Knee Massacre-Indian File, Case Collection, University Archives, McGovern Library, DWU; James Brown Dog to Francis Case, April 20, 1937, Wounded Knee Massacre-Indian File, Case Collection, University Archives, McGovern Library, DWU.

82. Francis Case to Ralph Case, April 1, 1937, Wounded Knee Massacre-Indian File, Case Collection, University Archives, McGovern Library, DWU; Francis Case to James Brown Dog, April 26, 1937, Wounded Knee Massacre-Indian File, Case Collection, University Archives, McGovern Library, DWU.

83. Francis Case to Charles Blindman Sr., April 2, 1937, Wounded Knee Massacre-Indian File, Case Collection, University Archives, McGovern Library, DWU; Ralph Case to Francis Case, April 29, 1937, Wounded Knee Massacre-Indian File, Case Collection, University Archives, McGovern Library, DWU.

84. West to Rogers, April 28, 1937, HR 2535, *Hearings*, 2.

85. West to Rogers, April 28, 1937, HR 2535, *Hearings*, 3.

86. West to Rogers, April 28, 1937, HR 2535, *Hearings*, 2, 3–4.

87. J. E. Hi Hawk to Francis Case, April 8, 1937, Wounded Knee Massacre-Indian File, Case Collection, University Archives, McGovern Library, DWU.

88. J. E. Hi Hawk to Francis Case, May 17, 1937, Wounded Knee Massacre-Indian File, Case Collection, University Archives, McGovern Library, DWU.

89. On the continued use of Big Foot Survivors Association, see James Hi Hawk, Philip Blackmoon, and Richard Afraid of Hawk, Justification for a Relief Bill, draft, June 20, 1935, Main Decimal File, 053 Historical Data 1932–1938, RG 75, NARA-KC; J. E. Hi Hawk to Francis Case, June 5, 1937, Wounded Knee Massacre-Indian File, Case Collection, University Archives, McGovern Library, DWU. On the use of the Wounded Knee Survivors Association name or close variant, see James Pipe on Head, Charles Blindman Sr., Louis Iron Hawk, Richard Afraid of Hawk, Jackson He Crow, Alfred Frog, Peter Stands, and John Little Finger, Resolution, February 14–15, 1933, Main Decimal Files, 036 Departmental Relations War Department, RG 75, NARA-KC and Scott Hart, "The Federal Diary," *Washington Post*, August 8, 1937, Wounded Knee Massacre-Indian File, Case Collection, University Archives, McGovern Library, DWU.

90. J. E. Hi Hawk to Francis Case, May 17, 1937, Wounded Knee Massacre-Indian File, Case Collection, University Archives, McGovern Library, DWU.

91. J. E. Hi Hawk to Francis Case, June 5, 1937, Wounded Knee Massacre-Indian File, Case Collection, University Archives, McGovern Library, DWU.

92. Francis Case to J. E. Hi Hawk, June 29, 1937, Wounded Knee Massacre-Indian File, Case Collection, University Archives, McGovern Library, DWU.

93. Jeffrey Ostler, *The Lakotas and the Black Hills*. The Penguin Library of American Indian History (New York: Viking, 2010), 136.

94. Francis Case to Ralph Case, July 6, 1937, Wounded Knee Massacre-Indian File, Case Collection, University Archives, McGovern Library, DWU; Ralph Case to Francis Case, July 9, 1937, Wounded Knee Massacre-Indian File, Case Collection, University Archives, McGovern Library, DWU.

95. Francis Case to J. E. Hi Hawk, July 10, 1937, Wounded Knee Massacre-Indian File, Case Collection, University Archives, McGovern Library, DWU.

96. See Francis Case to James Pipe on Head, December 28, 1937, Wounded Knee Massacre-Indian File, Case Collection, University Archives, McGovern Library, DWU; Edward Stover to Francis Case, October 4, 1937, Wounded Knee Massacre-Indian File, Case Collection, University Archives, McGovern Library, DWU.

97. Leo Iron Hawk, ca. 1939, Wounded Knee Massacre-Indian File, Case Collection, University Archives, McGovern Library, DWU.

98. Francis Case to James Pipe on Head, March 10, 1938, Wounded Knee Massacre-Indian File, Case Collection, University Archives, McGovern Library, DWU.

99. W. O. Roberts to Francis Case, February 23, 1938, Wounded Knee Massacre-Indian File, Case Collection, University Archives, McGovern Library, DWU; Jim Pipe on Head to Francis Case, February 26, 1938, Wounded Knee Massacre-Indian File, Case Collection, University Archives, McGovern Library, DWU. Charles White Wolf served as their interpreter.

100. Francis Case, statement, HR 2535, *Hearings*, 9.

101. Ralph Case, statement, March 7, 1938, HR 2535, *Hearings*, 8. On anti-attorney allegations, see Rosenthal, *Their Day in Court*, 22–27.

102. Ralph Case, statement, March 7, 1938, HR 2535, *Hearings*, 8–16.

103. Pipe on Head, statement, March 7, 1938, HR 2535, *Hearings*, 17.

104. Pipe on Head, statement, March 7, 1938, HR 2535, *Hearings*, 21.

105. Pipe on Head, statement, March 7, 1938, HR 2535, *Hearings*, 17.

106. Pipe on Head, statement, March 7, 1938, HR 2535, *Hearings*, 18.

107. The paintings were reproduced in "Present the Bill for the Historic 'Wounded Knee Massacre,'" *American Weekly*, April 24, 1938, 11, Wounded Knee Massacre-Indian File, Case Collection, University Archives, McGovern Library, DWU.

108. Pipe on Head, statement, March 7, 1938, HR 2535, *Hearings*, 19.

109. Pipe on Head, statement, March 7, 1938, HR 2535, *Hearings*, 21.

110. Dewey Beard, statement, March 7, 1938, HR 2535, *Hearings*, 22.

111. Beard, statement, March 7, 1938, HR 2535, *Hearings*, 22.

112. Beard, statement, March 7, 1938, HR 2535, *Hearings*, 22.

113. Beard, statement, March 7, 1938, HR 2535, *Hearings*, 24.

114. Rosier, *Serving their Country*, 53.

115. Pipe on Head, statement, March 7, 1938, HR 2535, *Hearings*, 21; Beard, statement, March 7, 1938, HR 2535, *Hearings*, 21–22.

116. Vine Deloria Jr. and Clifford M. Lytle, *American Indians, American Justice* (Austin: University of Texas Press, 1983), 162. See also David E. Wilkins and Heidi Kiiwetinepinesiik Stark, *American Indian Politics and the American Political System*, 3rd ed. (Lanham, MD: Rowman and Littlefield, 2011), 74; Royal B. Hassrick, *The Sioux: Life and Customs of a Warrior Society* (1964; repr., Norman: University of Oklahoma Press, 1967), 48–50.

117. Beard, statement, March 7, 1938, HR 2535, *Hearings*, 21–22.

118. Beard, statement, March 7, 1938, HR 2535, *Hearings*, 24.

119. Francis Case to James Pipe on Head, March 10, 1938, Wounded Knee Massacre-Indian File, Case Collection, University Archives, McGovern Library, DWU.

120. "Wounded Knee Survivors to Plead for Indemnity," *Omaha World Herald*, March 5, 1938, 10; "Massacre Survivors Ask Government Cash," *Omaha World Herald*, March 5, 1938, 30; "Wounded Knee Veterans," *Time*, March 14, 1938.

121. Collier, editorial, *Indians at Work* 5, no. 8 (April 1938): 1–2; John Collier to Francis Case, April 5, 1938, Wounded Knee Massacre-Indian File, Case Collection, University Archives, McGovern Library, DWU; Francis Case to Louie L. Lavatta, April 7, 1938, Wounded Knee Massacre-Indian File, Case Collection, University Archives, McGovern Library, DWU; Francis Case to James H. McGregor, April 12, 1938, Wounded Knee Massacre-Indian File, Case Collection, University Archives, McGovern Library, DWU.

122. As quoted in Rosier, *Serving Their Country*, 80.

123. "Present the Bill for the Historic 'Wounded Knee Massacre,'" *American Weekly*, April 24, 1938, 11, Wounded Knee Massacre-Indian File, Case Collection, University Archives, McGovern Library, DWU.

124. Francis Case to James Pipe on Head, May 3, 1938, Wounded Knee Massacre-Indian File, Case Collection, University Archives, McGovern Library, DWU; Francis Case to H. Merritt, May 9, 1938, Wounded Knee Massacre-Indian File, Case Collection, University Archives, McGovern Library, DWU; Francis Case to Frank G. Wilson, June 7, 1938, Wounded Knee Massacre-Indian File, Case Collection, University Archives, McGovern Library, DWU.

125. Francis Case to Charles Brooks, June 8, 1938, Wounded Knee Massacre-Indian File, Case Collection, University Archives, McGovern Library, DWU.

126. Limerick, *The Legacy of Conquest*, 35 54.

127. Brennan, statement, May 12, 1938, HR 2535, *Hearings*, 33–34.

128. Miles to G. W. Baird, November 20, 1891, quoted in Jerry Green, ed., *After Wounded Knee: Correspondence of Major and Surgeon John Vance Lauderdale while Serving with the Army Occupying the Pine Ridge Indian Reservation, 1890–1891* (East Lansing: Michigan State University Press, 1996), 33.

129. Brennan, statement, May 12, 1938, HR 2535, *Hearings*, 36.

130. Brennan, statement, May 12, 1938, HR 2535, *Hearings*, 38.

131. Rep. John R. Murdock, statement, May 12, 1938, HR 2535, *Hearings*, 41.

132. Rep. Francis Case, statement, May 12, 1938, HR 2535, *Hearings*, 41–42.

133. George M. Paulus, statement, May 12, 1938, HR 2535, *Hearings*, 43.

134. On the Piegan survivors' compensation claims, see pp. 134–35 and Andrew R. Graybill, *The Red and the White: A Family Saga of the American West* (New York: Liveright, 2014).

135. A bill to liquidate the liability of the United States for the massacre of Sioux Indian men, women, and children, HR 953, January 3, 1939, 76th Cong., 1st sess., copy in Wounded Knee Massacre-Indian File, Case Collection, University Archives, McGovern Library, DWU.

136. Harold L. Ickes to Will Rogers, April 12, 1939, Wounded Knee Massacre-Indian File, Case Collection, University Archives, McGovern Library, DWU.

137. Francis Case to Ralph Case, July 19, 1939, Wounded Knee Massacre-Indian File, Case Collection, University Archives, McGovern Library, DWU; House Committee on Indian Affairs, Liquidating the Liability of the United States for the Massacre of Sioux Men, Women, and Children at Wounded Knee, Report 2317, May 28, 1940, HR 953, 76th Cong., 3rd sess., copy in Wounded Knee Massacre-Indian File, Case Collection, University Archives, McGovern Library, DWU.

138. See Alan Brinkley, *The End of Reform: New Deal Liberalism in Recession and War* (New York: Knopf, 1995); Prucha, *The Great Father*, 993–1012.

139. Francis Case to James Pipe on Head, June 10, 1940, Wounded Knee Massacre-Indian File, Case Collection, University Archives, McGovern Library, DWU.

140. Rosenthal, *Their Day in Court*, 64.

141. Francis Case to John Cochran, May 31, 1940, Wounded Knee Massacre-Indian File, Case Collection, University Archives, McGovern Library, DWU.

142. E. D. Scott, "Wounded Knee: A Look at the Record," *Field Artillery Journal* 29, no. 1 (January–February 1939): 5–24.

143. Scott, "Wounded Knee," 22.

144. Scott, "Wounded Knee," 23.

145. Scott, "Wounded Knee," 22–23.

146. Scott, "Wounded Knee," 16, 19–20.

147. Scott, "Wounded Knee," 13–14, quote on 23.

148. Scott, "Wounded Knee," 16–21.

149. Scott, "Wounded Knee," 21.

150. Scott, "Wounded Knee," 23, 24.

151. Frank McNitt to Francis Case, February 16, 1939, Wounded Knee Massacre-Indian File, Case Collection, University Archives, McGovern Library, DWU.

152. Francis Case to Will Rogers, August 7, 1939, Wounded Knee Massacre-Indian File, Case Collection, University Archives, McGovern Library, DWU.

153. Report 2317, 3–5; Francis Case to James Pipe on Head, June 10, 1940, Wounded Knee Massacre-Indian File, Case Collection, University Archives, McGovern Library, DWU.
154. Francis Case to Willis Mountain, January 17, 1941, Wounded Knee Massacre-Indian File, 3–13, Case Collection, University Archives, McGovern Library, DWU.
155. Francis Case to Ralph Eagle Feather, November 28, 1940, Wounded Knee Massacre-Indian File, Case Collection, University Archives, McGovern Library, DWU.
156. Francis Case to Boyd Leedom, November 22, 1947, Wounded Knee Massacre-Indian File, Case Collection, University Archives, McGovern Library, DWU.

CONCLUSION

1. Philip Burnham, *Song of Dewey Beard: Last Survivor of the Little Bighorn* (Lincoln: University of Nebraska Press, 2014), 176. As Burnham notes, Beard's birthyear was recorded inconsistently over the years, making his exact age at the time of death impossible to calculate with precision (1–2).
2. "Dewey Beard Dead," *New York Times*, November 4, 1955, 29.
3. Dewey Beard, affidavit, March 12, 1917, Wounded Knee Massacre Claims, No. 31678—1920—260, RG 75, National Archives and Record Administration, Washington, DC.
4. Dewey Beard, statement, March 7, 1938, *Hearings Before the Subcommittee on Indian Affairs*, HR 2535, To Liquidate the Liability of the United States for the Massacre of Sioux Indian Men, Women, and Children on December 29, 1890, 75th Cong., 3rd sess., March 7, and May 12, 1938 (Washington, DC: Government Printing Office, 1938), 22.
5. H. D. Rosenthal, *Their Day in Court: A History of the Indian Claims Commission* (New York: Garland Publishing, 1990); David E. Wilkins, *Hollow Justice: A History of Indigenous Claims in the United States*. The Henry Roe Cloud Series on American Indians and Modernity (New Haven, CT: Yale University Press, 2013).
6. "Indians Seek Claims for Sioux Massacre," unidentified clipping, September 17, 1948, Wounded Knee Massacre Indian File, Case Collection, University Archives, McGovern Library, DWU; Francis Case to Boyd Leedom, November 22, 1947, Wounded Knee Massacre-Indian File, Case Collection, University Archives, McGovern Library, DWU; "Case Wants 1890 Indian Massacre Investigated," *Daily Republic* (Mitchell, SD), August 29, 1951, 22; A bill to authorize and direct the Indian Claims Commission to determine the liability for the engagement in the vicinity of Wounded Knee, South Dakota, on December 29, 1890, H.R. 9304, May 25, 1954, 83rd Cong., 2nd Sess.

7. *Hearings Before the Committee on the Judiciary,* S. 1147 and S. 2900, To Liquidate the Liability of the United States for the Massacre of Sioux Indian Men, Women, and Children at Wounded Knee on December 29, 1890, 94th Cong., 2nd sess., February 5–6, 1976 (Washington, DC: Government Printing Office, 1976).

8. Marie Not Help Him, oral statement, September 25, 1990, in *Hearing Before the Select Committee on Indian Affairs,* S. HRG. 101-1184, To Establish Wounded Knee Memorial and Historic Site and Proposal to Establish Monument Commemorating Indian Participants Little Big Horn and to Redesignate Name of Monument from Custer Battlefield to Little Big Horn National Monument Battlefield, 101st Cong., 2nd sess., September 25, 1990 (Washington, DC: Government Printing Office, 1991), 14.

9. Not Help Him, written statement, S. HRG. 101-1184, *Hearing,* 53.

10. Mario Gonzalez and Elizabeth Cook-Lynn, *The Politics of Hallowed Ground: Wounded Knee and the Struggle for Indian Sovereignty* (Urbana: University of Illinois Press, 1999); Wanbli Sapa and William Cooper, "Wounded Knee: Are we about to do it again?" 1995, www.dickshovel.com/WKc.html, accessed February 10, 2015.

11. James H. McGregor, *The Wounded Knee Massacre from the Viewpoint of the Sioux* (Baltimore: Wirth Bros., 1940). The sixteenth printing was by Fenwyn Press in 2010 (Rapid City, SD).

12. Dee Brown, *Bury My Heart at Wounded Knee: An Indian History of the American West* (1970; repr., New York: Henry Holt, 2000), vii.

13. Brown, *Bury My Heart at Wounded Knee,* xviii.

14. Brown, *Bury My Heart at Wounded Knee,* 439–55; McGregor, *The Wounded Knee Massacre.*

15. Sherry L. Smith, *Hippies, Indians, and the Fight for Red Power* (Oxford: Oxford University Press, 2012), 149.

16. Ari Kelman, *A Misplaced Massacre: Struggling Over the Memory of Sand Creek* (Cambridge, MA: Harvard University Press, 2013), 211–12.

17. According to the publisher, Brown's book has been translated into seventeen languages. On the international turn away from historical narratives emphasizing "progress" toward accounts focusing on "regret" in the twentieth century, see Jeffrey K. Olick, *The Politics of Regret: On Historical Memory and Historical Responsibility* (New York: Routledge, 2007).

18. Vine Deloria Jr., "This Country Was a Lot Better Off When the Indians Were Running It," *New York Times Magazine,* March 8, 1970, 48.

19. "A New Indian War Threatened," *(NY) World,* June 6, 1897.

20. Paul Chaat Smith and Robert Allen Warrior, *Like a Hurricane: The Indian Movement from Alcatraz to Wounded Knee* (New York: New Press, 1996), 117, 127–68; Troy R. Johnson, *The American Indian Occupation of Alcatraz Island: Red Power and Self-Determination* (1996; repr., Lincoln: University of Nebraska Press,

2008); Akim Reinhardt, *Ruling Pine Ridge: Oglala Lakota Politics from the IRA to Wounded Knee* (Lubbock: Texas Tech University Press, 2007).

21. Smith and Warrior, *Like a Hurricane*, 171–268.

22. Elizabeth Rich, "Remember Wounded Knee: AIM's Use of Metonymy in 21st Century Protest," *College Literature* 31, no. 3 (Summer 2004): 70–91; Michelene E. Pesantubee, "Wounded Knee: Site of Resistance and Recovery," in *Religious, Violence, Memory, and Place*, eds. Oren Baruch Stier and J. Shawn Landres (Bloomington: Indiana University Press, 2006), 75–88.

Bibliography

ARCHIVAL PRIMARY SOURCES
Assumption Abbey Archives

McLaughlin, James, Papers. Assumption Abbey Archives, Richardton, North Dakota.

Brigham Young University

Camp, Walter Mason, Papers, 1905–1925. MSS 57. L. Tom Perry Special Collections, Harold B. Lee Library, Brigham Young University, Provo, Utah.

Dakota Wesleyan University

Case, Francis H., Collection. University Archives, McGovern Library, Dakota Wesleyan University, Mitchell, South Dakota.

Indiana University

Camp, Walter Mason, Collection. Manuscripts Department, Lilly Library, Indiana University, Bloomington, Indiana.

Little Bighorn Battlefield National Monument

Camp, Walter Mason, Papers. Archives, Little Bighorn Battlefield National Monument, Crow Agency, Montana.

Montana Historical Society

Bureau of Indian Affairs. "Claims of the Heirs of Chief Heavy Runner, SB 287, Letters & Affidavit," MF 53a-d, Montana Historical Society, Helena, Montana.

National Archives and Records Administration-Kansas City, Missouri

Bureau of Indian Affairs. Pine Ridge Reservation Finance Records, RG 75. National Archives and Records Administration, Kansas City, Missouri.

Bureau of Indian Affairs. Letters Sent to the Commissioner of Indian Affairs, RG 75, NARA-KC.

Bureau of Indian Affairs. Main Decimal File, RG 75, NARA-KC.

Bureau of Indian Affairs. Misc. Letters and Telegrams, RG 75. NARA-KC.

Bureau of Indian Affairs. Misc. Letters Received from the Office of Indian Affairs, RG 75, NARA-KC.

National Archives and Records Administration-Washington, DC

Bureau of Indian Affairs. Letters Received, 1881-1907, 1905-36010, RG 75. National Archives and Records Administration-Washington, DC.

Bureau of Indian Affairs. Wounded Knee Massacre Claims, No. 31678—1920—260, RG 75, NARA-W.

Nebraska State Historical Society

Gilmore, Melvin R., Papers. RG3308.AM. Nebraska State Historical Society, Lincoln, Nebraska.

Ricker, Eli S., Collection. RG 1227. NSHS.

Wounded Knee Massacre Photographs, RG 2845-19-3, NSHS.

South Dakota State Historical Society

Box 3563B, H76.1. South Dakota State Historical Society, Pierre, South Dakota.

Brennan, John R., Collection. H72-2. SDSHS.

Sioux Miscellany Manuscripts, Box 3549B, H 75.321. SDSHS.

Wounded Knee Compensation Papers, 1891-1976, H 76-24. SDSHS.

University of South Dakota

Abourezk, James G., Papers, Archives and Special Collections, University Libraries, University of South Dakota, Vermillion, South Dakota.

Bureau of Indian Affairs. Application for Rations, Wounded Knee Injury 1917, Archives and Special Collections, University Libraries, USD.

Case, Ralph H., Papers. Archives and Special Collections, University Libraries, USD.

Wounded Knee Survivors Association Correspondence 1971-1973, Archives and Special Collections, University Libraries, USD.

PUBLISHED PRIMARY SOURCES

Barrere, Albert, ed. *A Dictionary of Slang, Jargon, and Cant*. London: George Bell and Sons, 1897.

Beach, Rex E. "Wounded Knee." *Appleby's Booklover's Magazine* 7 (January–June 1906): 731–37.

Bland, T. A., ed. *A Brief History of the Late Military Invasion of the Home of the Sioux*. Washington, DC: National Indian Defence Association, 1891.

"Book of Interments in the Pine Ridge Agency at Pine Ridge, S.D." *US, Burial Registers, Military Posts and National Cemeteries, 1862–1960*, http://search.ancestry.com/search/db.aspx?dbid=3135. Accessed December 2, 2010. Provo, UT: Ancestry.com Operations, Inc., 2012.

Camp, W. M. "Ghost Dance and Battle of Wounded Knee." *Winners of the West* 10, no. 11 (October 30, 1933): 4.

"The Case of General Forsyth." *Army and Navy Journal*, February 14, 1891.

"Census of the Sioux Indians Belonging to the Cheyenne River Reservation Who Were in the Battle of Wounded Knee and Are Yet at Pine Ridge Agency, S.D. Taken June 30/91." http://oyate1.proboards.com/index.cgi?board=census&action=print&thread=550. Accessed April 1, 2013.

Collier, John. Editorial. *Indians at Work* 5, no. 8 (April 1938): 1–2.

Danker, Donald F. "The Wounded Knee Interviews of Eli S. Ricker." *Nebraska History* 62, no. 2 (Summer 1981): 151–233.

Desmore, Frances. *Teton Sioux Music*. Smithsonian Institution, Bureau of American Ethnology, Bulletin 61. Washington, DC: Government Printing Office, 1918.

Eastman (Ohiyesa), Charles A. *From the Deep Woods to Civilization: Chapters in the Autobiography of an Indian*. Boston: Little, Brown, 1916.

Foley, Thomas W., ed. *At Standing Rock and Wounded Knee: The Journals and Papers of Father Francis M. Craft, 1888–1890*. Norman, OK: Arthur H. Clark Company, 2009.

Gilmore, Melvin R. "The Truth of the Wounded Knee Massacre." *The American Indian Magazine: The Quarterly Journal of the Society of American Indians* 5, no. 4 (October–December 1917): 240–52.

Gonzalez, Mario, and Elizabeth Cook-Lynn. *The Politics of Hallowed Ground: Wounded Knee and the Struggle for Indian Sovereignty*. Urbana: University of Illinois Press, 1999.

Green, Jerry, ed. *After Wounded Knee: Correspondence of Major and Surgeon John Vance Lauderdale while Serving with the Army Occupying the Pine Ridge Indian Reservation, 1890–1891*. East Lansing: Michigan State University Press, 1996.

Greene, Jerome A. *Lakota and Cheyenne: Indian Views of the Great Sioux War, 1876–1877*. Norman: University of Oklahoma Press, 1994.

Indian Census Rolls, Pine Ridge Agency, 1916. *US, Indian Census Rolls, 1885-1940*, http://search.ancestry.com/search/db.aspx?dbid=1059. Accessed December 20, 2012. Provo, UT: Ancestry.com Operations Inc, 2007.

Jensen, Richard E., ed. *Voices of the American West*. Vols. 1 and 2. Lincoln: University of Nebraska Press, 2005.

Jensen, Richard E., R. Eli Paul, and John E. Carter. *Eyewitness at Wounded Knee*. The Great Plains Photography Series. Lincoln: University of Nebraska Press, 1991.

"Joseph Horn Cloud." *The Indian Sentinel* 2, no. 7 (July 1921): 332–34.

The Journals of the Lewis and Clark Expedition Online. http://lewisandclarkjournals. unl.edu.

Leupp, Francis E. *The Indian and His Problem*. New York: Scribners and Sons, 1910.

Lindberg, Christer, ed. "Foreigners in Action at Wounded Knee." *Nebraska History* 71, no. 4 (Fall 1990): 170–81.

Mattes, Merrill J. "Report on Historical Investigation of Wounded Knee Battlefield Site, Pine Ridge Indian Reservation, South Dakota." October 3, 1952. www.nps.gov/ parkhistory/online_books/wokn/wokn_battlefield_site.pdf. Accessed July 15, 2013.

McGregor, James H. *The Wounded Knee Massacre from the Viewpoint of the Sioux*. 1940. Reprint, Rapid City, SD: Fenske Printing, 1993.

McLaughlin, James. *My Friend the Indian*. New York: Houghton Mifflin, 1910.

"Medal of Honor Recipients: Indian Wars Period." www.history.army.mil/html/ moh/indianwars.html. Accessed July 3, 2012.

Mooney, James. *The Ghost-Dance Religion and Wounded Knee*. In *Fourteenth Annual Report of the Bureau of Ethnology to the Smithsonian Institution, 1892–93*.Washington, DC: Government Printing Office, 1896.

National Council of the Congregational Churches of the United States, 18th Regular Meeting, Grand Rapids, Michigan, October 21–29, 1919. New York: Office of the National Council, 1919.

The Passing of the Redman: Being a Succinct Account of the Last Battle that Wrested Idaho from the Bondage of the Indians. Preston, ID: Franklin County Historical Society and Monument Committee, 1917. http://archive.org/details/passin-gofredmanboofranrich. Accessed May 15, 2012.

Publications of the Nebraska State Historical Society 18 (1917): 290.

Reports And Correspondence Relating To The Army Investigations Of The Battle At Wounded Knee And To The Sioux Campaign Of 1890–1891. Washington, DC: Government Printing Office, 1975. M-983.

Report of the Secretary of War; Being Part of the Message and Documents Communicated to the Two Houses of Congress at the Beginning of the First Session of the Fifty-Second Congress. Washington, DC: Government Printing Office, 1892.

Rogers, Robert. *A Concise Account of North America*. London: For the Author, 1765.

Scott, E. D. "Wounded Knee: A Look at the Record." *The Field Artillery Journal* 29, no. 1 (January–February 1939): 5–24.

Sixtieth Annual Report of the Commissioner of Indian Affairs to the Secretary of the Interior, 1891. Washington, DC: Government Printing Office, 1891.

US Congress. House. A Bill to Liquidate the Liability of the United States for the Massacre of Sioux Indian Men, Women, and Children at Wounded Knee on December 29, 1890, HR 11778, March 12, 1936, 74th Cong., 2nd sess.

US Congress. House. A Bill to Liquidate the Liability of the United States for the Massacre of Sioux Indian Men, Women, and Children at Wounded Knee on December 29, 1890, HR 2535, January 11, 1937, 75th Cong., 1st sess.

US Congress. House. A Bill to Liquidate the Liability of the United States for the Massacre of Sioux Indian Men, Women, and Children, HR 953, January 3, 1939, 76th Cong., 1st sess.

US Congress. House. A Bill to Liquidate the Liability of the United States for the Massacre of Sioux Indian Men, Women, and Children at Wounded Knee, HR Report 2317, May 28, 1940, HR 953, 76th Cong., 3rd sess.

US Congress. House. *Hearings Before the Subcommittee on Indian Affairs,* HR 2535, To Liquidate the Liability of the United States for the Massacre of Sioux Indian Men, Women, and Children on December 29, 1890, 75th Cong., 3rd sess., March 7, and May 12, 1938. Washington, DC: Government Printing Office, 1938.

US Congress. House. Piegan Indians. 41st Cong., 2nd sess., 1870. H. Ex. Doc. 49.

US Congress. House. Piegan Indians. 41st Cong., 2nd sess., 1870. H. Ex. Doc. 185.

US Congress. House. Piegan Indians. 41st Cong., 2nd sess., 1870. H. Ex. Doc. 197.

US Congress. House. Piegan Indians, 41st Cong., 2nd sess., 1870. H. Ex. Doc. 269.

US Congress. Senate. A Bill to Establish a Wounded Knee National Tribal Park, and for Other Purposes, S.382, February 9, 1995, 104th Cong., 1st sess.

US Congress. Senate. A Bill to Liquidate the Liability of the United States for the Massacre of Sioux Indian Men, Women, and Children at Wounded Knee on December 29, 1890, S. 1147, March 11, 1975, 94th Cong., 1st sess.

US Congress. Senate. A Bill to Liquidate the Liability of the United States for the Massacre of Sioux Indian Men, Women, and Children at Wounded Knee on December 29, 1890, S. 2900, January 29, 1976, 94th Cong., 2nd sess.

US Congress. Senate. *Hearings Before the Committee on the Judiciary,* S. 1147 and S. 2900, To Liquidate the Liability of the United States for the Massacre of Sioux Indian Men, Women, and Children at Wounded Knee on December 29, 1890, 94th Cong., 2nd Sess., February 5–6, 1976. Washington, DC: Government Printing Office, 1976.

US Congress. Senate. *Hearing Before the Select Committee on Indian Affairs,* S. HRG. 101–1184, To Establish Wounded Knee Memorial and Historic Site and Proposal to Establish Monument Commemorating Indian Participants Little Big Horn and to Redesignate Name of Monument from Custer Battlefield to Little Big Horn National Monument Battlefield, 101st Cong., 2nd sess., September 25, 1990. Washington, DC: Government Printing Office, 1991.

US Congress. Senate. *Letter from the Secretary of the Interior, In Relation to the Affairs of the Indians at the Pine Ridge and Rosebud reservations in South Dakota*. 52nd Cong., 1st sess., 1892. S. Ex. Doc. 58.

US Congress. Senate. To Acknowledge the 100th Anniversary of the Tragedy at Wounded Knee Creek, State of South Dakota, December 29, 1890, Wherein Soldiers of the United States 7th Cavalry Killed and Wounded Approximately 350–375 Indian Men, Women, and Children of Chief Big Foot's Band of Minneconjou Sioux, and to Recognize the Year of Reconciliation Declared by the State of South Dakota Between the Citizens of the State and the Member Bands of the Great Sioux Nation, S. Con. Res. 153, October 15, 1990, 101st Cong., 2nd sess.

US Congress. Senate. Treaty with the Sioux—Brulé, Oglala, Miniconjou, Yanktonai, Hunkpapa, Blackfeet, Cuthead, Two Kettle, Sans Arcs, and Santee—and Arapaho. April 29, 1868. In *Indian Affairs: Laws and Treaties*, compiled and edited by Charles J. Kappler, 2:998. Washington, DC: Government Printing Office, 1904.

Walker, James R. *Lakota Belief and Ritual*, edited by Raymond J. DeMallie and Elaine A. Jahner. 1980. Reprint, Lincoln: Bison Books, 1991.

Wells, Philip F. "Ninety-Six Years Among the Indians of the Northwest—Adventures of an Indian Scout and Interpreter in the Dakotas." *North Dakota History* 15, no. 4 (1948): 265–312.

The William F. Cody Archive: Documenting the Life and Times of an American Icon. http://codyarchive.org. Accessed January 24, 2015.

"Wounded Knee." National Historic Landmarks Program. http://tps.cr.nps.gov/nhl/detail.cfm?ResourceId=540&ResourceType=Site. Accessed July 15, 2013.

"Wounded Knee Medals of Dis Honor." www.ipetitions.com/petition/12-20-1890/. Accessed July 15, 2013.

ARTICLES AND BOOK CHAPTERS

Andrews, John. "Saving Their Language: Speakers Try to Revive Lakota and Dakota Before They Disappear." *South Dakota Magazine: Celebrating Life in South Dakota* (March/April 2009). http://southdakotamagazine.com/lakota-saving-their-language. Accessed May 18, 2013.

Borst, John C. "The John R. Brennan Family Papers at the South Dakota Historical Resource Center." *South Dakota History* 14 (1984): 68–72.

Chenoweth, Richard R. "Francis Case: A Political Biography. *South Dakota Historical Collections* 39 (1976–78): 288–433.

Clow, Richmond L. "The Lakota Ghost Dance After 1890." *South Dakota History* 20, no. 4 (Winter 1990): 323–33.

Coates, Lawrence. "The Mormons and the Ghost Dance." *Dialogue: A Journal of Mormon Thought* 18 (Winter 1985): 89–111.

Deloria, Ella Cara. "Dakota Treatment of Murderers." *Proceedings of the American Philosophical Society* 88, no. 5 (November 7, 1944): 368–71.

DeMallie, Raymond J. "Pine Ridge Economy: Cultural and Historical Perspectives." In *American Indian Economic Development*, edited by Sam Stanley, 237–312. The Hague: Mouton Publishers, 1978.

DeMallie, Raymond J. "The Lakota Ghost Dance: An Ethnohistorical Account." *Pacific Historical Review* 51, no. 4 (Nov. 1982): 385–405.

Dickson III, Ephraim D. "Honoring the Fallen: Establishment of the Fort Douglas Cemetery." *Fort Douglas Vedette: Newsletter of the Fort Douglas Museum Association* 34, no. 3 (Fall 2009): 3–6.

Edy, Jill A. "Journalistic Uses of Collective Memory." *Journal of Communication* 49, no. 2 (Spring 1999): 71–85.

Ellinghaus, Katherine. "Reading the Personal as Political: The Assimilationist Views of a White Woman Married to a Native American Man, 1880s–1940s." *Australasian Journal of American Studies* 18, no. 2 (December 1999): 23–42.

Ellison, George. "Introduction: James Mooney and the Eastern Cherokee." In *History, Myths, and Sacred Formulas of the Cherokees*, by James Mooney, 1–24. Fairview, NC: Bright Mountain Books, 1992.

Fisher, Robert L. "The Treaties of Portage Des Sioux." *Mississippi Valley Historical Review* 19, no. 4 (March 1933): 495–508.

Gedi, Noa, and Yigal Elam, "Collective Memory—What is It?" *History and Memory* 8, no. 1 (Spring–Summer 1996): 30–50.

Green, Jerry. "The Medals of Wounded Knee." *Nebraska History* (Summer 1994). www.dickshovel.com/GreenIntro.html. Accessed April 19, 2012.

Greene, Jerome A. "The Uses of Indian Testimony in the Writing of Indian Wars History." *Journal of the Order of the Indian Wars* 2, no. 1 (Winter 1981): 1–7.

Hämäläinen, Pekka. "The Rise and Fall of Plains Horse Cultures." *Journal of American History* 90, no. 3 (December 2003): 8333–62.

Hedren, Paul L. "The Contradictory Legacies of Buffalo Bill's First Scalp for Custer." *Montana: The Magazine of Western History* 55, no. 1 (Spring 2005): 16–35.

Ho Tai, Hue-Tam. "Remembered Realms: Pierre Nora and French National Memory." *American Historical Review* 106, no. 3 (June 2001): 906–22.

Howe, Craig. "Lewis and Clark among the Tetons: Smoking Out What Really Happened." *Wicazo Sa Review* 19, no. 1, American Indian Encounters with Lewis and Clark (Spring 2004): 131–43.

Hoxie, Frederick E. "From Prison to Homeland: The Cheyenne River Indian Reservation before WWI." *South Dakota History* 10, no. 1 (Winter 1979): 1–24.

Huntzicker, William E. "The 'Sioux Outbreak' in the Illustrated Press." *South Dakota History* 20, no. 4 (1990): 299–322.

Hutton, Paul. "Phil Sheridan's Pyrrhic Victory: The Piegan Massacre, Army Politics, and the Transfer Debate." *Montana: The Magazine of Western History* 32, no. 2 (Spring 1982): 32–43.

Jacobs, Margaret D. "The Eastmans and the Luhans: Interracial Marriage between White Women and Native American Men, 1875–1935." *Frontiers: A Journal of Women Studies* 23, no. 3 (2002): 29–54.

Johnson, Walter. "On Agency." *Journal of Social History* 37, no. 1 (Autumn 2003): 113–24.

Kammen, Michael. "Commemoration and Contestation in American Culture: Historical Perspectives." *Amerikastudien/American Studies* 48, no. 2 (2003): 185–205.

Kammen, Michael. "Frames of Remembrance: The Dynamics of Collective Memory by Iwona Irwin- Zareka." *History and Theory* 34, no. 3 (October 1995): 245–61.

Kerstetter, Todd. "Spin Doctors at Santee: Missionaries and Dakota-Language Reporting of the Ghost Dance and Wounded Knee." *Western Historical Quarterly* 28, no. 1 (Spring 1997): 45–67.

Klein, Christina. "'Everything of Interest in the Late Pine Ridge War Are Held by Us for Sale': Popular Culture and Wounded Knee." *Western Historical Quarterly* 25, no. 1 (Spring 1994): 45–68.

Kupperman, Karen Ordahl. "English Perceptions of Treachery, 1583–1640: The Case of the American 'Savages.'" *The Historical Journal* 20, no. 2 (June 1977): 263–87.

Linenthal, Edward Tabor. "'A Sore from America's Past That Has Not Yet Healed': The Little Bighorn." In *Sacred Ground: Americans and Their Battlefields*, 127–71. Urbana: University of Illinois Press, 1991.

McDonnell, Janet. "Competency Commissions and Indian Land Policy, 1913–1920." *South Dakota History* 11 (Winter 1980): 21–34.

Means, Jeffrey D. "'Indians Shall Do Things in Common': Oglala Lakota Identity and Cattle- raising on the Pine Ridge Reservation." *Montana: The Magazine of Western History* 61, no. 3 (Autumn 2011): 3–21.

Medicine, Beatrice. "'Warrior Women'—Sex Role Alternatives for Plains Indian Women." In *The Hidden Half: Studies of Plains Indian Women*, edited by Patricia Albers and Beatrice Medicine, 267–80. Lanham, MD: University Press of America, 1983.

Middleton, David, and Derek Edwards. "Conversational Remembering: A Social Psychological Approach." In *Collective Remembering*, edited by David Middleton and Derek Edwards, 23–45. London: Sage Publications, 1990.

Meyer, Melissa L., and Kerwin Lee Klein. "Native American Studies and the End of Ethnohistory." In *Studying Native America: Problems and Prospects*, edited by Russell Thornton, 182–216. Madison: University of Wisconsin Press, 1998.

Moore, Laura Jane. "Lozen: An Apache Warrior Woman." In *Sifters: Native American Women's Lives*, edited by Theda Perdue, 92–107. Oxford: Oxford University Press, 2001.

Nash, Gary B. "The Image of the Indian in the Southern Colonial Mind." In *The Wild Man Within: An Image in Western Thought from the Renaissance to Romanticism*, edited by Edward Dudley and Maximilian E. Novak, 55–86. London: Henry M. Snyder and Co., 1972.

Nora, Pierre. "Between Memory and History: Les Lieux de Memoire." *Representations* 26 (Spring 1989): 7–24.

Nora, Pierre. "General Introduction: Between Memory and History." In *Realms of Memory: Rethinking the French Past*, directed by Pierre Nora. Vol. 1, *Conflicts and Divisions*, edited by Laurence D. Kritzman. Translated by Arthur Goldhammer, 1–23. New York: Columbia University Press, 1996.

Nora, Pierre. "General Introduction." In *Rethinking France: Les Lieux de Memoire*, directed by Pierre Nora. Vol. 1, *The State*, translated by Richard C. Holbrook, vii–xxxiii. Chicago: University of Chicago Press, 2001.

Olick, Jeffrey K. " 'Collective Memory': A Memoir and Prospect." *Memory Studies* 1, no. 1 (2007): 19–25.

Olick, Jeffrey K. "From Collective Memory to the Sociology of Mnemonic Products and Practices." In *Cultural Memory Studies: An International and Interdisciplinary Handbook*, edited by Astrid Erll and Ansgar Nunning, 151–61. Berlin: Walter de Gruytar, 2008.

Olick, Jeffrey K., and Joyce Robbins. "Social Memory Studies: From 'Collective Memory' to the Historical Sociology of Mnemonic Practices." *Annual Review of Sociology* 24 (1998): 105–40.

Paul, Andrea I. "Buffalo Bill and Wounded Knee: the Movie." *Nebraska History* 71, no. 4 (Winter 1990): 183–90.

Paul, R. Eli. "The Investigation of Special Agent Cooper and Property Damage Claims in the Winter of 1890–1891." *South Dakota History* 24, no. 3 (Winter 1994): 212–35.

Pesantubee, Michelene E. "Wounded Knee: Site of Resistance and Recovery." In *Religious, Violence, Memory, and Place*, edited by Oren Baruch Stier and J. Shawn Landres, 75–88. Bloomington: Indiana University Press, 2006.

Pessah, Tom. "Violent Representations: Hostile Indians and Civilized Wars in Nineteenth-Century USA." *Ethnic and Racial Studies* 37, no. 9 (July 2014): 1628–45.

Popular Memory Group. "Popular Memory: Theory, Politics, Method." In *Making Histories: Studies in History-Writing and Politics*, edited by Richard Johnson, Gregor McLennan, Bill Schwarz, and David Sutton, 205–52. Minneapolis: University of Minnesota Press, 1982.

Potts, Steve. "American Horse." In *The Encyclopedia of North American Indian Wars, 1607–1890: A Political, Social, and Military History*, edited by Spencer C. Tucker, 1:13–14. Santa Barbara: ABC-Clio, 2011.

"The Purge of 1917." www.homeofheroes.com/moh/corrections/purge_army.html. Accessed May 15, 2013.

Pratt, Scott L. "Wounded Knee and the Prospect of Pluralism." *Journal of Speculative Philosophy* 19, no. 2 (2005): 150–66.

Prucha, Francis Paul. "Forts." In *The New Encyclopedia of the American West*, edited by Howard R. Lamar, 387–90. New Haven, CT: Yale University Press, 1998.

Radley, Alan. "Artefacts, Memory and a Sense of the Past." In *Collective Remembering*, edited by David Middleton and Derek Edwards, 46–59. London: Sage, 1990.

Ratledge, Mark. "Observing the 1870 Baker Massacre." *The Buffalo Post: A News Blog About Native People and the World We Live In.* February 23, 2010. www.buffa-lopost.net/?p=7108. Accessed May 11, 2013.

Rich, Elizabeth. "Remember Wounded Knee: AIM's Use of Metonymy in 21st Century Protest." *College Literature* 31, no. 3 (Summer 2004): 70–91.

Savage, Kirk. "Faces of the Dead." www.kirksavage.pitt.edu/?p=209. Accessed October 1, 2011.

Schudson, Michael. "The Past in the Present and the Present in the Past." *Communication* 11 (1989): 105–13.

Schwartz, Barry. "The Social Context of Commemoration: A Study in Collective Memory." *Social Forces* 61, no. 2 (December 1982): 374–402.

Skocpol, Theda. "America's First Social Security System: The Expansion of Benefits for Civil War Veterans." *Political Science Quarterly* 108, no. 1 (Spring 1993): 85–116.

Slotkin, Richard. "Massacre." *Berkshire Review* 14 (1979): 112–32.

Smith, Sherry L. "Reconciliation and Restitution in the American West." *Western Historical Quarterly* 61, no. 1 (Spring 2010): 5–25.

Turner, Frederick Jackson. "The Significance of the Frontier in American History." In *The Frontier in American History*, 13–42. 1920. Reprint, n.p.: BiblioBazaar, 2008.

Welsch, Robert L. "Introduction." In *Prairie Smoke*, by Melvin R. Gilmore, xi–xxiii. 1929. Reprint, St. Paul, MN: Minnesota Historical Society, 1987.

White, Richard. "Frederick Jackson Turner and Buffalo Bill." In *The Frontier in American Culture*, edited by James R. Grossman, 7–66. Berkeley: University of California Press, 1994.

White, Richard. "Using the Past: History and Native American Studies." In *Studying Native America: Problems and Prospects*, edited by Russell Thornton, 217–43. Madison: University of Wisconsin Press, 1998.

White, Richard. "The Winning of the West: The Expansion of the Western Sioux in the Eighteenth and Nineteenth Centuries." *Journal of American History* 65, no. 2 (September 1978): 319–43.

Wolfe, Patrick. "After the Frontier: Separation and Absorption in US Indian Policy," *Settler Colonial Studies* 1, no. 1 (2011): 13–51.

Wolfe, Patrick. "Settler Colonialism and the Elimination of the Native." *Journal of Genocide Research* 8, no. 4 (December 2006): 387–409.

Zabeki, David T. "Decorations, Medals, and Military Honors." In *The Encyclopedia of North American Indian Wars, 1607–1890: A Political, Social, and Military History*, edited by Spencer C. Tucker, 2:881. Santa Barbara: ABC-Clio, 2011.

BOOKS

Adams, David Wallace. *Education for Extinction: American Indians and the Boarding School Experience, 1875–1928.* Lawrence: University Press of Kansas, 1995.

Anderson, Benedict. *Imagined Communities: Reflections on the Origins and Spread of Nationalism.* 2nd ed. New York: Verso, 1991.

Andersson, Rani-Henrik. *The Lakota Ghost Dance of 1890*. Lincoln: University of Nebraska Press, 2008.

Appleby, Joyce, Lynn Hunt, and Margaret Jacob. *Telling the Truth about History*. 1994. Reprint, New York: Norton, 1995.

Barkan, Elazar. *The Guilt of Nations: Restitution and Negotiating Historical Injustices*. New York: Norton, 2000.

Blackhawk, Ned. *Violence Over the Land: Indians and Empires in the Early American West*. Cambridge, MA: Harvard University Press, 2006.

Blight, David W. *Race and Reunion: The Civil War in American Memory*. Cambridge, MA: Belknap Press of Harvard University Press, 2001.

Bodnar, John. *Remaking America: Public Memory, Commemoration, and Patriotism in the Twentieth Century*. Princeton, NJ: Princeton University Press, 1992.

Brinkley, Alan. *The End of Reform: New Deal Liberalism in Recession and War*. New York: Knopf, 1995.

Brooks, Roy L. ed. *When Sorry Isn't Enough: The Controversy over Apologies and Reparations for Human Injustice*. New York: New York University Press, 1999.

Brown, Dee. *Bury My Heart at Wounded Knee: An Indian History of the American West*. 1970. Reprint, New York: Henry Holt, 2000.

Brumble III, H. David. *American Indian Autobiography*. Berkeley: University of California Press, 1988.

Bruyneel, Kevin. *The Third Space of Sovereignty: The Postcolonial Politics of US–Indigenous Relations*. Minneapolis: University of Minnesota Press, 2007.

Burnham, Philip. *Song of Dewey Beard: Last Survivor of the Little Bighorn*. Lincoln: University of Nebraska Press, 2014.

Choay, Franciose. *The Invention of the Historic Monument*, translated by Lauren M. O'Connell. Cambridge: Cambridge University Press, 2001.

Christensen, Scott R. *Sagwitch: Shoshone Chieftain, Mormon Elder, 1822–1887*. Logan: Utah State University Press, 1999.

Colas, Dominique. *Civil Society and Fanaticism: Conjoined Histories*, translated by Amy Jacobs. Mestizo Spaces/Espaces Métissés. Redwood City, CA: Stanford University Press, 1997.

Calloway, Colin. *One Vast Winter Count: The Native American West before Lewis and Clark*. History of the American West. Lincoln: University of Nebraska Press, 2003.

Colwell-Chanthaphonh, Chip. *Massacre at Camp Grant: Forgetting and Remembering Apache History*. Tucson: University of Arizona Press, 2007.

Cothran, Boyd D. *Remembering the Modoc War: Redemptive Violence and the Making of American Innocence*. Chapel Hill: University of North Carolina Press, 2014.

Cubitt, Geoffrey. *History and Memory*. Historical Approaches. Manchester: Manchester University Press, 2007.

Deloria, Philip J. *Indians in Unexpected Places*. Lawrence: University Press of Kansas, 2004.

Deloria, Vine, Jr. and Clifford M. Lytle. *American Indians, American Justice*. Austin: University of Texas Press, 1983.

DeMallie, Raymond J., ed., *The Sixth Grandfather: Black Elk's Teachings Given to John G. Neihardt*. Lincoln: University of Nebraska Press, 1984.

DeMontravel, Peter R. *A Hero to His Fighting Men: Nelson A. Miles, 1839–1925*. Kent, OH: Kent State University Press, 1998.

Dippie, Brian W. *Custer's Last Stand: The Anatomy of an American Myth*. 1976. Reprint, Lincoln: Bison Books, 1994.

Dippie, Brian W. *The Vanishing American: White Attitudes and US Indian Policy*. Lawrence: University Press of Kansas, 1982.

Doss, Erika. *Monument Mania: Public Feeling in America*. Chicago: University of Chicago Press, 2010.

Edmunds, R. David. *The Shawnee Prophet*. Lincoln: University of Nebraska Press, 1983.

Elliott, Michael E. *Custerology: The Enduring Legacy of the Indian Wars and George Armstrong Custer*. Chicago: University of Chicago Press, 2007.

Fellman, Michael. *Citizen Sherman: A Life of William Tecumseh Sherman*. Lawrence: University Press of Kansas, 1995.

Fenn, Elizabeth A. *Encounters at the Heart of the World: A History of the Mandan People*. New York: Hill and Wang, 2014.

Fixico, Donald L. *Indian Resilience and Rebuilding: Indigenous Nations in the Modern American West*. The Modern American West. Tucson: University of Arizona Press, 2013.

Fleisher, Kass. *The Bear River Massacre and the Making of History*. Albany: State University of New York Press, 2004.

Flood, Renee Sansom. *Lost Bird of Wounded Knee: Spirit of the Lakota*. New York: Scribner, 1995.

Fluhman, J. Spencer. *"A Peculiar People": Anti-Mormonism and the Making of Religion in Nineteenth-Century America*. Chapel Hill: University of North Carolina Press, 2012.

Foote, Kenneth E. *Shadowed Ground: America's Landscapes of Violence and Tragedy*. Rev. ed. Austin: University of Texas Press, 2003.

Forsyth, Susan. *Representing the Massacre of American Indians at Wounded Knee, 1890–2000*. Lewiston, NY: Edwin Mellon Press, 2003.

Foucault, Michel. *Language, Counter-Memory, Practice: Selected Essays and Interviews*, edited by Donald F. Bouchard. Translated by Donald F. Bouchard and Sherry Simon. Ithaca, NY: Cornell University Press, 1977.

Graybill, Andrew R. *The Red and the White: A Family Saga of the American West*. New York: Liveright, 2013.

Green, Jonathan. *Cassell's Dictionary of Slang*. 2nd ed. London: Weidenfeld & Nicholson, 2005.

Greene, Jerome A. *Stricken Field: The Little Bighorn Since 1876*. Norman: University of Oklahoma Press, 2008.

Greene, Jerome A. *American Carnage: Wounded Knee, 1890*. Norman: University of Oklahoma Press, 2014.

Greenspan, Henry. *On Listening to Holocaust Survivors: Beyond Testimony.* 2nd ed. New York: Paragon House, 2010.

Halbwachs, Maurice. *The Collective Memory.* Translated by Francis J. Ditter Jr. and Vida Yazdi Ditter. New York: Harper Colophon Books, 1980.

Halbwachs, Maurice. *On Collective Memory.* Edited and translated by Lewis A. Coser. The Heritage of Sociology. Chicago: University of Chicago Press, 1992.

Hargreaves, Alex, ed. *Memory, Empire, and Postcolonialism: Legacies of French Colonialism.* Lanham, MD: Lexington Books, 2005.

Harjo, Joy, and Gloria Bird, eds. *Reinventing the Enemy's Language: Contemporary Native Women's Writings of North America.* New York: Norton, 1997.

Hassrick, Royal B. *The Sioux: Life and Customs of a Warrior Society.* 1964; Reprint, Norman: University of Oklahoma Press, 1967.

Hatamiya, Leslie. *Righting a Wrong: Japanese Americans and the Passage of the American Civil Liberties Act of 1988.* Redwood City, CA: Stanford University Press, 1994.

Hawke, David Freeman. *Those Tremendous Mountains: The Story of the Lewis and Clark Expedition.* New York: Norton, 1980.

Hertzberg, Hazel W. *The Search for an American Indian Identity.* Syracuse, NY: Syracuse University Press, 1971.

Holm, Tom. *The Great Confusion in Indian Affairs: Native Americans and Whites in the Progressive Era.* Austin: University of Texas Press, 2005.

Hoxie, Frederick E., ed. *Talking Back to Civilization: Indian Voices from the Progressive Era.* The Bedford Series in History and Culture. Boston: Bedford/St. Martin's, 2001.

Hoxie, Frederick E. *A Final Promise: The Campaign to Assimilate the Indians, 1880-1920.* Lincoln: University of Nebraska Press, 1984.

Hoxie, Frederick E. *Parading Through History: The Making of the Crow Nation in America, 1805–1935.* Cambridge: Cambridge University Press, 1995.

Hoxie, Frederick E. *This Indian Country: American Indian Activists and the Place They Made.* New York: Penguin, 2012.

Hughes, Mark. *Bivouac of the Dead.* Bowie, MD: Heritage Books, 1995.

Hutton, Patrick H. *History as an Art of Memory.* Hanover: University Press of New England, 1993.

Hyde, Anne F. *Empires, Nations, and Families: A History of the North American West, 1800–1860.* History of the American West Series. Lincoln: University of Nebraska Press, 2011.

Jacoby, Karl. *Shadows at Dawn: A Borderlands Massacre and the Violence of History.* New York: Penguin, 2008.

Janson, H. W. *The Rise and Fall of the Public Monument.* New Orleans: The Graduate School Tulane University, 1976.

Johnson, Troy R. *The American Indian Occupation of Alcatraz Island: Red Power and Self-Determination.* 1996. Reprint, Lincoln: University of Nebraska Press, 2008.

Jortner, Adam. *The Gods of Prophetstown: The Battle of Tippecanoe, the Holy War for the American Frontier.* Oxford: Oxford University Press, 2011.

Juster, Susan. *Doomsayers: Anglo-American Prophecy in the Age of Revolution.* Early American Studies. Philadelphia: University of Pennsylvania Press, 2003.

Kammen, Michael. *Mystic Chords of Memory: The Transformation of Tradition in American Culture.* New York: Knopf, 1991.

Kasson, Joy S. *Buffalo Bill's Wild West: Celebrity, Memory, and Popular History.* New York: Hill and Wang, 2000.

Kelman, Ari. *A Misplaced Massacre: Struggling Over the Memory of Sand Creek.* Cambridge, MA: Harvard University Press, 2013.

Kerstetter, Todd M. *God's Country, Uncle Sam's Land: Faith and Conflict in the American West.* Urbana: University of Illinois Press, 2006.

Kidd, Colin. *The Forging of Races: Race and Scripture in the Protestant Atlantic World, 1600–2000.* Cambridge: Cambridge University Press, 2006.

Kolbenschlag, George R. *A Whirlwind Press: News Correspondents and the Sioux Indian Disturbances of 1890–1891.* Vermillion, SD: University of South Dakota Press, 1990.

Lazarus, Edward. *Black Hills, White Justice: The Sioux Nation versus the United States, 1775 to the Present.* 1991. Reprint, Lincoln: Bison Books, 1999.

Le Goff, Jacques. *History and Memory.* Translated by Steven Randall and Elizabeth Claman. New York: Columbia University Press, 1992.

Lyons, Scott Richard. *X-Marks: Native Signatures of Assent.* Minneapolis: University of Minnesota Press, 2010.

Limerick, Patricia Nelson. *The Legacy of Conquest: The Unbroken Past of the American West.* 1987. Reprint, New York: Norton, 2006.

Limerick, Patricia Nelson. *Something in the Soil: Legacies and Reckonings in the New West.* 2000. Reprint, New York: Norton, 2001.

Limerick, Patricia Nelson, Clyde A. Milner II, and Charles E. Rankin, eds. *Trails: Toward a New Western History.* Lawrence: University Press of Kansas, 1991.

Mackintosh, John D. *Custer's Southern Officer: Captain George D. Wallace, 7th U.S. Cavalry.* Lexington, SC: Cloud Creek Press, 2002.

Maddra, Sam A. *Hostiles? The Lakota Ghost Dance and Buffalo Bill's Wild West.* Norman: University of Oklahoma Press, 2006.

Madsen, Brigham D. *The Shoshoni Frontier and the Bear River Massacre.* Salt Lake City: University of Utah Press, 1985.

Mason, Patrick Q. *The Mormon Menace: Violence and Anti-Mormonism in the Postbellum South.* Oxford: Oxford University Press, 2011.

McKale, William, and William D. Young. *Fort Riley: Citadel of the Frontier West.* Topeka: Kansas State Historical Society, 2000.

McMillen, Christian W. *Making Indian Law: The Hualapai Land Case and the Birth of Ethnohistory.* New Haven, CT: Yale University Press, 2007.

Mikaelian, Allen. *Medal of Honor: Profiles of America's Military Heroes From the Civil War to the Present.* New York: Bill Adler Books, 2002.

Misztal, Barbara A. *Theories of Social Remembering.* Berkshire: McGraw-Hill, 2003.

Moses, L. G. *The Indian Man: A Biography of James Mooney.* 1984. Reprint, Lincoln: Bison Books, 2002.

Moses, L. G. *Wild West Shows and the Images of American Indians, 1883–1933.* Albuquerque: University of New Mexico Press, 1996.

Nabokov, Peter. *A Forest of Time: American Indian Ways of History.* Cambridge: Cambridge University Press, 2002.

Nash, Gerald D. *Creating the West: Historical Interpretations, 1890–1990.* 1991. Reprint, Albuquerque: University of New Mexico Press, 1993.

Neff, John R. *Honoring the Civil War Dead: Commemoration and the Problem of Reconciliation* Modern War Studies. Lawrence: University Press of Kansas, 2005.

O'Brien, Jean M. *Firsting and Lasting: Writing Indians Out of Existence in New England.* Minneapolis: University of Minnesota Press, 2010.

Olick, Jeffrey K. *The Politics of Regret: On Historical Memory and Historical Responsibility.* New York: Routledge, 2007.

Olick, Jeffrey K., Vered Vinitzky-Serouissi, and Daniel Levy, eds. *The Collective Memory Reader.* Oxford: Oxford University Press, 2011.

Ong, Walter J. *Orality and Literacy: The Technologizing of the Word.* 1982. Reprint, n.p.: Taylor and Francis e-Library, 2001.

Ostler, Jeffrey. *The Lakotas and the Black Hills: The Struggle for Sacred Ground.* The Penguin Library of American Indian History. New York: Viking, 2010.

Ostler, Jeffrey. *The Plains Sioux and US Colonialism from Lewis and Clark to Wounded Knee.* Studies in North American Indian History. Cambridge: Cambridge University Press, 2004.

Owens, Ron. *Medal of Honor: Historical Facts and Figures.* Paduca, KY: Turner Publishing Co., 2004.

Parman, Donald Lee. *Indians and the American West in the Twentieth Century.* Bloomington: Indiana University Press, 1994.

Pearce, Roy Harvey. *Savagism and Civilization: A Study of the Indian and the American Mind.* Rev. ed. Berkeley: University of California Press, 1988.

Petrucci, Armando. *Writing the Dead: Death and Writing Strategies in the Western Tradition,* translated by Michael Sullivan. Redwood City, CA: Stanford University Press, 1998.

Pfaller, Louis. *James McLaughlin: The Man With an Indian Heart.* New York: Vantage Press, 1978.

Philp, Kenneth R. *John Collier's Crusade for Indian Reform, 1920–1954.* Tucson: University of Arizona Press, 1977.

Piehler, G. Kurt. *Remembering War the American Way.* Washington, DC: Smithsonian Institution Press, 1995.

Powers, Marla N. *Oglala Women: Myth, Ritual, Reality*. 1986. Reprint, Chicago: University of Chicago Press, 1988.

Powers, William K. *Oglala Religion*. 1975. Reprint, Lincoln: University of Nebraska Press, 1982.

Prucha, Francis Paul. *The Great Father: The United States Government and the American Indians*. Lincoln: University of Nebraska Press, 1984.

Reeve, W. Paul. *Religion of a Different Color: Race and the Mormon Struggle for Whiteness*. Oxford: Oxford University Press, 2015.

Reinhardt, Akim. *Ruling Pine Ridge: Oglala Lakota Politics from the IRA to Wounded Knee*. Lubbock: Texas Tech University Press, 2007.

Richardson, Heather Cox. *Wounded Knee: Party Politics and the Road to an American Massacre*. New York: Basic Books, 2010.

Ronda, James P. *Lewis and Clark Among the Indians*. Bicentennial Edition. Lincoln: University of Nebraska Press, 2002.

Rosenthal, H. D. *Their Day in Court: A History of the Indian Claims Commission*. New York: Garland Publishing, 1990.

Rosier, Paul C. *Serving Their Country: American Indian Politics and Patriotism in the Twentieth Century*. Cambridge, MA: Harvard University Press, 2009.

Sagala, Sandra K. *Buffalo Bill on the Silver Screen: The Films of William F. Cody*. The William F. Cody Series on the History and Culture of the American West. Norman: University of Oklahoma Press, 2013.

Savage, Kirk. *Standing Soldiers, Kneeling Slaves: Race, War, and Monument in Nineteenth- Century America*. Princeton, NJ: Princeton University Press, 1997.

Sengupta, Indra, ed. *Memory, History, and Colonialism: Engaging with Pierre Nora in Colonial and Postcolonial Contexts*. London: German Historical Institute London, 2009.

Skogen, Larry C. *Indian Depredation Claims, 1796–1920*. Legal History of North America. Norman: University of Oklahoma Press, 1996.

Slotkin, Richard. *The Fatal Environment: The Myth of the Frontier in the Age of Industrialization, 1800–1890*. 1985. Reprint, Norman: University of Oklahoma Press, 1994.

Slotkin, Richard. *Gunfighter Nation: The Myth of the Frontier in Twentieth-Century America*. 1992. Reprint: Norman: University of Oklahoma Press, 1998.

Slotkin, Richard. *Regeneration through Violence: The Mythology of the American Frontier, 1600–1860*. 1973. Reprint, Norman: University of Oklahoma Press, 2000.

Smith, Linda Tuhiwai. *Decolonizing Methodologies: Research and Indigenous Peoples*. 2nd ed. London: Zed Books, 2012.

Smith, Paul Chaat, and Robert Allen Warrior. *Like a Hurricane: The Indian Movement from Alcatraz to Wounded Knee*. New York: New Press, 1996.

Smith, Sherry L. *Hippies, Indians, and the Fight for Red Power*. Oxford: Oxford University Press, 2012.

Smith, Sherry L. *The View from Officers' Row: Army Perceptions of Western Indians.* Tucson: University of Arizona Press, 1991.

Smoak, Gregory. *Ghost Dance and Identity: Prophetic Religion and Ethnogensis in the Nineteenth Century.* Berkeley: University of California Press, 2006.

South Dakota's Ziebach County, History of the Prairie. Dupree, SD: Ziebach County Historical Society, 1982. http://files.usgwarchives.net/sd/ziebach/history/z-hst-21.txt. Accessed July 9, 2013.

Standing Bear, Luther. *Land of the Spotted Eagle.* 1933. Reprint, Lincoln: Bison Books, 1978.

Taysom, Stephen C. *Shakers, Mormons, and Religious Worlds: Conflicting Visions, Contested Boundaries.* Religion in North America. Bloomington: Indiana University Press, 2011.

Torpey, John, ed. *Politics and the Past: On Repairing Historical Injustices.* Lanham, MD: Rowman and Littlefield, 2003.

Utley, Robert M. *Last Days of the Sioux Nation.* 2nd ed. New Haven, CT: Yale University Press, 2004.

Volf, Miraslov. *The End of Memory; Remembering Rightly in a Violent World.* Grand Rapids: Eerdmans, 2006.

Warren, Louis A. *Buffalo Bill's America: William Cody and the Wild West Show.* New York: Knopf, 2005.

White, Richard. *"It's Your Misfortune and None of My Own": A New History of the American West.* 1991. Reprint, Norman: University of Oklahoma Press, 1993.

White, Richard. *The Middle Ground: Indians, Empires, and Republics in the Great Lakes Region.* Cambridge: Cambridge University Press, 1991.

White, Sophie. *Wild Frenchmen and Frenchified Indians: Material Culture and Race in Colonial Louisiana.* Early American Studies. Philadelphia: University of Pennsylvania Press, 2014.

Wilkins, David E. *Hollow Justice: A History of Indigenous Claims in the United States.* The Henry Roe Cloud Series on American Indians and Modernity. New Haven, CT: Yale University Press, 2013.

Wilkins, David E., and Heidi Kiiwetinepinesiik Stark. *American Indian Politics and the American Political System,* 3rd ed. Lanham, MD: Rowman and Littlefield, 2011.

Wilson, Angela Cavendar. *Remember This! Dakota Decolonization and the Eli Taylor Narratives.* Lincoln: University of Nebraska Press, 2005.

Wilson, Dorothy Clarke. *Bright Eyes: The Story of Susette LaFlesche, an Omaha Indian.* New York: McGraw-Hill, 1974.

Michael Witgen, *An Infinity of Nations: How the Native New World Shaped Early North America.* Early American Studies. Philadelphia: University of Pennsylvania Press.

Wooster, Robert. *Nelson A. Miles and the Twilight of the Frontier Army.* Lincoln: University of Nebraska Press, 1993.

Zerubavel, Yael. *Recovered Roots: Collective Roots and the Making of Israeli National Tradition.* Chicago: University of Chicago Press, 1995.

THESES AND DISSERTATIONS

Lamport, Nancylee. "Francis Case: His Pioneer Background, Indian Legislation, and Missouri River Conservation." MA thesis, University of South Dakota, 1972.

Roberts, Gary L. "Sand Creek: Tragedy and Symbol." PhD diss., University of Oklahoma, 1984.

Scolari, Paul. "Indian Warriors and Pioneer Mothers: American Identity and the Closing of the Frontier in Public Monuments, 1890–1930." PhD diss., University of Pittsburgh, 2005.

Index